Zoé Oldenbourg was born in St Petersburg in 1916 and was educated at the Lycée Molière and the Sorbonne in Paris. The author of a number of novels, including *The Cornerstone*, which won the Prix Fémina in 1953, her historical works include *The Crusades* and *Catherine of Russia*. *Le Bûcher de Montségur* was published in 1959 and was first published in English in 1961 as *Massacre at Montségur*.

Massacre at Montségur

A History of the Albigensian Crusade

by

Zoé Oldenbourg

Translated from the French by Peter Green

A PHOENIX GIANT PAPERBACK

First published in Great Britain
by George Weidenfeld & Nicolson Ltd in 1961

This paperback edition published in 1998
by Phoenix, a division of Orion Books Ltd,
Orion House, 5 Upper St Martin's Lane,
London WC2H 9EA

First published in France under the title
Le Bûcher de Montségur in the Gallimard series
'Trente journées qui ont fait la France'

Copyright © 1959 Librairie Gallimard
English translation © 1961 George Weidenfeld & Nicolson Ltd
and Pantheon Books, a Division of Random House Inc, New York

A CIP catalogue record for this book is available
from the British Library.

Printed and bound in Great Britain by
Butler & Tanner Ltd, Frome and London

CONTENTS

LIST OF ILLUSTRATIONS

1 Painting by Berruguete (1477–1503) of Saint Dominic at the Tribunal of the Inquisition, from the Prado Gallery in Madrid (Photo: Mansell Collection)

2 Painting by Fra Angelico (1387–1455) of Saint Dominic and the Miracle of the Book, from the Louvre in Paris (Photo: Giraudon)

3 A thirteenth century fresco of Pope Innocent III from the church at Subiaco in Italy (Photo: Mansell Collection)

4 A drawing of Simon de Montfort taken from a stained glass window in the cathedral at Chartres in France (Mansell Collection)

5 Mediaeval seals. (*a*) Simon de Montfort and the crest he used on his shield from a wax impression in the British Museum, London (Photo: British Museum) and (*b*) enlarged drawings of wax impressions of seals from the Archives Nationales in Paris showing (i) a Knight from Languedoc, (ii) Raymond Pelet, Squire of Alais, (iii) Raymond Trencavel, Viscount of Béziers, (iv) Raymond VI, Count of Toulouse, and (v) Raymond VII, Count of Toulouse

6 & 7 Two manuscript pages from the *Chanson de la Croisade* by William of Tudela showing the taking of the town of Béziers and Count Raymond VII re-entering the town of Toulouse. The book is in the Bibliothèque Nationale in Paris

8 Drawing from a bas-relief in the thirteenth century St Nazaire Church in Carcassonne believed to depict the death of Simon de Montfort (Mansell Collection)

TRANSLATOR'S NOTE

The anglicization of mediaeval French names always presents some difficulty: I cannot claim to have been consistent in this respect. The better-known names I have converted according to traditional English usage—as, for example, in Sir Steven Runciman's *The Mediaeval Manichee*. Elsewhere I have been somewhat arbitrary, and acted as the context seemed to demand in terms of euphony or convenience: thus, variously, William de Puylaurens, [Pierre des] Vaux de Cernay (where Sir Steven reads Peter de Vaux-Cernay), Peter Amiel, or Blanche of Castille. I trust that readers will take this captious attitude in the spirit with which T. E. Lawrence treated the proof-reader of *The Seven Pillars of Wisdom*.

I would like to express my thanks publicly to Mme Oldenbourg for reading my entire typescript with scrupulous care, saving me from several egregious errors, and on occasion putting me to shame by suggesting a better English phrase than I could have thought of myself. It is a rare pleasure for a translator to be blessed with so amiable and co-operative an author.

PETER GREEN

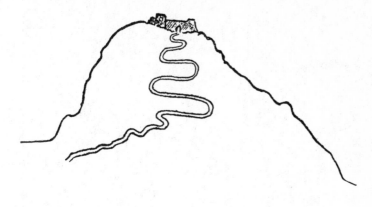

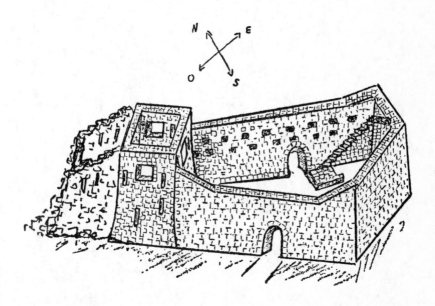

Diagrammatic sketch of the fortress of Montségur with the road leading up to it

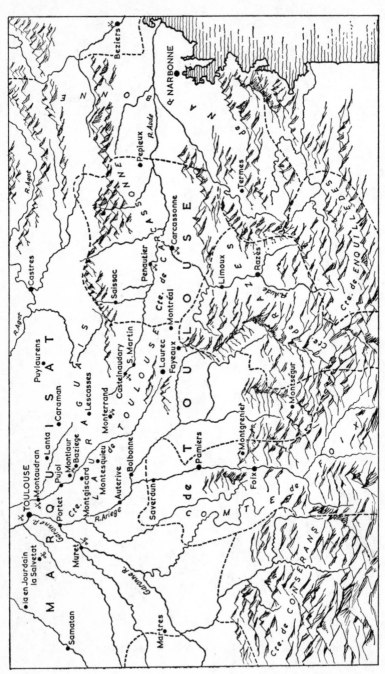

THE GEOGRAPHICAL BACKGROUND OF THE ALBIGENSIAN CRUSADE

CHAPTER I

THE BACKGROUND OF
THE CRUSADE

1. *The Initial Facts*

ON 10TH MARCH 1208 His Holiness Pope Innocent III issued a
solemn call to arms, summoning all Christian nations to launch a
Crusade against a country of fellow-Christians. This Crusade, he
claimed, was not only justifiable but a matter of dire necessity; the
heretics who inhabited this land were 'worse than the very Saracens'.

The Pope's appeal came four years after the capture of Constantinople by a Crusaders' army. The new enemy was Raymond VI,
Count of Toulouse, a cousin of the King of France and brother-in-
law to the Kings both of England and of Aragon. Besides being bound
by ties of homage to these three monarchs he owed a similar allegiance to the German Emperor; he was, further, Duke of Narbonne,
Marquis of South-West Provence, a feudal sovereign whose authority
extended over the regions of Agenais, Quercy, Rouergue, Albigeois,
Comminges and Carcassès, not to mention the County of Foix. He
was, in short, one of the greatest princes in Western Christendom,
premier baron of all the territories where the *langue d'oc* was spoken.

Since this was a period when actual power was firmly in the hands
of the nobility, and since this nobility, from the monarch down to
the smallest landed proprietor, was by definition a military caste, it
follows that war achieved a permanent, necessary status in their
lives. Christian princes were never short of an excuse for invading
their neighbours' territories. But the preceding century had seen,
first a slackening, then a sharp falling off in that enormous enthusiasm with which Western Europe had hitherto regarded the Holy
Land. In the hey-day of the twelfth century, the warrior-pilgrim,
though he might frequently be pursuing material ends, felt confident
that he was fighting on God's behalf. But the nobility, their ranks
decimated on the battlefields of Palestine, chafed bitterly against the
useless sacrifices they were called upon to make, while the various

local campaigns they had to conduct struck them as being both petty and dull.

Later, at the time of the Fourth Crusade, Simon de Montfort (a warrior whose appetite for warfare even the most sceptical could hardly question) was to refuse flatly to bear arms against a Christian city, or to put himself in the Doge's service rather than that of the Pope. Even though the bulk of the Crusaders failed to copy his example, and followed up their capture of Catholic Zara with an assault on Constantinople, nevertheless the scandal occasioned by this deflection of a Crusade from its true goal left the French nobility with a certain feeling of disillusion, despite the perennially powerful lure of conquest and pillage. The Crusade itself was gradually becoming a dead end, and the Holy Land, increasingly threatened though it was, now attracted only a minority of enthusiasts. For a good many knights and men-at-arms this way of obtaining God's forgiveness (which allowed them to cover themselves with glory on the battlefield as well) had become an habitual practice. Sometimes genuine passion inspired it; more often the motive was material need.

What are we to make of this new type of Crusade, imposed upon Christendom by the Pope's emergency decree? One factor we should bear in mind is how cosmopolitan in their connections the aristocracy of this period were. In England the nobles all spoke French. Italian and Spanish poets were composing in the *langue d'oc*, and German *Minnesinger* took lessons from the Troubadours. Above all, the intricate and complex ties created by feudal obligations, coupled with a whole network of political intermarriage, had ensured that all the great princes throughout Western Christendom were mutually bound by responsibilities of vassalship, or kinship, or both. In such conditions it is hard to see how a Holy War preached against the Count of Toulouse ever reached the point of actually being fought.

When, on this March day in 1208, Rome's Bull of Anathema was flung down on the soil of Languedoc, it cut the history of Catholic Christendom clean in two. The Papal sanction granted to a war conducted against a Christian people was to destroy, for ever, the moral authority of the Church, and to undermine the very foundations on which that authority rested. What the Pope regarded as a mere casual police action, dictated by particular circumstances, was soon to grow, under the pressure of events, into a methodical system of oppression; and for millions of Western Christians Rome was to become an object of hatred and contempt.

The circumstances which led Innocent III to take such severe action against the Count of Toulouse suggest, *a priori*, some justification for the Pope's appeal. Every single district throughout the Count's domains was a hotbed of heresy; and on 14th January 1208 Brother Peter of Castelnau, the Papal Legate, had been assassinated at Saint-Gilles by one of Raymond VI's officers.

The murder of a Legate—that is, of the Pope's Ambassador and Envoy Plenipotentiary—was a capital crime, which fully justified a declaration of war. But the Church was not, in theory, a temporal power, and so could only answer this bloody affront with chastisement of a spiritual order. Nevertheless, such spiritual sanctions were formidable enough. Faced with a threat of excommunication or interdiction kings would at once yield, making chaos of their political alliances or private lives in order to avoid the Church's thunderbolts.

In 1170 King Henry II of England had been excommunicated for the murder of Thomas à Becket, and had only received the Pope's pardon after a public apology and act of humiliation. Frenchmen had by no means yet forgotten those long months of interdiction their country had suffered in 1200 as a result of King Philip II's illegal divorce. Excommunication made its victim no better than dead in the eyes of the law, and released his relatives or subjects from all obligations towards him; while interdiction paralysed a country's life, by debarring its inhabitants from any participation in religious observances, and especially from Communion—a thing as essential for the bulk of Christians as their daily bread.

We see the Pope intervening in the election of an Emperor, trying to impose his own candidate against the will of the German princes. We see him putting England under an interdict because King John obstinately preferred to select the archbishop he, rather than the Pope, had in mind. Philip II made submission, while John suffered the humiliation of surrendering his crown and receiving it back at the hands of the Papal Legate. The King of Aragon, a Catholic monarch engaged in a perpetual Crusade against the Moors, made the journey to Rome in order to offer the Pope his oath of allegiance and be crowned by His Holiness: he knew very well that Rome's friendship was a guarantee of internal stability. Innocent III was a Pope determined to treat any Catholic monarch as his vassal.

But when the Pope pronounced his excommunication against the County of Toulouse, he knew that his usual weapons were powerless: there was no point in putting an interdict on a land that had already, more or less openly, severed itself from the Church of Rome.

Raymond VI's crime was that of ruling a country where the authority of the Church was in decline, and of doing nothing to remedy such a state of affairs. The avowed aim of the Crusade, directed as it was against a country that had been Christian for a thousand years, was the overthrow of a prince whose very legitimacy made him somewhat over-prone to side with his own people. To save the Church from the danger threatening its continued existence in the Midi, it was essential that this country should be placed under the control of an alien, external government, that would have the courage to act firmly and without compromise. The outline of this far-reaching operation can already be traced, in its entirety, in the letter that Innocent III sent to the King of France before the assassination of his Papal Legate. On 10th March 1204 he wrote: 'It is your responsibility to harry the Count of Toulouse out of those lands which at present he occupies; to remove this territory from the control of sectarian heretics; and to place it in the hands of true Catholics who will be enabled, under your beneficent rule, to serve Our Lord in all faithfulness.'

The territories under the Count of Toulouse's jurisdiction had been a notorious nest of heresy for something over a hundred years. In every Christian country, ever since the foundation of the Church itself, there had existed various permanent heretical enclaves, of greater or lesser importance. At the time of the Crusades not only the Slav countries but the whole of Northern Italy had become a battleground where Catholics and heretics waged unceasing warfare. In the French Midi, though the heretics remained a minority group, they had, nevertheless, long since formed a most important section of the population. This caused the Church considerable distress. Every kind of sanction was brought into play, including excommunication and the use of the secular arm; but, in this area at least, such efforts proved increasingly ineffectual. Heresy—or rather, a variety of heresies—began to gain ground everywhere, with increasing speed. For over four years now Innocent III had realized that the only real chance of extirpating this heretical movement lay in a full-scale expeditionary force.

The murder of Peter of Castelnau, even more than that of the Duke of Enghien, was something of which it could well be said that 'it was worse than a crime: it was a mistake'. There are, besides, good grounds for supposing that the Count himself had nothing to do with it.

Peter of Castelnau, latterly Legate to the Apostolic See of Languedoc, had been Archdeacon of Maguelonne and a monk of the Cistercian Abbey of Fontfroide. For a long while now he had been engaged in a struggle to prevent government policy and the Church's work from coming into direct collision. In order to convert the rebellious, he had plunged into political activity of the most violent sort. First, accompanied by his colleague Arnald-Amalric, the Abbot of Cîteaux, Peter of Castelnau had set about those Languedoc prelates who were suspected of looking on heresy with a friendly, or at least a tolerant eye. In 1205 he suspended from office two bishops, those of Béziers and Viviers. Next, the two Legates ordered proceedings to be taken against Bérenger II, Archbishop of Narbonne, and Primate of all Languedoc. But Bérenger refused to be intimidated, and indeed openly defied the Papal envoys.

Finally, towards the end of 1207, Peter of Castelnau managed to establish a league of Southern barons, the purpose of which was to hunt down heretics. When Raymond VI was asked to join this league, he refused. As Pierre des Vaux de Cernay observes, the man of God [i.e. Peter of Castelnau] actually incited the *seigneurs* of Provence to rebel against their liege lord.[1] But he went further still. Undaunted by the Count's disaffection, the Legate excommunicated him in public, put his territory under interdict, and wound up a most lively occasion by pronouncing his anathema in round terms: 'He who dispossesses you will be accounted virtuous, he who strikes you dead will earn a blessing.' Despite Raymond's obstinacy the excommunication had its effect: the Count of Toulouse made his submission, and renewed the promises required of him. The interview— an extremely stormy one—took place at Saint-Gilles. Directly after it Peter of Castelnau, together with the Bishop of Couserans, left the city. The following morning, just as the Papal party was about to cross the Rhône, an officer in the Count's service flung himself upon the Legate and ran him through with his sword.

This brief summary of Peter of Castelnau's activities offers ample proof that the Legate was by no means accommodating by nature, and that he had no fear of making enemies. But at a moment when relations between the Count of Toulouse and the Church were already seriously strained, the murder of an Ambassador from the Holy See was the last drop that made the cup brim over. Innocent III had long been contemplating the idea of a Crusade against this heresy-tainted land. He only needed one solid, explosive incident, something that would fire the public imagination and justify a declaration of war.

The Papacy had no armies in its pay. Crusades, which in the previous century had been a pretty popular kind of war, remained, above all, *voluntary* campaigns, despite the fact that kings and princes took part in them. The Pope could not force the French King to launch a Crusade, and in the event failed to persuade him. The success of the venture was wholly dependent on the goodwill of the landed gentry, great and small, who would agree to join it. Accordingly the Pope dispatched letters to every French bishop, with the intention of launching a propaganda campaign in support of this new Crusade.

His emissaries, strengthened by the evocation of Peter's blood-stained white habit, went the rounds of the French churches, expatiating on the tragic condition of a country thus abandoned to the ravages of heresy. Arnald-Amalric, we are told by William de Puylaurens,[2] seeing that he was powerless to bring back these straying sheep to God,

made his way to France, a land that has ever fought in God's cause; there he reached an agreement with the King and the barons, while sundry men of the people, suitable for such a task, began, in the name of the Apostolic authorities, to preach a war against the heretics, entailing indulgences comparable to those habitually dispensed to Crusaders who crossed the seas in order to bring succour to the Holy Land.

The author of the *Chanson de la Croisade*[3] puts the following words into the mouth of Arnald-Amalric during his journey to Rome: 'May the man who abstains from this Crusade never drink wine again; may he never eat, morning or evening, off a good linen cloth, or dress in fine stuff again to the end of his days; and at his death may he be buried like a dog!' Such sentiments could not have been uttered in Rome, since at the time the Legate was actually in France; but they doubtless convey a faithful enough representation of his characteristic fierceness in discourse. The propaganda drive was so successful that the King of France (who had, initially, tried to limit a movement that seemed likely to rob him of troops at a time when he was liable to need them) found himself forced to change his tune almost at once.

Volunteers streamed in from all quarters: from Normandy and Champagne, Anjou and Flanders, Picardy and Limousin. Not only knights, but peasants and burghers, too, enrolled themselves for this Crusade, eager to serve under the colours of their liege lord or their bishop. It is impossible to judge the strength of this army with any precision: such figures as the historians record are vague in the extreme. But certainly it was a large army as armies went in that period, and its strength made a considerable impression on contemporary witnesses.

2. *The Crusaders*

Before we make a detailed examination of the heresy which provoked the Albigensian Crusade, or sketch in the background of the country where one of the cruellest dramas in French history was destined to be played out, we must, first, study the Crusaders themselves. What manner of men were these, who dared to invade a Christian country that had never molested them, and which was closely allied to them both by speech and by racial descent?

We have already seen that Crusades as such had long formed part of the *mores* peculiar to the Western European aristocracy. Quite apart from the four major Crusades, the whole of the twelfth century had witnessed an endless stream of small private wars, led and financed by various *grands seigneurs* at their own expense. It was not only their vassals who took part in these forays either, but numerous volunteers, of all sorts and conditions: many of the expeditionary forces were commanded by bishops. The bulk of the Crusaders were Frenchmen, from the Midi no less than from the North. The Christian empire now gradually foundering in the Near East was a French empire; it stood in need of continual reinforcements, and the Christian kingdoms of the West had for a century now paid a heavy tribute in human lives to the Holy Land. These warrior-pilgrims were by no means all fired with a pure and disinterested passion; a great number of them were ambitious adventurers. But the unreserved approval with which the Church regarded such a pious undertaking as a Crusade had an odd effect. Those who fought in it were convinced that, by practising a profession which in different circumstances would have contributed nothing to their salvation, they were both serving God and saving their own souls. Crusaders who campaigned in the Holy Land enjoyed indulgences granted by the Pope, while anyone who had taken part in such a Crusade not only won forgiveness for his sins, but also had the chance to acquire both fame and fortune.

There was, on the face of it, something most attractive about such doubly profitable enterprises; but a series of defeats, and the progressive decay of the French empire in Syria and Palestine, tended to discourage would-be adventurers. The new Latin Empire of Constantinople appeared to hold out greater opportunities, though it lacked the special appeal of the Holy Sepulchre. There were, nevertheless, a good many soldiers, especially in France, who needed a Crusade much in the same way as a Moslem needs his pilgrimage to Mecca. It is not, therefore, surprising that the Pope's appeal met with so favourable a reception in the provinces of Northern France.

The indulgences promised in respect of this Crusade were comparable to those that had been bestowed on Crusaders in the Holy Land—and the effort involved was considerably less. Furthermore, to go on a Crusade was a very handy way of holding up the payment of one's debts, and keeping one's property clear of any ultimate claims that might be made upon it, since a Crusader's goods were declared sacrosanct for the whole period of his absence.

It is very probable, indeed, that the larger part of this Crusading army (a point which applies to the nobility just as much as to the burghers and common people) was composed either of sinners anxious to win God's pardon, or else of debt-ridden wretches who hoped in this way to escape being harried by their creditors; or else, again, of those who had already vowed their services to the Holy Land, and were anxious to wriggle out of this liability by taking part in a shorter, less wearying Crusade. The third category was probably the largest.

A large number of these Crusaders were, indeed, little better than professional mercenaries, always glad of an honourable excuse for fighting. At the same time we should not forget that the army now being made ready for its venture, whether in great castle or parish armoury, in beflagged tiltyard or private guardroom, princely palace or stately ecclesiastical pile, was an army of men who wore the Cross sewn upon their surcoats. The mere fact of bearing this Cross provided even the most lukewarm with a symbol eloquent enough to stir their enthusiasm.

Another point: how did the Papal anathema contrive to transform Raymond of Toulouse, overnight, into a pagan and an infidel?

Languedoc was not separated from France by the high seas and several thousand miles; but it was, nevertheless, a foreign if not an actively hostile country. The great Southern barons, jealous above all else of their personal independence, were continually shifting their allegiance: sometimes they leaned towards the King of France, sometimes to the King of England; again, they might ally themselves with the German Emperor or the King of Aragon. The thread which bound the Count of Toulouse in vassalship to the French King was somewhat tenuous. High liegeman of the Crown the Count might be; yet he could not even be regarded as the King's safe ally, but rather as a somewhat doubtful neighbour, always liable to support the political aims either of the English King (who was his brother-in-law, and the uncle of his only son) or of the Emperor. The great barons of the North, the land of the *langue d'oïl*, though they were by no means all loyal to the French King, still remained

French by culture and tradition: they would not dream of allying themselves with those whom they somewhat contemptuously referred to as 'Provençals'.

The most notable of the great barons who joined the Crusade were Eudes II, Duke of Burgundy, and Hervé IV, Count of Nevers. These *seigneurs* were in no doubt why they were going to the wars. Heresy had already penetrated their own domains, and they had good cause for wanting to check its further expansion. Knights such as Simon de Montfort or Guy de Lévis were animated by sincere enthusiasm for what they regarded as God's cause: there were a great number of such 'soldiers of God' in the Crusaders' army that assembled in answer to Pope Innocent's appeal. The French nobility had long become accustomed to regarding its own interests and God's interests as identical.

The faith held by these Crusaders, who never hesitated to exterminate their fellow-men for the greater glory of God, may strike us as extraordinary—indeed, as somewhat contemptible. Possibly it was not always like this: ordinary human morality was never considered for a moment when God's interests appeared to be at stake. These interests could take on a surprisingly mundane character, though this did not shock anyone: God, after all, was so closely bound up with human affairs. Faith, in France as in other Christian countries (perhaps especially in France), was deep, sincere, and violent—a fact which ensured fierce attachment on the part of devotees to the Faith's external manifestations. The religious feeling which permeated every aspect of men's social and private life achieved a species of symbolism. This symbolism was treated in so literal a fashion that we might easily mistake the attitude involved with that of the fetichist. When we study the history of the Albigensian Crusade, we should not forget that there were other motives behind it apart from the purely political ones—motives of sentiment or passion without which the war might never have taken place, or, at least, would have avoided that peculiarly brutal quality which was destined to mark it out. This war was not simply the business of a few fanatics or adventurers. It was not even a simple expression of the Catholic Church's opposition to heresy. It symbolized, in a profound way, a special sort of Western civilization, a particular view of God and the Universe.

I have described the faith held by these men in the twelfth and thirteenth centuries as being, in a sense, 'mundane', since it seems clear that during this period the urge to delimit the supernatural within increasingly concrete and coherent patterns developed with hitherto unsurpassed vigour. By either outlawing ancient mythology, Roman and Celtic, or else taking it over and turning it to profitable use, the Church had transformed the Saints into characters from folklore—and, by a converse process, turned gods and demi-gods into saints. As a result the Christian lived in a world where the lives of the Saints and readings from sacred works largely filled the place occupied today by theatre, cinema, illustrated weeklies and fairy-tales. Secular and folk literature, alien by nature to religious in-fluence, were still restricted to minor media or reserved for the pleasure of a small *élite*. The creative energy of these Western nations—so young, so avid of new experience, so touched with poetry even in their humblest occupations—was almost wholly canalized into the religious life, which very soon took on the appearance of pure paganism, thinly veneered with Christianity.

It has been said that the cathedrals were the poor man's Bible, and something more: the great book by means of which the devotee was brought into contact with history, with the sciences both moral natural, with the mysteries of past and future alike. The remains of those twelfth century cathedrals give us no more than a partial notion of their splendour. It must not be forgotten that they were painted and gilded outside as well as in; that the statues and tympana that adorned their great portals were tricked out in poly-chrome; that the naves were not only smothered with frescoes but, over and above this, decked with richly-woven tapestries, Eastern fabrics, and silken banners all embroidered with gold; and that the altars, shrines, and miraculous images, on account of their superb craftsmanship no less than the rare materials which had gone to their making, constituted a treasure of incalculable value.

The mass of the common people were poor; the bourgeoisie had already become rich, but, like the bourgeoisie everywhere, was wholly self-regarding. The nobility practised a certain ostentatious extravagance, while the prelates of the Church frequently copied the nobility, both in their luxurious habits and their addiction to warfare. The country was constantly ravaged by famine, fire, battles great and small, plague epidemics, and every sort of banditry; and yet from that same soil there arose these extraordinarily rich cathedrals. We have (if we want to reconcile these facts) to grant that men's faith in this age possessed a special temper all its own. This frantic urge to incarnate the divine, to give it concrete shape, suggests both a deep regard for material objects and the created world, and a pro-found contempt for human life. The cathedrals rose on the faith of those who also offered adoration to relics.

The men of Northern France were by no means all fervent supporters of the Papacy: far from it. In 1204 the French bishops stood
out against the Papal Legates when they tried to force Philip II into
peace with England. The barons continually squabbled with the
bishops and abbots in the furtherance of their various private interests, and the common people continually resented the tithes they
were forced to pay. This does not alter the fact that, during the
period under discussion, the French people as a whole were deeply
Catholic, and clung to their churches, religious customs, and centres
of pilgrimage as though they formed a kind of national heritage.
Now the heresy that had gained ground in the districts of Languedoc
was fiercely opposed in principle to all outward manifestations of
ecclesiastical life; so those emissaries whom Arnald sent out to
preach the Crusade had little trouble in working up the indignation
of their large audiences against 'God's enemies'.

The stories which reappear like a faint echo in the chronicle of
Pierre des Vaux de Cernay must have formed the subject of endless
discussion and comment throughout the length and breadth of
France; nor, we may be certain, do they represent all the incidents
that took place, or even the worst of them. One man defiled a church
altar. Some soldiers in service with the Count of Foix took a certain
Canon and chopped him into pieces; they also used the arms and
legs of a crucifix to grind up spices with, in lieu of a pestle. Such
things must have haunted the minds of even the most casual believer.

These heretics desecrated Communion chalices and asserted that
by receiving the Sacred Host one swallowed a devil; they uttered
blasphemies against the Saints, declaring that they were all damned.
The Pope's words—'they are worse than the very Saracens'—were
quite literally true. Those who listened to Rome's envoys, however,
were not humanitarian by nature, and probably found the idea of a
mutilated crucifix more distressing than that of chopping a man
to pieces.

The King, whose mind moved along political lines, was not (so
far as we can judge) extravagantly moved by the development and
spread of this heresy. He showed himself, indeed, about as unen-
thusiastic over the proposed Crusade as he could, within the bounds
of common decency. He wrote to Innocent III saying that he would
not go on this Crusade unless the Pope forced the King of England
to refrain from attacking France, and levied a special tax to finance
the expedition. In any case he had doubts concerning the legitimacy
of the scheme. In February 1209, when military detachments were

gathering throughout every province, with contributions pouring in and the leaders busy preparing for the great day of departure, Innocent III wrote to King Philip:[4]

It is to you that We especially entrust the cause of God's Holy Church. The army of the Faithful that is forming to combat heresy must have a leader to whom its members will owe unquestioning obedience. We therefore beg your Serene Highness to choose, on your own initiative, some loyal, discreet, and vigorous gentleman who may lead the champions of Our Holy Cause to final triumph under your banner.

The King, however, refused. He would not go to the wars himself, or let his son go; he would not even accept the responsibility of choosing a deputy who could act in his name. The Pope wanted to use the King of France as a legal, secular agent of Divine Justice in this Crusade; but the Crusade remained what in sober fact it was, a war launched by the Church itself. The barons who followed the Cross would be soldiers of the Church; and the leader whom the Crusaders' army appointed over themselves was that Papal Legate Arnald-Amalric, the Abbot of Cîteaux.

The King of France was to have his turn later.

Among the barons who joined the Crusade in 1209 we know the names of Eudes II, Duke of Burgundy, Hervé IV, Count of Nevers (both already mentioned above); Gaucher de Châtillon, Count of Saint-Pol; Simon de Montfort; Pierre de Courtenay; Thibaud Count of Bar; Guichard de Beaujeu; Gauthier de Joigny; Guillaume de Rocher, the Seneschal of Anjou; Guy de Lévis, and many others. But Church dignitaries, too, figure as military leaders. The Archbishops of Rheims, Sens and Rouen, together with the Bishops of Autun, Clermont, Nevers, Bayeux, Lisieux and Chartres, all joined the Crusade. Each of them led a contingent composed half of seasoned fighters, and half of pilgrims who knew nothing of war, but were aflame with the desire to serve God's holy Cause.

A year had passed since the death of Peter of Castelnau, and now the threat looming over Languedoc began to take more precise shape. The Count of Toulouse, whose rank and position could still inspire some respect among those of the Crusaders who were bred in the same caste, had been much discredited by rumours accusing him of complicity in the Legate's murder. But this crime might not suffice in itself to arouse wholehearted execration against him, since the French barons were themselves constantly at daggers drawn with the clergy. Accordingly the propagandists were obliged to blacken his portrait yet further. Pierre des Vaux de Cernay, a faithful interpreter of the extremist movement among the Crusaders, makes the Count a perfectly odious figure.

His private habits, we learn, were abominable. He had little respect for the sanctity of marriage—a venial sin, considering that among the barons of the period a faithful husband was something of a rarity. The facts were simple: he had been married five times, and two of his divorced wives were still alive. Better still, the Count had, as a young man, seduced certain of his father's mistresses. (Since the Count was now fifty-two, the complaint seems to have come a little late in the day.) His part in the murder of Peter of Castelnau, we are told, was notorious—and this though the Pope himself dared make no more than a half-hearted assertion on the subject! In order to prove his statements, the chronicler tells us that Raymond VI paraded the murderer throughout his domains, saying to anyone who cared to listen: 'Do you see this man? He is the only person who truly loves me and knew how to fulfil my desires . . .'[5] The remark would appear to be bitterly ironic; but in any case Raymond could not allow himself little pleasantries of this nature. The Count of Toulouse was a politically cautious man, always anxious to keep on good terms with everyone. Even if he had, in fact, ordered the Legate's murder (which is most improbable) he would be forced to disown the agent he had used. If he failed to punish the man, it was out of concern for public opinion in his own domains. The man who killed so unpopular a Legate was doubtless regarded by his fellow-countrymen as a hero.

The Pope and the leaders of the Crusade saw very clearly that it was the country as a whole which bore the responsibility for this crime, and that the Count should not suffer the abuse of the mob except in his capacity as the country's leader. His crime was, it must be said, a heinous one in the eyes of every faithful member of the Church. He was not content with mere indifference where heresy was concerned; he seemed actively to encourage it.

On this point we possess a wealth of evidence, though since it comes from the Count's enemies it must be regarded with some suspicion. It was alleged that he surrounded himself with known heretics whom he treated in the most courteous fashion. He even had a notion to get his son taught by their ministers. His impiety was notorious: it was not enough for him to practise systematic persecution of churches and monasteries; when he attended Mass he made his jester parody all the gestures of the priest. He was observed to prostrate himself before various heretical ministers, and one day, in a fit of rage, he exclaimed: 'I can see that it was, indeed, the Devil who created this world; nothing goes as I wish it!' In short, the Church (as embodied by Pierre des Vaux de Cernay, a man of somewhat intemperate language but still, doubtless, a fairly accurate guide to the general opinion of his kind) regarded Count Raymond as 'a limb of Satan, a child of perdition, a hardened criminal, a parcel of sinfulness'.[6] Pope Innocent himself is scarcely more charitable: 'impious, cruel tyrant, creature both pestilent and insane' is the way he addresses him.[7]

But this was where Church and Crusaders alike struck one of the biggest stumbling-blocks in their scheme: things turned out to be far more complex than they would have liked. The 'impious tyrant' performed an abrupt *volte-face*, reminding his adversaries that he was still the sovereign lord of a Christian country. After a bungled attempt to get both the King of France and the German Emperor to intercede on his behalf—a remarkable piece of stupidity, since the two monarchs were at daggers drawn, and neither of them was to forgive the Count for approaching the other—Raymond finally declared himself an obedient son of the Church, ready to submit to every condition which the Pope might impose on him.

This decision of the Count's has been severely criticized by historians, who have regarded it as a proof of feebleness, if not downright cowardice. But Raymond VI was by no means the kind of man liable to exclaim 'All is lost save honour'; his personal honour seems to have been a matter of little concern to him; his main concern was to minimize the damage done. We must remember that the majority of his subjects were Catholics, and that consequently they, no less than the heretics in their midst, were liable to suffer if war came.

The Count owed his Catholic subjects this proof of his good faith—and could also use it to cut the ground from under his enemies' feet. If *he* was no longer the foe, against whom were they marching out to war? Heresy as such was a faceless enemy: it possessed neither army, nor headquarters, nor defensive positions—let alone a Pope or a King. By depriving them of a concrete objective the Count destroyed half the *raison d'être* of the Crusade.

But it was far too late to check the mounting enthusiasm which now blazed throughout the Army of God. The Count's submission did not make anyone lay down his arms; it merely served to exasperate his enemies still further, since such a manoeuvre weakened their moral position without in any way advancing the interests of the Church. So it came about that this army, with its 'soldiers of

Christ', invaded a country which felt itself the victim of a flagrant injustice; and what had begun as a religious war became an attack upon an entire nation.

3. *The Land of Languedoc*

While the Crusaders were busy making preparations for war, Innocent III was simultaneously invoking every sort of curse in heaven and earth on the Count of Toulouse in public, and conducting negotiations with him privately. The Count promised to make complete submission, with one *caveat*: he would prefer to discuss the terms of his capitulation with some other Legate than Arnald-Amalric, who was his sworn enemy. The Pope sent him Milo, the Lateran Apostolic Notary, together with Master Thédise, a Genoese Canon. If the Count supposed he now had to do with less rigorous judges, he soon found out his mistake. These two men were merely there to execute orders which came from the Abbot of Cîteaux. Pope Innocent must have told Milo that it was the Abbot who would continue to make decisions; he, Milo, was to be no more than an agent.

In point of fact the Pope had decided to beat the Count at his own game, and match Raymond's feigned submission with an equally feigned clemency. To his special representatives—that is, the Abbot of Cîteaux, together with the Bishops of Riez and Couserans—he wrote as follows:

We have received many and urgent enquiries as to what attitude the Crusaders should take in respect of the Count of Toulouse. Let us follow the advice of that Apostle who said: 'Being crafty, I caught you with guile.' Use a certain judicious dissimulation: leave him [*i.e.* the Count] alone to begin with, and concentrate on the rebels. It will be a far harder task to crush these minions of Antichrist if we give them time to unite their scattered groups into a single body of resistance. If the Count does not come to their aid, on the other hand, nothing should be easier than to finish them off; and perhaps the spectacle of their defeat will bring him back to his senses. However, if he persists in his evil purposes, we will be able (when he is isolated, and thrown back on his own unaided strength) to defeat and crush him without overmuch effort.

The ceremony of the Count's public apology took place in June 1209 at Saint-Gilles, where Peter of Castelnau had been killed. It looks as though the Church were intent, before striking at her enemies, on demonstrating to the people—through the persons of her Legates—just how much the worldly power of the great was worth when confronted by the might and majesty of God.

In the great church of Saint-Gilles (a splendid edifice, which even today hints at both the piety and the luxuriousness which characterized the ancient Counts of Toulouse) there had gathered three archbishops and no less than nineteen bishops; while a great throng of other high dignitaries, together with their liegemen and various clerics, crowded both the church and the square outside. Between the two great lions that guarded the entry to the West Door were set out various relics of Christ and the Saints. The Count, wearing a penitent's garb, with a cord round his neck and a candle in his hand, was brought into the square, stripped to the waist; and here, over the reliquaries, he swore allegiance to the Pope and the Legates. Then Milo draped his stole round the penitent's neck, gave him Absolution, and marched him into the church, beating him smartly about the shoulders with a bundle of birch-twigs as they went. The crowd that surged in behind him was so close-packed that he could not get out the way he had come, and was taken down through the crypt—where Peter of Castelnau was buried. His contemporaries, prone to find signs and portents everywhere, regarded this coincidence as a just punishment for the crime he was assumed to have committed.

Before this cruel ceremony was enacted, the Count had been obliged to subscribe to the following conditions:

(a) He must offer apologies to every bishop and abbot with whom he was at loggerheads.

(b) He must relinquish his rights over the bishoprics and religious houses throughout his domains.

(c) He must rid himself of the bands of veterans and mercenaries whom he employed to defend his territories.

(d) He must no longer entrust any Jew with public office.

(e) He must give up his practice of protecting heretics, and deliver them up to the Crusaders.

(f) He must regard as heretics all those denounced as such by ecclesiastical authority.

(g) He must abide by the Legates' decisions concerning all the complaints that had been laid against him.

(h) He must himself observe, and enforce the observance in others, of every clause in the peace treaty drafted by the Legates.

In short, by making this Act of Submission the Count had accepted a virtual Church dictatorship over his country. He must have calculated that the various clauses of the treaty would be hard to enforce in practice, and doubtless supposed that time would work on his side.

As soon as he had got his Absolution, Count Raymond took the initiative in an unforeseen way: he asked to be allowed to join the Crusade himself. This decision was somewhat startling, coming as it did from a prince who had always done his utmost to accommodate heretics. 'A further example of his double-dealing,' Vaux de Cernay wrote. 'His only motive for joining the Crusade was to render his person and property immune from seizure, and to provide a cloak for his nefarious schemes.'[8] With this view the evidence seems, indeed, to agree well enough. But Raymond was also trying to go over the Legates' heads (there was, clearly, nothing more to be hoped for from them) and to win the trust of the Pope himself. And indeed, on 26th July Innocent wrote to him: 'From an object of scandal to many, lo, you have been transformed into a model subject. . . . We have no wish but for your welfare and your honour. You may rest assured that We shall not allow any wrong to be done you if you have not deserved it.' This was the language of diplomacy, and did not perhaps by intent commit the writer to any very weighty obligation; but it was a card which Count Raymond was to play to its uttermost limit.

The Count of Toulouse was not merely the main actor in the drama that was to be played out across his territory: his character resembles a scaled-down projection of all his country's weaknesses and contradictions, virtues and misfortunes. His behaviour was not so much due to personal, individual decisions, whether for good or ill, as to the general condition of Languedoc at the time of the disaster—a condition which it in some sort reflects. His private character vanishes when confronted with the public rôle he was obliged to play. We cannot even say that the task was too heavy for his shoulders to bear, since he seems to have identified himself so closely with his people's cause that in the end they saw him as something very much more than a mere leader. He was their rightful sovereign, in the full sense of that term: a sovereign whose function was to be his people's symbolic representative, and the slave of his subjects' wishes or needs. With all his faults and weaknesses, he remains human to the end—especially when contrasted with adversaries whom bigotry, fanaticism, ambition or plain ignorance had robbed of all humane qualities. In an age when people were judged and condemned according to the conduct of their princes, Count Raymond VI had committed a crime which carried such dire consequences that it was impossible to let him get off scot free: he had been a tolerant ruler,

Tolerance did not pass for a virtue in that period, and doubtless Raymond never boasted of possessing it. His ancestors—indeed, his own father—had burnt heretics, as their neighbouring monarchs had also done. But towards the end of the twelfth century heresy had become so widespread that any attempt to observe the letter of the law would have entailed burning people by the thousand and reducing whole provinces to beggary. The Count could no longer persecute heretics, for the excellent reason that they now formed a large proportion of his subjects. What in other countries was still regarded as a monstrous scandal had become in the Midi a sort of necessary evil, which in the end would no longer be regarded as an evil at all. When Foulques, the Bishop of Toulouse, asked the Chevalier Pons Adhémar why they did not break up the nest of heretics in their territories and drive them out, Adhémar replied: 'We cannot do it. We were all brought up together. Many of them are related to us. Besides, we can see for ourselves that they live decent, honourable lives.'[9] William de Puylaurens, who tells the story, adds: 'In this way heresy, shielding itself hypocritically behind the pretence of an honourable life, concealed the truth from these somewhat impercipient souls.'

Such were the facts; but we still have to discover how a country with so lengthy and well-established a Catholic tradition could reach the point where it tacitly accepted a creed the avowed aim of which was to destroy the Church utterly. In order to understand this phenomenon we must cast a rapid glance over the history of Languedoc during the twelfth century, examining its social and political condition and, in particular, analysing the spiritual and moral climate which prevailed there. This cluster of provinces was, after all, one of the main centres of Western culture during our period.

The lands actually under the sovereignty of the Counts of Toulouse were almost as extensive as those that owed direct allegiance to the French Crown; but Languedoc itself, the area where the Occitan dialect was spoken, was not a major Power. Nevertheless, it remained an independent territory. In theory the Count of Toulouse was vassal to the King of France; but in fact he was less a vassal than the Count of Champagne or even the Duke of Burgundy. Paris was a long way from Toulouse; Northern speech was different from that of the Midi; and the French King's power in the Midi remained purely nominal. On the other hand the Count held part of his domains in fief from the King of England, an equally distant and theoretical sovereign. Certain important vassals of the Count's also owed allegiance to the King of Aragon; and this monarch controlled certain areas in the heart of Languedoc—Montpellier for one, and the viscountcies of Carlat and Millau. Arles, again, belonged to the Emperor. Such a diversity of overlords was in itself a guarantee of independence. Provided the Emperor kept his distance; provided the King of England remained busy defending his vast domains against the growing power of successive Kings of France; provided the King of Aragon (whose main concern in any case was to add to his territories beyond the Pyrenees) continued to be caught up with his endless campaign against the Moors; provided the French King's desire to extend his boundaries led him towards lands that marched with his own along geographically dictated frontiers—why, then the Count of Toulouse had nothing to fear. In their struggle to maintain a dominant influence over his terrain, the Count's rival overlords were not so much his masters as, virtually, his protectors.

But this picture is still too clear-cut: more remains to be told. During the course of the twelfth century the County of Toulouse was successively invaded by both the English and the Aragonese, who ravaged the Rouergue district and the environs of Toulouse. Raymond V, Raymond VI's father, spent his whole life defending himself against his dangerous 'protectors'. In 1181, among the allies of his adversary, the King of Aragon, he had to reckon his own major vassals: the Counts of Montpellier, Foix and Comminges, and the Viscount of Béziers. He was Louis VII's brother-in-law by virtue of his marriage to Louis's sister Constance; and the King did, in the event, come to his aid to protect him against the English. But his conduct towards his wife was such that very soon he had to break off relations with the King of France and transfer his homage to the House of Plantagenet. Unfortunately the old English King, Henry II, was at war with his own son, Richard Coeur-de-Lion; and the latter invaded the Toulouse area at the head of his army of mercenaries. All this goes to show that a policy based on maintaining the balance of power has its dangers; nevertheless, the Counts of Toulouse clung stubbornly to their independence. The kings of France, England and Aragon all gave them their sisters in marriage and angled for their alliance; each successive Raymond remained a free agent when he set foot on their soil, owing obedience to no man.

Yet these same Counts had very little more authority over their own provinces than the kings of France did over the County of Toulouse. The Trencavel family, hereditary Viscounts of Béziers, possessed domains that embraced the districts of Carcassès, Albigeois and Razès; these lands of theirs, which stretched in all from the

Tarn to the Pyrenees, were in vassalage to the King of Aragon. Throughout the twelfth century the Counts of Toulouse were to struggle, unsuccessfully, against the growing power of the Trencavels. The Counts of Foix, too, safe in their mountain fastnesses, remained equally impervious to the authority of the Counts of Toulouse, and only formed alliances with them in order to fight against the Trencavels. Various vassal leagues were continually being formed against the Count, and as frequently dissolved, according to the state of each member's aims and interests.

These examples would give a poor notion of the political situation in Languedoc on the eve of the Crusade if we did not bear in mind that the same conditions prevailed in almost every Western kingdom. The kings of France were constantly compelled to defend themselves against vassal leagues. In England a systematic fight conducted by feudal barons against the royal prerogative culminated in Magna Carta. Germany and Italy were the scenes of continual warfare, ranging from parish-pump rivalry to the grim struggle for the Empire. In this period, when the moral ties binding a man to his *seigneur* and his Church were a real and indisputable bond, each individual's conduct seemed inspired by the old saying about a man's home being his castle.

These people never talked about liberty. Yet they acted, for the most part, as though their freedom was the one ideal, the only possession that they had to defend. We see towns rising in revolt against their lawful *seigneur* through fear of having their rights of self-government curtailed. Bishops stood their ground against kings, even against Popes, while the *seigneurs* in turn attacked the bishops. All of them, apparently, made it a special point of honour not to accept any form of constraint. In the Midi this attitude had just about reached its apogee, for the country was wealthy, endowed with an ancient traditional culture of which it was most proud, and at the same time eager for progress.

We see, then, that the Count of Toulouse was not in control of his own vassals; but, odder still, even within his personal domains, which were traditionally loyal to him, he found himself unable to raise an army, and was forced to rely upon mercenaries. It was very often the case that he simply had no vassals on whom he might call, for this reason: whereas in the North a *seigneur*'s heritage would pass, after his death, to his eldest son, in the Midi the fief was split up equally amongst all his children. Thus after three generations or so a château could belong to fifty or sixty '*co-seigneurs*', who in their turn, whether by marriage or the rights of succession, might also be *co-seigneurs* of other châteaux besides. The result was that the big estates did not have a true owner, but merely a kind of manager. Furthermore, since brothers and cousins were frequently liable to quarrel among themselves, a fief, even an important one, did not form a military unit, as was the case in France.

Nor was the Count master of the major towns, which formed small autonomous republics, only acknowledging their overlord provided he left them alone. Since trade flourished in Languedoc, and several great trade-routes passed through it, its cities, notoriously, achieved a greater degree of prosperity than those elsewhere. A burgher's privileges were substantial indeed. Every inhabitant became a free man the moment he took up residence there, and his citizenship was so strong a guarantee of his security that no external authority possessed the right to bring him to trial. Though he committed a crime a hundred leagues outside the walls, only that city's tribunal could pass judgment upon him.

The towns were governed by consuls—a survival from Roman Law. This code still formed the basis of all local jurisdiction. The consuls (or *capitouls*) were elected from among the city nobility and bourgeoisie; and in this respect the burgher was the knight's equal, *de facto* no less than *de jure*. Here we may observe a relaxation of the caste-tradition which the Northern nobility were to hold against both classes in the Midi, and for which they could not forgive them. The rich burgher was a *grand seigneur*, and so confident of his rights that he would stand his ground against any knight. In the defence of their precious liberties these burghers shrank from nothing. During the year 1161 the citizens of Béziers, for example, murdered their Viscount and beat up their Bishop in the Church of the Madeleine. It is true that this crime provoked frightful reprisals; but the spirit of independence that glowed in these tiny republics was tempered and strengthened by their long battle against the abuse of princely power.

In the midst of this organized chaos stood the Church, a supra-national body, disciplined in theory, and obedient to one supreme Head; yet the Church too was forced, by pressure of circumstance, to yield before the prevalent contagion. In her capacity as temporal power she drew most cruel persecution upon herself; her wealth excited all manner of covetousness, while her authority seemed a standing threat to all individual liberty. The bishops were haughty of speech and masterful in their actions; they considered themselves —after God and the Pope—the country's rightful masters. In point of fact there was no justification for their claims: here as elsewhere

B

—perhaps here especially—they were great feudal landlords, who had at their disposal vast territories and very considerable revenues. They were frequently more concerned with the defence of their temporal interests than the spiritual direction of those who dwelt in their diocese. They had an excuse for this. It was essential, they said, to cry with the pack, since the Church's earthly patrimony was a guarantee of her moral freedom, and that patrimony was very severely threatened.

These bishops were both indifferent to Papal authority and extremely unpopular in their own dioceses. The people refused to back them against the barons, and instead reviled them for their luxury, their lack of concern for the poor, and their passionate addiction to Crusades. The abbots, who, thanks to their richly endowed monasteries, could boast no less princely a state, were almost equally ill-regarded. The common clergy, through the neglect of their superiors, had fallen into such discredit that the bishops were hard put to it to find fresh priests, and would ordain the first candidates who came to hand. According to the unanimous testimony of every contemporary Catholic writer, the Church in the Midi at this period had neither authority nor prestige: it was spiritually dead.

So the Catholic population was reduced to one of two alternatives. Either they had to make do with a Church that might well lead even the best of them astray; or else they must seek some other outlet for their spiritual aspirations.

The evidence cited hitherto might lead one to suppose that Languedoc was a kind of hell where discord and anarchy reigned. It was in fact a country where life was far less rigorous than elsewhere, a country that possessed a sort of unity. But this unity was internal rather than apparent, lying as it did in the civilization of which each inhabitant partook, and which formed an invisible bond between them, a bond expressed by a certain common mode of thought and feeling. It was not merely the burgher's wealth that made the knight respect him; and though these Counts of Toulouse were for ever embroiled in disputes with their bishops and vassals, the people continued to show them unconditional love and respect.

There were, indeed, numerous wars, which, though they involved a small number only of actual combatants, always caused much damage to the crops. Despite this the people as a whole were by no means poverty-stricken. From contemporary witnesses (such as Etienne, Abbot of Ste Geneviève, the future Bishop of Tournai[10]) we learn that the roads were unsafe, being infested by Basque and

Aragonese freebooters; that the fields were burnt and the houses in ruins. (For lack of regular troops the barons in the Midi used to employ mercenaries.) But villages on the main roads were comparatively rare, being mostly fortified burghs or overflows from a nearby city; thus the peasant was often a townsman too, and hoed his vines under the shadow of the city-walls. The soil was fertile, and the towns' prosperity was reflected in the lives led by the peasantry. Not only the burghers but a great number of peasants as well were free men; and in many of the fiefs the absence of one paramount *seigneur* meant that the serfs were not really responsible to anyone.

The burgher was a privileged person: he not only had his freedom, but was also protected by his community. The increasing development of trade, too, had made its impact on the working classes. Even humble artisans were gradually being transformed into a powerful class, with full realization of their rights.

The influence and authority exercised by the bourgeoisie played a prominent part in the social evolution of Languedoc. The land of the troubadours was also the land of trade *par excellence*: a country in which the burgher's social position was beginning to eclipse that of the nobility. It is true that the burghers, whether out of snobbishness or through some lingering sense of inferiority, still made efforts to acquire noble escutcheons; but this was, in their case, mere gratuitous self-satisfaction. When any bourgeoisie is treated on an equal footing by the aristocratic society of the day, this means, in fact, that it has the upper hand.

The Rhône and the Garonne were great arteries, along which was borne all merchandise and raw material exchanged between the North and the Midi. Marseilles, Toulouse, Avignon and Narbonne had been major ports since ancient times. The Crusades enriched all the cities of the West; but Languedoc in particular, on account of its position as half-way house and key to the Near East, made a veritable fortune out of them. Those about to embark bought their stores and equipment for the voyage there, while returning veterans sold their booty to Languedoc traders; the local nobility, a feckless and footloose lot, were often forced to sell their lands and goods for a mere song to the bankers who financed expeditions to the Holy Land. From these perennially out-of-pocket overlords the common people in due course purchased various privileges and liberties which, once having got, they were never again to surrender. Since the burghers acknowledged no master apart from their consuls, it followed that the Count of Toulouse lacked any legal authority in his own city, and was only obeyed so long as he respected local common law.

Every burgher had the right to buy, sell, or engage in barter without paying any duties or taxes on such transactions. There were no restrictions placed upon marriage. Resident aliens enjoyed full citizens' rights, regardless of their nationality or creed. These 'free towns' formed the centres of the country's social life: the election of a consul was a great public event, celebrated with processions and a universal hammering of church bells, its pomp and splendour rivalling any religious festival. A citizen's life, from the cradle to the grave, was closely bound up with the life of the city itself. The nuptial blessing pronounced by the priest could not, for sheer solemnity, match the moment when bride and bridegroom were brought before the consuls, magnificent in their ermine-trimmed robes, and made their offering of flowers and fruit-laden branches. As an instrument of secularization (albeit permeated with both the spirit and the external ritual of religious faith) this flourishing public life in the 'free towns' stood very high.

Being predominantly commercial cities, the townships of the South attained an opulence which the North had every reason to envy. There was no comparison between Paris and Toulouse, and neither Troyes nor Rouen was a match for Avignon. The splendour of such Catholic churches in the Midi as war and the passage of time have spared helps us to imagine just how magnificent these cities must have been in their hey-day—great centres of religious and cultural development, where business, industry, and every sort of craft and art flourished. The larger ones could boast schools of medicine, philosophy, mathematics and astrology: not only Toulouse, but also Narbonne, Avignon, Montpellier and Béziers were in fact university cities before the nominal foundation of their universities. At Toulouse, the course on Aristotle embodied various recent discoveries made by Arab philosophers; since the ecclesiastical authorities in Paris refused to release this material, the philosophical school at Toulouse gained considerable prestige as a result of their censorship.

Regular contact with the Moslem world had been established very early on, mainly through the medium of Arab merchants and doctors, who reached Languedoc either from the East, or across the Pyrenees. The infidel could no longer be regarded as a natural enemy. The Jews, who formed a large and powerful community in every major business centre, were not debarred from public life through any sort of religious prejudice. Their doctors and savants were held in high regard by the general populace throughout the cities of the area; they had their own schools, where they gave free courses of lectures, some of which were open to the public. Catholic students had no objection to attending such lectures. For instance, we hear of a Doctor Abraham from Beaucaire, and in Saint-Gilles we find a scholar named Simeon and a Rabbi Jacob. The influence of Jewish and Moslem apocryphal writings was widespread among the clergy, and even reached the common people. In some towns, indeed, Jews were appointed to the office of consul or magistrate.

For good or ill, one thing is certain: in this area secular life was considerably more flourishing than its religious counterpart—to a point where the latter seemed likely to be snuffed out altogether.

The nobles drifted with the tide of events. Some historians present them as a vain, ineffectual, degenerate body; others see in them the finest flowering of the knightly *esprit courtois* that the age could show. What is certain, however, is that the bulk of this nobility had acquired a strong bourgeois streak; that its members were cultured gentlemen more addicted to civil than to military matters, even though, on occasion, the knights of Languedoc could show themselves every whit as brave as their Northern rivals. Here, in short, was an aristocracy which was beginning to forget that its main purpose, indeed, its traditional *raison d'être*, was the profession of arms. Yet this did not prevent its members from being very fierce-tempered indeed when their personal interests were at stake.

There were no more great causes to fight for; decentralization and the parcelling out of the estates had seen to that. The result was that each baron fought merely for his own advantage, and yesterday's foes were only too likely to become today's friends—or *vice versa*. In the end such petty local rivalries were no longer taken very seriously, even by the interested parties. Besides, though nobles and burghers did not always see eye to eye with one another, they at least united to encroach systematically upon the rights of the Church. The Church's powers had been weakened, and her unpopularity made her all the easier to attack. Many bishops were ruined as a result of the wars they were forced to wage against the great or lesser barons. There was nothing uplifting for the nobility in campaigns of this nature; and in any case, their minds were elsewhere.

The time was long past when the Church had a virtual monopoly in the production of what we may term the intellectual class. For over a century now the laity had enjoyed a mastery of the written word, and the literary language used in Christian countries was no longer Latin. Literature, indeed, was coming to play an increasingly important part in the lives, not only of the aristocracy, but of the middle classes as well. Northern Frenchmen, Germans, and Englishmen were all great readers of romances. Secular drama began, somewhat shyly, to appear side by side with its religious counterpart. The arts of poetry and music had become an essential daily perquisite even for the lesser nobility and the bourgeoisie.

It is a curious fact that the Midi has left us no literature in the field of fictional romance. On the other hand its poetic heritage stands supreme in European history, being not only most ancient, but also unique in the quality of its inspiration. Its genius was universally recognized, and imitated as far afield as Germany. For French, Italian, and Catalan poets alike, the Occitan tongue was the language of literature *par excellence*; we should not forget that Dante originally intended to compose his *Divina Commedia* in it.

If we cannot think of the Southern French nobility without immediately evoking the name of the troubadours, the fact remains that these aristocrats were genuinely and passionately devoted to poetry, and tried, as best they could, to carry out in practice the literary ideals of their age. It is easy to accuse them of having their heads in the clouds; but when we consider the matter more closely, they appear more realistic than, say, Louis XIV's courtiers, whose highest ambition was to have the honour of helping the King get up in the morning. For a Southern gentleman of the twelfth century, honour consisted in a certain disdain for the good things of this world, coupled with an unbounded exaltation of one's own personality. The adoration of the Lady, that marvellous and inaccessible Lover, is nothing else, surely, but the urge to proclaim a triumph of self-will? Even though one may be offering one's devotion, it is not to some divinity whom the whole world shares, but to a private deity of one's own, freely chosen.

Some commentators have gone so far as to claim that the Lady was purely symbolic, and represented either the Cathar Church or some esoteric revelation; and it is true that the poems of certain troubadours bear considerable resemblance, in style and tone, to those of the Arab mystics. This can almost certainly be ascribed to mere literary imitation, for at the time it occurred to no one to regard such poetry as being anything other than love-poetry. Nevertheless it remains true that troubadour verse appears to deal primarily, not with love itself, so much as with a method of attaining moral and spiritual perfection through love's agency. These sighs and torments, these protracted vigils and metaphorical deaths seem at once passionately sincere and, somehow, a little unreal. What the poet seems to be admiring, all through these bouts of suffering, is his own exquisite soul.

A turbulent, restless, egotistical society, this; given to prodigal extravagance (e.g. the Seigneur de Venous, who out of sheer bravado had thirty horses burnt alive in the presence of his guests), obsessed with most apparently impractical arts, hungry for unattainable loves. Yet behind such qualities there is evident a certain way of life which by no means lacked nobility. That superficial appearance of frivolity perhaps masked a desire for withdrawal, an unwillingness to treat unworthy subjects seriously. When the time of peril came upon them, and the initial surprise was over, the nobles of Languedoc proved themselves warriors indeed: there was a stubborn, even a ferocious quality about their patriotism. The political weaknesses they showed cannot on any count be taken to signify a lack of vital energy.

One thing we know, at all events, is that the nobles of Languedoc were not only indulgent towards heresy, but became its most steadfast (and, indeed, notorious) supporters. It was because this new religion had won over the only class of the population who were in a position to defend the Church's cause by force of arms, that the Crusade was deemed essential in the first place.

Languedoc was Catholic both in theory and actuality: yet by a wholly natural process, quite smoothly and without any overt rebellion, it had become a land of heresy. The new doctrine was now so well acclimatized that it was already impossible to distinguish the wheat from the tares: the only alternatives were to strike indiscriminately or to do nothing at all. Throughout this pitiless ten years' war the heretics came more and more to seem a mere excuse for the Crusaders' real aim: the destruction of the entire country. Yet far from eradicating this heresy, the Crusade in fact renewed and redoubled its strength. A century was to elapse before Catharism was finished, and then its end was only achieved by the gradual obliteration of everything which went to make up the living tradition of Languedoc.

CHAPTER II

HERESY AND HERETICS

1. *Origins*

THE EXISTENCE OF HERESY cannot be considered apart from the
existence of the Church itself: the two run *pari passu*. Dogma is
always accompanied by heresy; from the very first the history of the
Christian Church was a long catalogue of battles against various
heresies—battles no less bloody or bitter than those which the
Christian communities fought against their pagan neighbours. But
from the sixth century onwards Western Europe, still barely recovered from the shock of the great invasions, and constantly
threatened with the possibility of fresh inroads, nevertheless enjoyed
relative stability in its religious affairs. The authority of the Church
was (in theory at least) respected and obeyed.*

Yet heresy—or rather, heresies—proliferated everywhere. Survivals from those supposedly defeated creeds, the Arian and the
Manichaean, cropped up incessantly, sometimes in the shape of a
tacit compromise with orthodoxy, sometimes in open opposition
to it. Furthermore, the inevitable abuses characteristic of an Established Church were in evidence here, and provoked a never-ending
stream of protest and would-be reforms; these often became heresies
by definition—that is, they diverged from official doctrine. Heresies
appeared in the country districts, where they probably represented
a barely Christianized survival of Celtic mysticism; and in the
monasteries, as the fruit of much meditation on the part of monks
with minds of their own. They were uttered *ex cathedra* by learned
Professors of Theology, and also turned up in the towns, where they
tended to be identified with some sort of social revolution.

---

* The Schism of 1054, which brought about final separation between the
Churches of Rome and Byzantium, was no more than the ratification of a *fait
accompli*. For all their community of doctrinal belief, the two Churches had long
since parted company in a political and historical sense, and had no good
reason for prolonging their mutual dependence. Rome was now, as far as the
West was concerned, sole arbiter in matters of religious truth—which meant, in
effect, that she had a monopoly of truth in general.

But in Northern Italy and the French Midi Rome was confronted with a very different sort of situation. It was no longer a matter of local or individual manifestations of independence; a rival religion, no less, had planted itself in the very heart of Christendom and was gaining ground fast—largely by presenting itself as the one true Faith. The traditional means of persuasion which the Church employed against her straying flock here ran into an absolutely immovable brick wall. These heretics were no longer dissident Catholics: they drew their strength from the consciousness of belonging to a faith that had never seen eye to eye with Catholicism, and was more ancient than the Church itself.

We should not, however, lose sight of one important fact. Very many of the heretics, both in Italy and in Languedoc, were not Cathars: they belonged to various 'reforming' sects, such as the Waldensian, which the Church would have almost certainly contrived, in the long run, to draw within her orbit by means of a more liberal and comprehensive policy. But as such vaguely extremist movements of reform were afterwards confused with the great central heresy, Catharism, it is this which we must primarily consider.

The religion of the Cathars, or 'pure ones', came from the East. Their contemporaries labelled them as Manichaeans or Arians: indeed, the majority of heretical sects that appeared in Western Europe from the eleventh century onwards were given the common title of 'Manichaean'. This was merely a figure of speech: the heretics themselves never claimed any connection with Mani, and it is clear that the various Churches with avowed Manichaean tendencies (e.g. those established in Spain, North Africa, and even in France) had for long now renounced so alarming an affiliation, with the anathemas and bonfires that it brought in its wake. There was no longer such a being as a 'Manichaean'; by now there were only 'Christians'.

Some modern historians—F. Niel, for example—have gone so far as to claim that Catharism was not in fact a heresy at all, but an alien religion that had nothing whatsoever in common with Christianity. It might be more accurate to say that it had nothing in common with the Christianity that ten centuries of Church history had produced. The Cathar religion was indeed a heresy, one which can be dated back to a time when the Church's doctrines had not yet hardened into dogma. During this period the ancient world was searching around desperately, by every means at its disposal, to find some formula capable of assimilating so wholly alien a creed.

Christianity was too explosive and dynamic: its contradictions, whether apparent or genuine, were not calculated to reassure minds addicted to clarity.

One answer was Gnosticism, an attempt to make a synthesis of ancient philosophy and Christianity, which denied the possibility of God having created either evil or physical matter. Though speedily condemned by the Early Fathers, this system never completely disappeared. Its spirit remained very much alive in the Eastern Churches, and its influence on the Western tradition was much greater than is commonly supposed. The Gnostics influenced the doctrine of Mani, who, as the heir to Zoroastrianism, believed in two essential principles, those of Good and Evil. Mani, in his turn, also influenced Gnosticism: of this interpenetration there was born that great Dualist tradition which bore the name of Manichaeism, and which, by various underground routes, crept into the citadel of orthodox Christianity.

But the Manichaeans proper, after having spawned a series of powerful sects that spread right across Europe and Asia, even penetrating as far as China, suffered a series of cruel persecutions and finally vanished. The name of Mani was obliterated by that of Christ. There remained the Paulicians, a Manichaean sect with strong Christianizing tendencies, which flourished in Armenia and Asia Minor; but in 872 they were conquered by the Greeks and forced into submission, many of them being deported to the Balkan peninsula on the Emperor's orders. It was here that there formed the nucleus of that Church which was later to be identified with the Cathars.

In the seventh century an Asiatic people called the Bulgars had reached the Balkans and established a kingdom there, to the south of the Danube. When, during the eleventh century, the Greek and Latin Churches were simultaneously busy converting the Slav population of Bulgaria, it was here that the deported Paulicians, too, were still engaged in their own missionary activities. And it was in Bulgaria that Catharism—the Catharism which spread through the Midi—also appeared in the tenth century, under the name of Bogomilism.

We do not know whether the founder of this sect was really called Bogomil (that is, the Beloved of God), and applied his ordinary surname to the creed he professed; or whether, in accordance with a tendency common among the Slavs, the word was intended to suggest some symbolical, generalized personality. In the latter case, for lack of accurate information, devotees of the sect must ultimately have assumed the existence of a real, flesh-and-blood founder. The orthodox writers of the period also refer to a certain 'Papa' Jeremiah. The origins of the sect are shrouded in obscurity; but it spread rapidly, and there was no denying its dynamic force. In Bulgaria, despite a series of persecutions (due to the creed's revolutionary tendencies, which worried the ruling classes), the Bogomils increased and multiplied. Not only that: they very soon began to send out field missionaries, throughout the whole Mediterranean world. The new religion gained ground in Bosnia and Serbia, where it maintained itself so effectively that it frequently figured as the official State religion, and was not finally blotted out till the Turkish invasion in the fifteenth century.

By the eleventh century Bogomil doctrines had been disseminated throughout Northern Italy and the Midi. We cannot tell just what, exactly, there may have been in the way of Manichaean survivals here to allow so rapid an assimilation of Bulgarian Catharism. It remains true that the Cathar faith became so firmly established in these countries (its effect rather resembles that of yeast on bread) that from the middle of the twelfth century it emerges as a quasi-official, albeit persecuted, religion. It had its own local history and traditions, its own organized hierarchy. The Catharist movement was beginning to throw off, with increasing boldness, its hitherto clandestine and ineffectual nature. In 1167 the Bulgarian Bishop Nikita, or Nicetas,* arrived from Constantinople for the purpose of confirming the young Churches of Languedoc in the true Bogomil tradition, and called a Council of Cathar bishops and ministers at Saint-Félix de Caraman, near Toulouse. This one piece of evidence shows us how far the Cathar Church had gone towards proclaiming its own universality and supra-national unity, in direct defiance of the Church of Rome. It was no longer merely a sect, or an opposition movement aimed against the Established Church: it had become a Church of its own.

The authorities, scared by the size of this movement, at first responded by attempts to intimidate its members. The Count of Toulouse, Raymond V, even dreamed of a Crusade in which the Kings of both France and England would participate. Pope Alexander III sent his Cardinal Legate, Peter of Chrysogonus, to Toulouse at the head of a powerful delegation. But when the Legate saw that there were far too many heretics for him to hunt down and bring to book, he contented himself perforce with making an example instead.

* Referred to by Catholic chronicles as *papa*, a fact doubtless due to some confusion between the terms for 'Pope' and 'priest'.

He got hold of a wealthy and universally respected old man, Peter Mauran, who was a burgher of Toulouse known for his friendliness towards the heretics, and had him publicly whipped. After three years' exile in the Holy Land, Mauran returned to Toulouse, and amid scenes of great pomp and rejoicing was elected *capitoul*. The Legate's *démarche* had merely served to increase the popularity of the new faith.

It is easy to explain the success which Catharism achieved by pointing out such factors as the spiritual insolvency of the Catholic hierarchy in Languedoc; or the greedy ambition of burghers and nobility alike, both only too grateful for an excuse to plunder Church property without scruple; or the weakness which both classes had for anything that smacked of novelty. We have already observed that conditions were favourable for the blossoming of a new religion. But favourable conditions do not of themselves explain very much. The reasons for this religion's extraordinary success must be sought inside the religion itself.

2. Doctrine and Dogma

This is not the place to make a detailed study of the doctrine and ideas held by the Catharist Church. In the first place, even the little evidence we possess concerning it would provide enough material for several volumes; and in the second, such evidence would not of itself tell us what this vanished creed was really like. As well might we try to reconstruct a dead man's living features from a study of his skull. We can make a few brief hints, and any number of guesses. Not only did the Cathar faith suffer a peculiarly violent demise; it was also subjected to so systematic a process of denigration, slander, and distortion that even those who were not *a priori* biased against it ended up by finding it somewhat contrary to the normal dictates of reason. Such is the case with all dead religions; besides, mediaeval Catholicism on occasion seems just as strange to us as does the Catharist faith.

The best we can do is to give a brief outline of essential doctrine, draw what conclusions we may from such concrete facts as remain in our possession and attempt to form some sort of notion, however vague, of the spiritual climate in which this religion was enabled to develop and ripen.

One question immediately poses itself: did Catharism embody any sort of esoteric teaching? There are certain facts which suggest that this might conceivably be the case—among others, the existence of the stronghold of Montségur, and its very curious, not to say unique, design. But if this religion *did* have its mysteries and secret rites, their secret has been kept extraordinarily well. Even those *perfecti* who were converted to Catholicism and joined the ranks of the Inquisition, such as Raynier Sacchoni, never breathed a word concerning them. Certain specific items of Catharist doctrine, in particular those relative to fasting and feast-days, remain obscure, for the excellent reason that it never occurred to the Inquisitors to interrogate any heretic on such matters. Of a once abundant and varied Catharist literature nothing remains except one or two documents that accidentally escaped destruction[1]: and we cannot tell whether these were important works, or even if they faithfully reflect the spirit of the Catharist Church as a whole. Besides, like all Churches, this one too embraced numerous 'heresies' or divergent opinions within its main body; doubtless it might also have contained one or two especially 'esoteric' sects unknown to the majority of the faithful.

What is quite certain is that the Cathars were great preachers, and made no secret of their beliefs. On several occasions we see them taking part in theological debates, or attending meetings at which their learned doctors argue with bishops and Legates. These public discussions continued from 1176 (Lombers) until the missionary campaign conducted by St Dominic and his companions between 1206 and 1208. They proved that the Cathars of Languedoc were men very much of their place and time: mighty orators, passionate logicians who never tried to take refuge behind vague but ineffable mysteries that could not be revealed to the profane. On the contrary, they claimed that their doctrine rested on sound, reasonable common sense, and attacked the 'mysteries' of the Catholic Church, which they charged with being mere superstition and magic.

But it is equally true that our knowledge of this doctrine is restricted to those points over which it came into conflict with the Church—that is, in a sense, its negative side. It might be alleged that, granted the fact of Catharism being opposed to the Church in almost all respects, merely to list the points of disagreement should give a fairly complete picture of the Cathar's doctrinal position. But this is not at all certain; indeed, the chances are that the whole positive side of Catharist teaching is lost to us, and that, after all, was what gave the movement its very real success.

Our knowledge of this religion, then, is limited to two sources of evidence. First, there are its 'errors'—that is, the points in which it diverged from Catholic doctrine; and secondly, there are certain features of its external organization—the lives and customs of its adherents, its rites and ceremonies. Here we find ourselves rather in the position of a man who knows nothing about Christianity, and is trying to understand a description of the Mass that omits all mention of its spiritual, emotional, or symbolic significance. All we can do is to regard it with the respect that any profound mystical experience deserves, and not attempt to explain it.

The 'errors' of Catharism are legion. They date back to that Gnostic tradition which proclaimed the absolute separation of Spirit and matter. As Manichaeans the Cathars were dualists, and believed in the existence of two opposed principles of Good and Evil. Some Cathar theologians held that these two principles had existed since the beginning of the world, while others regarded the principle of Evil as a later creation, a fallen angel. But whether the origin of Evil was set outside time altogether, in primeval Chaos, or supposed to be the result of ill-will on the part of one of God's creatures (and God was both unique and good), all Cathars were at one in the belief that God, though good, was *not* omnipotent; that Evil warred implacably against Him, for ever challenging His claim to supremacy. (The end of Time would, however, give the final victory to God.) In a period when men believed just as firmly in the Devil as they did in the Deity, this theory need hardly cause surprise.

The most difficult tenet for Christians to accept was the one which formed the very keystone of all Catharist doctrine: that is, the assertion that the material world was never created by God, being in fact wholly the work of Satan. Without entering into a detailed discussion of various extremely complex cosmogonies, which explain the Fall of Satan and his Angels, and the Creation of matter, we can simply state that Cathars regarded the visible, tangible world (including, for most sects, the sun and stars) as a diabolical phenomenon and a manifestation of Evil.

Then what about Man? He too, insofar as he was a creature of flesh and blood, was regarded as a creation of the Devil. The Spirit of Evil, however, was incapable of creating life, and therefore was supposed to have asked God for His help—by breathing a soul into a body of clay. God of His bounty agreed to assist this depressingly sterile creator; but the wisp of divine Spirit thus breathed into the gross envelope that Satan had wrought for it refused to remain there. However, by a series of ruses, the Devil succeeded in binding it prisoner. Our first parents, Adam and Eve, were supposed to have been impelled by the Devil towards that carnal union which finally consummated their position as creatures of matter. According to the doctrine of certain schools, the Spirit breathed by God transmitted itself, via the act of procreation, to Adam's descendants, like a flame undergoing infinite subdivision and multiplication. But the more generally accepted theory was as follows: The Devil (otherwise Lucifer or Lucibel) either brought down in his Fall, or else lured down from Heaven by various seductive deceits, a great crowd of souls who had been created by God and were living close to Him, in a state of beatitude. It was from this inexhaustible reserve of fallen or captive angels that human souls derived, and were then condemned to a yet more frightful degradation by being thrust into a fleshly body. In the Catharist cosmogony the material world represented the very lowest aspect of reality, that which lay for all eternity at the furthest remove from God: there was a whole graded sequence of other worlds, which offered various possible degrees of salvation.

The Devil was none other than the God of the Old Testament, Sabaoth or Jaldabaoth, whose crude attempts to emulate the creative scope of the Good Deity merely produced a wretched universe in which, despite all his efforts, he never contrived anything lasting. The souls of those angels who had been forced, on account of their own weakness, into a material body remained utterly alien to this world; their life there, cut off from the Spirit which had been in them prior to their fall, was one of unimaginable suffering.

In this respect, too, the various Cathar sects show certain discrepancies between one another. Some of them claimed that the total number of these 'lost souls' was limited, and that they merely migrated from one body to another, in a continual sequence of births and deaths—a view very much akin to the Hindu doctrine of metempsychosis and *karma*. Others again believed the opposite of this. Each new birth, they thought, brought down one of those diabolically corrupted angels, if not from Heaven, at any rate from the region between heaven and earth. Hence the Cathars' notorious horror of procreation, the cruellest act of all in their view, since it dragged a heavenly soul into our world of material matter. Be that as it may, the Cathars, generally speaking, acknowledged the doctrine of metempsychosis as held by the Hindus, with the same precise calculations governing posthumous retribution for the individual. A man who had led a just life would be reincarnated in a body better suited for his further spiritual development; whereas the criminal was liable, after his death, to be reborn in a body full of flaws and hereditary vices—or even, in extreme cases, in that of an animal. But apart from these endless and most depressing rebirths, the fallen souls were allowed no glimmer of hope, and could never return to their proper home unless a Messenger from the Good Deity came down into the world of matter on their behalf.

The Good Deity was all pureness and joy; yet though He might be unaware of evil, He knew that certain heavenly souls had been cut off from Him, and longed to bring them back into His heaven. He could do nothing to aid them Himself, since a great gulf was fixed between Him and them, and He could have no contact with the universe created by the Prince of Evil. So He sought, among those blessed beings who surrounded Him in His glory, for a Mediator to re-establish contact between Heaven and the fallen souls. In the end God chose and dispatched Jesus, who was, according to the Cathars, either the most perfect of the angels, or else one of the Sons of God —the second, that is, Satan having been the first. This title, Son of God, carried no implication of equality between the Son and the Father. Jesus was at best a sort of emanation, an Image made in God's likeness.

It was pity that enabled Jesus to descend into this impure world of matter, and not to shrink from so defiling a contact: pity for the souls to whom he must needs show the way back to their true home. But it was unthinkable that purity should have any *real* contact with impurity, and so Jesus was assumed to possess the appearance only of a body: he underwent, not incarnation, but what might be termed adumbration, a shadowing forth. He was, then, in some sense a phantom; and if he made a show of submitting himself to the laws of earthly nature, this was all part of his plan to deceive the Devil's eternal vigilance. But the Devil, having recognized the Messenger of God, sought to encompass his death; and God's enemies, blinded by appearances, were to hold it as an article of faith that Jesus had *really* suffered and died on the Cross. The truth, however, was far otherwise: Jesus' body, being non-fleshly, could neither suffer, die, nor achieve resurrection. He had endured no outrage of this sort, and when he had shown his disciples the proper path to salvation, he reascended into Heaven. His mission was accomplished: he had left behind on earth a Church impregnated with that Holy Spirit which alone could offer true consolation to the souls dwelling in exile.

But the Devil, the Prince of this world, showed great skill in leading men astray. He destroyed Jesus' work in a most complete and diabolical fashion, by substituting a false Church for the true one. This false Church claimed the title of 'Christian', but it was in fact the Church of the Devil, and taught doctrines diametrically opposed to those of Jesus. The authentic Christian Church, the repository of the Holy Spirit, was that of the Cathars.

The Church of Rome, then, figured as the Great Beast, the Whore of Babylon; and none who remained obedient to her could hope to be saved. Everything appertaining to this Church was wicked and blasphemous. Her sacraments were not only worthless in themselves, but a snare set by the Devil, since they led men to believe that wholly material rites and mechanical gestures could bring them salvation. Neither the water of Baptism nor the bread of the Host could be vehicles for the Holy Spirit, since they were impure matter. The Host itself could not be the Body of Christ; for, the Cathar preachers declared, with somewhat ingenuous irony, if all the Hosts dispensed throughout the world during the past ten centuries were put together, they would make up a 'Body' rather larger than a mountain.

The Cross, they claimed, should not be an object of veneration. On the contrary, it should inspire horror, since it had formed the instrument of Jesus' humiliation. When a roof-beam falls and crushes the son of the house, they argued, it is not set in the place of honour and offered adoration or incense. This line of reasoning suggests that the Cathars in fact attached rather more importance to the Crucifixion than is supposed: why should the Cross inspire horror if Jesus had not, in some way or other, really suffered because of it?

If the Cross was the Devil's instrument *par excellence*, all the images and objects which the Church held to be sacred were equally the work of the Evil One. In the name of Christianity he had initiated a reign of paganism pure and unalloyed. Holy images were no more than idols, and relics worse still—mere bits of crumbling bone, wooden splinters or scraps of cloth being picked up any old where, and passed off by a pack of plausible rogues as parts of saints' bodies or other venerable objects. Those who bowed before such objects were adoring matter, and matter was the Devil's handiwork. In any case, they said, all the Saints were really sinners, because they had served the Devil's Church; they were blasted with the same anathema as the Just of the Old Testament, being reckoned the creatures and servants of the Evil Deity.

The Blessed Virgin was never the Mother of Jesus, since Jesus never had a body. If He had decided to give the appearance of being born of Her, this meant that the Virgin too was a non-material being, an angel who had taken on the lineaments of a woman.

Perhaps she was even no more than a symbol, representing the Church fostering within herself the Word of God.

Having stated as a principle that this world had been created by the Spirit of Evil, the Catharist Church was consequently obliged to condemn every manifestation of earthly life. All that was not pure Spirit was doomed to utter destruction, and merited neither affection nor respect. If the Church was the most visible embodiment of evil in this world, secular authority ran it a close second, since its power rested on constraint, and frequently on murder (i.e. war and penal legislation). The family was condemned as a cause of earthly attachments; and marriage was, in addition, a crime against the Spirit, since it entangled men in the life of the flesh, and was liable to bring destruction upon yet more souls by dragging them down to the world of matter. All murder, including the killing of animals, was a crime: by taking life a man deprived one soul of the chance to achieve reconciliation with the Spirit, and improperly cut short its penitential span. Even when lodged in the body of an animal, a soul was entitled to infinite consideration, for it still might have some unforeseeable chance of being reborn in better circumstances. There-fore the carrying of arms was forbidden, to avoid the risk of killing even in self-defence. To eat food of animal origin was also banned, on the ground that such food was essentially impure: even eggs and milk products, together with every other by-product of procreation, were to be strictly avoided. The Cathar must never lie, or utter an oath; nor was he permitted to own worldly property. But even the fulfilment of all these conditions did not *per se* guarantee salvation. One could not be saved—i.e. reconciled with the Holy Spirit— except by entering the Catharist Church, which necessitated a laying on of hands by one of that Church's ministers. In this way alone could a man be reborn, and cherish the hope of entering, after his death, a condition of divine beatitude—unless, that is, various fresh sins plunged him into the Devil's hellish Abyss.

Hell itself, however, did not exist spatially, but rather consisted of reincarnation in another body. Nevertheless, a long sequence of evil lives could, ultimately, deprive a soul of any hope for salvation. There were, too, certain souls actually created by the Devil, a fact which ensured that the persons they inhabited could never be saved. It was difficult to distinguish them from the rest; but presumably kings, emperors, and prelates of the Catholic Church were among those thus predestined to damnation. All other souls were, finally, to be saved, and the torture of earthly incarnations would continue as long as there remained one heavenly soul who had not found the path to salvation. In the end the tangible world would vanish, the sun and stars be extinguished, while fire consumed the waters and the waters in turn quenched the fire. The souls of all 'demons' would perish in this holocaust, and nothing would remain but eternal joy in God.

This *résumé* of Catharist doctrine might well lead the reader to wonder how, with so many points separating the Cathar's faith from traditional Christianity, a Catholic population could so easily discard the faith of their fathers in favour of so glaring a heresy.

Two points may be noted here. In the first place, as a result of the Church's pastoral incompetence—a failing castigated by the Popes themselves—the people often knew little or nothing about niceties of religious orthodoxy. Secondly (and this needs strong emphasis) the opponents of the Catharist faith were particularly concerned to expose its doctrinal *errors*, giving these a prominence which they probably did not have in the eyes of the Cathars themselves. So much was this the case that many points may have been based upon differences of interpretation and expression rather than genuinely heretical opinions.

We must not, admittedly, neglect the unorthodox aspects of the Catharist creed; but we should endeavour to view it in its true perspective. When we examine the facts we see that the 'errors' which seemed most shocking in Catholic eyes were precisely those that had the appearance of stemming logically from orthodox contemporary doctrine. That was why they were considered so dangerous.

To take an example: Catharist dualism (so wildly exaggerated by the Cathars' opponents) was simply a natural development from belief in the Devil, who assumed vast importance for Christians throughout the Middle Ages. Catholic doctrine had always contained a latent streak of Manichaeism. The Devil was a very solid fact, and his power continually attested by Catholic preachers, who never lost an opportunity of condemning as diabolically inspired every manifestation of the secular spirit—sometimes even the most harmless, such as music and dancing. Indeed, the Church itself (at least as far as its more respectable representatives were concerned) had gone so far in this direction that it is hard to see how the Cathars could have improved on it. Mediaeval civilization, having been formed originally in a monastic mould, regarded the material world with undiluted loathing and contempt. It may not have actually claimed that matter was the work of the Devil, but it *behaved* exactly as though it thought so. Where, before St Francis of Assisi, can we find a Catholic saint moved to glorify the beauties of the natural world which God created? How often do we hear of priests extolling marriage, going into raptures over little children, or speaking in praise of earthly joys? Most of those festivals or religious customs in which love of life on earth bulks large were survivals— either from paganism, or else from Jewish tradition. Any purely Christian contribution to the love of Creation has been weak in impulse and wholly theoretical.

Such an attitude was not, doubtless, representative of the Church as a whole; but it was certainly held by its holiest and most venerable members, such as St Bernard—who opposed not only the frivolous outlook of the laity, but also what he considered over-rich ornamentation in the churches. Beauty which seduced the eye could not achieve anything except to distract one's spirit from meditation. Here was a period in which the need to give material form to the divine, to *embody* it, was stronger than ever before; when towns or entire regions were beggaring themselves in order to honour the Virgin, or their local saint, with a house beside which a royal palace seemed no more than a poor hut. Yet during this same period every sincere Catholic believed that the world was hopelessly corrupt, and that the cloister offered the only true road to salvation. Between a universe created by the Devil, which was merely tolerated by God, and a universe created by God, but wholly corrupted and perverted by the Devil, there might seem to be no great difference—not, at least, in practice.

The Cathars condemned marriage and the flesh, then; so rigorously, indeed, that they abstained from any food which was a by-product of the procreative act. But as we shall see, this condemnation was not absolute. Nevertheless, the Catholic Church held a very similar attitude to marriage itself. The priest, just like a Cathar minister, could not marry; and the institution was only tolerated among the faithful as a means of propagating the species and a remedy against concupiscence. Indeed, with regard to women the attitude of the Catholic Church was even harsher than that of the Cathars. When St Peter Damian fulminates against the mistresses of the clergy, calling them 'Satan's bait, poison for men's souls, the delight of greasy pigs, inns where unclean souls turn in', we sense a real horror of woman *qua* woman, who is seen as the Devil's eternal lure. This general, barely concealed condemnation of marriage and the flesh carries an implicit denial of a world in which all life, from the very flowers of the field upward, is subject to procreative laws.

When Catholic priests declared, in opposition to the Cathars, that a man *could* achieve salvation within the marriage-bond, they were merely showing their indulgence towards human frailty. As we shall see, this was exactly the case with the Cathars, too.

Though life in the eleventh and twelfth centuries showed a tremendous upsurge both of civilization and of artistic achievement— and though, despite its worst miseries, it would appear to have been brimming over with a deep, intense *joie de vivre* (for the people were, after all, young)—we cannot say that the thoughts of the Church were consciously orientated in this direction. Catholicism was, like Catharism, a self-avowed 'religion of souls': salvation was its sole aim. If the Church also possessed a body—a material, indeed at times an all-too-material body—that was through the pressure of circumstances, and quite at odds with her declared doctrine.

Of the Catharist dogmas which Catholics found particularly shocking, those concerned with the Trinity and the Incarnation may have worried theologians and philosophers, but left the bulk of the faithful relatively unperturbed. The Cathars, it seems, were really Arians insofar as they refused to admit the equality of the three Persons of the Trinity. Nevertheless, certain words in the Creed—*et ex Patre natum ante omnia saecula*—suggest (despite the saving *consubstantialem*) a certain original supremacy for the Father. For the Cathars, too, Jesus was a Son 'born of the Father before time began': we cannot tell whether their adversaries interpreted their views exactly or not. But one thing beyond any doubt is the fact that the Cathars always displayed a devotion to the person of Christ such as no Catholic could exceed: we can argue with everything except (in this sense) their Christianity. As far as the Incarnation is concerned, were not such tenets as Jesus' miraculous birth, or that apocryphal tradition according to which Mary's virginity remained intact after the Nativity, or indeed the Resurrection and the Ascension—were not these calculated to cast doubt and confusion in men's minds? The Catholics themselves appeared to admit, if only by implication, that Jesus' body was, in some way or other, different from those of ordinary human beings.

In point of fact the Catharist dogma which Catholics found absolutely inadmissible was the denial of the Catholic Church herself. But—and this is something which has not, perhaps, been sufficiently emphasized—what this faith had to offer its flock was, quite simply, Christ and the Gospel. The Book, the one and only true Book, the Book that took the place both of Cross and Chalice,

was the Gospel—a Gospel read in the vernacular, available to young
and old alike, brought home all the closer to them by constant preaching and discussion. All we know concerning the Catharist interpretation of the Gospels is what can be glimpsed through a haze of
polemic. But the preachers who addressed themselves to the faithful
were not now dealing in polemics. Their faith brought Christ close to
His worshippers: it ripped off the swathes of dogmas, tradition and
superstition that had, century by century, gathered about primitive
Christianity. We only have to read something like the *Golden Legend*
(composed in the thirteenth century, but embodying oral and written
traditions of much greater antiquity) to become aware how little
popular piety had, on many occasions, to do with Christianity.

Since the Church actively discouraged any attempts to translate
the Scriptures into the vernacular tongues, it had scant defence
against this particular danger. Even the most irreproachably orthodox Catholic became suspect of heresy if he displayed any inclination
to read the Gospels in his own language; and yet even the priests
themselves sometimes knew no Latin. The Church in the Midi had
reached such a point of decadence that its priests no longer gave
religious instruction—and if they did, no one paid any attention to
them. The Church had hidden the Key of Knowledge; and she
found it all the harder to combat her adversary since that adversary
was attacking her in the name of Christ.

What was more, the Cathars declared themselves the heirs of a
tradition that was older than that held by the Church of Rome—
and, by implication, both less contaminated and nearer in spirit to
the Apostolic tradition. They claimed to be the only persons who
had kept and cherished the Holy Spirit which Christ had bestowed
upon His Church; and it looks as though this claim was at least
partially justified. The Catharist Ritual (of which we possess two
texts, both datable to the thirteenth century) demonstrates, as Jean
Guiraud proves in his *magnum opus* on the Inquisition, that this
Church undoubtedly possessed certain most ancient documents,
which were directly inspired by the traditions of the Primitive
Church.

In fact—and Guiraud shows this too, by a comparison of initiation
ceremonies among the Cathars with the Baptism of the Catechumens
in the Primitive Church—the parallelism between the two traditions
is so consistent that it could not conceivably be due to mere coincidence. The Cathar neophyte, like the Christian catechumen, was
received into his Church only after a probationary period and a vote

of approval by the Elders of the community. Baptism in the Primitive Church, like admission into the Catharist Church, was only granted to adults in full possession of their faculties, and was seldom demanded by believers except on their deathbeds. The minister who received the neophyte into the Catharist Church was known as 'the Ancient' (*Senhor*)—an obvious translation of *presbyter*. The catechumens' renunciation of Satan has a parallel in the Cathars' renunciation of the Church of Rome. Apart from the anointing with oil, symbolizing the Holy Spirit, and the immersion in the baptismal *piscina*—both of which sacraments were too closely connected with matter, and therefore rejected by the Cathars, who only preserved the laying on of hands—the admission of a catechumen into the Primitive Church was at all points identical with that of a Cathar postulant into his new Faith. The same comparison can be drawn between the devout Catholic's Act of Confession and the Remission of Sins dispensed by the Cathars in assembly.

Certain Inquisitors, particularly Bernard Gui in the fourteenth century, were struck by the proportion of Christian observances in the rites of the heretical Church, and assumed that they had to do with a kind of parody of Catholic baptism. Today we are better informed than they were concerning the practices of the Early Church, and have to admit that the Cathars merely followed a tradition somewhat more ancient than that of the Church herself. It was with some appearance of reason that they claimed Rome as the party guilty of 'heresy' through her falling-off from that original purity which had characterized the Church of the Apostles.

The very text of the Ritual as we possess it today certainly goes back to an extremely early date, even though the two versions which survive, one in Occitan and the other in Latin, can be attributed to the thirteenth century. Was this text brought from the East and translated by Bulgarian missionaries? Where, and in what conditions, was it preserved? What was its precise origin? It consists for the most part of quotations from the Gospels and Epistles, with brief commentaries. There are constant references to the Father, the Son and the Holy Ghost, and to various episodes in the Gospels themselves: any good Catholic could have read it approvingly and, as he perused its text, have got the impression that he was savouring the full flavour and vigour of primitive Christianity, rather than the theological speculations of a sect that was credited with the most highly unorthodox doctrines.

Now this Ritual, which was a book of prayer and initiation, was not meant for ordinary eyes; it contained the most formal and sacred expression of Catharist beliefs, a verbal rendering of this Church's highest sacrament. When we find nothing in it that could suggest, even remotely, any tinge of Manichaean dualism or the theory of metempsychosis, any denial of the Incarnation and the Eucharist; when we even come upon statements that run contrary to Catharist doctrine as we know it on baptism by water—then we can only conclude that these texts go back a long way beyond Catharism in the accepted sense of the term. But the very fact that the Cathars (who lacked neither the courage of their convictions nor a taste for speculative theology) had not felt inclined to modify their ritual in any way—this, surely, proves that such a ritual accurately expressed their doctrine as they conceived it, and that the 'errors' of which the Catholic Church accused them were, in all likelihood, only secondary aspects of their teaching: not so much basic elements of faith as a cosmogony, a philosphical approach to life and the universe.

If we are to judge a religion by its prayers and its ritual—this is still the best approach to any estimate of its true essence—the little we know concerning the Catharist faith cannot but lead us to respect its simplicity, moderation, and high spiritual qualities. The Ritual which so miraculously escaped destruction is of infinitely greater weight than all the sworn testimony of the Cathars' adversaries, and every word that has been written or spoken about them through the centuries.

3. *Organization and Expansion*
The Cathar religion endeavoured to make an absolute and literal application of its doctrines in practice. The road to salvation was narrow, and seems to have been reserved for a minority only of the elect. Here, however, in a somewhat unexpected way, Catharist observance coincides with that of Catholicism, both in its concern for the weaker brethren and by reason of its faith in the absolute value of the sacraments. The Cathars, just like the Catholics, required, as a necessary condition of salvation, one act of a sacramental nature: reconciliation in the Spirit by the laying on of hands, this being done by ministers of the sect who had already received the Spirit themselves. We are not concerned here with any sort of symbolical gesture: there is no doubt that this rite, the *consolamentum*, contained genuine supra-natural virtues for the Cathars. In their eyes it actually brought down the Holy Spirit upon its beneficiary. The degree of sanctity achieved by the administrant was immaterial; what conferred the Holy Spirit was the physical laying

on of hands, and this act formed the keystone, the central truth of the Catharist Church.

Whether or not the Cathars admitted the doctrine of Apostolic Succession, they certainly held that the Spirit could only be passed on by untainted hands. However, such purity was a prime requirement in their ministers, and there were very few cases of the *consolamentum* being adjudged void by reason of an unworthy celebrant. The Spirit truly descended upon the man who received it; henceforward he was a 'Christian' (in the Cathar sense), and his death to this world was followed by a rebirth in the life of the Spirit. He had to submit himself, without *caveat* or compromise, to every obligation which his new faith might impose—and these obligations were more exacting than those required of any monk on taking his monastic vows. Only a very tiny minority of believers had the strength and resolution to achieve salvation in this way. But the Catharist Church also granted the *consolamentum* to those on the point of death; and thus we find a large number of persons receiving this sacrament with no other guarantee of the purity of their faith apart from the knowledge of their imminent decease. Thus the sacrament could, in fact, be bestowed upon people who were not *a priori* either pure or among the elect; and here the Catharist faith seems open to the same criticism which Cathars levelled against Catholics—that of turning a sacrament into a mere mechanical ritual, independent of the spiritual condition of its recipient. But though the principle might be the same, at least the Cathars contrived to surround *their* sacrament with the requisite degree of solemn grandeur by making it a precious and unique gift—unique in the sense that unless a man were prepared to sacrifice his life entirely for it, he might not obtain the *consolamentum* until the moment when death's agony had already torn him from this world.

Once the Spirit had descended upon a believer, he was thereby at once made a 'new creature', and henceforth the slightest sin on his part became an act of sacrilege which was liable to destroy or lose him the Spirit in which he stood 'clad'. In practice there can be found instances of *perfecti* who received the *consolamentum* several times during their life, either as a result of some sin, or else because their faith had temporarily weakened. This seems to prove that the sacrament did not possess that binding and irrevocable power with which it is generally credited.

The *consolamentum* had elements in common with at least five of the seven Catholic sacraments—baptism, Holy Eucharist, confirmation, ordination, and extreme unction. Yet it was a very simple ceremony. It was preceded by a long period of probation or initiation; the postulant had to spend some time—a year, or even on occasion two years—in a Catharist seminary or *maison des hérétiques* where his sense of vocation was subjected to long and rigorous tests. This formed a species of novitiate; and if, at the end of his preliminary trial, the postulant had not managed to satisfy his superiors as to his sincerity and powers of endurance, he was often liable to find himself refused the *consolamentum* altogether. If he was adjudged worthy, he was presented before the community of *perfecti* that must elect him; after which he prepared for the day of his consecration with lengthy fasts and vigils, and unending prayer.

When the day came, the postulant was brought into the hall or chamber where the faithful were gathered. The Cathars possessed no temples, and conducted their rites in private houses; but in the towns they had houses specially set apart for services, doctrinal instruction, and the care of the sick. In these houses they lived as a community, each individual *perfectus* being obliged to surrender his goods to the Church. Most of the larger towns generally reckoned on having several such *maisons des hérétiques*.

The room where the faithful assembled for prayer contained no outward sign of their cult. The walls had to be bare, and were usually whitewashed. The furnishings, too, were as simple as possible: some benches, and a table covered in spotlessly white linen, on which lay the Book, that is, a text of the Gospels. This table, which served in lieu of an altar, would also have on it several napkins, again of the purest white; and on a side table or chest there stood a ewer and basin for the washing of hands. The only decoration in this austere chamber took the form of countless white candles, their flames symbolizing the Holy Spirit as it descended in tongues of fire at Pentecost upon the Apostles. In the presence of a congregation of the faithful the new postulant was led towards the table, before which there stood those ministers whose business it was to receive him—deacons or ordinary *perfecti*, clad in the long black robes that symbolized their withdrawal from the world. The officiating minister and his two assistants now washed their hands, so as to be able to touch the holy Gospels. Then the ceremony began.

The minister expounded to the postulant both the dogmas of the creed he was about to embrace, and the obligations to which he must needs submit himself. Next he recited the Our Father, glossing each phrase as he went, and the postulant had to repeat it after him. After this the neophyte had to solemnly abjure the Catholic faith in which he had been brought up, and (after prostrating himself thrice) ask for permission to be received into the true Church. He had to 'give himself to God and the Gospel'. He swore to abstain in future from meat, eggs, and all food of animal origin; from all carnal intercourse; and from lies and oaths, for ever. He swore never to renounce his faith, through fear of death by fire, water, or any other means. Finally he made a public confession of his sins and asked those present to forgive him. After his absolution he had to repeat once more all the solemn vows he had just taken. Only then was he ready to receive the Spirit.

The moment of consecration took place when the minister placed the Gospels on the postulant's head, and, together with his assistants, laid his hands on the future *perfectus*, praying God to receive him and send His Holy Spirit upon him. In that instant the man became a wholly new creature, he was 'born of the Spirit'.

Those present now recited the Our Father aloud, after which the minister read the first seventeen verses of St John's Gospel: 'In the beginning was the Word. . . .' Then he once more recited the Our Father.

The newly-elected *perfectus* now received the kiss of peace—first from the officiating minister, then from his assistants. He in his turn bestowed the kiss of peace on the member of the congregation standing nearest to him; and so, like a torch passed from hand to hand, this brotherly salutation was transmitted to every single one of those present. If the postulant was a woman, however, the kiss of peace was replaced by a more symbolical gesture: the minister would touch her shoulder with the Gospel, and her elbow, briefly, with his own.

The new recipient of the *consolamentum* would henceforth wear the black robe proper to his condition, the mark of his special status: it was an outward and visible sign of the dignity lately conferred upon him, and therefore never to be put aside. Later, however, when the *perfecti* were forced, by reason of the persecutions, to exercise some caution in their calling, the robe was replaced by a cord worn under their clothes—for men, round the neck, and for women, about the waist. But the very importance attached to this robe, or 'vesture' —the heretical adepts were most often referred to by the title of *revestiti*—demonstrates that the *consolamentum* was in essence both sacramental and sacerdotal. Its recipient entered fully into the religious life, in every sense of that term which a Catholic would admit. He surrendered all his goods and chattels to the community; after which, following the example set by Christ and His Apostles, he embarked upon a wandering life devoted to prayer, preaching, and charitable works.

The local deacon or bishop would allot the new *perfectus* a companion, chosen from among his fellow-*perfecti*. This companion was destined to be his *socius* (or *socia* in the case of two women), an inseparable comrade who would henceforth share all his labours and hardships.

It has been said, with some justice, that the Catharist Church proper was composed only of those who had partaken of this sacrament; that it was, in fact, a Church made up solely of priests. Our postulant, having received the terrible privilege of admission to the ranks of the *perfecti*, was now a 'Christian', cut off from the rest of mankind. Wherever he went ordinary 'believers' or *credentes* were obliged to offer him 'adoration', or, more accurately, to show their respect for his office by kneeling or bowing before him thrice, with this ritual salutation: 'Pray God to make a good Christian of me, and bring me to a good end.' The *perfectus* would pray to God as requested; but he would not reply, as a Catholic might, 'Pray for me, a sinner'. That theoretical equality which exists between all orthodox Christians, from the Pope down to the lowest criminal, seems to have been absent in this realistic creed. According to their own doctrine, the *perfecti* constituted a sort of higher echelon among mortals: the Spirit conferred upon them by the *consolamentum* did not, and could not, dwell in the souls of those who had not received this sacrament. (We should evidently take the term *perfectus* in its etymological sense of 'finished' or 'complete': man being composed of body, soul, and spirit, the *perfecti* were those who, by virtue of this sacrament, had contrived to win back their 'spirit', that divine portion of the self which their original Fall had taken from them.) Thus we find ourselves faced with something of a paradox. Here was a powerful Church, constantly gaining fresh territory, which numbered amongst its adherents a good proportion of the country's nobility, bourgeoisie, and craftsmen; which held châteaux, walled cities, entire districts under its sway; and which nevertheless had only a few hundred, at the very most several thousand, fully effective members.

We shall return later to this question of the *credentes*, the rank-and-file believers, and the precise role they performed in a Church which, at first sight, would appear to have regarded them as being of little importance. It is certain that some vital clue is eluding us here, since, despite this apparent fundamental distinction between the *perfectus* and the ordinary believer, the religious conduct of the latter was (as we shall see) exactly that of a good Catholic towards the Church of Rome, while the attitude of the *perfectus vis-à-vis* the *credentes* hardly differed from that of a conscientious parish priest towards his flock. In Languedoc every province had its Catharist bishop, and each town or important district its own deacon: such bishops and deacons were not appointed for the sake of a handful of *perfecti* alone. The Catharist bishops regarded themselves as spiritual shepherds responsible for large communities. In all probability they showed greater solicitude for their as yet uninitiated brethren than the Catholic bishops did where their own faithful were concerned, for this simple reason: that a faith obliged to struggle for its very existence will treat its adherents with much greater consideration than will any established religion. The *credentes* were very far from resembling a flock without shepherds, and never had any need to regard themselves as deprived of all contact with spiritual matters.

But it nevertheless remains true that the kernel, the living soul, of the Catharist Church was formed by the *perfecti*. We know what they were: confessors, in the sense which the Church understands by that term. This ultra-select body of men, chosen and ordained in their calling with such caution that even an already flourishing Church could have produced no more than a few of them, compelled the admiration even of their worst enemies. To judge from the number of heretics burnt during the period of the Crusade (only the *perfecti* were normally condemned to the stake) it would seem that there must have been several thousand of them in the Midi—making allowance, that is, for those who managed to escape detection throughout, those who got away into Italy, and those others who must have fallen victims in the general slaughter. Moreover, throughout the entire history of the Crusade and the years that followed it, scholars have only noted three instances of a *perfectus* recanting. Even here the first, who embraced conversion *in extremis* and only escaped the fire by a miracle, was a neophyte still, and had not received the *consolamentum*; the second, Pons Roger, who was converted by St Dominic, is merely assumed to have been a *perfectus* because of the rigorous penance imposed upon him by the Saint. The third case was that of William de Solier, who in 1229 recanted to avoid going to the stake, and bought his own life at the price of denouncing his brethren. If we consider what death by fire means, we may well be amazed when we reflect that out of hundreds of men and women threatened with such an end, only *one* can be found who turned traitor.

But it was not their courage that won admiration for the *perfecti*; in any case, before the Crusade they had not yet shown this quality to the full. What their adversaries unanimously admitted was the purity of their moral lives. The Pope and St Dominic paid them a striking tribute on the day that they decided to war against them 'with their own weapons', and the saintly Catholic took the road himself as a preacher, bare-footed, living by alms, following the good example set him by the heretics.

The *perfecti* were not, however, merely austere men who won admiration through their contempt for the good things of this world: the people also dubbed them *bons hommes*, a phrase which in modern French has lost its true, original significance. They were, quite literally, 'good men'. This appellation alone would appear to give the lie to those who depict Catharism as a miserable kind of religion, indifferent to the wretchedness of a world which in any case it despised. These lean, black-clad men, with their long hair and pale features, did not catch people's imagination so much by reason of their austere habits as through their sheer goodness. A crabbed, sour asceticism would not have attracted anybody. These dedicated men and women, who went forth, two by two, to visit village, château, or city street, were received everywhere with the most rapturous veneration. When the Count of Toulouse pointed to an ill-clad, crippled *perfectus* and said: 'I would rather be this man than a king or an emperor,'[2] he was merely expressing publicly, opinions which had been current among the common people for some time.

These men exercised such powerful moral authority that the Church was very shy of openly charging them with hypocrisy. The most they were accused of was being over-ostentatious in their asceticism. The *bons hommes* were, indeed, most uncompromising over the matter of fasts. It was not enough for them to abstain from all 'impure' nourishment, and to observe three Lenten periods in the year, during which they ate nothing but bread and water for three days in the week; they would actually rather die than swallow so much as a crumb of any food forbidden by their religion. The practice of fasting, prominent throughout the ages in all religions, though far further developed in the East than in the West, seems to have played a very special part in the lives of the *perfecti*. At all events, for the common people no less than the Church, they were, first and foremost, men who fasted. Cosmas Presbyter* had already described

---

* A Bulgarian priest of the tenth century, author of a *Tract against the Bogomils* (ed. Père Joseph Gafort, *Theologia antibogomilistica Cosmae Presbiteri*, Rome 1942).

the Bogomils as pale-faced, emaciated, and bearing all the characteristics of privation.

Like yogis or fakirs, certain *perfecti* were so passionately addicted to extreme fasting that they incurred the charge of wanting to put an end to their own lives. This is the explanation behind the legend of the *endura*, or voluntary death by starvation. There is only one detailed case on record, in the fourteenth century, by which time Catharism was in its death-throes, and had already lost its genuine characteristics. In fact the *perfecti* could not possibly have countenanced suicide in any circumstances: their horror of murder was so great that we find instances (e.g. those heretics who were hanged at Goslar, in Germany, in 1052) where they actually preferred to die themselves rather than kill a hen. Though their contempt for this earthly life was so great, they nevertheless retained an absolute respect for the fact of life itself; they would not allow any violent intervention by the human will (which they regarded as invariably evil and arbitrary) in the fate of a soul pursuing its road to salvation. These men did not court martyrdom, and their bravery in the face of death sprang less from indifference to life than from the burning ardour of their faith.

The *perfecti* were also distinguishable by their grave and moderate utterance, and their habit of constant prayer coupled with endless discourse concerning God. In this Cosmas affected to discern a skilful ruse—not to mention symptoms of spiritual pride. They never raised their voices, that was true enough; they never uttered an offensive word, or so much as opened their mouths except to speak piously; they were always praying in public places, just like the hypocritical Pharisees whom Our Lord denounced. They were wolves in sheep's clothing, and it was this aggressive pietism of theirs which seduced the ignorant.

It is possible that the method of prayer among the *perfecti* followed certain special rules and observances, in all likelihood of Eastern origin. There is a frequently cited example of the *perfectus* whom Berbeguera, the Seigneur of Puylaurens' wife, went to visit, and found sitting on his chair 'motionless as a tree-trunk, entirely oblivious of his surroundings'.[3] This puts one in mind of some Hindu sage in a state of trance. But clearly hearts are not won by sitting still; and the *perfecti* were, above all, famous for their charitable works.

Though poor themselves, they had at their disposal contributions from the faithful for succouring those who were distressed; and even when they had no gifts to offer, they were there in person, bringing the comfort of their friendship and discourse, never shunning the

vilest outcast's company. They were often skilled in medicine—
something of a paradox in the case of men who so despised the
body. Agreed that this offered a powerful avenue for propaganda;
but no one becomes a good doctor unless he bestows a certain
degree of attention and love upon the body he is tending. Charity
addresses itself to the body rather than the soul. The records
of the Inquisition refer to the testimony of one William Dumier,
a knight who was tended with great care by one such medically-
trained *perfectus* until the day came when he formally refused
to recant his Catholicism, after which he received no further
treatment. This cannot have been a very common occurrence. Any
doctor who made a habit of acting in such a way must very soon
have lost, at a single stroke, both his patients and any future converts
he might have made.

The same applies to the evidence of William Viguier's wife.
Although her husband tried to convert her to Catharism 'by beating
her with a stick'[4]—not a very effective method of persuasion—she
refused, because the *bons hommes* had told her that the child she
was carrying was a demon. The husband and wife were both clearly
very ignorant, and the *bon homme* in the case was not, we may feel,
over-tactful. But it is clear that this is one of the exceptions which
confirm the rule. Preachers who always used such gambits with their
parishioners would hardly have acquired a reputation for charity
or kindness.

All the testimony agrees in stating that it was by the example
they set that the *perfecti* won the hearts of their flock. Of their inner
spiritual life or personal magnetism nothing survives today apart
from the striking, though vague, evidence offered by the amazing
success of their apostolic mission.

The secondary causes favouring a spread of Catharism at this time
are so numerous and obvious that merely to list them might well
make us think that the new Church did not need such formidable
apostles in order to turn the folk of the Midi away from Rome.

The most spectacular side of Catharism, and also the most
revolting as far as Christendom was concerned, was the Cathars'
absolute rejection of Catholic dogma, and even of the Church's
most sacred symbols. This sent a wave of sheer horror through every
country in which the Church was strong and heresy of infrequent
occurrence. But in the French Midi the progress of heresy went
pari passu with the increasing decadence of the Church itself, and
it is hard to say which of these two factors determined the other.

What we know of the ecclesiastical dignitaries in the Midi during the Fourth Crusade suggests that such bishops might have caused even the most devoted Catholic to doubt the sanctity of his Church.

Here is what Innocent III has to tell us about the clergy in the Languedoc area, and especially their leader, Bérenger II, the Archbishop of Narbonne:[5]

They are blind creatures, dumb hounds who can no longer bay, simoniacs who sell justice, damning the poor and giving absolution to the rich. They do not even observe the laws of the Church. They acquire endless benefices, entrusting the priesthood and other ecclesiastical responsibilities to unworthy pastors and illiterate children. Hence the insolence of the heretics; hence the contempt in which both gentry and people hold God and His Church. Throughout this region the prelates are the laughing-stock of the laity. But the root of all this evil lies in the Archbishop of Narbonne. This man knows no other God but money, and keeps a purse where his heart should be. During the ten years that he has held his office he has not once visited his own diocese, let alone the province as a whole. He extracted five hundred *sous d'or* as a fee for consecrating the Bishop of Maguelonne; and when We asked him to raise subsidies for the relief of Christians in the East, he refused to obey Us. When a church living falls vacant, he refrains from nominating a fresh incumbent so that he can enjoy the revenues himself. He has reduced the number of Canons in Narbonne by half in order to appropriate their prebendaries, and similarly is keeping the vacant archidiaconates under his own control. In this diocese one may observe Regular monks or Canons who have cast aside their monastic habit, taken wives or mistresses, and are living by usury; some, indeed, have set up as lawyers, *jongleurs*, or doctors.

This picture speaks so eloquently for itself that it might seem difficult to add any significant detail to it; but the Pope's enquiry also revealed that the Archbishop's bailiff was a captain of Aragonese mercenaries—which means, in effect, a common highway robber. But it was in vain that the Pope fulminated against Bérenger: the stubborn old man, so much more zealous in the defence of his own interests than in the business of his diocese, was to hold out against Legate after Legate for years. He refused to be deposed until 1210, after the Crusade had been triumphantly concluded by force of arms.

The Bishop of Toulouse, Raymond de Rabastens, who was born of a strongly heretical family, spent most of his life fighting against his own vassals; in order to provide himself with the sinews of war he was obliged to put his episcopal estates under mortgage. Finally, in 1206, he was deposed for simony; but his successor, Foulques de Marseilles, Abbot of Thoronet, found nothing in the episcopal coffers save ninety-six Toulousain *sous*, and did not even have an escort to take his mules to the drinking-trough—the bishop's authority being so little respected that he dared not send his mules to the common drinking-trough without one. He was, quite literally, hounded down by his predecessor's creditors, who would even come and disturb him while the Chapter was in session. The bishopric of Toulouse, as William de Puylaurens said, was a dead letter.

Councils held in Languedoc during this period ordered abbots and bishops to wear the tonsure and habit of their order, and forbade them to wear costly furs, play at games of chance, swear, introduce actors or musicians as guests at table, hear Matins in bed, indulge in frivolous gossip during Divine Office, or practise excommunication wilfully and at random. They were recommended to convoke their synod at least once a year, and to avoid taking fees for conferring Holy Orders, celebrating illegal marriages, or quashing legitimate wills.

What could the attitude of the laity be when confronted with clergy who neglected their duties to such a degree? We know what it was: no respectable person would any longer consider having his son trained for the priesthood, and, according to William de Puylaurens,[6]

the laity became inspired with such disdain for all ecclesiastical offices that they gave rise to a form of oath, as in the case of the Jews. Just as people say 'I would rather be a Jew', so now they declared: 'I would rather be a priest than do so-and-so'. When the clergy showed themselves in public they concealed their small tonsures by combing the long hair forward from the back of their head. It was seldom that the nobility put a son into the priesthood; they contented themselves with pushing their retainers' sons into such livings as brought them tithes. The bishops conferred the tonsure on anyone they could, as circumstances permitted.

The lower clergy, being thus casually recruited, ignored by their bishops, and held in contempt by the people at large, lived an exceedingly miserable life: so much so, indeed, that according to Innocent III (as cited above) priests began to desert their calling *en masse* for richer and more potentially profitable occupations.

This lamentable state of affairs elicited indignant protests not only from the Pope, but also from foreign bishops and abbots—especially those, such as John of Salisbury, who were brought up in the Cistercian tradition. Geoffrey of Vigeois makes no bones about criticizing the monastic clergy. He observes that monks frequently wear lay garments, eat meat, and quarrel with each other; adding that he personally has seen one monastery with four rival abbots in residence.

Lay critics condemned these clerical failings in even rounder terms. The Troubadours composed various *sirventés** full of angry railing against the luxury, debauched habits, and venality of the local prelates. Their stables, it was claimed, were better than those of any Count; they only dined off the most costly fish, garnished with equally expensive and exotically spiced sauces; they made presents of rich jewellery to their mistresses. They were hypocrites, too: they would fulminate against some quite innocent practice such as feminine self-adornment, yet remain wholly indifferent to the virtues of charity and justice. They loved the rich and oppressed the poor. Violent attacks on ecclesiastical morality had become a commonplace of satirical literature, even in ecclesiastical circles.

Many churches were abandoned for lack of a priest-in-charge; some of them were used by the people to hold dances in, or for the singing of profane songs. Moreoever, this state of affairs developed *pari passu* with the growing influence of the Catharist Church: very often those parishioners who abandoned their own services went along to hear the sermons preached by the *bons hommes*. We must also take into account the fact that clerical negligence had, with the passage of time, brought people to a state of comparative indifference where religious matters were concerned. As for the upper classes, most of them were active heretics; and those who were not displayed such extreme tolerance as in that Age of Faith was bound to be a matter of public scandal. If there were (as there must have been) a number of sincere Catholics in this society, their Catholicism was not that of the Pope or his Legates, nor indeed that of the bulk of believers in other countries. Finally, the nobility as a class must have numbered among them very many who were either sceptical or indifferent to the whole matter, and who, with all the sincerity in the world, declared that the Pope and his Holy Roman Empire were as nothing compared to a kiss from their Lady.

We must, it is true, always be on our guard against taking the diatribes of Popes and monks, or the furious invective of satirists, in too literal a fashion. A Church that could still allow itself self-expression of this sort, and endure such violent attacks unmoved,

* A type of Provençal lay, usually satirical, which was employed to attack political, personal, or moral enemies, or to ventilate military rivalries. Notable exponents of the *genre* include Bertran de Born, Pons de Capdueil, and Guilhem Montanhagol. The form is variable: one popular version consists of three rhymed hendecasyllables followed by a quinary rhyming with the next three: a a a$_{11}$ b$_5$; b b b $_{11}$ c$_5$; c c c$_{11}$ d$_5$, etc. (Trs.)

was, beyond doubt, a strong Church. The dioceses of Languedoc were not all under the charge of bishops such as Bérenger of Narbonne. Not all the churches were abandoned. Indeed, we may well hazard a suspicion that Catholic chroniclers like William de Puylaurens blackened the picture somewhat in order to prove how desperate a necessity the Crusade itself was. We frequently find a régime that has established itself by force exaggerating the shortcomings of its predecessor—in all good faith, too. Even at the time of the Fourth Crusade the Midi cannot have lacked for peaceful parishes administered by decent priests; and those who heard Mass in the great Cathedrals of Albi and Toulouse cannot all have nursed secret contempt for their Church. It nevertheless remains true that very many Catholics found no great difficulty in breaking away from a Church that was so enfeebled and discredited.

The facts outlined above also show that in the areas where the Cathars conducted their apostolic missionary work the people were not sufficiently well instructed in their faith to stand up against the arguments of these formidable logicians. Among the converts we find burghers, noblemen, the occasional *grand seigneur*, priests, monks, artisans—but scarcely ever an abbot, bishop, professional theologian, or Doctor of the Church. (One exception was William, a former Dean of Chapter at Nevers; in the years preceding the Crusade he became one of the best-known Catharist preachers in Languedoc under the name of Theodoric.) It is true that such people had little to gain from being converted to heresy; but it is not always self-interest that determines a conversion. This particular heresy triumphed just as much through the religious ignorance of a largely secularized laity as it did by virtue of its own forceful teaching. Indeed, this blazing heresy may well have appeared to many sincere Catholics as an expression of orthodoxy in its purest form.

Lastly, whatever charges of inhumanity or exclusiveness may be levelled against a creed centred upon its 'Elect', it remains true that Catharist ministers stood far closer to their flock than any Catholic priest did. They were poor; they mixed with people in their daily lives, and shared their labours. They were not above working at a loom or giving the reapers a hand with the harvest. They gave fresh courage to the poverty-stricken through the example of their own lives, which were harder than that of the meanest peasant. To their followers they embodied that genuine sort of power and authority which needs no pomp or ceremony in order to impose its will. As they themselves proclaimed, they were the Church of Love, and did violence to no man. So their Church flourished throughout the land, and grew prosperous, because those who were converted to it could feel that they now formed part of a community which offered greater unity, a richer spiritual life, and more inner life than Catholicism.

We know really very little about the Catharist *credentes*, the body of the faithful; not even their approximate numbers. We do know that the population of certain boroughs and country estates was composed wholly of heretics; that in some districts—such as the Ariège Valley—they formed a comfortable majority; and that they were more numerous in some guilds than others—for instance, 'weaver' was a popular nickname for any heretic. But when we have assembled such facts as we possess, this mass of believers cannot but seem to us today both vaguer, more irresolute, and less organized than in fact it was. No official document contains so much as an outline of the way in which the Catharist Church was organized: as we shall see from subsequent events, these people had nothing to gain by getting themselves officially registered as heretics.

Nevertheless, this organization did in fact exist. To begin with, each province had its own bishop, together with two assistants, known respectively as the bishop's *filius maior* and *filius minor*, or elder and younger son. Before he died the bishop would ordain the *filius maior* as his successor; the *filius minor* in turn now became *filius maior*, and the regional congregation of *perfecti* elected a new *filius minor*. Each important locality had its deacon, assisted by a varying number of *perfecti*, both men and women. We know that there were never all that many of them. The whole financial and administrative side of the Church's organization was in the hands of ordinary *credentes* who had not renounced the world: they ranged from rich merchants, who were entrusted with the funds necessary to maintain various *maisons communes*, down to the common folk, both men and women, who acted as messengers, guides, or liaison agents. Wherever the *bons hommes* halted to preach, they would find asylum for the night with some faithful member of the Church, well known for his upright way of life or his religious zeal. When we read in the Inquisition's transcripts that such-and-such a man or woman had sheltered *perfecti* under their roof, we may suppose that the *credentes* judged worthy of this honour were not picked at random, and that already they formed something of an *élite* among the general body of the faithful.

In such communally maintained houses there were always to be found a number of persons whose desire it was to receive the Holy

Spirit, and whose life was therefore devoted to prayer, and to study of the Church's teachings. They might be young people (often entrusted to the *perfecti* by their parents while still mere children) or converts of any age; and though they had not yet received the *consolamentum*, they were no longer classed with the rank and file of the *credentes*. There were also those believers who, while still living in the secular world, still observed a proportion of the restrictions imposed upon *perfecti*—i.e. those concerned with fasting, chastity, and prayer. The greater majority, however, lived perfectly normal lives, and contented themselves with attending meetings and showing reverence to the *bons hommes*.

Theoretically, the ordinary Cathar had only one ritual obligation, and that was to perform his *melioramentum* or act of veneration before the *bons hommes*. This very simple ceremony consisted in his bowing three times to the *perfectus* and saying: 'Pray God to make a good Christian of me, and bring me to a good end.' The *perfectus* would then bless him, and say: 'May God make a good Christian of you, and bring you to a good end.' The believer had no other religious obligation apart from this, and could even continue, out of prudence, to attend Mass in Catholic churches. The *credentes*, in fact, were people who had either given up going to church, or only did so out of fear or habit; and as we have seen, there were very many parishes in which there was no need for them even to do this.

Those whose faith was strong and sincere, and who despite this were still debarred from the sacrament, would regularly (once a month on the average) make their *aparelhamentum*, or self-correction: this involved a public declaration of their sins, and a begging of God's forgiveness. It was not exactly a public confession in the full sense, but rather akin to an Act of Contrition, cast in sufficiently wide terms to include every sort of sin—especially those of indolence or neglect in fulfilling God's wishes. The *perfectus* officiating at this ceremony then absolved the congregation, one by one, from their sins, and imposed penances upon them in the form of fasting and prayer. The Cathars prayed a great deal, but most of their devotion consisted in repeating the Our Father in the Occitan tongue (with the phrase 'suprasubstantial bread' substituted for 'daily bread'*) and meditation on the commentaries with which they glossed the

---

* This Cathar variant on the normal version of the Lord's Prayer results from a different interpretation of the Greek word *epiousios*, which is almost impossible to render precisely, and contains a certain ambiguity of form. 'Suprasubstantial' is a quite feasible rendering. Cf. Runciman, *The Mediaeval Manichee* (1947), p. 166, who explains it as a 'literal translation of the so-called Nikolski gospel, the Slavonic gospel of the Bosnian heretics' (Trs.).

Lord's Prayer. Specifically Catharist prayers do survive,* but the creed's one great central prayer, its focal point of truth, the daily nourishment of *perfectus* and *credens* alike, remained the Our Father.

We see, then, that a Catharist *credens*, despite his non-participation in the sacraments, led a truly religious life; and thanks to the simple fact that his Church was, if not actively persecuted, at any rate illegal and still a partially clandestine organization, his personal faith functioned at a deeper and more intense level than could that of the majority of Catholics. It is true that in many districts the Cathars no longer made any pretence of concealment; indeed, by the time of the Crusade a large number of people must already have gone over to Catharism for motives of self-interest, or simply to be in line with the rest of the community. But the new Church still retained, unchanged, its original characteristics, which were those of a persecuted creed. The man who turned heretic through conviction could always steel his faith with the memory of still-recent burnings.

At the close of the twelfth century the Catharist community had considerable resources at its disposal. Not only did the *perfecti* (most of whom were men of substance) will over all their property to the Church; many *credentes* also bequeathed their entire fortunes on their deathbeds to the support of this new faith. Many rich and influential *credentes* made special donations to the *bons hommes*, not only in cash, but also in the shape of land, houses, even whole châteaux. Despite the vow of absolute poverty which they had taken—and which they never broke—the *perfecti* nevertheless accepted all these gifts, and disposed of them according to the best interests of the Church. They were already being accused of rapacity and greed—by their enemies, at least, if not yet by their friends. Besides emergency relief for the poor and needy, the Cathar communities were also obliged to maintain their *maisons communes*, which fulfilled the simultaneous rôles of school, monastery and hospital. They also founded working craft guilds, especially large weaving establishments; these served a double secondary function, being both educational centres for the young, and training establishments for the novitiate. Furthermore, a very large number of noble ladies surrendered their homes and wealth to the community, thus fostering the development of what were, in effect, Catharist convents. Here they brought up both the daughters of poor *credentes*, and such

* See Appendix III.

children of the nobility as were chosen by their parents to spend their lives in God's service. In the Ariège mountains there were established various hermitages, where widows, or young girls who wished to keep their virginity for ever, and even some married women who had left their husbands the better to serve God, all gathered together, living in grottoes or tiny isolated huts, spending their time in prayer and meditation. These groups of recluses acquired a great reputation for saintliness throughout the area.

The importance of the part played by women in the Cathar communities has frequently been emphasized. There is nothing surprising about it, however. To begin with, it is a generally accepted fact that on the appearance of any new religion, some great preacher will infallibly turn up and unleash a wave of mass enthusiasm—mass hysteria, we might almost say—to which women are more prone by nature than men. Every zealous propagator of a new religious sect— indeed, every priest with a strongly-marked personality—finds himself at once surrounded by a group of devoted and fanatical women, ready to receive his every utterance as though it were the Gospel itself. We should not forget that even here, in heresy-ridden Langue-doc, it was the women rather than the men who also responded to the preaching of St Dominic. The same applies to the Cathar *perfecti*: the women, as a rule, appear to have been more ardent than the men in acceptance of this new faith; frequently it was they who dragged a more cautious or less enthusiastic husband along in their wake.

Besides, in the Midi women enjoyed a far greater degree of moral independence than did their Northern sisters. If respect for women had been a commonplace in literature for more than a century, that was because Provençal women had long known how to compel men's respect. It was from Languedoc that the tradition of *amour courtois* spread throughout Europe, and if the *seigneurs* of the Midi were not always too chivalrous in their actions, at least verbally, they remained beyond reproach. We may recall that famous remark which St Dominic's companion, Brother Stephen of Minia, ad-dressed to Esclarmonde, the sister of the Count of Foix: 'Go tend your distaff, madam; it is no business of yours to discuss matters such as these.'[7] It is not hard to imagine the astonishment and indig-nant disdain which that great lady must have experienced on being thus put in her place by so utterly crude a remark: the more since she was mistress of her own lands, a dignified and elderly widow who had borne six children and now, as a *perfecta*, was revered by all Cathar believers. Brother Stephen must beyond doubt have been both a foreigner and a boor to allow himself such licence in the circumstances. The ladies of Languedoc (and indeed, the same could be said of French noblewomen) were not all accustomed to being dismissed to their distaffs: they were often better educated than their husbands. Such, at any rate, was their position in secular society; according to the Catholic dispensation, however, they remained minors by definition.

The Catharist faith, by denying the 'reality' of the sexes—as it denied the 'reality' of all life in the flesh—was at least implying an equality between men and women. It is true that Catholicism did not openly deny this equality; but it remained in practice at least a staunchly anti-feminist creed. Catharism favoured women a great deal more: those who had received the Holy Spirit possessed, just as men did, the power to transmit it by the laying on of hands—though as a rule they only did so in cases of emergency, and far less frequently than men. We do not find any women among the Cathar bishops or deacons; this active branch of the aspostolate was reserved for men, since they were better fitted to endure the danger and fatigue of a wandering, vagabond existence. Nevertheless the *perfectae* enjoyed very great esteem, and some of them were regarded virtually as the Mothers Superior of their particular communities.

Among the *perfecti*, then, there were fewer women than men— but not markedly fewer. When the historians of the period speak of the heretical *vestiti* captured by the Crusaders, they do not give us any precise figures; but there does not appear to have been an overwhelming predominance of males. These '*bonae Christianae*' conducted their apostolate primarily among women *credentes*: as we have already observed, they were much concerned with girls' education, and also very often acted as nurses or doctors, since at this period women preferred a medical attendant of their own sex. Moreover, more of them devoted themselves to the contemplative life than was the case among the male *perfecti*.

Among the ordinary *credentes*, on the other hand, there seems to have been a greater number of women than men; and certainly the women on the face of it were bolder and more fearless. From the great lady surrounded by her poets and admirers to the widow who devoted her life to prayer and works of charity—not to mention the peasant women who served the *bons hommes* at table and carried their messages throughout the length and breadth of Languedoc— the female *credentes* are more in evidence on the whole than their male counterparts. There was a fairly obvious reason for this. The men, even those of unquestioned and impassioned sincerity, had certain obligations—professional, social, or military—which they could not renounce. In this society a large proportion of men's dealings with one another rested upon the use of the oath; so one could not be too open in one's adherence to a religion which forbade all swearing whatsoever. In this respect women enjoyed greater liberty, and could devote themselves more wholeheartedly to their religious activities without scamping their other obligations.

Besides, even before the Crusade, simple caution prevented people from making too obvious a parade of their convictions. Though the Count himself and the majority of the great feudal landlords in the area were well disposed towards the new heresy, such a state of affairs might not last: the Church of Rome was still powerful, and still partially at least in control of local administration. That is why we so often find heretics being given shelter in women's houses (e.g. Blanche de Laurac, Guillelmine de Tonneins, Fabrissa de Mazeroles, Ferranda, Serrona, Na Baiona, etc.). In this way their fathers, brothers and husbands remained technically innocent before the law, since heresy was only tolerated, not given official recognition. Later we find the Count of Foix (himself a protector of heretics, and both husband and brother to *perfectae*) disclaiming all responsibility for the actions of that 'notorious heretic', his sister Esclarmonde: 'If my sister were in truth an evil and sinful woman, that is yet no reason why I should perish because of her sins. . . .'[8] This is not to say that men, on occasion, failed to show at least as great zeal for their faith as women did.

4. Catharism in its Social and Moral Aspects

All evidence concerning the morality—or rather the immorality—of those holding the Cathar faith is worth a lengthy and detailed scrutiny, since it is precisely on these grounds that most of the sect's adversaries tended to attack it. Since the essential value of any faith must be judged by the effect it produces in the lives of its devotees, those whose business it was to fight against Catharism could hardly proclaim that this heresy rendered its adherents both charitable and virtuous. That was why they continually emphasized the hypocrisy of the *perfecti*, and the immoral conduct of the ordinary believer.

As far as the *perfecti* are concerned, their behaviour in the very face of death must forever free them from any taint of hypocrisy. Nevertheless, their austerity struck contemporary Catholics as so odd that they were repeatedly accused of secret and shameful vices, and in particular of homosexuality—a charge which arose from the fact that both male and female *perfecti* lived in pairs, and were never parted from their *socius* or *socia*. Even when they conceded moral purity to the *perfecti*, Catholic polemicists regarded such a condition as most unnatural, and asserted that these ascetics felt sourly envious of men who had not renounced the pleasures of this world. This suggests that the majority of priests and monks during the period under discussion were very far from observing the rules of poverty and chastity; for if it had been otherwise, no one would have been astonished at the virtues displayed by the Cathar ministers.

In a society where even the clergy did not set a virtuous example— far from it, in fact, as the writings of various Popes, abbots, and bishops testify, not to mention the evidence to be adduced from profane literature—is it to be supposed that the laity were given to more austere habits of morality? What was said concerning the immorality of various Cathars could equally well be applied to their Catholic contemporaries; while the private life of the *grands seigneurs* (we know very little about that of lesser individuals) shows that licentiousness was the rule rather than the exception. Mediaeval society in general, and that of the Midi in particular, was by no means given to hypocrisy: vanity, greed and luxuriousness were not vices that anybody would be at pains to conceal.

On the other hand one charge frequently levelled at the *perfecti*— that they consorted with undesirable persons—is far too reminiscent of that brought against Jesus by the Pharisees to be taken over-seriously. In any case their apostolic zeal must have led them (the same applies to all Christian missionaries in a country with a well-organized religion of its own) to take a special interest in every sort of pariah and *déclassé*: such people tend to be of doubtful morality, which, we may assume, was not invariably reformed by the *bons hommes'* sermons. Besides, since the charity of the *perfecti* was well known, there must have been numerous parasites who feigned conversion in order to find with them a refuge from their destitute lot. But it is not by its weakest and least disinterested members that a community should be judged.

The principal complaint made against the true *credentes*, those who were devoted body and soul to their Church, who witnessed the *consolamentum* and received the ministers of the sect under their own roofs, seems to have been that they cohabited with 'concubines', and that some of them had sired bastards. Cases are frequently cited of *credentes* attending some heretical ceremony accompanied by their concubines (*amasia*=mistress): '*Willelmus Raimundi de Roqua et Arnauda, amasia ejus*; *Petrus aura et Boneta, amasia uxor ejus*;

Raimunda, amasia Othonis de Massabrac,' etc.[9] As far as the Catholic hierarchy were concerned, any woman not married in church was automatically classed as a 'concubine' and Cathar believers might well object to being married within a Church whose rites they abhorred and despised. Otho de Massabrac provides an excellent example: he was a young man, a knight of the Montségur garrison whose family had been Cathars for three or four generations, and who was proscribed as such himself under the Inquisition. In any case, the fact that a person was not married in church does not *per se* afford proof of immorality. Towards the end of the nineteenth century we find many extremely strait-laced ladies proudly asserting their right to a civil marriage. It is well known that, as a general rule, devotees of new religions tend towards puritanism rather than any relaxation of moral standards.

On the other hand the Inquisitors are unanimous in their declaration that the heretics regarded marriage as an institution of the Devil. 'They claim,' Bernard Gui wrote,[10] 'that for a man to have carnal knowledge of his wife is no less heinous a fault than incestuous commerce with his mother, daughter, or sister.' Can we really believe that the *perfecti* sought, in their sermons, to spread such dangerous 'truths' as these among their followers? And might not such statements encourage the faithful actually to commit incest with their mothers or daughters? It seems most likely that the sort of proposition which Gui cites (if authentic) was only addressed to adepts; that is, to the *perfecti* themselves and those who aspired to such initiation, men for whom marriage—even a marriage blessed by God —would have been no less a scandal than it would for a Catholic monk or priest. The Catholic Church herself has always maintained that for a monk even the most serious failings—provided they are casual rather than persistent, and followed by true contrition— weigh less heavily than the sacrilege caused by an officially conse- crated yet sinful marriage. It is in this sort of context that the rigorous austerity of the *perfecti* must be viewed.

The *bons hommes* incurred censure for condemning procreation, often in violent language, and declaring that a pregnant woman was in a state of sin and impurity; but, as the churching of women proves, the Catholic Church, too, admitted procreation and child- birth to be basically impure acts. For Catholics, however, a child represented God's grace rather than a curse: their theology accepted the inexplicable mystery of God's love for the material world, even in its corrupt aspects. But this wisdom, which stemmed from ancient Judaism and possibly incorporated certain pagan traditions, presented the Church with a problem: how was it to be integrated with her close-knit system of moral values? The Middle Ages dearly loved logic; they were very much an epoch of reasoned argument. The consequence was an apparent denial of the possibility of a Fourth Dimension—even with God.

The accusations of immorality made against the Cathars are all the odder in that for many of them, especially women, marriage symbolized their reconciliation with the Church. Covinens de Fanjeaux, having been converted by St Dominic, 'abandoned her heresies and took a husband'. 'Bernarda,' we learn, 'lived three years as a heretic, but afterwards she married and had two children.'[11] We are not told that these girls led a dissolute life prior to marrying, but merely that they kept their virginity. The same applies to the young woman heretic from Champagne who was burnt at Rheims in 1175[13]: her belief in Catharism was revealel solely by her desire to remain a virgin at all costs. It was, then, by their purity rather than any taint of self-indulgence that sincere Cathar believers got themselves specially noticed.

These, it may be objected, were only a small *élite*: what about the rest? It is very likely that a certain number (of enthusiastic convictions but too little strength of will to resist temptation) actually abandoned the conjugal state in order to renounce this world, but thereafter fell into various sins of the flesh which caused a public scandal and brought discredit upon their community as a whole. Even if the *perfecti* did not turn their faces against these strayed sheep, they could hardly promote active support of immorality, since it was, precisely, just such moral licence which they denounced most violently among their Catholic adversaries.

The case of the young girl from Rheims is very typical in the light it sheds on the mentality of the Cathars' opponents. Radulph, Abbot of Coggeshall, relates that one day the Archbishop of Rheims was taking a stroll outside the city accompanied by some of his clergy; and that one of these, Gervais Tilbury, noticing a young girl walking on her own through a nearby vineyard, went up and accosted her with amorous intent ('although,' as Radulph says, 'he was a Canon'). His proposals must have been blunt and direct in the extreme, since the girl, 'with modest and solemn mien, scarce daring to look at him', replied that she could not give herself to him; for, said she, 'if I were to lose my virginity, my body would be corrupted on the instant, and I should be damned irremediably for all eternity'. From these utterances the holy clerk perceived that he had to do with a heretic, and denounced her as such to the Archbishop, who meanwhile had come up with his suite. The girl herself, together with the woman who had instructed her in the Cathar faith, was condemned to the stake, and died with a courage that won great admiration from those who witnessed her end. It is hard to know which element in this story is more surprising: the heroism of the anonymous martyr, or the moral callousness displayed by judges and chronicler alike. It seemed quite natural to them that a cleric should not only try to seduce a young girl, but also that he should utilize the very fact of his shameless conduct as an argument against his victim. A Church in which such moral decadence flourished was hardly qualified to cast the first stone against anyone else.

The majority of the rank-and-file *credentes* would not appear, then, to have led lives any worse than those of the Catholics. Better still, when we examine the lists of those noble families who openly adhered to the Cathar faith (such lists are the only ones which have survived) there is not a vestige of evidence that this religion attempted, in any way whatsoever, to undermine family life by condemning marriage or procreation. On the contrary: the social edifice of the Catharist Church depended in great measure precisely on these great families, with their traditions handed down unbroken from father to son. The catalogue of names conjures up a picture of a society in which ties of kinship were both powerful and well-respected. Those particularly zealous *credentes* who were forced into feigned 'conversion' under pressure of persecution all agreed that they had been brought up in the Cathar faith by their mother, grandmother, uncle, aunt, or some other relative; they married their sons to the daughters of fellow-Cathars; they received the *consolamentum* in the home of their brothers or in-laws. Great ladies such as Blanche de Laurac appear to have acted in all respects as head of their clan, with countless sons, daughters, grandchildren, sons-in-law and daughters-in-law all brought up as fervently devoted Cathars. The *seigneurs* of Niort, Saint-Michel, Festes, Fanjaux, Mirepoix, Castelbon, Castelverdun, Carabet, Miraval and many other châteaux were notorious and open heretics; and the testimony of witnesses constantly refers to the various members of these *seigneurs'* families in every degree of kinship—a fact which suggests that throughout this area (as in any feudally ruled district) the sense of family solidarity was very strong. The disruptive influence of Catharist doctrine would not appear to have been exercised here, at any rate: indeed, these families must be considered among the staunchest supporters of the new religion, and had been for several generations. It would be absurd, therefore, to claim that Catharism constituted a danger to society through the disintegrating effect it was liable to have upon family life.

It is true that certain women of extreme piety retired into conventual life while their husbands were still alive; but in general they did this at an advanced age, when their children were already grown up and married. More often they waited till they were widows, as Blanche de Laurac and Esclarmonde de Foix did—both of whom had numerous children.

Another less common criticism which Catholics made against the Cathars was that of driving their followers into anarchy by the contempt they displayed for public authority, coupled with their rejection of all force and their refusal to take oaths. At first sight this complaint would appear to be better founded than its predecessor. The Cathars did, in fact, preach that temporal authority was originally established by Satan rather than God. Yet neither the Cathars in Languedoc nor the Vaudois sect* (whose morality was closely akin to that of the Cathars) had ever shown any revolutionary tendencies, such as had characterized the Bogomils. Though the Vaudois (or Waldensians) might insist on their followers observing a rule of poverty, this was by no means the case with the Cathars, whose most zealous adepts tended to come from the most wealthy sections of the community. In any case, the Cathars certainly did not incite their supporters to rebel openly against public authority; they had, with some logic, come to the conclusion that in a universe governed by the Prince of this world, no social organization whatsoever could be wholly satisfactory.

Nevertheless the *credentes*, though living in this world, professed a creed that denied every principle on which their society rested. Must it not inevitably follow that their sense of discipline, or of obligation to their *seigneurs* and the law of the land, was thereby seriously unsettled? Sincere believers, it would appear, even though they might be excellent citizens, must needs have performed their civic duties in the knowledge that what they were doing was a useless task, and of entirely secondary importance. Yet did not the Catholic Church herself teach the faithful that the Kingdom of Heaven was worth far more than the principalities of this world? Would anyone accuse the official hierarchy of sowing the seeds of anarchy by such pronouncements?

* The heretical sect of the Vaudois [Waldensians] was formed independently of the Cathars at Lyons, about 1170: it showed distinct characteristics, with a bias towards evangelicism. See C. Schmidt, *Histoire et Doctrine de la secte des Cathares ou Albigeois* (1849), p. 68; and Runciman, *The Mediaeval Manichee* (1947), pp. 124–5. (Trs.)

Various sorts of charges were brought against the *credentes*, and
repeated over and over again. Though Pierre des Vaux de Cernay
may be a most partial witness, he cannot surely have been wholly
mistaken when he claimed that these *credentes* were addicted to
'usury, rapine, murder, perjury, and every kind of perversion'. He is
here referring, clearly, to the Cathar *seigneurs* and knights; and we
should not forget that identical accusations were brought against the
nobility of countries untouched by any taint of heresy. The perennial
hostility between clergy and nobility would, indeed, give us a most
sinister impression of the Catholic nobility if we had no evidence to
go on save the writings of monks and churchmen: apart from a few
'soldiers of Christ', these knights are drawn as men given over to
every base instinct, bursting with brutality, glutted with honours and
luxuries, only happy when engaged in warfare or rapine. Secular
literature, on the other hand, either ignores or despises the clergy;
here the bishops—unless, like Turpin, they happen to be cracking
Saracen skulls—figure at best as mere decorative additions to the
narrative. In the countries where Catholicism was most firmly
established the nobility and the ecclesiastic hierarchy seemed to live
in completely separate worlds, as rivals and indeed as enemies to
one another. Now the aristocracy of the Midi, though not worse
than its counterpart in any other country, numbered among its
plentiful shortcomings that of holding the Catholic religion in open
contempt: so why should we be surprised at its incurring clerical
censure, seeing that the clergy habitually kept up a running fire of
criticism against the Catholic nobility as a whole?

The great barons in the North by no means always honoured
their oaths of allegiance: they seized the least excuse to rebel against
overlords whom they had sworn on the Gospels to serve faithfully.
Those of the Midi (those at least who also happened to profess the
Cathar faith, which compelled them to treat *any* oath as illicit) must
have regarded such oaths as they were obliged to take as merely
simple formalities, void of any moral force; or at any rate, they
were quite at liberty to do so when it suited their book. Possibly then
this meant that they 'perjured' themselves more often than the men
from the North? But, as against this, their religion also condemned
any kind of lie—which meant, by implication, that they had to preserve a certain scrupulousness in their conduct. The only people who
were liable to be driven into perjury by reason of their religion were
those who would have perjured themselves under any circumstances.
Still, even the most honourable of them were often obliged to maintain some sort of relationship with the Catholic Church, since the

latter controlled a large proportion of the country's official administration; and this necessarily encouraged hypocrisy. It is only fair to say that many of the smaller landed proprietors had made a clean and open break with the established Church. In Ariège, Carcassès, and the region round Toulouse whole villages—indeed, sometimes whole districts—had long since abandoned the practice of Catholicism. All the inhabitants received the *consolamentum* on their deathbeds; the *perfecti* conducted their rites in the deserted churches; and one extreme case is cited, that of the Château de Termes, where, until the arrival of the Crusaders, no religious service had been held for over a quarter of a century. The *seigneurs* described as *faidits*—that is, whose who abandoned their lands when the Crusaders came— were too intransigent in their faith even to feign submission to the Church; and there were a great many of them. It is reasonable to assume that men who were capable of sacrificing both property and security for the sake of their religious beliefs were not likely also to be addicted to usury, rapine, and debauchery.

The burghers of the towns in the Midi seem to have been pugnacious folk; the nobility, rich or poor, when they were not at Court or celebrating various feast days, had scarcely nine months in the year to get on with their own affairs. In order to keep their domains intact they had to conduct continual guerilla warfare against bandits, aggressive neighbours, and insubordinate vassals or bailiffs. The Cathar Church had not succeeded in transforming these wolves into lambs, any more than the Catholics had; but doubtless the Cathars were more vehement in their denunciation of murder. The Cathar believer could never feel that he was fighting for a sacred and righteous cause. This, at any rate, was how things stood during the first years of the Crusade.

The Cathars held most lofty notions concerning the value and dignity of life; thus they would not admit that the God of the Old Testament could have been a righteous God, since He had drowned the entire pre-Deluge population of the world, annihilated Pharaoh and his army, destroyed the inhabitants of Sodom, and done much more of the same sort. In fact, they pointed out, He actually *approved* of murder: witness his orders to the Israelites, commanding them to massacre the peoples of Canaan. To Catholics the destruction of evil-doers seemed to present no particular problem; Cathar morality was both subtler and more demanding. Taking the Gospels as their authority, they utterly condemned the death penalty, and indeed punitive measures of any sort; they claimed that criminals should not be punished, but rather given treatment designed to make them better citizens. Doubtless it was easy enough for them to talk in this way, since their adversaries were responsible for the execution of justice; but it is, nevertheless, highly disturbing to find such humane doctrines being denounced by the Church as scandalous. Nor should we be surprised at notions of this sort appealing to a great many people: the times, we may conclude, were less brutal and primitive than superficial observers are wont to assume.

Those who listened to the preaching of the *perfecti* must have possessed an awareness of common humanity lacking in such crude noblemen as supposed they could win entry to Paradise by cleaving numbers of Saracens to the chine. The declaration that to kill a Saracen was just as great a crime as parricide or fratricide was certainly not immoral, though it may have been somewhat imprudent. As we shall see later, however, the war eventually compelled the *perfecti* to modify their uncompromising attitude and allow their followers into battle—though perhaps not with much active degree of encouragement. Still, it remains possible that their pacifism contributed to the relative weakness of resistance in Languedoc at the outset of hostilities.

5. *The Struggle against 'Babylon'*

These few considerations show us that Catharist doctrine might present certain dangers from the social viewpoint—though any objective study of the situation is virtually impossible for lack of concrete evidence. What *is* certain is that the public authorities in Languedoc, from princes and barons to consuls and leading burghers, were, in general, well disposed towards this heresy and its adherents. In fact the anarchic aspects of Catharism worried the *grands seigneurs* and the consuls so little that they were prepared to embrace it themselves, and to allow their wives and sisters to do so. If the Cathar faith had an aggressive side to it, this was directed against the Church rather than those in temporal authority.

As has been suggested above, the Church was the rival, and frequently the enemy, of the aristocracy: a state of affairs which had prevailed for centuries. The Church, indeed, profited by the Crusades to harness the nobles' warlike instincts for conquest, at least partially, to her own advantage; but those *seigneurs* who abstained from crusading, in whatever country, had one eye on the Church's local property, and hoped to win it by simple *force majeure*. The Church, for her part, had been steadily enriched through the centuries by gifts, bequests, and the increasingly numerous dues that she levied from town and countryside alike; this meant that she was now to a great extent secularized. She administered vast domains, and employed an armed militia to defend them; as we have seen, certain bishops, such as Bérenger of Narbonne, went so far as to have their dues collected by mercenary captains in their employ, and though such instances may have been rare, this one detail shows that the Church stood no nonsense over non-payment of tithes. By levying these dues on an already poverty-stricken population, the Church was setting up in competition with the *seigneurs*, whose greed she had already excited by reason of her rich estates and châteaux: warriors seldom felt anything but contempt for those who wore the tonsure. Wherever possible the *seigneurs* either took legal proceedings against the bishops and abbots, or else made open war upon them. By the end of the twelfth century the prelates were beginning to abuse their powers of excommunication. This still constituted a serious annoyance from the administrative point of view, but no longer struck terror into its victims; indeed, such spiritual thunderbolts often remained ineffectual through having been aimed at random.

If such a chronic antagonism between Church and nobility existed in countries where Catholic doctrine as such remained unquestioned, it followed that where heresy flourished, this enmity took on the character of open warfare. Must we then deduce that the reason why so many *grands seigneurs* turned heretic was one of pure self-interest, and that what they wanted was to lay hands on Church property? There is no doubt that the great barons of Languedoc, and above all the Count of Toulouse, were mighty despoilers of such ecclesiastical possessions. In 1209 Raymond VI himself admitted to having taken violent action against the persons of monks and abbots; to having imprisoned the Bishop of Vaison and deposed the Bishop of Carpentras; and to having confiscated towns and châteaux from the Bishops of Vaison, Cavaillon, and Rodez, from the Abbots of Saint-Gilles, Saint-Pons, Saint-Thibéry, Gaillac, and Clarac, and many more besides. This list not only demonstrates the Count's rapacity, but also serves to show how well endowed these abbeys and bishoprics were.[13] The nobility no less than the common people criticized the Church because of her excessive wealth, which was out of all proportion to the services she rendered in return for them.

Now while the Counts of Toulouse and of Foix, and successive Viscounts of Béziers, all confiscated Church property for their own enrichment, they also made generous gifts to various churches and abbeys. Such actions would appear to have been dictated by specific local interests and personal obligations; they were not, so far as we can tell, due to any well-defined general policy. What the appearance of Catharism (and later of the Waldensian heresy) had provoked, or rather revealed, in the Languedoc area was a deep and widespread hatred of the Catholic Church: hatred which found a sympathetic response at every level of society.

It would be wrong to assume that it was the propaganda put out by the *perfecti* which whipped up this atmosphere of hatred; feeling must have been running very high already, since the most violent attacks on the Church were favourably received by a large number of Catholics themselves. Furthermore, the anti-clerical bias of the Cathars' preaching has been regarded as one of the major reasons for their success; and this explanation (which constitutes *per se* the most damning indictment one could conceivably bring against the Church) has been advanced by various Catholic historians, who could scarcely be suspected of anti-clerical leanings themselves. But though the Church may indeed have been unpopular in Languedoc, and incapable of fulfilling her duties there, it also has to be admitted that her enemies' propaganda often provoked the most scandalous disorders, besides providing fuel for passions of the very lowest order.

Such confiscations of Church lands by great or lesser *seigneurs* could, taken all in all, be regarded only as a reaction, legitimate enough, against the vastly swollen appetites displayed by certain prelates of the day. But for the poor folk, who must have heaved a sigh of relief at the thought of no longer paying tithes, and those numerous other dues wrung from them in return for the Sacraments, to abandon the Faith of their fathers could not be merely a matter of money. Those who turned their back on a Church in which they had once believed (even though with an ill grace and vague understanding) were driven by frequently indiscreet propaganda to commit various crimes of the most odious nature. The *perfecti* doubtless did not approve such acts, but they were at least partially responsible for them. Once the new faith had taken root in Languedoc, it aroused a wave of pure fanaticism. This, doubtless, was not the case with the majority of Cathar believers, since on the whole Catholics and heretics got on excellently; but the phenomenon cannot be written off, either, in terms of irresponsible atrocities committed by brigands and highway robbers.

Pierre des Vaux de Cernay cites the case of one Hugues Faure, who defiled a church altar in the crudest fashion; he also refers to those heretics from Béziers who set upon a priest, tore the chalice from his hands, and proceeded to desecrate that in the same way.[14] From the files of the Inquisition we learn of a certain B. from Quiders, who urinated on a priest's tonsure.[15] Such incidents must have been rare, since the heretics' adversaries had every reason to publicize them, and in fact only quote a few isolated instances. But Vaux de Cernay also tells us a revealing anecdote about the Count of Foix. The Count, it seems, was engaged in litigation with the monks of St Antoninus, who held the *seigneurie* over the town of Pamiers, and sent two of his knights there to avenge the affront done a noble *perfecta* by these same monks, who had expelled her from the town limits. The knightly messengers cut one reverend Canon to pieces, and gouged out the eyes of another. Later the Count himself burst into the monastery, held a feast on the premises, and then set fire to it. He did the same to the monastery of Our Lady, after laying siege to the monks, starving them out, and pillaging their chapel. In another church he had the arms and legs torn off a crucifix, and his soldiers used the bits to pound up spices in a mortar; one of his squires ran another crucifix through several times with a spear, mockingly calling upon the figure of Christ to ransom itself.[16]

Are we dealing here with mere slanderous inventions? It is possible, but if the Catholic Count Raymond could be accused of burning a church together with those inside it, such violent conduct on the part of the Count of Foix should not surprise anyone. In the case under discussion behaviour of this sort shows not so much brutality as genuine anti-clerical passion: such acts were surely inspired by a most lively hatred of the Catholic Church. And though, later, Raymond Roger of Foix was to make a declaration of orthodoxy before the Pope, he doubtless only did so in obedience to the orders of his spiritual advisers. This tireless fighter and redoubtable foe to all Crusaders was one of the most striking examples of a particular type of Cathar nobility: at once passionately devout and militant to the point of fanaticism.

Such *seigneurs* as the Count of Foix had the power to do a great deal of harm to the Church. Believers with fewer resources (but equally fierce zeal) did not burn down monasteries, or commandeer them for the housing of *perfecti*; but they did manhandle priests and pillage churches and cemeteries. These were doubtless reinforced by numerous footloose soldiers of fortune, not to mention plain crackpots, who were always glad of any excuse for making trouble: by pretending to be heretics, they could do what they wished without incurring any public censure. The authorities, being sympathetic towards Catharism, took no steps against crimes of this nature; while the people as a whole approved of what was done, either through zealous fanaticism or merely because they detested the clergy. Contemporary testimony is quite explicit on the subject: not only did whole districts go over to heretical beliefs, but even in those which remained nominally Catholic there was no hint of reprisals for the acts of sacrilege committed by heretics, whether genuine or false.

The Cathars professed especial hatred both for the Cross, as the instrument of God's agony, and for the Mass, which was in their eyes supremely sacrilegious, since it regarded as the true Body of God a scrap of gross matter destined to decompose in the guts of the faithful. This hatred led them into violent attacks upon the Catholic Church's most sacred doctrines; and the mere fact that such attacks no longer seemed to arouse any protests shows how universally the Church, here at any rate, was held in contempt. Those towns which retained their Catholic allegiance did not attempt to defend the Faith by local Crusades or massacres; and while this is very much to their credit, it shows primarily that in Languedoc it was the Catharist Church which had the upper hand. Many bishops and abbots came from heretical families, and showed marked indulgence towards heresy as such. Priests and Canons habitually fraternized with *credentes*, and even with *perfecti*, either from opportunistic motives or out of sympathy for a doctrine the moral force of which they could hardly fail to recognize. Yet for the Cathars themselves the Church was the Enemy *par excellence*, the Great Whore of Babylon, Satan's citadel and the seat of all damnation; not in any circumstances could they tolerate what they described as her superstitious practices and gross material errors.

All our testimony is agreed upon the following points. In a Catholic country, where a large proportion of property, wealth, and public authority was in the hands of the Church, and where moreover the Church had control and sanction over every act in men's lives, whether public or private, the population as a whole were either indifferent or actively hostile towards Catholicism. A new Church had been established, and had won general approval and regard. It was already an integral part of the country's national life, and continued to gain ground without recourse to civil strife or spectacular public riots. Its avowed aim was the destruction of the Established Catholic Church, which constituted the one target against which this half-popular, half-mystical movement directed its hostile energies. Thus Catholicism slowly began to lose all contact with the country's deeper spiritual needs; by progressive self-identification with a specific social caste, concerned above all else to defend its own interests, the Church became increasingly isolated from reality.

On the eve of those events which brought upon Languedoc the catastrophe that was to cost her her independence, the Church stood neither for justice, order, peace, charity, nor God; what she represented was the Papacy. The genuinely tragic position in which she found herself led her into a most terrifying confusion of values, and made her subordinate all moral considerations to the defence of her temporal interests.

Catholic historians—those of the thirteenth century no less than their modern successors—have all emphasized the point that this heresy constituted a most serious danger to the countries which it had 'infected'. This is perfectly true, and indeed borne out by events: the 'danger' thus described, however, was in fact none other than the Crusade itself, the Church's threat of violent reaction against the peril to which she stood exposed. It should never be forgotten that, for all her many abuses of the power she held, the Church formed an integral part of society—was, indeed, a very large cog in the machinery of government, flawed perhaps, but to all practical intents and purposes irreplaceable. Though they might filch her wealth, princes and consuls continued to make use of her, and never so much as considered her suppression. At the same time popular sentiment, fuelled by Catharist doctrine, sapped and harried her, steadily cutting down her whole *raison d'être*. It would be false to say that a spirit of tyrannical intolerance and sectarianism could be found only on the Catholic side: when two parties are in open strife they contaminate each other progressively. The *perfecti* (and even this only applies to some of them) went no further than verbal violence themselves; but they already had wide enough influence to attract rather more fanatical followers.

Let us for one moment try to imagine a Pope, inspired by evangelical enthusiasm, who issued a Bull deposing and dispossessing every abbot and bishop, ordering them to distribute the Church's property among the poor, to live by alms, and to go forth on foot as wandering preachers. If such a radical remedy had been applied, it would have provoked the most frightful disorders. Yet what other way was there of reforming a Church whose inner ills sprang directly from her vast temporal powers? The Cathars' strength derived in part from their comparative poverty, and the fact that they were not responsible for the administration of public affairs; whereas the Catholic Church, though on occasion she might behave harshly, or temper justice to her own interests, nevertheless possessed great administrative experience, and was forced to cope with practical difficulties the very existence of which remained unknown to her adversaries.

The most serious charge that can be brought against the Cathars is precisely that which (with good reason) has been foisted on their opponents: religious intolerance. They did not indict Catholics, nor did they go in for bonfires, having neither the means nor the wish to do so; but they did denigrate and deride (often in the most indiscriminately abusive fashion) a religion which *per se* should have commanded their respect. Doubtless the blame for this can be attributed to the unseemly conduct of prelates and priests, the harshness of ecclesiastical administration, and the idiosyncratic Provençal temperament: even in the days of paganism the Church Fathers sometimes rebuked those who insulted a pagan cult or desecrated the images of its gods.

The Cathars in Languedoc, then, had by now coalesced into a semi-official Church, a society which was no longer secret or clandestine, and which numbered among its members both high-born nobles and the lowest of the land. Nor was their Church the only heretical Church in the area. In his informative sketch of Languedoc as it was before the Crusade, Pierre des Vaux de Cernay admits that one group of these Provençal heretics, the Vaudois, were 'evil, but much less so than the others', and that 'in many respects their beliefs are the same as ours'.[17] The Vaudois [Waldensians] were less numerous than the Cathars, and it was in general the common folk who supported them—though one of the Count of Foix's sisters was herself a member of the sect. Their preaching, to judge from the testimony quoted above, tended to convert those who were sickened by ecclesiastical abuses, but remained true to the Catholic Faith. Doctrinally the creed was far less revolutionary than Catharism, but it showed itself equally abhorrent of the Church, the ecclesiastical hierarchy, and any kind of Catholic ritual.

The Waldensian sect was of recent origin. Its founder, Peter Waldo, began preaching about 1160, in Lyons; this is why the movement's followers were often referred to as Leonists, or the Poor Brethren of Lyons. Peter Waldo, a rich merchant of that town, was a pious man who, desiring to become better acquainted with the Scriptures, had them translated by one of his friends, Stephen d'Anse. When

this Stephen was killed in an accident, Peter Waldo was so heart-
broken that he decided to devote the rest of his life to God's service:
he sold his goods and distributed the proceeds among the poor,
henceforth living only for preaching and charitable acts. Other
people followed his example, and so a pious Society was formed,
a group of laymen whose aim was to practise absolute poverty, in
emulation of the Apostles, and to preach God's Word among the
people.

Waldo acquired large numbers of disciples, whom he sent out to
preach in the towns and villages around Lyons, in public squares and
even on occasion inside the churches themselves. The Archbishop of
Lyons, Jean de Bellesmains, was disturbed by the way this popular
movement spread: it was scandalous to see these simple, ill-read
laymen, *idiotae et illiterati*, without benefit of any authoritative
ecclesiastical mandate, taking it upon themselves to expound Holy
Writ as they pleased. By this time the movement had already won
countless adherents. In 1180 the Archbishop forbade Peter Waldo
and his followers to preach any more; but they replied that it was
better to obey God than men, and cited the example of St Peter
before the Sanhedrin. The preaching continued, and an appeal was
made to the then Pope, Lucius III, who upheld the veto which Jean
de Bellesmains had pronounced. Three years after this the Poor
Brethren of Lyons are already being mentioned as *heretics*, in the
same breath as the Cathars, in the Constitutio *Ad Abolendam*
promulgated by Lucius at Verona.[18]

Thus the disciples of Peter Waldo, having begun as Catholics
who would not knuckle under to authority, now found themselves
transformed into genuine heretics; and from this point onwards
their 'heresy' grew steadily. Little by little they moved towards open
rebellion against the Church's institutions, and thence against the
very principles for which she stood. 'Heretics,' wrote Bernard of
Fontcaude, in his tract against the Waldensians, 'are those who
either adhere to an ancient heresy or succeed in manufacturing a
new one from the old. Such are they who declare that we owe no
obedience either to the Church of Rome or to her priests—*quod dictu
horribile est!*—but solely to God.' The position of the Waldensians
is here clearly defined: they were men who had constructed a new
heresy (as opposed to the Cathars, who were bracketed with the
Manichaeans) and their particular heresy consisted in their resolve to
obey God only, and not the Church of Rome.

The principle which the Waldensians took for the basis of their
condemnation of the Church was as follows. Since the prelates of

the Church were corrupt, they could not therefore be vehicles of Grace; in rejecting the principle of the priesthood, the Waldensians also rejected the other sacraments, including baptism and the Eucharist. They reached a point, indeed, at which they denied not only the whole body of Catholic ritual but also a large proportion of Catholic doctrine. They no more believed in the Real Presence of Christ in the sacrifice of the Mass than they did in the Communion of Saints or in Purgatory. Jesus, they claimed, should be man's sole Mediator (to the exclusion of the Saints) and the sole recipient of human prayers. It was wrong to pray for the dead, since from the moment when he departed this life every man was either saved or damned. (We should remember that prayers for the dead and the cult of the Saints both flourished during the Middle Ages to an extent hard for us to imagine today. Nor should it be forgotten that one of the Church's largest sources of revenue was obtained from the administration of the sacraments—baptism, marriage, extreme unction—and, above all, from Masses for the Dead.) The Waldensians, then, would not celebrate religious festivals; nevertheless, they did observe Sundays, the feasts of the Blessed Virgin, and those of the Apostles and Evangelists besides.

Thus their religion was a kind of Christianity, still partially orthodox, but simplified to a very great degree. They, like the Catholics, believed in the divine inspiration of the Old Testament; they also believed in the doctrines of the Trinity and the Incarnation; in the historical truth of Christ's Passion and Resurrection; in Hell, in the last Judgment, and, in short, in every article of the Creed, which they accepted according to the Church's own traditional interpretation. (However, they never recited the Creed, just as they never recited any prayer that the Church had adopted, with the single exception of the Our Father.) They asserted that the Catholic Church had fallen into heresy through the fault of Pope Sylvester, who in their eyes was the founder of the Roman Church; and that everything this Church had promulgated and laid down since the fourth century was false and worthless.

Therefore we may say that the heresy of the Waldensians—despite their denial of certain fundamental dogmas such as the Eucharist—consists almost entirely in their absolute rejection of the Roman Church. They were not so much heretics as over-zealous reformers, and seemed not to have invented any new doctrines. Although they had their own formulaic professions of faith, not to mention their own prayers and apologetic literature, their thought was neither so coherent nor so constructive as that of the Cathars. Their greatest successes were primarily made among the working classes, whom they attracted by their preaching of poverty, their addiction to hard work, and their personal piety—which seemed to many Catholics more genuinely Christian than that of most priests. Though they had been officially listed as a heretical body since 1184, even in the early years of the thirteenth century they continued to attract the sympathy of various Catholics who regarded them as 'the poor ones of God', freely bestowed alms upon them, and allowed them to chant their prayers in the churches.[19] Despite all this, the Waldensians were subjected to Papal denunciation on the grounds that they were dangerous heretics, no less detestable than the Cathars.

The truth of the matter is that, in Languedoc at least, these two heretical movements (which had relatively little in common, and on occasion would clash with one another in bursts of the most furious polemic) were often so hopelessly mixed up that it is hard for us to determine just which heretics the authorities in such-and-such a place were dealing with—at any rate so far as ordinary rank-and-file believers were concerned. This confusion stemmed from two causes. In the first place, since both heresies were equally hostile to the Church, the latter was inclined to treat them in the same way; and secondly, since the Waldensians were of more recent origin, they tended to model both their organization and their moral code on those of the Cathars.

The Waldensians, exactly like the Cathars, had their *perfecti* and their *credentes*; the former were raised to this dignity by means of a ritual known in the same way as the *consolamentum*, which similarly consisted of a laying on of hands, and was followed by the surrender of one's property to the community and a vow of poverty and chastity. Though the Waldensian communities did not have any bishops, they were nevertheless controlled by superior ministers, both deacons and priests, and their organization very much resembled that of a normal religious Order. They had their own religious houses, very similar to monastic establishments, where the Waldensian *perfecti* spent their time in fasting, study, and prayer. Their periods of abstinence were not so rigorous as those of the Cathars, nor were they based upon any particular dogma; but despite this, the Waldensians, like the Cathars, were regarded as notable ascetics.

They devoted their lives to preaching, and above all to the expounding of the Scriptures, which they brought within reach of the common people by distributing a large number of Bibles translated into the vernacular. Despite the accusations of ignorance which some of them incurred, they were eager to teach the people; again like the Cathars, they had their schools, where they taught children the meaning of the Gospels and the Epistles.[20]

The Waldensian women *perfectae* were also preachers, and claimed, in fact, that any Christian enjoyed the right to preach. In this respect the Waldensians were more revolutionary than the Cathars, since among the latter it is only very rarely that women appear to have functioned as preachers.

As with the Cathars, their main and almost sole prayer was the Our Father, which they would recite a certain number of times every day—often thirty or forty in all. They differed from the Cathars, however, in the matter of absolution. The Cathars only practised confession in the form of a public absolution from sin performed by the whole assembly of the faithful; whereas the Waldensians could confess to one of their own brethren and get absolution from him.

Like the Cathars, again, the Waldensians were very fierce against the Church of Rome (which they referred to as the Whore of Babylon); and they never missed any opportunity of lashing out against Catholic 'superstitions' and abuses. In this respect, at any rate, they made common cause with the real heretics, though they were distinguished from them locally by the title of *ensabatés* or *ensabatatz*. And it is very likely that in Languedoc, where the Cathars predominated (the Waldensians being most numerous in the Alpine districts and Lombardy) Waldensian communities had, in the end, been infiltrated by the beliefs and customs of their Catharist neighbours.

There is no doubt that there were very many Waldensians among the country folk and the working class generally; but the ruling classes contained fewer of them. To take a random example: on the list of two hundred and twenty-two heretics who were arraigned at Béziers in 1209, a mere dozen names are accompanied by the phrase *val*—that is, *Valdenses*. And if their enemies themselves admitted that they were 'very much less evil' than the others, it would not seem probable that any distinction was ever made, at the time of the persecutions, between Cathars and Waldensians. The Catharist Church, being the stronger and the better organized, had in the end overshadowed the small Waldensian Church in Languedoc, and the ensuing war was to bind them still closer together in a common martyrdom.

At the time of the Crusade, it seems likely that a large proportion of the population of Languedoc consisted either of heretics or of those who at least were openly sympathetic towards heresy. Nevertheless we cannot be entirely sure about this: it is possible that the people merely tolerated Catharism, since in order to fight against the Crusaders it was enough to possess a sense of honour and patriotism. To be an adept of the Cathar faith was not a necessary prerequisite. This war of religion was by no means a civil war.

My intention is not to discuss the intrinsic value of the Cathar religion, but simply to put before the reader a concrete historical situation. Such facts as we possess show us the development of a newly-formed religion, which was in a strong position because of its origin as a semi-clandestine movement. This religion had little difficulty in taking root in a society the corruption of which it was free to denounce as much as it liked, since it had no official connections. It was indeed confronted with an Established Church that had grown over-sure of her privileges, and was now both corrupted and discredited by that habit of compromise to which the defence of her own interests had now for too long habituated her.

The Church of Rome could no longer refrain from striking at this heresy with all the strength she could muster—just as a man whose clothing is on fire has no alternative but to put the flames out in any way he can. It remains true that even in such a case not all means are legitimate. But as we shall see, the Church had, with the passage of centuries and under the pressure of circumstance, become a totalitarian power. As such she naturally tended towards oppression and was already inclined to regard as legitimate only such acts as furthered her own temporal interests.

CHAPTER III

THE PRE-HERETICAL CHURCH

1. *The Period before Innocent III*

IT IS NOT A MATTER for surprise that the Catholic Church's reaction when confronted by Catharism was one of absolute and uncompromising intolerance—though it by no means possessed a monopoly of such intransigence. Once any powerful religion has become a State religion, it will commit oppressions in all good faith, since it regards any opposition as a sacrilege and an offence against God. A Church can no more get rid of its fanatics than a man could amputate his own arm or leg. Without fanaticism very few religions would have managed to survive at all—certainly not in Western Europe.

St Francis of Assisi was the friend of St Dominic, and St Dominic was the friend of Simon de Montfort. It was no less than the very life of the Church which was at stake, and this justified some fanaticism; we must avoid under-estimating beliefs which drove into acts of violence men whose first duty should have been to condemn violence of any sort.

In the French Midi, it was neither public morality nor social life nor yet again civil authority which was threatened by the Catharist heresy; what *was* threatened was the Catholic Church. As we have already seen, in the twelfth century this Church was a veritable State within a State, a well-organized, frequently despotic power against which Kings themselves waged incessant and more or less open warfare: a struggle seldom crowned with success. The Church was still, as much as she had ever been, an organic part of mediaeval society; but her progressive decadence in the Languedoc area during the twelfth century, together with the spread of Catharism, had ended by bringing about a state of affairs such as up till then had appeared inadmissible, indeed unthinkable, in the eyes of any sincere Catholic. Here was a country, at the very heart of Christen-

dom, a prosperous, comparatively powerful country with a long
established tradition of Christianity behind it, a major centre of
trade, and the home of a culture that had won universal admiration
—yet this same country was in the process of reaching a point where
it could not only do without the Catholic Church, but (to all appearances) openly spurn its authority in favour of an entirely new
religion.

It was not only the material interests of the Church, its hierarchy
and privileges that were threatened by this new faith, but also its
spiritual life: a life that had been won at great cost, matured over
the centuries, and sanctified by the prayers of thousands of saints,
both known and unknown; a mystical life wholly based on the daily
sacrifice of the Mass and on the Presence, as real as it was eternal,
of Christ in His Church. The Catholic faith had both assimilated and
transfigured the civilizations of antiquity; it had built cathedrals and
given protection to the poor; it had founded schools, discovered or
re-discovered the sciences, produced works of art of an incomparable
splendour, set God within reach of the humblest of his creatures,
and, on occasion, put down the mighty from their seats. The foundations upon which its tradition rested could no longer be shaken
without imperilling the entire edifice of mediaeval civilization; the
Cross and the Host were no mere accessories of the Christian faith,
but constituted its very heart and centre.

A new Church which not only denied the Catholic Church's most
sacred traditions, but even questioned its most fundamental doctrines, could not, in a period when man refused to admit that truth
might be two-faced, maintain a position of peaceful co-existence.
To tolerate heresy was to admit by implication that the Host was not
the True Body of Christ; that the Saints of the Church were liars,
and that the crosses which adorned churches and cemeteries were
little more than handy perches for ravens. There are things about
which one has no right to be tolerant: one would not describe as
'tolerant' a man who let his mother be publicly insulted.

The indignation felt by the Catholic Church, then, was quite
legitimate; all the more so since her opponents were men who had
been brought up in a Catholic tradition and reared on Christian
soil. Moreover the weapons these dissident elements used to attack
Catholicism were those which the Church herself had given them:
who else but the Church had inspired such heretical converts with
the need for those Christian qualities of purity and charity in the
name of which they condemned the Church herself? It was only the
Church of Rome—whether she were 'the Church of the Devil' or not

—that had rendered possible the expansion of the Catharist faith; her adversaries were attacking her in the name of that Christ whom for centuries she had taught them to love.

The use of force was not scandalous *per se*; it formed part of those inevitable compromises which every Established Church is forced to make with the secular authorities. In every Christian country there were ecclesiastical courts which punished crimes committed by the clergy, cases of moral delinquency, and also such things as sorcery and commerce with the Devil.

Nevertheless the Church did not *a priori* bracket the heretic with the sorcerer, and on occasion displayed a rather more understanding attitude than did the civil authorities. Thus we find St Bernard writing to the Pope, about the heretics massacred at Cologne, in the following words: 'The people of Cologne have exceeded all decent bounds. Though we may approve of their zeal we most emphatically do not approve of what that zeal has brought about; for faith is a work of persuasion, and cannot be imposed by force.'[1] In the eleventh century we find Wazon, Bishop of Liège, protesting against the cruelties committed by those Frenchmen who, in their frantic loathing of heresy, had set about slaughtering every person of pale complexion that they could lay hands on. The reputation for asceticism which the *perfecti* enjoyed was as long-established as it was widespread.

The Church before the period of the Inquisition was by no means more intolerant than secular society. Doubtless she could be accused of having herself created that spirit of intolerance whose excesses she occasionally condemned; but all the same, any attempt to treat the conscience of the Church and that of the Christian peoples she ruled as two separate entities would be a vain undertaking. Catholicism was a good deal more than a mere system of international administration represented by an army of bureaucrats directed by the Bishop of Rome.

The powers which the Church had at her disposal were too great for her not to yield, on occasion, to the temptation of abusing them. Generally, however, she contented herself with maintaining public order in those domains which lay under her jurisdiction, in a more or less harsh manner according to the circumstances of the case. It is no more immoral to burn one man for sorcery than to hang another for stealing a side of bacon. If the Church took upon herself the administration of criminal justice, that was simply because a great proportion of all such administrative offices lay in her hands. It had not been necessary for her to usurp these functions: she had assumed them during a period when no other body was capable of taking the responsibility for them.

Those persons who professed religious opinions manifestly contrary to the teaching of the Church, and who refused to renounce the error of their ways, were liable, under the laws then in force, to be condemned to death at the stake. But, in theory at least, the Church's true weapon in the struggle against all heresy was persuasion: a persuasion which most often took the shape of intimidation pure and simple. The presumed heretic ran the risk of excommunication, with all its consequences: once he was cut off from the Church an excommunicated person was to all intents and purposes a social outcast. In a country like Northern France where people and clergy were both equally fanatical, the Apostolic See had to concern itself more with curbing the zeal of its bishops than with sending out missionaries. In the Midi, on the other hand (this being a notorious nest of heretics) the Popes organized preaching campaigns and made every effort to reform ecclesiastical morals.

If we turn back to the evidence of Innocent III concerning the Occitan clergy, it will be seen that this latter measure had very little result; and the preaching was hardly more successful.

Yet it was St Bernard himself who became the apostle of Catholicism and came to preach in the Midi in 1145, together with the Papal Legate Albéric, Bishop of Ostia, and Geoffrey, Bishop of Chartres. His is a formal testimony to the triumph of heresy:[2]

The churches lack their congregations of the faithful; the faithful lack priests; and the priests lack all honour. All that remains are a few Christians without Christ. The sacraments are abused, and the Feasts of the Church are no longer celebrated. Men are dying with their sins still upon them. By refusing children the Grace of Baptism these people are depriving them of all life in Christ.

Such was the position sixty years before the Crusade. Even if we assumed that St Bernard, in his pious consternation, exaggerated the extent of the disaster, his words furnish proof enough of the Church's decadence in such districts as he visited.

On the day of his arrival in Albi, St Bernard preached in the Cathedral to a congregation of thirty persons. It is true that two days later the vast building was too small to contain the throng of enthusiastic worshippers who flocked there to hear the Saint preach; but their enthusiasm doubtless soon burnt itself out, and St Bernard's evangelical mission proved fruitless.

Despite the forced recantation and spectacular condemnation of

D

Peter Mauran, known as 'St John the Evangelist', the preaching Crusade launched by Pope Alexander III in 1179 had even less result. One or two easily-impressed heretics made an outward show of submission, but after the Legates had gone the people as a whole, irritated by this crude interference in their internal affairs on the part of a foreign Power, showed their respect for heresy yet more openly. The following year the Pope first began to consider an appeal to the secular arm. At the Ecumenical Council of the Lateran (1179) he declared:

> Although the Church, as St Leo has said, contents herself with spiritual judgment, and makes no use of bloody executions, yet she must needs have recourse to secular law and invoke the aid of princes, *that fear of temporal punishment may force men to seek a spiritual cure for their shortcomings.* Therefore since these heretics, whom some call Cathars, others *patarini*, and others again *publicani*, have made great advances in Gascony, and the lands about Albi and Toulouse and elsewhere, and are there publicly teaching false doctrine and striving to pervert the simple-minded, We hereby declare them under Our anathema, together with all who protect or shelter them. . . . [Cf., Appendix IV.]

This is already a confession of impotence: the Pope is admitting that the Church can no longer fight this heresy by her own proper methods. But in Northern Italy and here in the French Midi, Rome ordered local authority, both secular and ecclesiastical, to conduct against these heretics what amounted to a campaign of political repression. After the Council of Verona Pope Lucius III enjoined his bishops to travel through their respective dioceses specifically to search out heretics, and commanded all *seigneurs* and consuls to aid the bishops in their task on pain of excommunication and interdict. The Papal Legate, Henri Abbot of Clairvaux (later to become Bishop of Albano), not content with setting up councils to reform clerical morality, actually deposed the Archbishop of Narbonne, and succeeded in gathering together a certain number of Catholic knights from the area: this body proceeded in 1181 to lay siege to Lavaur, one of the main centres of heresy in Languedoc.

The tactics employed by the great feudal barons of Languedoc when dealing with Rome varied very little: their main gambit consisted in making promises which they never kept. From their point of view this was the only course open to them. Though Raymond V, urged on by considerations of a political nature, still inclined to side openly with the Church, his son, realizing how important the heretical element was in the country as a whole, later did all he could to keep the peace between the two rival religions.

Raymond VI succeeded his father in 1194. Four years later Lothario Conti, a Cardinal-Deacon aged only thirty-eight, was elected Pope, and took the title of Innocent III. He came from an old patrician Roman family, and was not only well thought of in ecclesiastical circles in Rome, but equally popular in his own home town. The admiration that his character and capacities inspired was so great that despite his youth, despite the way his predecessor, Celestinus III, had kept him out of public affairs (he was an Orsini, and the Contis and Orsinis were traditional enemies), and despite the fact that he had not yet been ordained priest, the Cardinals' decision was almost unanimous. The very morning after Celestinus III's death, the young Cardinal-Deacon found himself promoted Head of the Christian Church.

It was with genuine and indeed implacable sincerity that he assumed this high role. During the eighteen years of his Pontificate he was to act as a veritable vicegerent of God on earth, dictating his will to monarchs and peoples without regard for individual interests, never hesitating when faced with practical difficulties that might prove an obstacle to his commands. He was both a theoretician and a man of action, who laid down as his prime axiom the Church's absolute supremacy, and saw himself as one called to guide kings and emperors, and compel them to serve God's interests.

Innocent III contrived to bring both Philip II and John Lackland to heel. He won direct homage from the King of Aragon. He launched the German knights against the Northern paynims, and sent the flower of French chivalry crusading against the Saracen. (This latter expedition was to culminate, against his wishes, in the capture of Constantinople; he nevertheless took advantage of the situation to try and extend his sway over the Greek Church.) He successfully imposed his Papal Legates everywhere in the capacity of Ministers charged with the guidance of princely politics. Taking all this into consideration, it is plain that he, even less than his predecessors, could hardly tolerate such a scandal as was presented by a country in which the Church had become a public laughing-stock, both among the common people and among those set in authority over them.

Yet Innocent III, though primarily responsible for launching the Crusade against the Catharist heresy, was by no means a fanatic. His pastoral letters reveal to us a circumspect man, one anxious to act with justice and moderation. When dealing with cases of heresy referred to him by the Bishop of Auxerre or the Archbishop of Sens, he wavered hesitantly, asked for further proof, further enquiries, and in the end, somewhat uncertainly, came to the conclusion that the accused were innocent.

When he dispatched his Legates into Languedoc, Innocent III, seeking to attack the root cause of the trouble rather than its symptoms, began by investigating the local bishops and secular authorities. He judged it to be the evil example set by the clergy which gave rise to 'heretical insolence'. But this Pope, who flattered himself that he could reduce kings to begging his mercy, found his own subordinates somewhat more refractory: the authority of the Church could be a two-edged weapon. It is true that certain prelates—William de Roquessels, Bishop of Béziers; Nicholas, Bishop of Viviers; Raymond de Rabastens, Bishop of Toulouse; and Bérenger, Archbishop of Narbonne—were all declared suspended from office by the Pope's Legates. This revolutionary measure was scarcely calculated to win the Pope the sympathetic regard of his higher clergy. The Archbishop of Narbonne and the Bishop of Béziers refused to obey, alleging that the Legates were incompetent to pronounce such a sentence, and dragged out their trials to quite inordinate length: it took a full-scale Crusade to depose Bérenger, and William de Roquessels was assassinated in 1205, before even the preliminary investigation of his case had been completed. Raymond de Rabastens, who had so scandalously ravished the episcopal domains of Toulouse, was to hold out for months. But the attempt at reform which the Pope had launched soon began to take on the appearance of a clash between two rival clans: on the one side the local clergy, on the other those regular Orders more directly under the Pope's jurisdiction, in particular the Cistercians. It was they who, right till the end, decided which way the game would go.

The Pope could no longer count on the support of his bishops; he was obliged to give his Legates *carte blanche*, and let them act according to their several capacities, as the occasion arose. Now when they were dealing with local prelates, these Papal envoys found that the ill-will which met them was more or less successfully disguised; but when they turned to the civil authorities, they encountered nothing but open hostility or sly evasions.

Seigneurs and consuls alike protested their fidelity to the Church —but refused to hunt down heretics. The Count of Toulouse, who had earlier been excommunicated by the previous Pope for persecuting monks, now made his peace with the Church, and obtained a pardon from Innocent III. This done, he continued to protect Cathars, despoil abbeys, and turn various monasteries into private fortresses. The Papal Legate, Peter of Castelnau, obtained further formal engagements and promises from him, which were no more regarded than their predecessors. A *modus vivendi* had been worked out in Languedoc between the Church and its heretical adversaries; Catharist leaders, who were in theory liable to the most severe penalties, did not fear to appear publicly side by side with bishops, and to engage in theological controversy against them.

During the first ten years of his Pontificate, especially during the period between 1203 and 1208, Innocent III concentrated most of his efforts on the preaching campaign. Being a man of absolute self-assurance, certain that he held a monopoly of truth, he had strong hopes of bringing back his strayed sheep simply by dissipating that ignorance in which the incompetence of their spiritual leaders had kept them. Exactly like his predecessors Gregory VII and Alexander III, he made special efforts to convert such presumed heretics as seemed to him to diverge less from orthodox belief than the rest.

To take an example: in 1201 the *humiliati*, 'humbled ones', the fore-runners of St Francis of Assisi, who had been unjustly accused of heresy, received from him rules for their Order in which the influence of Waldensian practices could be clearly seen. In 1208 he took under his protection a converted Waldensian named Durand de Huesca, whom he allowed to found an Order the organization of which was highly reminiscent of the heretical communities; and these 'poor Catholics', whom the clergy as a whole continued to distrust, were actively encouraged by the Pope, who regarded their movement as one that might well sow the seeds of a radical reform inside the Church by means of lay or semi-lay preaching.

But where self-declared heretics were concerned such a policy of conciliation was out of the question. The Pope was at this point still prepared to see the faults of the Church Militant condemned by public opinion; but he could not tolerate open attacks on Catholic dogma. Moreover he showed himself hardly less severe towards the Waldensians than towards the Cathars.

Accordingly he sent out preachers. These consisted, in the first instance, of the Legates themselves: men tried and tested in their faith, Cistercians who belonged to that Order as St Bernard had reformed it. The Cistercians now stood, within the body of the Church, for austerity, discipline and moral reform. They formed the Church's active spearhead, intransigent and uncompromising. As we have already seen, the Legates were active enough; but they also sought to convince. The result was that since Languedoc had slipped outside the Church's control, the Legates visiting it were no longer plenipotentiary ministers of the Pope, but found themselves reduced to the role of mere preachers—and preachers at that who found it difficult to command an audience.

They began with threats, but for some time now threats had been useless. Accordingly they were forced to descend into the arena, which also made them recognize that the adversaries whom they so despised had at least a right to existence. The result was that they now invited them to meetings to discuss matters as equals.

We have already had occasion to mention Peter of Castelnau, Archdeacon of Maguelonne, and a monk in the Cistercian abbey of Fontfroide. He had as his companion a certain Brother Raoul, also from Fontfroide. Finally, to lend somewhat greater authority to their mission, the Pope gave them as their leader the Abbot of Cîteaux himself, who was the General of the Order and, as such, one of the leading personalities within the Church. Arnald-Amalric was a cousin of the Viscounts of Narbonne. He had previously been Abbot of Grandselve, one of the largest Cistercian monasteries in Languedoc. He was a native of the area himself, and all the more zealous against heresy since he had come to know it at close quarters.

How could an Order re-established by St Bernard in the sternest traditions of austerity, obedience, and prayer have chosen for their leader this born fighter, this man of extremes, this impassioned individual who was about as far from any idea of Christian charity as was conceivably possible? Though he might not possess those evangelical virtues which would bring the strayed sheep back inside the fold of the Church, at least he knew how to organize a major preaching campaign. But however strong their apostolic zeal, these monks were suspect in advance to their audience. How could they hope to succeed where St Bernard himself had failed?

Accordingly the Legates brought their personal authority into play. They organized a series of debates, and these enjoyed considerable success. In order to arouse the interest of their listeners still further, they decided to have a jury chosen in every town where they went to preach. The members of this jury would be asked to pronounce on the relative value of the arguments put forward by either side. From being official custodians of absolute truth, then, the Legates had descended to acting as mere preachers, who were obliged to use reason both to convince their hearers and to prove the worth of their doctrine. The jury, which was composed half of

Catholics and half of heretics, possessed (in theory at least) the right to reject their views and award the prize to their adversaries. The Legates claimed that their victories were due to the fact that Catholic orthodoxy alone possessed the truth.

In 1204 Peter of Castelnau and Brother Raoul held one of these large public meetings at Carcassonne, in the presence of that deeply Catholic monarch Peter II of Aragon. Thirteen Catholics and thirteen Cathars were selected as members of the jury. The Catharist bishop of Carcassonne, Bernard de Simorre, preached quite openly on this occasion, expounding the doctrines of his Church. Though the presence of the King might seem to have weighed the balance in favour of the Legates, there were no conversions. Neither Peter of Castelnau nor Arnald-Amalric could have had many illusions about the matter: their propaganda attracted a large crowd of curious onlookers (folk in the Midi being great lovers of such rhetorical contests), but their arguments only succeeded in convincing those who were Catholics already. To the heretics they were a mere dead letter.

These discussions did not even arouse popular passions: they do not seem to have provided any excuse for scuffles or brawls between supporters of the rival faiths. The Catholics in this area were decidedly lacking in the spirit of aggression. Besides, the Papal envoys, surrounded as they were with a glittering escort, superbly mounted, their baggage and provisions borne in a most luxurious train, contrasted rather unfortunately with the austere simplicity affected by the Catharist ministers. One witness observed: 'Here was a God who always went on foot—yet today his servants ride in comfort. Here was a God of poverty—yet today his missionaries are wealthy. Here was a God humble and scorned of men—yet today his envoys are loaded with honours.'[3]

Though this mission was condemned to failure in advance, it was to receive unexpected aid in the persons of certain Spanish monks. They turned up burning with apostolic zeal, hotfoot from Rome, where the Pope had just refused them permission to go to South Russia to conduct missionary activities among the pagan tribesmen. Doubtless Innocent III thought that these would-be missionaries could find better employment in Languedoc. In August 1205 the Legates had a meeting in Montpellier with Don Diego de Acebes, the capital Bishop of Osma, together with the Sub-Prior of his Chapter, Dominic de Guzman. The old Bishop and his still youthful companion (Dominic was thirty-five at the time) offered the Legates their help in the struggle against heresy. They did something better than that: they gave them some practical advice. This advice perhaps came a little late, but in itself it was excellent. The Spanish missionaries advised the Legates and their envoys to come down off their horses, cancel their escort, and no longer insist on being received and lodged with the honours due to their rank. Instead they should go on foot, live off alms, and retain no outward sign of their dignified rank apart from their monastic habit. As provisions for their journey they should take nothing except a Book of Hours and such works as were indispensable to theological controversy.

Those who had already witnessed the Abbot of Cîteaux surrounded with all the honours due to a Prince of the Church may well have been astonished to see him thus change his apparel, and have accused him—not without reason—of being a 'wolf in sheep's clothing', since the Catharist missionaries had not waited for anyone's advice before practising a life of poverty. As far as the Legate was concerned, and the dozen or so Abbots he assembled in 1207 after a meeting of the Chapter of the Order, such an attitude was nothing more in fact than a convenient method of propaganda. As we shall see later, Arnald-Amalric had not the least taste for either humility or poverty. With the Spanish monks it was another matter entirely.

Dominic de Guzman was canonized thirteen years after his death; and even during his own lifetime he enjoyed a very great reputation for sanctity. Such information as we possess concerning his life has come down to us from his enthusiastic disciples, who were naturally inclined to exaggerate their hero's merits; but there is no doubt that, from his youth onwards, Dominic must have made a most powerful impression both on his fellow-monks and his superiors in the Order by the ardour of his faith and his most vigorous intelligence. Together with his future Bishop, Diego de Acebes, he played an active part in reforming canonical duties in his diocese; in 1201 he was appointed Prior and Dean of his Chapter.

We have already seen that he dreamed of converting pagan souls to God, and that only the Pope's formal order had diverted him from this undertaking and made him a missionary to the heretics. To be sure, the Church had no lack of enthusiastic preachers, but Dominic's activities alone led to practical results. As William de Puylaurens put it: 'It was necessary that heresy should manifest itself in our time and in our country that thereby the most venerable Order of Dominicans might come into existence—an Order which has borne fruit so abundantly and to such great profit, not so much here among us as throughout the entire world.'[4]

2. *The Mission and Failure of St Dominic*

This vast movement of religious reform (which in the event was to be given a somewhat sinister flavour by its association with the Inquisition) first saw the light along the stony roads of Languedoc, where one day two men marched forth under a burning summer sun, trudging bare-footed through the dust to beg for two things: their daily bread and the right to a hearing.

The Bishop of Osma, after a year of this, was forced by age and exhaustion to return to Spain, where he died. Nevertheless he accompanied St Dominic on the majority of his travels and took part in the two-sided discussions held at Servian, Béziers, Carcassonne, Verfeil, Montréal, Fanjeaux and Pamiers. In the intervals between these public meetings (to which the leaders of the Cathar Church were always invited) Dominic travelled indefatigably round the countryside, visiting villages, towns, and châteaux, and setting an example by his way of life, which was more austere than that of the *perfecti* themselves.

He was not always kindly received; far from it. 'The enemies of truth,' wrote Jordanus of Saxony, 'made mock of him, throwing mud and other disgusting stuff at him, and hanging wisps of straw on him behind his back.' Such treatment was not calculated to worry a mind as enthusiastic as Dominic's.

From the same source we learn the reply which the Saint made to those heretics who asked him: 'What would you do if we seized you by force?' He told them: 'I should beg you not to kill me at one blow, but to tear me limb from limb, that thus my martyrdom might be prolonged; I would like to be a mere limbless trunk, with eyes gouged out, wallowing in my own blood, that I might thereby win a worthier martyr's crown!'[5]

The characteristically Spanish exaggeration of these remarks must have discouraged his adversaries. Even though they persisted in regarding Dominic as an envoy of the Devil, they were forced to realize that with such a madman they could do nothing. He went singing through villages where men and women pursued him with threats and jeerings; when he was exhausted he would sleep by the roadside.

But even his most fervent apologists concentrated more on his miracles (which were not very convincing) than on the number of conversions which he had obtained.

A detailed examination of the debates which he held is in itself revealing. St Dominic and the Bishop of Osma preached at Montpellier—without any success. When they preached at Servian, the

Cathar ministers Baudouin and Thierry, observing their humble attitude and naked, bleeding feet, agreed to participate in a discussion with them. After eight days of public argument, the two Catholic missionaries withdrew without having obtained any results apart from the warm respect of the local Catholics. At Béziers both the Spaniards, together with the Legates, preached for over a fortnight and debated with the *perfecti* at length; yet all they got out of it was the conversion of one or two *credentes*.

At Carcassonne they preached for eight days and drew a complete blank. At Montréal they came up against Guilhabert de Castres, who was *filius maior* to the Catharist Bishop of Toulouse, and the greatest Cathar preacher of the period, together with the deacons Benoît de Termes and Pons Jordan and a great number of *perfecti*. According to William de Puylaurens a Cathar named Arnald Hot maintained in public that:

. . . the Church of Rome defended by the Bishop of Osma was neither holy nor the Bride of Christ; rather was it espoused of the Devil and its doctrine diabolical. It was that Babylon which St John called, in his Apocalypse, the mother of fornications and abominations, drunk with the blood of the Saints and of Christ's martyrs. Moreover the Bishop's ordination was neither sanctified nor valid nor, indeed, established by Our Lord Jesus Christ. Christ and his Apostles had never ordained or laid down the Canon of the Mass as it now existed.

The Bishop of Osma offered to prove the contrary by citing evidence from the New Testament.

'O dolorous case!' the historian exclaims. 'To think that among Christians the ordinances of the Church and of the Catholic Faith should have fallen into such disregard that secular judges were called in to pronounce upon such blasphemies!'[6] A pertinent enough remark; moreover the judges who were called upon to give a verdict in this debate found themselves so divided in their opinions that they were discharged without having come to any decision.

At Verfeil, where St Bernard had already met with an unfavourable reception, the Papal envoys debated with the Cathars Pons Jordan and Arnald Arifat. The two parties seem to have had some trouble in understanding one another, either because of linguistic difficulties (some Cathars did not speak Latin) or else through lack of clarity in the speeches themselves. The Bishop of Osma withdrew in a huff, having somehow got the impression that the heretics pictured God as a man sitting in Heaven, whose legs were so long that they dangled down to earth. 'God's curse be on you!' he exclaimed. 'I hoped to find some subtlety of intelligence among you, but in vain: you are heretics of the grossest sort.'

The final debate took place at Pamiers, under the noble patronage of the Count of Foix, who threw open his home, the Château du Castela, for the purpose. The Bishop of Osma and Dominic were supported on this occasion by Foulques, the new Bishop of Toulouse, and Navarre, the new Bishop of Couserans. Since there were as many Waldensians as Cathars in Pamiers, the two sects each sent their own speakers. The Count's sister, Esclarmonde, a *perfecta* herself and a famous protector of all heretics, also took part in the discussions. On this occasion the Catholic mission gained rather more success than it had done elsewhere, since Durand de Huesca the Waldensian did penance afterwards, together with a number of his friends. But in general their successes were something less than mediocre.

At this point the mission broke up. The Bishop of Osma returned to Spain, Raoul the Legate also departed, and Arnald-Amalric was recalled to France to deal with the affairs of his own Order. Peter of Castelnau (who was, besides, extremely unpopular in Languedoc) was far too busy squabbling with the feudal barons to devote his time to preaching. Dominic alone went on indefatigably with the task he had set himself, preaching in villages and by the wayside, winter and summer alike, living on nothing but bread and water, sleeping on the bare earth, astonishing everyone who saw him by his powers of endurance and the fiery, authoritative tone of his utterances.

When we consider that he began his preaching career in 1205, and that in June 1209 the Crusaders' army invaded Languedoc, we may well regret that this genuine Apostle of the Church had so little time to bring to any good conclusion a task that might well have produced enduring results. Yet despite this, we find another Dominican in the time of St Louis, Stephen de Salagnac, crediting the Founder of his Order with cruel words which suggest that Christian patience was not one of St Dominic's virtues. To a large crowd assembled at Prouille he is supposed to have said:

For several years now I have spoken words of peace to you. I have preached to you; I have besought you with tears. But as the common saying goes in Spain, Where a blessing fails, a good thick stick will succeed. Now we shall rouse princes and prelates against you; and they, alas, will in their turn assemble whole nations and peoples, and a mighty number will perish by the sword. Towers will fall, and walls be razed to the ground, and you will all of you be reduced to servitude. Thus force will prevail where gentle persuasion has failed to do so.

Yet what are 'several years' in an evangelizing mission? St Dominic seems to have abandoned his task before it was well begun.

It was not such missionaries of whom the Catholic Church stood in need. There was too much in her conduct that needed forgiveness for her to allow herself to utter threats, certainly if she wanted to regain the affections of the faithful. One remark like that quoted above was quite liable to alienate for ever the trust of those who had been converted by the example of St Dominic's charity or courage. The Cathar ministers never threatened that those who held out against *their* preaching would perish by the sword.

When we take into account what we know of St Dominic's powerful personality—his energy, the quality of his faith, and the way in which he subordinated himself entirely to his work—we might well, at first sight, feel astonishment at the small number of conversions which he managed to obtain: especially since this was a Christian country, where the doctrines which he preached must have been close to his listeners' hearts, despite everything. Even though his apostolic mission was so short, one would have expected the influence of his personality to have drawn a large number of proselytes to him. Yet the evidence shows a few bare names only: some young hermits from Fanjeaux, Pons Roger, and a few women and children of whom we know nothing. There can be little doubt that he would have done better in South Russia.

But this final paradox can be explained by the equivocal situation in which he found himself. Since he was the representative of a Church that was always ready to flourish the big stick, he could hardly expect to inspire confidence. It needed almost superhuman courage to become converted, by one's own free choice, to a religion that boasted of imposing its will by force. At the very same time that St Dominic was cheerfully exposing himself to the mockery and insults of his adversaries, the Pope was writing one letter after another to the King of France, exhorting him to take up arms against heresy; the Legates were bringing every sort of pressure to bear upon the Count to make him persecute these same heretics; and while the Church was quite ready to engage in theological debate with Cathar ministers, she did not renounce her powers of legislation. These, if put into effective action, would have sent those ministers to the stake, and driven their followers into ruin or exile. In such conditions even the most sincere and impassioned preaching could only appear as a most odious species of hypocrisy.

The Church, then, was obliged to fight for her own; but the contestants were singularly ill-matched. The Roman Church, Holy,

Catholic and Apostolic, strong in her secular tradition of political wisdom and authority, was, at any rate in the French Midi, beginning to take on a somewhat different appearance. Now she seemed rather more like a police force, and a foreign police force at that: a mocked and despised body, which people hoped to deceive by feigned submission. In short, she had become so wretched a thing that it was enough to make all her followers weep tears of blood at the sight. Her efforts to regain the ground she had lost were to lead her into yet lower stratagems. Who can tell by what implacable sequence of errors, compromises, personal ambitions, ill-founded loyalties, and conscious or involuntary abuses of power such a state of affairs came about? The evil was of such long standing that it would be unfair to lay full responsibility for it on Innocent III or his over-zealous ministers.

If a saint like Dominic could be so affected by the scandal (as he considered it) of heresy as to forget that the big stick is not a weapon worthy of Christ, we can hardly be surprised if weaker men than he believed that they had authority to defend their Church by force of arms. And if things had come to such a pass that even a saint could do nothing but play the unrewarding role of a policeman in disguise, we can hardly be surprised at the perfectly reasonable resistance which the people of the Midi displayed to Catholic preaching.

St Dominic did succeed, however, in making one notable convert. This was Pons Roger of Tréville in the Lauraguais district, and on him Dominic imposed the following penances. On three successive Sundays the penitent was to walk from the boundary of his village to the church bare-backed, and followed by a priest who would flog him with a birch. He was to wear a monk's habit, with two small crosses sewn on either side of his breast. For the rest of his life, except at Easter, Pentecost and Christmas, he was to eat neither flesh, eggs nor cheese; and three days a week he was also to abstain from fish, oil and wine. He was to observe three Lenten periods every year, and hear Mass daily. He was to maintain himself in a state of perpetual chastity. Once a month he was to show his letter of recantation to the parish priest in Tréville. If he disobeyed any of these injunctions, he would be excommunicated as a heretic and a perjurer.[7]

This one authentic case of conversion apart—and it is the only one of which any record has been preserved—the result of St Dominic's work, during these years before the Crusade, can be reduced to the foundation of the nunnery at Prouille. This establishment was the forerunner and starting-point for the Order of

Preaching Friars, which was so quickly to fulfil a major rôle in the life of the Church.

One evening in the year 1206 St Dominic went into the church at Fanjeaux to pray, after delivering an open-air sermon. Several young girls then came and threw themselves at his feet, declaring that they had been brought up by *perfectae* in the heretical faith, but that his saintly discourse had made them doubt the truth of their religion. 'Pray God,' they said, 'to reveal to us that faith in which we shall live, die, and achieve salvation.' 'Take courage,' the Saint replied, 'Our Lord God, who wills no man's destruction, will show you what manner of master you have served hitherto.' One of them told later how immediately afterwards the Devil appeared to them in the shape of a hideous cat.[8]

Whether this strange vision was due to St Dominic's powers of suggestion, or to the nervous condition of excitement into which the girls had got themselves, it is hard to take a conversion of this sort seriously. Could it be that the Saint's preaching inspired more horror and loathing of heresy than it did love for the eternal verities of the Church? At all events, these young converts were afraid lest their new faith might weaken when confronted with the supplications or threats of their relatives; and St Dominic decided to create a place of refuge for them, where they might live beyond temptation's reach.

The convent very soon began to receive endowments. In 1207 the Archbishop of Narbonne made over the church of St Martin of Limoux to this new foundation, and somewhat later, after the successful completion of the Crusade, the convent was further enriched with spoils taken from heretical *seigneurs*.

We shall return later to St Dominic's activities during the Crusade and to the foundation of the Order of Preaching Friars. Let us leave him for the moment in (as he would put it) heresy-infected Languedoc, where the execution of his mission was made all the more difficult since his adversaries were preachers who showed themselves as fearless, ascetic, and firmly grounded in their faith as he was himself —and who were, in addition, known and venerated throughout the entire countryside. We may well believe that the *perfecti*, following his example, thought fit to present *his* faith and charity as a hypocritical and diabolically inspired stratagem. But though these evangelical campaigns converted virtually no heretics, they did at least serve to arouse the zeal of part of the Catholic population.

Ever since 1206 what amounted to a Catholic resistance movement against heresy had been growing up in Toulouse, both in the town itself and the surrounding countryside. The movement was organized by a man of the most prodigious energy and enthusiasm: no less a person than the Bishop of Toulouse himself.

Foulques of Marseilles, who had been elected to succeed that undesirable character Raymond de Rabastens, was to have the glorious privilege, forty-eight years after his death, of figuring in Dante's *Paradiso*. Here he was described as a soul so rich with delight that its brilliance, blazing laughter-bright, struck the eye like some ruby caught in the sun's full glory. This fortunate being was placed by the poet in Venus's quarter of the heavens, since he burnt with love more fiercely than ever Dido did—'for so long as the colour of his hair permitted'.[9] He was in fact a man of bourgeois origin, born in Genoa, who spent most of his life in Marseilles; a wealthy business man turned troubadour, who had enjoyed very considerable reputation as a poet, and had employed his verses to sing of the noble ladies whom he had loved. Having arrived at the age when his hair turned grey, he threw over these ardent passions of his for a piety more ardent still. In 1195 he made his profession of faith at the Abbey of Thoronet; and ten years later he was nominated to the Bishopric of Toulouse. His zeal and energy were familiar to everyone; moreover as a Provençal he had no connections in the Toulouse area and was not, therefore, likely to act in an obliging or compromising way. Finally, he was a man well acquainted with the world, an excellent speaker, and a writer of repute who still aroused his public with *sirventés* and religious lyrics, just as in bygone days he had charmed them with his love-poems.

In 1206 Foulques arrived in a ruined and to all intents and purposes non-existent bishopric. Yet he not only contrived to pay off all episcopal debts and set the affairs of the diocese in order (it was not for nothing that he came of a long line of businessmen); he also managed to acquire genuine personal popularity in his see, at any rate among the Catholics. The historian William de Puy-laurens, who from 1241 was notary to the Toulouse bishopric, and from 1242 to 1247 chaplain to the Counts of Toulouse, speaks of this Bishop (who had been dead for at least forty years at the time when William composed his narrative) with admiration and reverence: Foulques must have left a good reputation behind him among ecclesiastical circles in the Toulouse area. It is only fair to recall this, since those to whom his memory smelt anything but good must have been legion.

In point of fact, this strange troubadour-bishop, who survived to the age of eighty and died while composing a canticle on the coming

of the Heavenly Dawn, inspires astonishment rather than respect. As
we shall see, his energetic behaviour was more appropriate to the
leader of an extremist political party than to a bishop. William de
Puylaurens praises him for giving the citizens of Toulouse 'not a
shameful peace but a just war'. His platform eloquence roused men
to concrete action and deeds; and it is Foulques who has the doubtful
honour of being one of the only people who succeeded in the attempt
to raise the Catholic population against their heretical brethren.
Even in this case, however, we are only concerned with a limited
number of militant fanatics; to the people as a whole Foulques
remained, as the burghers of la Bessède area were one day to call
him, 'the Devils' Bishop'.

The Church could rely on the Legates and their missionaries; she
could rely on new-style and recently appointed bishops such as
Foulques of Marseilles and Navarre, Bishop of Couserans. There
were also the Bishops of Comminges, Cahors, Albi, Béziers, and
several others whose fidelity to the Church was never in doubt, but
whose efforts in the struggle against heresy remained, as it were,
entirely Platonic. What other support could the Church rely upon
in the Occitan provinces?

A certain proportion of the aristocracy must have remained
faithful to Catholicism. The Papal Legate, Peter of Castelnau, had
succeeded in forming a league of barons for the purpose of combating
heresy—though it seems fairly certain that these barons only acted
as they did in order to annoy the Count of Toulouse. The Crusaders
in the Midi came, above all, from Provence, an area relatively untouched by heresy, or else from Quercy and Auvergne. The Bishops
of Cahors and Agen managed to assemble several armed bands of
pilgrims who were later to take part in the Crusade; but it seems as
though in the entire region that lies between Montpellier and the
Pyrenees, stretching from Comminges in the south to Agen in the
north, the Church had only isolated groups of supporters. These
in any case took little action on her behalf, being more strongly
aware of the unity that bound them to their fellow-citizens, however
heretical, than of their obligations to Rome—at least when these
obligations demanded that they should expel and persecute such
heretics. What was more, the heretics were powerful enough to
defend themselves. Even had he wished it the Count did not command sufficient strength to provoke a civil war.

The Church's healthier elements, then, remained both vigorous
and aggressive, and some of her leaders were genuine fanatics. She

still held great administrative and financial control over Languedoc. Yet despite all this—not to mention the Pope's various attempts at persuasion and intimidation—she found herself incapable of checking this new religion's advance: indeed, it was beginning to paralyse all will to resistance among the Catholic bulk of the population. The Pope and his Legates could envisage no other way of continuing the struggle than by force of arms. It was at this point that the murder of Peter of Castelnau gave the signal for battle to be joined. The Church surrendered her task to the power of the sword.

CHAPTER IV

THE CAMPAIGN OF 1209

IN JUNE 1209 Raymond VI underwent his scourging at Saint-Gilles and was solemnly reconciled with the Church. The army of warrior-pilgrims that had come into being in answer to the Pope's appeal was now ready, all its preparations made, and assembled at Lyons. The date of its departure was fixed for St John's Day, 24th June. The Count, having abandoned all hope of averting war, now played his last card by turning Crusader himself.

War had been officially declared the day after the murder of Peter of Castelnau; but it was only now that it entered its active phase. The Crusading forces were ready for battle, and it was high time they were on the march. A Crusader would follow the Cross for forty days of active campaigning only; so the commanders concerned had no time to lose.

During the winter of 1208-9 their adversaries do not appear to have taken the threat of danger very seriously, and neglected to organize any real defence system. Indeed, nothing could have been further from their thoughts. They had considerable differences of opinion amongst themselves as to what their line should be; right up to the last moment they continued to hover, still hoping to disarm the Pope and his representatives by promises of submission. According to the *Chanson de la Croisade*,[1] the Count of Toulouse vainly begged his nephew, the Viscount of Béziers, 'not to make war upon him, not to quarrel with him; let both stay on the defensive', to which the Viscount is supposed to have replied 'not with a Yes, but a No', and the two barons parted on bad terms—a fact which should cause no surprise when we recall that the great houses of Béziers and Toulouse had been constant enemies and rivals for centuries past.

Those historians who have been at pains to deplore the lack of agreement between the country's rulers when faced with a common danger seem to forget how difficult and equivocal the position of these men was. In June 1209 they could not foresee what turn events might take. It was not a foreign power that was marching against them, but Soldiers of Christ. It was the Head of their own Church who had declared war upon them. Their enemies had powerful and numerous allies in Languedoc itself. On the other hand the various Western European monarchs (to whom, either directly or indirectly, they owed allegiance) were maintaining an attitude of somewhat enigmatical neutrality. Though they did nothing in support of the Crusade, they did not seem inclined to oppose it, either.

We may infer, then, that the policy followed by the Southern barons was dictated by a species of elementary caution. They intended to budge no more than they had to, and, by bowing before the storm, hoped to come through the whole business with as little loss or annoyance as possible. The Count of Toulouse, who seems to have understood better than anyone what open conflict with the Church would mean, went over to the camp of his personal enemies. By so doing he placed his domain (a notorious hotbed of heretics) under the protection of that law which declared Crusaders' property inviolable. The more powerful of his vassals would not go so far along the road to submission, and prepared to defend themselves. The reason they bungled the job was not, surely, through lack either of courage or of military equipment, but because a war declared *against heresy* was still too vague and imprecise a concept to guarantee the absolute loyalty of their retainers. These were, in any case, already only too willing to avail themselves of the flimsiest excuse for disobedience or plain rebellion.

Thus the country into which the Crusaders' army marched had no desire for war, was unprepared to deal with it, and right up to the very last moment still hoped to avoid bloodshed by depriving the invader of any excuse for military action.

1. *Warfare in the Middle Ages*
However, the Crusaders were quite determined about the matter: military action they would have.

It will be convenient at this point to examine the scope and nature of warfare as practised during the period under discussion—warfare that dispensed with such things as guns, bombardments, and compulsory military service. But before describing what such a war was like in itself, we should try to get some idea of the dangers and liabilities it imposed upon a country as a whole—on its army, its populace, its economy, and the entire fabric of its social life. Though our ancestors were lacking in our more technical facilities for destruction, it would be doing them an injustice to suppose either that war was less cruel then than it is today, or that they did not possess more effective weapons for terrorizing their opponents than those at our disposal.

It is true that a pitched battle in the open countryside was infinitely less costly of life than its modern equivalent, even if we allow for the far smaller population in those days as compared to our own times. A mediaeval army of twenty thousand men was reckoned very large indeed; that which took part in the First Albigensian Crusade can hardly have numbered more, and may well have been smaller. The vagueness which most chroniclers of the period display with regard to the effective strength of this or that army is due to the fact that for the most part they calculated an army's size from the number of knights it contained. But a knight was somewhat unpredictable as a unit of military strength: the retinue which followed him might be anything between four men and thirty. Every knight was accompanied by a small troop of foot-soldiers and cavalry, generally drawn from among his friends and relations, and always vassals whose loyalty was tried and certain. These men fought at their lord's side in battle, squires and sergeants alike; and though in the thirteenth century notions of military discipline were somewhat rudimentary, there was a military camaraderie between a knight and his followers which still (especially among the Northern nobility) preserved an almost mystical quality about it. Many men who remained totally indifferent to the cause which they were defending accomplished prodigies of bravery simply to maintain the reputation of that particular *seigneur* whose liegemen they happened to be. The knights, then, formed a military *corps d'élite* in every army; and for this reason an army's strength was judged by the number no less than the mettle of its knights.

Mediaeval warfare was, on the face of it, an aristocratic affair. The fighter who really mattered was the knight; he was constantly obliged to risk his neck, but—for this very reason—was less exposed to danger than the rest of his men. His armour protected him so effectively that arrows, indeed even sword-strokes and spear-thrusts, could be rained upon him without his coming to any harm: the verse-chronicler Ambrose tells how King Richard returned from one battle so bristling with arrows that he resembled a hedgehog. Yet though these arrows were so light, a single lucky shot could kill a man who lacked a coat of mail; and chain-mail was expensive equipment, comparatively rare, and reserved for the fighting *élite*. The knight's armour covered his entire body; that of the squire barely reached to his knee. The mere sergeant-at-arms wore a *broigne*, a kind of jerkin sewn with strips of leather, tough enough in all conscience, but incapable of withstanding the cutting edge of a sword. All the common foot-soldier had was a tall shield, some five feet high: the infantry's defensive equipment was rudimentary in the extreme. Though a battle caused comparatively few fatal casualties among the knights, or indeed their mounted retainers, for the bulk of the army—the mere anonymous fighter, sergeant or varlet—it was a very different matter. Every battlefield was strewn with their corpses, and they lay thick outside the walls of every besieged town.

Over and above its regular units, those battalions or small companies under the personal command of a knight, a mediaeval army also contained various auxiliary troops, which handled the technical side of the campaign. These were, first and foremost, *professional* soldiers, who specialized in various military arts: they included archers, crossbowmen, sappers, miners, and siege-engineers. The more highly qualified amongst them performed their duties as conscientiously as any other professional, and showed exemplary loyalty to the employers who hired them.

Lower in the military hierarchy, yet an element of prime importance when it came to the actual conduct of operations—whether pitched battle or siege—were the *routiers*, or mercenary companies, who formed a large part of the infantry. They were the most formidable weapon the commanders of the period had at their disposal: notoriously brutal, forbidden by the Church, yet put to good use by all parties alike. If to the aristocracy war stood, above all, for the opportunity to cover oneself with glory or to defend a more or less noble cause, the common people simply identified it with the terrifying threat of the *routier*.

It is impossible to discuss warfare in the Middle Ages without dwelling for a moment on the extraordinary misery and horror which was aroused by the mere thought of the *routier*—that godless, lawless, fearless being, who had no rights and showed no mercy. He inspired the same sort of terror as a mad dog, and was treated as such not only by his opponents, but often by those who made use of him. His mere name was a sufficient and natural explanation for any sort of brutal or sacrilegious behaviour, however outrageous. He seems to have been viewed as a living emblem of Hell on earth.

These large mercenary bands had not yet the importance they were to attain during the Hundred Years' War; but they were already a public menace, and one of the principal complaints the Pope made to Raymond VI concerned the fact that the Count had recourse to *routiers* for the furtherance of his private wars. Raymond and his vassals were short of troops, and the *routiers* formed a large proportion of their effective strength. These men were pure brigands, and all the more formidable through being trained as professional soldiers. They also levied constant blackmail on the barons who employed them, since if their pay got into arrears they would threaten to pillage the barons' own domains. During a war they would similarly plunder conquered territory, and squabble with the regular army over the division of spoils: victories frequently ended in brawls between knights and mercenaries. As we shall see, the Crusaders' army (despite the fact that it marched in God's cause) readily made use of those same *routiers* whom the Count of Toulouse was forbidden to employ.

The officers and better-trained cadres of these mercenary bands were for the most part strangers to the countries in which they fought: in France the *routiers* most frequently employed were Basques, Aragonese or Brabantians. But during this period, when war, fire and famine continually ravaged the countryside, an endless stream of young men was driven out on to the highways, determined to make a living by any means they could; and so the wandering bands tended to recruit a fair number of hotheads, rebels and would-be adventurers from every district they passed through.

The *routiers* were poorly armed, and frequently threadbare. They went barefooted, without any sort of order or discipline, and would only obey their own officers. Nevertheless from the military viewpoint they possessed two great advantages. In the first place they were famous for their utter contempt of death. They were desperate fellows, with nothing to lose, and therefore would plunge on through thick and thin regardless: nothing could hold up their mad advance. They formed a series of shock-battalions, all the easier to utilize since no one had the slightest qualms about sacrificing them. The most important thing about them, however, was the terror they inspired in the civilian population. They had no respect for God, so they held orgies in the churches and mutilated sacred images. Not content with mere pillage and rape, they indulged in massacre or torture for the sheer fun of the thing, roasting children over slow fires and chopping men into small pieces.

In addition to these fighting elements—the knights and their retainers, the technicians, and mercenaries of every sort—the army also included a considerable non-combatant force. A great deal of baggage had to be carried on the march: caseloads of arms and armour, tents, field-kitchens, entrenching-tools and equipment for digging fortifications or building siege-engines. The army had its female camp-followers, too, in the shape of washerwomen, sempstresses and common whores. Furthermore, the richer combatants sometimes took their wives and even their children along with them. Lastly, the passage of a great army inevitably attracted a crowd of tramps, beggars and mountebanks—in short, a mass of civilians whom the army did not need in any way, but who hoped to get a living from it, and who in fact became a supplementary charge on any invaded country.

Such, more or less, was the composition of an army in the field. However insignificant it might be, its mere presence in a country tended *per se* to foment disorder. It blocked traffic on the roads, spread panic wherever it appeared, and ransacked the country round about in order to keep itself supplied with food and forage.

On the whole, warfare in the Middle Ages was a matter of sieges rather than pitched battles, and here the artillery played a major part in the operation. The besieged town's walls and bastions were bombarded with stone-guns, or giant catapults that had a range of some four hundred yards and hurled projectiles weighing anything up to eighty pounds. These siege-engines were mounted either on wooden platforms or mobile towers known as *chattes*; they often succeeded in breaching walls several yards thick, not to mention the annoyance they could cause inside the besieged town when the attackers built their wooden towers high enough to overlook the ramparts. Under cover of this artillery fire the besiegers would fill in the moat, while sappers dug subterranean galleries and undermined the foundations of the guard-towers. Direct assault was generally carried out with scaling-ladders, and very rarely succeeded. In order to storm a strong fortress it was essential first to breach its walls. This work of demolition tended to be both lengthy and dangerous. During the entire operation the besieged were generally at a distinct advantage. They set the mobile towers alight, and fairly mowed down their assailants (who had no ramparts to protect them) with arrows and crossbow fire. In point of fact most siege warfare was conducted on the principle of slow attrition.

On the first appearance of the enemy, the country folk would flee for safety to château or fortified town; and these strongholds (which in any case were more than likely to be besieged, and therefore to lose access to their normal sources of supplies) found their population increased by a large number of useless mouths, not to mention extra cattle. A siege, then, was apt to produce famine and epidemics. On the other hand an army advancing through enemy territory would ravage the countryside, looting or burning the stored grain and cutting down the fruit-trees—unless the defending forces had already done so themselves, with the intention of starving out the aggressor. Both sides were in the habit of poisoning wells, and famine and sickness between them killed more men than died in battle, even in the case of a besieging army. It was very seldom that a large military force managed to maintain itself for any length of time on enemy soil.

The common people, who did not go to war, suffered more during a campaign than those who did—especially from famine and the activities of the mercenary bands. For many years now the Midi had been accustomed to wars or guerilla skirmishes between feudal factions; it had become a nation of townsfolk, in fact. Most of the towns and villages were fortified, and the farms themselves were dependencies of the châteaux: at the first sign of trouble the peasant hastened to take shelter there. We know that the Counts of Toulouse and Foix, and the Viscounts of Béziers, were constantly at war with one another; such squaring of accounts between neighbours did not, apparently, much disorganize day-to-day life in the area. People came to regard war as a necessary evil, and made the best of it they could. The *routiers* who provoked such bitter complaints to the Count of Toulouse cannot have been so very frightful, or, indeed, so very numerous, since later on this same Count was to be regarded throughout the countryside as the very embodiment of peaceful law and order.

Perhaps this may explain why the threat of a Crusade did not disturb the population overmuch in advance: they were convinced they could give a good account of themselves notwithstanding. It may well be that the Occitans were expecting just another ordinary military expedition (they had seen scores of them already) against which ordinary means of defence could be employed. If things went against them, they would submit for the duration of the campaign, which was bound to be a short one.

But by early July 1209 news had begun to come in of the Crusaders' advance: news which convinced those in the threatened areas that this army was something quite out of the ordinary. According to the *Chanson de la Croisade*, nothing like it had ever been seen in Languedoc before. Soon the first groups of refugees came streaming back to the towns, and sentries, high in their watch-towers above the châteaux that dominated the Rhône Valley, saw that endless ribbon of moving troops, foot and horse, unwinding for mile upon mile in their innumerable thousands; saw, too, the great river itself crowded

with long strings of barges bearing the army's baggage and provisions. Allowing for the fact that this evidence comes from the
losing side, it must still have largely corresponded with reality. The
chronicler's description suggests that the spectacle of this armed
multitude coming down the Rhône Valley positively stupefied those
who witnessed it: there was something monstrous about it, something unnatural. Whatever the outcome of the war, the mere presence
of so many foreign soldiers in itself foreshadowed a vast and nation-
wide catastrophe.

From a distance this army appeared more formidable even than
it was. Over and above the bands of vagrants which tagged along
with any military formation on campaign, the Crusading host was
followed, surrounded, and generally cluttered-up by a crowd of
civilian pilgrims. These pilgrims were anxious to gain the Indulgences promised to all who joined a Crusade, and yearned, in their
saintly simplicity, to have some part in a pious work by helping to
exterminate heretics. The tradition of civilian 'Crusader' pilgrims
had been solidly established by a century of expeditions to the Holy
Land, and was responsible for dispatching these most curious
'pilgrims' on to heretic soil—pilgrims whose object was not the
veneration of holy relics, but a chance to watch burnings and take
part in massacres. These civilians were not a combatant force—
indeed, to the army they constituted a considerable source of annoyance; yet their presence did somewhat enhance the formidable
appearance of the Crusading troops, as the flood of invasion rolled
forward through Languedoc.

2. Béziers

Under the leadership of the Papal Legate, Milo, the Crusaders made
a rapid advance. They set out from Lyons at the beginning of July,
and by the 12th they had already reached Montélimar. In Valence the
Count of Toulouse joined them, the scarlet Cross sewn on his surcoat, and took his place among those other noble barons who were
leading the Crusade. Before the 20th they halted at Montpellier,
a friendly town, Catholic by tradition, and vassal to the King of
Aragon: this was to be their last stop before the campaign really got
under way. About the same time another, less important, Crusaders'
Army entered Languedoc by way of Quercy: it was commanded by
the Archbishop of Bordeaux, who had with him the Bishops of
Limoges, Bazas, Cahors and Agen, besides the Count of Auvergne
and the Viscount of Turenne. This force captured the town of

Casseneuil, where several heretics were taken and burnt at the stake.

Though Raymond VI was no longer an Enemy of the Faith, the Crusaders had not gone to all this trouble for nothing. The Legates had already marked down their first victim for destruction, the first of many 'abettors and instigators of heresy' in Languedoc. The property of the Viscount of Béziers had long been regarded as 'heretic's land' *par excellence*, and the young Viscount possessed neither the boldness nor the duplicity which characterized his uncle and liege lord, the Count of Toulouse.

In this month of July 1209, Raymond-Roger Trencavel, Viscount of Béziers and Carcassonne, found himself confronted with an army 'the like of which had never been seen', and which numbered among its ranks the Duke of Burgundy, the Count of Nevers, a whole multitude of bishops and nobles, not to mention his own liege lord the Count of Toulouse and the whole weight and spiritual authority of the Church into the bargain. His other overlord, the King of Aragon, seemed unlikely to support him: as a Catholic monarch he could not officially oppose an enterprise backed by the Church. The Viscount, having thus been pushed by force of circumstance into acting as the declared champion of heresy, and seeing that the enemy was at his very gates, at first attempted to negotiate. He went to Montpellier and tried to plead his case with the Legates there. When his youthfulness (he said) was taken into consideration, he could hardly be held responsible for things that had happened during his minority. He had never, himself, ceased to be a Catholic, and was perfectly willing to make his submission to the Church. By such purely conventional phraseology the Viscount, following the usual practice of the Midi nobility, was trying to use his name to protect the population of those provinces under his jurisdiction. The Legates refused to listen to him, and he was condemned for insubordination. All he could do now was to make ready his defences.

He had very little time. Here was a powerful army, which had already marched from Lyons to Montpellier in a fortnight, lying no more than fifteen leagues' distance from Béziers, the first important city on Trencavel soil; the road lay wide open, and the Viscount had not enough troops at his disposal to halt, or even to hold up, the Crusaders' advance. He hurried back from Montpellier to Béziers, but it was out of the question for him to shut himself up there. The town was the first to be threatened, and would certainly have to stand a siege; the Viscount, in his capacity as local generalissimo, could not risk being cut off from the rest of his domains. So he promised the consuls of Béziers that he would send them reinforcements, and went off himself to organize the defences of his capital city, Carcassonne, taking with him a few known heretics and all resident Jews.

The burghers of Béziers were left 'grieving and desolate' at their Viscount's departure, and hurriedly set about preparing the city's defences. They had no more than two or three days in which to accomplish this task, since the enemy army was already on the march, along the Roman road that runs straight from Montpellier to Béziers. The garrison, accordingly, helped by the civilian population, deepened the ditches round the city walls. These walls were solid enough, and the town was well victualled: they could look forward without perturbation to a lengthy siege. Besides, the very vastness of the Crusading Army (which popular imagination exaggerated yet further) tended to reassure its adversaries. Such an enormous body of men, they argued, would very soon be obliged to raise the siege, simply through shortage of supplies.

On 21st July the Crusaders' forces halted outside Béziers, and pitched camp along the left bank of the Orb. The city's deputy suzerain, the Bishop of Béziers, now in his turn attempted to negotiate before fighting actually broke out. This Bishop, Renaud de Montpeyroux, had been only lately appointed, after his predecessor, William de Roquessels, was assassinated in 1205. He returned from the Crusaders' camp with the proposal that Béziers should be spared—provided that the Catholic residents were willing to hand over their heretical brethren to the Legates, according to a list which the Bishop himself had drawn up. This list has survived. It contains two hundred and twenty-two names, some of which are marked with the abbreviation *val* (for *Valdensis*). All the evidence suggests that these 222 persons or families were either *perfecti* or else at least lay leaders of the sect, rich and well-known burghers.

The Bishop held a meeting in the Cathedral: his audience, naturally, was composed of Catholics. The heretics in Béziers were both numerous and powerful, and he did not think it remotely possible that they could be made to hand over their leaders. He accordingly suggested that the Catholic population should save their lives by leaving Béziers, and abandoning the heretics to their fate.

It is hard to tell whether these words hint at a specific threat, or whether the Bishop was merely referring to the risks incurred by the population of any town during a lengthy siege, and the excesses that invariably take place if that town is captured by storm. Whatever the answer, the consuls of Béziers indignantly rejected such a bargain, and declared that they 'would rather be drowned in the salt sea's brine' than surrender or betray their fellow-citizen. 'No one,' they said, 'would have so much as a brass farthing from them at the price of a change of allegiance.'[2] Their response, therefore, was an affirmation of loyalty both to the Viscount and to their privileged civic liberties. Béziers had already paid dear for her love of independence, and had no intention of letting any invaders impose their will upon her.

The attitude taken up by the men of Béziers showed the Crusaders that they could not rely upon the local Catholic population. Whatever the circumstances, the cities of Languedoc would place their national interests above anything else, against all comers; and from its very first day this religious war was to show all the characteristics of a national resistance movement—an attitude which it maintained to the very end. In this country the Church—even when represented by its own local bishops—was already a foreign power.

So Renaud de Montpeyroux withdrew from Béziers, taking with him one or two Catholics who were either more zealous or more nervous than their fellows; there could not have been many of them, since we know that a number of priests stayed behind.

The Crusaders' Army, under the command of the Abbot of Cîteaux, now set about investing the city. From their base on the shores of the Orb they began to make preparations for their final assault. On the fate of Béziers hung the whole fate of the Crusade, for if the Crusaders' forces were immobilized by a lengthy siege, they ran a risk of exhausting their supplies too quickly, and also of giving Raymond-Roger and his friends time to organize their defences. In addition, this all-powerful army was a Colossus with feet of clay. Its leaders were on far from friendly terms with one another (the Duke of Burgundy and the Count of Nevers were very much at loggerheads); the mercenary bands—not to mention the pilgrims—were quite liable to break camp and go off in search of plunder; while the knights themselves were only obliged, in theory, to stay with the army for their statutory forty days. Quick action was called for. Yet Béziers, with its massive fortifications, its moats and well-defended city gates, its lofty-towered cathedral and churches and keep, not to mention the mansions of its wealthy burghers, was an undoubtedly impressive sight. The Crusader commanders must have asked themselves whether the siege they were undertaking would not turn out a mere demonstration of strength, doomed in the long run to humiliating failure. There can be little doubt that they were exasperated beyond measure by the attitude of the burghers, who seemed almost wholly indifferent to their threats;

the hope of terrifying the enemy by a lightning-swift advance was now almost certainly lost, along with any chance of co-operation from the Catholics in the Midi.

On 22nd July, the feast day of St Mary Magdalene, both camps seemed comparatively quiet. The besiegers were not yet ready to launch their assault, while from behind their sheltering walls the besieged gazed out—with little fear and perhaps in somewhat ironical mood—at the vast expanse of tents and bivouacs, the solid mass of men, horses, and vehicles stretching away down the Orb and all round the city ramparts. Béziers was set in a commanding position, high above the valley, and could easily repulse any assault. In any case, the Crusaders who had pitched camp nearest to the walls hardly presented a formidable appearance. These were the groups of so-called 'pilgrims', and the mercenaries. The latter, dangerous enough at close quarters, presented a sorry enough spectacle when viewed from the ramparts. We have no alternative but to suppose that the sight of these tatterdemalion, ill-organized companies induced contempt rather than fear among the townsfolk. There is no other rational explanation of the strange events which, later, Arnald-Amalric and the Catholic chroniclers were to describe as a favour bestowed by divine Providence.

This day was to prove a decisive one in the history of the war, and one of the most tragic in the entire Crusade; yet it began unremarkably enough. Besieged and besiegers alike were in a casual mood, feeling that the real labours and perils were reserved for the days, possibly the weeks, that lay ahead. The garrison commanders were busy organizing their defence posts; the Crusader generals had summoned their chivalry to a council of war, and were working out their plans for the assault, which in all likelihood was not due to be launched for the next day or so. The troops were settling down to their breakfast.

About this time part of the garrison—or even, perhaps, a group of civilians, stirred by the threat of danger into turning soldier for the occasion—made a reconnaissance sortie through the gate overlooking the old bridge. This gate stands above the Orb, and is separated from it by a steeply inclined slope. William of Tudela cannot contain his indignation when commenting on the imprudence shown by these men. He describes the scene in such detail that he must have taken it from an eyewitness. From what he says it is clear that this was no *bona fide* military operation, but merely a piece of exhibitionism designed to annoy the enemy and make him look silly.

'Ah, it was an ill service that man did the townsfolk who counselled them to go forth from the city in broad daylight!' the chronicler exclaims. 'For mark well what these wretched creatures did, in their vast ignorance and folly: out they went, waving their coarse white linen banners, shouting at the tops of their voices, and thinking to scare the enemy thus, as one might scare birds in a wheatfield— bawling and hallooing, and waving their flags, and all this at crack of dawn, as soon as it was light.'[3]

Rash madness, the writer declares, having just been describing the army (for the sake of a French rhyme) as comparable to that of Menelaus, from whom Paris took Helen, and as one in which 'there was no French lord who came not to serve his forty days'. The army certainly did *not* number every French baron in its ranks; and the burghers who sallied out from the city were confronted only with virtually unarmed men, the rest being encamped at some little distance from the walls. The two parties could have expected no more than at most a little harmless skirmishing, some exchanges of badinage and insults. In an era when war aroused every combatant to a passion for the spectacular and for display, such exchanges formed a frequent preliminary to the serious business of fighting. At all events, the men of Béziers, having come forth from the city, approached very close to the pilgrims' encampment; and when one of these 'French Crusaders' advanced on to the bridge to answer their insults in kind they killed him, and threw his body into the Orb. The mercenaries, always quick to move into action, were stirred to considerable fury by this incident, and the demonstration began to turn into a brawl.

It was at this point, according to William of Tudela, that the Captain of the French mercenaries took a hand in the matter, and thus became the man most responsible for the subsequent victory. This officer was a person to be reckoned with: he commanded the most savage and daring troops in the entire army. Realizing the advantage which this situation offered, he gave the signal for an attack. The *routiers* charged forward, hurling their assailants back up the slope towards the gates of the city. 'There were more than fifteen thousand of them,' the *Chanson* relates, 'all barefooted, dressed only in shirts and breeches, and unarmed save for a variety of hand-weapons.' Doubtless fifteen thousand is a somewhat exaggerated figure, but the detachment from Béziers was certainly out-numbered, and its only chance lay in flight. The yelling, frenzied crowd of mercenaries went pounding up the slope, and reached the city gate just about the same time as the retreating members of the garrison. What happened at this point? William of Tudela writes that the *routiers* 'spread round the walls of the town and began to beat down the walls; they flung themselves into the ditches and set to work with picks and mattocks, while their comrades battered at the gates themselves'[4]—an exploit which it is somewhat hard to credit to half-naked men armed only with cudgels and the like. It seems a more likely supposition that some of the mercenaries managed to force their way into the city along with the retreating burghers, and in this way gained control of one of the gates, while the main body of the army launched its own assault on the walls with siege-engines better suited to such a task. But at all events the brawl was a lively enough affair to catch the attention of the commanders; and they, realizing that no time was to be lost, at once sounded the call to arms. Before the garrison had time to pull themselves together, the entire Crusader army was at the foot of the walls, and bands of mercenaries were charging through the streets of the town, spreading terror wherever they went.

After this initial setback the small garrison, under the command of Bernard de Servian, hurried to defend the ramparts, where the Crusaders had already set up their scaling-ladders. The fighting on and about the walls lasted only a few hours. The city was, in a manner of speaking, stormed before actually being taken, for while the troops were still locked in combat on the ramparts, panic and frenzy reigned in the streets, where the mercenaries were now in complete control. This fact made the garrison's continued resistance quite pointless; and they were in any case overwhelmed by assailants who were vastly superior to them in numbers, and elated by the unlooked-for, apparently miraculous windfall which this surprise attack had brought them.

The extreme violence of the assault transformed a comparatively peaceful town into a city of the damned, all in a few moments. 'The priests and clergy,' says the chronicler, 'vested themselves and had the bells tolled, as though they would sing a Requiem Mass at the burial of the dead; yet they could not stop these vagrant brigands bursting into the churches before Mass was done. . . ,'[5] For everyone, Catholics and heretics alike, the churches offered a last place of refuge. Those who had time to get away from their homes when the *routiers* broke in, hurried along the narrow crowded streets to one or other of the city churches—the Cathedral, the great Churches of St Mary Magdalene or St Jude—hoping to find shelter there till the attack was over. The mercenaries 'were already breaking into private houses, according to their fancy; there was a wide choice open to them, and each man took whatever he wanted, and plenty of it. The mercenaries were fierce for plunder, and had no fear of death; they cut the throats of any who stood in their way.'[6]

The war-whoops of the attacking knights and the still-resistant garrison, the shrieks of the wounded and dying, the mercenaries' exultant howls and their victims' screams of terror, the deathly tolling of every church bell in the city and the metallic clash of arms —all these must have produced a really appalling uproar, enough to disconcert the victors no less than the vanquished. The doors of the churches were forced open, the place of refuge was revealed as a trap. All inside were slaughtered wholesale—women, invalids, babies, and priests, the latter clasping the Chalice or holding aloft a crucifix. Pierre des Vaux de Cernay asserts that in the Church of the Madeleine alone seven thousand persons were done to death. This figure is obviously an exaggeration, since the church could not possibly hold so many; but the exact numbers are unimportant. What all the evidence confirms is that this was a general massacre, and that no individuals were spared; if one or two did manage to escape, they owed their lives either to speedy flight or some other accident quite independent of their conquerors' will.

In a few short hours the wealthy city of Béziers was a city of bleeding mutilated corpses, and nothing else. Its houses, streets and churches were now occupied by brigands, who went stamping through the blood they had spilt, dividing up and arguing over the vast spoils that these multitudinous deaths had bequeathed to them.

'Kill them all; God will look after His own.' The famous, too famous, remark, attributed to Arnald-Amalric by the German, Caesar von Heisterbach, is not so much a genuine historical *mot* as a critical comment on the nature of this episode. It might serve as the motto for any ideological or supposedly ideological war. Whether Arnald had sufficient imagination to coin a phrase of this sort, or whether he in fact never said the words at all, it remains true that the Crusaders' instructions at the sacking of Béziers do indeed seem to have been 'Kill them all'—with or without the rider concerning itself over how God might treat the souls of their victims.

William of Tudela is quite specific on the matter:[7]

The nobles of France, clergy and laity, Princes and Marquises, were agreed amongst themselves that whenever a château they invested refused surrender, and had to be taken by force, the inhabitants were to be put to the sword and slain; thinking that afterwards no man would dare to stand out against them by reason of the fear that would go abroad when it was seen what they had already done.

If 'the nobles of France' really did take such a decision, they calculated with some accuracy.

In his subsequent letter to the Pope, Arnald-Amalric preened himself on this unexpected and miraculous victory, announcing triumphantly that 'nearly twenty thousand of the citizens were put to the sword, regardless of age and sex'.

It would be useful, nevertheless, to know if the Crusaders' intentions were, in fact, what William of Tudela supposed them to be—and even if so, whether events did not go rather further than they intended. Normally if there was any question of putting a city's inhabitants to the sword after a siege, this referred solely to the male population. Women and children were only subject to such hazards of war as a measure of reprisal or when the fighting got completely out of hand; it was very rare for commanders to issue a decree of this sort in cold blood. However bloodthirsty he might have been, Arnald-Amalric would never have authorized the massacre of priests. With the *routiers*, however, it was another matter entirely. As the *Chanson* so picturesquely puts it, they had no fear of death and killed all who stood in their way. They were the first attackers into the city, and their lust for slaughter was notorious; it was they who were chiefly responsible for this massacre, and indeed they had neither the means nor the inclination to send a message asking the Commander-in-Chief what action they should take. There was no need to tell *these* men to 'kill them all'; they made not the slightest distinction between Catholic and heretic.

Those historians who favour the Crusade will, therefore, be tempted to place all responsibility for the massacre of Béziers on these bands of ruffians, these 'Basques and Aragonese' and other professional criminals, Godless men by definition and therefore possessing nothing in common with the Crusaders proper. But why did 'the army of Christ', as its chroniclers described it, make use of these diabolical auxiliaries at all? And in any case, as we shall see, when Béziers had been sacked and the time arrived to share out the spoil, the knights flung themselves on these 'ruffians' and clubbed them out of town. The mercenaries had not captured the city single-handed; they were not alone in their activities. They were far less well armed—perhaps even fewer in number—than those French Crusaders who scaled the battlements and stormed the walls; and none of the latter, being doughty fighters, wished to be last into the city.

It is, obviously, an easier business to rout a mob of drunken, incapable mercenaries than to stop a massacre; but the Crusaders

E

had better weapons than clubs at their disposal, and if their leaders
had given the order, there was nothing to prevent them bringing the
routiers to their senses. It is, indeed, hard to believe that they did not
take some part in the carnage themselves; are we to suppose that
victorious troops, confronted with catastrophe on such a scale,
simply stood by and did nothing? Though they might in the ordinary
way have been decent, honourable men, they could hardly have
helped being caught up in the general blood-lust and hysteria.

Nor should we forget that 'the Army of the Lord' also contained
its pilgrims. These people had been inflamed by violent propaganda,
and lived in a naïve and superstitious horror of heretics; they were
blood-brothers to those who, a century earlier, had seen every
foreign city as Jerusalem. Being simple souls, they were quite capable
of envisaging Béziers as the Devil's citadel. And if the French knights
contented themselves, more or less, with letting the mercenaries and
the rabble have their way (this is what the chroniclers allege, and it
seems likely enough), that, surely, was because they knew that this
way their work would be done for them, faster and better than they
could do it themselves. If they did nothing to stop this wholesale
massacre, it was because they actively desired it.

'After this', we read in the *Chanson*—'this' being a really quite
amazing outburst of sheer unbridled blood-lust, since in order to
kill *all* the inhabitants of a major city even the *routiers* and the most
hardened fanatics must have had their hearts in the business to a
phenomenal degree—'after this, the churlish soldiery broke into
houses everywhere, finding them full and running over with wealth.
But the French, *seeing this*, nearly choked with fury, and drove the
ruffians out, belabouring them with clubs and sticks as though
they had been mongrels.'[8] Nothing could be crueller than the
detachment with which the chronicler paints these hard-hearted
troops, who cared not a straw for the slaughter, but 'choked with
fury' when they saw other people making off with *their* plunder.
These Crusaders wasted no time singing a *Te Deum*, as had been
done after the sack of Jerusalem, and still less in horrified regret at
the spectacle of corpses piled up in their thousands—old men,
young girls, babies, mothers, growing boys, all mingled together.
The main object was to save their precious booty. The army needed
it to continue the campaign; besides, it was a golden opportunity for
lining one's pockets, and the knight could do with impunity what
was forbidden to the mercenary. So the soldiers of fortune were
stripped of their newly acquired possessions, and in a fit of more

than understandable pique, set fire to the town. The sight of blazing buildings spread panic among the looters; the Crusaders abandoned Béziers and its wealth; and a large part of the city burnt to the ground, burying the corpses of its inhabitants in the ruins. '. . . Burnt, too, was the Cathedral that Master Gervais built: so fierce were the flames that it burst asunder, cracked down the midst of it, and collapsed in two halves. . . .'⁹

As an epilogue to this terrible day the chronicler adds: 'Three days the Crusaders rested in the grassy meadows, and on the fourth day they departed, knights and sergeants all together, across open country. Their ensigns were raised and streaming in the wind, and nothing stopped their advance.'¹⁰ He remarks further that had it not been for those wretched mercenaries setting fire to the place, the Crusaders would all have been wealthy men for the rest of their days on the loot that was stored in Béziers. This reference to riches won or lost is one that recurs frequently in the *Chanson*: the right to booty was the soldier's natural privilege, and disinterestedness was not, in the knight's eyes, a prime virtue.

The antecedents and consequences of the sack of Béziers cannot be sufficiently emphasized. Merely to pause for a moment over the round figures involved (they vary from one historian to the next), and to treat this brutal episode as just another of those atrocities which crop up, inevitably, in any war is a critical mistake. From what we know of the brutal warrior code current during our period —and indeed more or less perennial—we might be led to make the *a priori* assumption that *any* soldiers, once the bonds of discipline had been removed, could only too easily behave in a similar fashion. But the facts show that such is not the case. Massacres such as that at Béziers are extremely rare; we are forced to accept the proposition that even human cruelty has its limits. Even among the worst atrocities which history has to show us through the centuries, massacres of this sort stand out as the exceptions; and yet it is the head of one of the leading monastic Orders in Catholic Christendom who has the honour of being responsible (while conducting a 'Holy War' to boot) for one such monstrous exception to the rules of war. We should be on our guard against underrating the significance of this fact.

Pierre des Vaux de Cernay, one of the Crusade's apologists, sees this collective punishment of an heretical city as a perfectly just act: in any case, had not the inhabitants murdered their Viscount forty-two years earlier to the very day? He does not add that they had been punished for this by the massacre of the male population the following year. He rejoices in such a miraculous coincidence, which proves that God willed the town's chastisement—a fact confirmed by the tragedy having taken place on the feast day of St Mary Magdalene, whose name the burghers of Béziers had allowed themselves to speak ill of. Moreover, it was in the Church of this same Mary Magdalene that seven thousand persons had been slaughtered(!). Singular though De Cernay's idea of God is, he cannot have been the only man who reasoned along these lines; but he appears to regard the misfortune that befell Béziers as a kind of cosmic catastrophe rather than the work of human hands. He would have described an earthquake in precisely similar terms. Perhaps the wind of madness which blew upon the aggressors during that hot July day was in fact the result of a collective frenzy, something that outstripped even the most implacable commander's individual will.

These soldiers had only just arrived on Occitan soil, with all their energy still intact: they had not even the excuse of being frayed by the hardships of a protracted siege. Their anger was, so to speak, hatred pure and unadulterated. The fury of the mercenaries (who were, after all, later whipped off like hounds) was only secondarily responsible; the massacre was due in the first place to a plain loathing of heretics. This emotion contained a good deal more that day than mere hypocrisy, a cloak for ambition or the urge to go looting.

So the atmosphere in which the war began was one of fierce hatred —so fierce, indeed, that the enemy was not even treated as a human being, but as some noxious animal to be got rid of, useless apart from the spoils he yielded when dead. There is no doubt that the Crusaders must have bitterly regretted the loss of all the rich plunder which went up in flames with the city. If they dared not treat Carcassonne in a similar fashion, it was only through fear of losing their booty. Such hatred is something our imagination cannot grasp. We are tempted to supply various other explanations for the Crusaders' behaviour—callousness in the common soldiers, the general cruelty of contemporary *mores*, military ambition among the commanders, the fighting man's natural contempt for the burgher, the well known antipathy between the Northern French and those of the Midi. All these factors were certainly involved; but above all there was a mood of white-hot religious enthusiasm, and the wish to wring a General Pardon from God by any possible means.

By this bludgeon-stroke the Crusaders' Army paralysed the will and resistance of their opponents. By the same token they lost all chance of winning over the Catholic population of the Midi. This Crusade was designed to succeed through terror; and the only 'converts' it won were those whom it terrorized into submission. Hardly had the Crusaders left Béziers, indeed, before they were met, at Capestang, by a deputation from Narbonne, with Archbishop Bérenger and Viscount Aimery at its head. The burghers of Narbonne promised full and complete submission to the Church, and severe repressive measures against their heretics.

The army resumed its triumphal march. It took the Crusaders no more than six days to get from Capestang to the walls of Carcassonne, and the *seigneurs* of the district came flocking in to hand over their châteaux and make formal submission to the Church. Others left home and fled into the mountains or forests with their families and vassals. Thus in a few days the Crusaders had won something like a hundred châteaux without a blow being struck.

3. Carcassonne

Raymond-Roger of Trencavel had decided to defend his own. Carcassonne was a stronger fortress than Béziers, and regarded as impregnable. In its present state, despite reconstruction by Philip the Fair and restoration work by Viollet-le-Duc, the city still looks much as it did at the beginning of the thirteenth century—dominating the Aude Valley, ringed with a wall of massive fortifications from which rise no less than thirty watch-towers. This formidable fortress offered little hope to the Crusaders that the 'miracle' of Béziers would be repeated: the presence of the Viscount, together with the cream of his fighting men, guaranteed the city at least some degree of security. But the outlying quarters beyond the walls of the city proper—Le Bourg to the north, Le Castellar in the south—were insufficiently fortified; besides which, the dwellers round about had sought refuge inside the city at the approach of the Crusaders, and had brought their cattle with them. There was also a great number of the Viscount's vassals, who had flocked in to Carcassonne to join their liege lord.

Even if we include the outlying quarters, the total area occupied by the city of Carcassonne seems curiously cramped to us today; even in peacetime the citizens put up with the minimum of living space, and though the palace apartments might be vast enough, ordinary houses were crammed on top of each other, higgledy-piggledy, with tiny rooms. Yet one of these rooms might house the entire family of a person of modest means. In war-time the city became a veritable anthill; and in August 1209, Carcassonne must

have contained some thirty or forty thousand persons (in addition
to horses and cattle), all in an area of some 9,000 square yards, or
15,000 if we include the outlying suburbs.

The Crusaders arrived outside the walls of Carcassonne on
1st August, elated by a success as overwhelming as it was unexpected.
On 3rd August they moved in to attack Le Bourg, chanting *Veni
Sancte Spiritus* as they went. Despite the heroic conduct of the
Viscount, this quarter (the weaker of the two outlying districts) could
not hold out against the Crusaders' assault: the defending garrison
and all the inhabitants were forced to abandon it and to withdraw
into the city. Le Castellar, on the other hand, being equipped with
sounder fortifications, withstood the attack, and its assailants
brought up their siege engines. Sappers undermined a section of the
ramparts, and breached them. The Crusaders occupied Le Castellar
on 8th August. However, they retired from this position for the
night, and the Viscount recaptured the quarter, and slaughtered the
holding garrison they had left behind.

For the first time this war had become a matter of genuine military
operations, and the Crusaders found themselves up against a
redoubtable opponent. The young Viscount was a brave warrior
himself, and had the cream of the country's chivalry behind him.
But that hot dry summer soon conjured up the traditional ally of a
besieging army: thirst. If the city was not short of provisions, it
very soon began to run out of water. The streets and ditches began
to fill up with decaying carcasses, and their rapid decomposition (it
being a hot August) spread a filthy stench throughout the entire
city, and attracted swarms of black meat-flies.

So it was that Raymond-Roger found himself obliged to parley
with the enemy. According to William of Tudela, he called upon
his liege lord, the King of Aragon, to mediate on his behalf. Peter II
did in fact make an attempt at intercession; together with the Count
of Toulouse, who was his brother-in-law, he went to see the Abbot
of Cîteaux, and spoke up for the young Lord of Trencavel, claiming
that he was innocent of his subjects' crimes. Arnald-Amalric, who
had long since grown tired of that well-worn equivocation by which
all subjects tended to be absolved of *their* crimes through the supposed innocence of their leaders, replied with an insulting ultimatum. Since the Viscount was personally innocent, his life would
be spared, and he would be granted safe-conduct out of the city,
together with twelve of his knights. The remainder of the inhabitants
were to be left behind, at the conqueror's mercy. Peter II returned to
the besieged city and laid this proposal before the Viscount, who

replied that he would rather be flayed alive than accept it. The King of Aragon now withdrew (somewhat piqued by the indifference that the Crusaders had shown to his intervention) and the siege continued. The position of the besieged steadily worsened:[11]

Bishop, priors, monks and abbots all cried out: 'Why do you hesitate? Remember the Indulgences you can gain!' The Viscount and his men stood their ground upon the walls, and discharged vaned quarrels from their crossbows; and on either side many were the men who perished. And had it not been for the mighty throng who took refuge in the city, not in a year would they have been stormed and sacked, for the towers were high and the walls well-fortified. But [the Crusaders] cut off their water supplies, and in the great heat of that scorching summer the wells dried up. They were plagued by many things: the stench of the sick, and of the numerous cattle flayed within the walls—from every district round these beasts had been herded in; the weeping and wailing of women and children, with whom the whole city was burdened; and swarms of flies, that bred in the heat and tormented them so fiercely that in all their lives they had never found themselves so distressed.

About the same time there took place a most controversial incident, which has not yet been satisfactorily explained—though it formed, in a sense, the crucial turning-point of this first 'Albigensian' Crusade. According to William de Puylaurens, 'Viscount Roger, in a sudden panic, made overtures for peace, proposing that the citizens should abandon Carcassonne, going forth clad only in shirts and breeches, while he himself remained as a hostage till the terms of the armistice were concluded.' William of Tudela, on the other hand, asserts that the Viscount went to the Crusaders' camp on the invitation of a certain 'wealthy military leader' (so far his account does not contradict that given by William de Puylaurens), but that once he had come into the Legate's presence, he was kept there by force. Such, at any rate, is the upshot of the chronicler's somewhat muddled, not to say reticent, account of the matter. He makes no mention of any peace treaty, or indeed of negotiations as such; he dwells on the fact that the 'rich man' (not named, but referred to as a relation of the Viscount) guaranteed his kinsman safe-conduct—not once, but on several separate occasions. Then the Viscount, who had a hundred knights with him, entered the pavilion of the Count of Nevers, where discussions were to take place. From this moment he fades out of the picture, so to speak, merely observing that 'he had given himself up as a hostage of his own free will, and had been out of his mind to do so'.[12] The breach of trust is not specifically described, but very clearly hinted at.

The Viscount was supreme military commander in his own domains, beloved of his people, and possessed (despite his youth) of incontestable moral authority. Is it conceivable that he would ever have agreed to give himself up as a hostage, and thus deprive the resistance movement of all leadership? The little evidence at our disposal on this incident all suggests that the Viscount's good faith was abused, and that there were neither proper negotiations nor a mutually agreed treaty. What seems most likely is that the Viscount refused the conditions proposed to him, and, having done so, was forcibly prevented from going back to the city.

With the Viscount a prisoner, Carcassonne was deprived of her commander, and had no choice but to surrender. In striking contrast to what had happened at Béziers, the inhabitants were able to leave the city safe and unharmed. How did this come about? According to the Anonymous Chronicler, by means of a hidden gateway and an underground passage, when the Crusaders' attention was distracted by other matters. This seems highly unlikely: such an escape might have been possible for a garrison, but not for the multitude of civilians, including women, children and invalids, who were cooped up in Carcassonne. In William of Tudela's account, however, 'they went out in great haste, half-naked, wearing shirt and breeches only, with no other clothes. [The Crusaders] left them no other possessions, not a farthing's-worth.' The condition for the surrender of the city, then, must have been this: the inhabitants' lives would be spared *if they left all their riches behind*—an assumption which explains that phrase about 'not a farthing's-worth'. We may note that there were a great many declared heretics living in Carcassonne; it is odd that the commanders of a Crusade launched for the extermination of heretics did not profit by so excellent an opportunity, and lay hands upon them.

Some historians have concluded from this that Raymond-Roger purchased his citizens' lives at the cost of his own freedom. It is more feasible to assume that the decision to surrender was taken by the defending forces who stayed behind in the city. The Crusaders had no need to wring such a personal sacrifice out of the Viscount; in any case their main objective was to capture the city intact, and the only way this could be done was by promising the inhabitants their lives.

After the inhabitants had departed (they appear to have evacuated the city before enemy troops entered it) the Crusaders marched in. Order and discipline were strictly kept; they were anxious, above all, to avoid another mass charge by the mercenaries and the rabble, since this might well endanger the profits which the operation could be expected to bring them. The fall of Carcassonne produced an immense haul of booty, which the army urgently needed.

In the first place, since the siege had lasted a bare fortnight, the Crusaders found abundant stores of victuals. They also discovered hoards of valuables: gold and silver (both coined and in the shape of jewellery or wrought metal), together with fine clothes, fabrics, and arms. They also acquired horses and mules, 'of which there was great abundance': this suggests that the position of the besieged was not all that desperate, and hints at treachery against the Viscount. If large numbers of horses and mules were still alive, water can only have been in relatively short supply. At all events, the city yielded so many commodities—either for direct use or cash conversion—that the army's fears of running short of supplies were finally stilled. What was more, the Crusaders now controlled a vital fortress, which had fallen into their hands almost intact, and was admirably suited to provide them with permanent quarters.

This time the commanders sorted out the booty systematically, inventoried it, and set a guard of armed knights over it, with orders to preserve it against the thievish greed of the common soldiers. This wealth was reserved by right for the furtherance of God's work, and any individual 'milking' of such treasure-trove was strictly forbidden. Arnald-Amalric declared publicly that 'we shall hand over these goods to some rich baron, who will maintain the land in a way pleasing to God'.[13] Many of the Crusaders who had come on this campaign in the hope of lining their pockets must have been bitterly disappointed; and the very knights assigned to guard the treasure were, at a later date, convicted of having embezzled five thousand *livres*'-worth from it themselves.

The fall of Carcassonne, then, must be regarded as an incontestable triumph for the Crusade. 'You see,' the Abbot of Cîteaux declared, 'what miracles are wrought on your behalf by the King of Heaven: nothing can stand against you.'[14] But the luckiest chance for the Crusaders was, perhaps, not so much having captured Carcassonne intact as having seized Raymond-Roger in person.

As we saw above, he was taken prisoner in circumstances which, to say the least, give rise to some concern. When the city surrendered, he, who was its overlord, with prime responsibility for its defence and safety, remained powerless in the background. Everything was done as though he no longer existed. He was treated, not as a commander who has surrendered his fortress, but rather as an item in the spoils of war. He was loaded with chains and flung into a dungeon cell; and when we remember that he was, after the Count of Toulouse, the premier baron in the whole of Languedoc, such conduct is only explicable on the assumption that he did not surrender himself of his own volition.

Such an act of treachery on the part of Arnald-Amalric is hardly surprising: he was an unscrupulous man, and quite capable (as an ecclesiastic, if for no other reason) of ignoring the rights of a great baron. But are we to believe that the *lay* commanders on the Crusaders' side could have treated one of their peers thus? If such was in fact the case, we must assume either that the Northern French barons had a peculiarly low opinion of the aristocracy of the Midi; or else that the stakes were too high for them to retreat, and that they were accordingly compelled to swallow any scruples they may have had. (In any case they had gone too far along the path of crime now to think of turning back.) There was yet another, somewhat fanatical, line they could take: this was that Raymond-Roger had, as a heretic, lost all rights to the consideration his rank would normally command.

Was the Viscount of Béziers in fact a heretic? William of Tudela describes him as follows:[15]

> In all the world you could find no nobler knight: more gallant, generous, courteous or amiable. . . . He was himself a Catholic, as many priests and canons could testify. . . . However on account of his great youth he was familiar with all alike, and those who dwelt in the domains of which he was *seigneur* neither feared nor defied him.

The author of the *Chanson* had no particular liking for the Viscount himself, and was here simply echoing a generally-held opinion. Raymond-Roger was, indeed, a most popular person. But the poet was writing in a period when freedom of expression was impossible; so we should not take him too literally when he guarantees the orthodoxy of any person whom he wishes to present in a favourable light. What is more, among all the countless characters in the *Chanson de la Croisade* we do not find one single heretic. The truth is that Raymond-Roger came from a family with a longstanding tradition of sympathy towards heretical opinions. His father, Roger II, had held the Cathars in such high esteem as to entrust his son's education to Bertrand de Saissac, a self-declared heretic. His mother, Adelaide, the Count of Toulouse's sister, had defended that heretical stronghold Lavaur against the Papal Legate Henry of Albano and his Crusaders; while his aunt, Beatrice of Béziers, wife to the Count of Toulouse himself, had retired into a 'convent' for *perfectae*. Having thus been brought up in a milieu where the Catharist Church was most highly regarded, young Raymond-Roger was, in all probability, as much a heretic as a *seigneur* of his rank could be: that is, he was Catholic by obligation and habit, but a Cathar at heart. This fact must have been more or less common knowledge: the Cathars always venerated the Viscount as a martyr of their faith. This partially explains the extraordinary lack of consideration which he suffered at the hands of his peers, the French barons.

By capturing the legitimate *seigneur* of the country they intended to conquer, the Crusaders had fulfilled one of the objects laid down by the Pope in his programme for this Crusade. They could now furnish the heresy-tainted land of Languedoc with a Catholic overlord whose business would be to enforce the triumph of the One True Faith. Legates, bishops and barons assembled in occupied Carcassonne, to take counsel together and choose a new master for the country: one who would rule not (as normal secular custom decreed) by virtue of feudal ascendancy, but through the *spiritual* authority he would command as a leader of Catholic Christendom. This, it must be said, was a revolutionary departure.

The position of the barons whose opinions Arnald-Amalric now solicited was by no means an easy one. However loyal they might be to the Pope and the Church's cause—and perhaps this loyalty was genuine enough—they were very well aware that the Pope was not the sole authority in matters of civil law, nor even the most competent. Besides, the Viscount of Béziers had never made a public profession of heresy. Whatever might be the motives that drove such great barons as the Duke of Burgundy, or the Counts of Nevers and Saint-Pol, it was hard for them to lend their support to any undertaking which violated feudal law for the benefit of the Church.

Yet it was to them, in the first instance, that the Legate offered—on the Pope's behalf—suzerainty over all lands now taken from the House of Trencavel. According to the *Chanson*, the Legates first approached Eudes of Burgundy, then Hervé, Count of Nevers, and after him the Count of Saint-Pol: they could hardly have done otherwise without gross discourtesy to the noble lords concerned. Each of these barons refused the offer in turn. The chronicler goes so far as to put lofty sentiments into their mouths for the occasion: they had not, we are told, joined the Crusade in order to acquire other men's lands; they had enough of their own already. 'No one,' wrote William of Tudela, 'could fail to feel himself dishonoured by accepting these domains.'[16]

Such an interpretation of the French barons' attitude contains elements both of truth and falsehood. It has been observed, with some justice, that Eudes II was in no position to make so haughty a disclaimer of any interest in other men's possessions: the reason for his being the last to arrive at the Lyons conference proves this. He had in fact dallied by the way in order to raid and plunder various merchant-convoys; the merchants concerned only regained their property thanks to the intervention of the King of France. We forget, however, that for a feudal baron a mere merchant was not another *person* at all; and a *seigneur* of this kidney, though he might boast of robbing burghers and monks, would still be likely to regard the property of a fellow-noble as sacrosanct. Though he had suffered defeat, and was not only a prisoner but a heretic into the bargain, Raymond-Roger still remained the legitimate suzerain of the domains under consideration.

The barons, then, might well fear to be stigmatized as 'dishonourable'; but if their cupidity once succeeded in outweighing this fear, they had little reason to accept the Legates' offer. In the first place, the Viscount's domains were feudal dependencies of the King of Aragon and the Count of Toulouse, to whom the Viscount himself owed homage and allegiance; and the Count in turn was vassal to the King of France. Though they might have little to fear from Raymond, the three barons knew that the offer made to them also infringed the rights of the King of Aragon. Besides, as the *Chanson* makes them say, they had 'enough lands of their own'; they could not afford to set aside a good proportion of their knights and other fighting men for the job of holding enemy domains as large as their own. Nor would they accept the title without the obligations it implied—simply to see, in due course, their garrisons slaughtered and their banners reversed and trailing in defeat. Despite the incredible speed of their initial conquests, what they were now offered was not a conquered country, but one still to be conquered.

So, whether through prudence or more honourable scruples, the three noble barons refused the title offered them: none of them chose to become Viscount of Béziers and Carcassonne. It was not, certainly, for reasons of political ambition that these feudal lords had joined the Crusade: neither now in 1209, nor at any later date, did a single one of them seek to establish a claim to conquered territory. Arnald-Amalric's choice was to fall upon a candidate who had less land of his own, and was therefore more likely to be tempted by the opportunity of adding to it—and more amenable to the orders issued him by the spiritual leader of the Crusade.

A commission made up of two bishops and four knights nominated Simon de Montfort, Count of Leicester.* This *seigneur* was a direct vassal of the King of France; he held an important fief between Paris and Dreux, which extended from the Chevreuse to the Seine Valley, and numbered a good many Ile-de-France châtelains among its vassals. Compared with the Duke of Burgundy or the Count of Nevers, of course, he was small enough fry; but he was far from being a man of no substance. Nor was he an unknown quantity. He came of an ancient aristocratic family, and had already distinguished himself in 1194 while serving with Philip II; later, in 1199, during the Fourth Crusade, he was one of those who refused to put themselves in the pay of the Venetians, and won a very solid reputation in the Holy Land, where he fought for a year or so.

Now he was a man of about fifty (or perhaps only forty-five), a proven warrior, and known for his sureness of judgment no less than his military qualities. Furthermore, during the siege of Carcassonne he distinguished himself (according to Pierre des Vaux de Cernay) by a remarkable piece of heroism: at the time of the attack on Le Castellar, just as the Crusaders were beating a retreat, Simon —accompanied only by a squire—plunged into the ditch, with a hail of stones and arrows pouring down on him from the walls, to rescue a wounded man.[17] Such a gesture, on the part of a captain already well advanced in years and renown, was enough to convince the Legates that here was a man with all the necessary qualities of leadership.

Simon de Montfort, too, began by refusing the offer made to him; and he only accepted it in the end after making the leaders of the Crusade swear to support him if he ever stood in need of their aid. This was a sensible, indeed an essential precaution. Simon saw that the barons were placing on his shoulders a burden they found too onerous for their own; he was afraid they might shrug off all their responsibilities once the new leader was duly proclaimed and recognized. When at first he declined this generally unwanted title, Simon de Montfort was not making a mere farcical gesture: this was, in sober truth, a most doubtful and perilous honour.

Finally, however, whether or not he was tempted by the prospect of playing a major role in the affairs of his time, Simon agreed to devote himself to the Church's cause and to become, on that account, Viscount of Béziers and Carcassonne. 'Elected' Viscount by the

---

* Since Simon's English possessions had been confiscated by the English King, his position as Count of Leicester (a title inherited on his mother's side) was purely nominal, and he enjoyed no rights appertaining to it.

leaders of a victorious foreign army, he was not—despite the approval of the Legates and indeed of the Pope himself—anything except the representative of a might-is-right policy; and it was only through force that he could hope to hold his position. Now the formidable army that had sown such terror in the areas it had invaded was only a temporary guest, soon to fold up its tents and depart. The Legates saw the end of the forty days' service approaching; and once that period had elapsed, the volunteers were under no obligation to stay, and could return home exactly as and when they chose. The enemy, however scared he might be now, knew very well that these barons and knights and pilgrims (whether civil or military) had not the slightest intention of spending the rest of their life in Languedoc, and that the Crusading Army would soon shrink into a series of insignificant garrisons.

Simon de Montfort therefore hastened to consolidate his position. He began with a lavish distribution of gifts to those local elements on whom he calculated he could rely—that is, the religious Orders, especially the monks of Cîteaux. Then he raised a levy of three deniers from each household, as his personal tribute to the Pope. He made a positively triumphal advance into his new domains: after the fall of Béziers and Carcassonne, towns and châteaux flung open their gates and welcomed the victors with open arms. Fanjeaux, Limoux, Alzonne, Montréal and Lombers were occupied, and garrisons left there by the Crusaders. Castres surrendered its heretics. Fortified by his new title, Simon de Montfort hastened to receive the homage of assorted châtelains, Viscounts, and consuls: the entire region between Béziers, Limoux and Castres made official submission to him, and he scarcely had time to hear all the countless protestations of fidelity. All he lacked was a pair of wings, to pass the quicker from one château to the next. It was a precarious triumph, this; but as a good feudal overlord he attached considerable importance to it. He wanted to assure himself, however dubiously, of his new subjects' loyalty.

Meanwhile the army began to break up. When his forty days' service were done, the Count of Toulouse withdrew, after assuring the new Viscount of his good wishes, and even offering to betroth his son to one of Simon's daughters. The Count of Nevers, who stood on such bad terms with the Duke of Burgundy that 'men feared daily the one would kill the other',[18] was furious at finding himself under Simon's orders, since Simon had joined the Crusade under the Duke of Burgundy's banner. So when *his* forty days were over, Hervé IV of Nevers went home for good.

The Duke of Burgundy still lingered on for a while, but finally withdrew too, discouraged by the failure of the siege of Cabaret. Now they all began to quit the country—barons great and small, the bishops' militias, pilgrims and looters, separately or by groups, draining away in a steady, uninterrupted flow, their Indulgences won by hook or crook, all their enthusiasm vanished. A few months, and this army could have overcome local resistance altogether (the country was singularly ill-prepared for war); but instead it dissolved like a puff of smoke, with not a thought for how it might exploit a success which was generally admitted to have been 'miraculous'. But, as the *Chanson* says, 'the mountains were wild, the passes narrow; and they had no desire to be slain in this country'.[19] Perhaps most of the Crusaders had simply come to realize that heretic and Catholic could not be distinguished by the colour of their skin, and that this Holy War was no more uplifting than any ordinary conflict. In any case, forty days was enough to gain the promised Pardon.

In September 1209 Simon de Montfort had only twenty-six knights left with him. It was little enough with which to control a country that remained only partly conquered—and that part by the terror which the presence of a reputedly invincible army inspired—while the rest, the larger part, was still to subdue. The situation in which Simon found himself (not wholly through his own fault) was desperate indeed; so desperate that one feels almost inclined to forgive him the crimes he afterwards committed. Only fear—indelible, uncontrollable fear, stronger than reason or the instinct for self-preservation, a fear inspired in the population of the Midi by the Crusaders' early exploits—could explain the fact that, with a mere handful of men and reinforcements as erratic as they were infrequent, Simon de Montfort not only survived but actively triumphed in a country which was fiercely hostile to him; a country where he was condemned to rule through fear alone.

CHAPTER V

SIMON DE MONTFORT

1. *Portrait of a General*

IN TWO BARE MONTHS' campaigning the Crusaders had achieved success on so stupendous a scale that they themselves could only attribute it to Divine intervention. But the main purpose of the expedition—the extermination of heresy—had not so far been attained; indeed, apart from the notorious 'kill them all' injunction, the Crusaders seem to have discovered no practicable method of doing so. Quite the contrary, in fact: apart from one or two isolated cases where heretics were surrendered by their fellow-countrymen (e.g. at Narbonne and Castres) the Crusaders had not as yet really come to grips with the enemy they sought to defeat.

The terror which they inspired put an insurmountable barrier between them and the inhabitants of the regions they invaded. The best-known Catharist ministers went to ground in various sure hiding-places; the *perfecti* put aside their black robes, and dressed themselves as burghers or artisans; the local *seigneurs* either protested their loyalty to the Catholic Faith, or else vanished into the mountains. As a result the heretical movement was rather harder to deal with than it had been a year before. The Crusaders had failed to make any distinction between Catholics and heretics at Béziers; now, as a result, they found themselves forced to treat the whole country as heretical.

The Church was thus compelled to abandon all hope of conquest by persuasion. At the same time her purely military resources left much to be desired, consisting as they did of a general who bore a usurped title, and could count on a mere handful of troops. How many fighting men, in fact, did the 'thirty or so' knights referred to by De Cernay have under them? Two or three hundred, perhaps: hardly more. Simon employed mercenaries—but not many, since he was hard put to it to pay them. The conquered towns, and such knights as had made their submission, would furnish him with further contingents (egged on by fear or self-interest); but such troops were seldom very reliable. The only soldiers he could really count on, in fact, were those few Frenchmen who formed his personal escort.

This small troop (as events were to prove) was utterly loyal, vowed body and soul to the service of its commander, and composed of most valiant warrior-knights. Some, such as Guy de Lévis, Bouchard de Marly, the three Amaury brothers, or William and Robert de Poissy, were relatives or neighbours of Simon's. Others were Normans, who, since they shared the same nationality, preserved the troop's homogeneity: among these were Peter de Cissey, Roger des Essarts, Roger des Andelys, and Simon the Saxon. From Champagne came Alain de Roucy, Raoul d'Acy, and Gobert d'Essigny; finally there were various knights from the other districts of Northern France and from England—Robert de Piquingny, William de Contres, Lambert de Croissy, Hugues de Lacy, and Gauthier Langton. Somewhat later Simon de Montfort was also to acquire a most valuable supporter in the person of his brother Guy, who returned from the Holy Land in order to join him. Most of these barons saw distinguished service at their leader's side during the various campaigns of the Crusade; many met their deaths. It was on them no less than on Simon de Montfort personally that the defence of the Church's interests in Languedoc was to rest. They were not so much mere subordinates as active and well-advised colleagues: from various passages in the chroniclers' narratives we see that Simon never came to a decision without holding a council of war and consulting his barons. Because of its unity and willingly accepted discipline, this troop—for all its numerical weakness—constituted a formidable fighting force. Whether in success or adversity, these men remained a single, cohesive body right to the end, their courage proof against all adversities.

And indeed, they had great need of their courage. To begin with, all the domains that came under their direct jurisdiction (and of which Simon was, theoretically, the Viscount) were up in arms against them: the districts around Limoux and Albi contained numerous apparently impregnable strongholds determined to resist them. Down in the South, among the Ariège mountains, the Count of Foix, Raymond-Roger (that valiant captain and noted protector of heretics) still had all his forces intact. Westward there lay the lands of the Count of Toulouse—ex-Crusader, legally sacrosanct, but an unreliable ally, ready to turn enemy at the first opportunity. Simon's only genuine allies were the Papal Legates, who hardly could be called a military body at all. The local clergy, encouraged by the success of the Crusade, were beginning to raise their heads again; but they, too, could hardly support the new Viscount except by giving him financial aid; and even now the higher prelates still tended to regard him primarily as a champion of *their* interests and benefices. The King of Aragon did not regard this new vassal of his with a favourable eye: despite Simon's repeated requests, he put off the official acceptance of his homage for some considerable time.

It is true that Simon de Montfort had several factors on his side. A certain proportion of the Languedoc nobility had sworn the oath of allegiance to him and his cause. There was, above all, the ever-present threat of further Crusades. Nevertheless, this did not make his position any the less uncertain; and his forces were ludicrously inadequate for the vast task he had before him. Despite all this the sheer volume of hatred he inspired is enough to confirm the vital role which he played in the country's conquest: for years to come the Church's policy in Languedoc was identified with the person and activities of Simon de Montfort.

What sort of a man was this, to whom the Papacy (using its Legates as intermediaries) had entrusted the defence of the Church throughout the French Midi? The judgments passed on him by the historians of the time vary according to each writer's personal convictions. The heroic figure, *sans peur et sans reproche*, painted by De Cernay becomes a ferocious and bloody tyrant for the chronicler who finished William of Tudela's work—while William himself refers to 'this wealthy, doughty, and valiant lord, this hardy warrior, full of wisdom and experience, a great and gentle knight, gallant, comely, frank yet soft-spoken . . .'[1] and William de Puylaurens, while praising Simon's conduct during the first years of the war, accuses him afterwards of rapacity and ambition. But all of them unanimously recognize his courage and, above all, the tremendous prestige, compounded of fear and admiration, which he enjoyed even among his enemies. The man was worth an army on his own. He became a legend during his own lifetime, the flail of God, a second Judas Maccabaeus; somehow, with the aid of a handful of troops, he had built himself up to the stature of a great tyrant, one of those at the mere mention of whose name all heads are bowed. In an ordinary fighting commander this was no mean achievement.

Contemporary testimony describes him as a splendid aristocratic figure of a man: immensely tall and endowed with herculean strength, 'wonderfully skilled in the use of arms'. Vaux de Cernay, his panegyrist, boasts in somewhat conventional style of his handsome and elegant bearing—not to mention his amiability, gentleness, modesty, chastity, prudence and fierce energy: he was 'indefatigable in his achievements, and wholly devoted to God's service'.[2]

The most striking thing about him, when we study the history of his campaigns—and they lasted nearly ten years—is his talent for being everywhere at once, the extreme rapidity of his decisions, the calculated audacity of his attacks. Here, moreover, was a soldier who risked his own neck well beyond the common claims of duty, as we saw during the siege of Carcassonne—and as he proved again later, while crossing the Garonne near Muret. He went back through the river (which was in spate) so as not to leave part of his infantry in the lurch; stayed with them for several days; and did not rejoin the main body of his army till the very last mercenary soldier had struggled across to the far side of the Garonne.

Many other passages, in the *Hystoria* no less than the *Chanson*, portray the leader of the Crusade as an impassioned, indeed an obsessional soldier, and one who showed great concern for his men. Once, when Simon was besieged in Castelnaudary, Vaux de Cernay relates how 'our Count came forth from the castle, eager to destroy the said engine of war; and as the enemy had hemmed it about with ditches and palisades, so that our men could in no wise reach it, this gallant warrior (I speak of the Count de Montfort) proposed to jump his horse over a certain dyke, very wide and deep, and thus to boldly set about the rabble by the engine. But certain persons on our side, perceiving the peril he would surely be at if he acted in such wise, seized his horse by the bridle and restrained him from exposing himself in this fashion. . . .'[3]

Historians speak of his austere morals and great piety. We can, if we like, interpret this as being no more than the piety of self-interest, since Simon owed his all to the Church, and could look to no other source of aid. Or it may have been quite sincere: after all, Simon was so redoubtable a warrior that he hardly needed to assume a pious front, a factitious air of godliness. No, he thought of himself, in all good faith, as a soldier of Christ; he believed it so implicitly, indeed, that when he suffered a reverse, he would blame God for negligence or ingratitude. The account given by Vaux de Cernay of the last Mass his hero ever heard reads like an extract from some pious *chanson de geste*; if it is true, it has a certain moving quality about it. Messengers were urging the Count [de Montfort] to hurry to join the assault. Without turning round he said: 'First suffer me to partake of these Divine Mysteries, and look upon the Holy Sacrament, that pledge of our Redemption.' When another messenger arrived, urging him to take the same course, and saying: 'Hurry,

hurry! The battle is becoming fiercer, and our men cannot sustain the brunt of it much longer', the Count replied: 'I shall not come forth till I have looked upon my Redeemer.' Then, at the elevation of the Chalice, he stretched out his arms, recited the *Nunc Dimittis*, and remarked: 'Come, then; and if we must, let us die for Him who deigned to die for us.'[4] This scene might well have been invented after the event by a narrator who knew that Simon was, in point of fact, going to be killed a few moments afterwards. There is nothing improbable about it: for a soldier the eve of every battle was a preparation for death. While we may assert that the piety of a man such as Simon de Montfort should more justly be regarded as an insult to any religion, it remains hard to deny that piety's intrinsic force.

Having said this, however, one is forced to admit that the soldiers of Christ could hardly have chosen a commander less worthy to be called a Christian.

In 1210, after the capture of Bram (which had resisted for three days only) Simon de Montfort seized the garrison, over a hundred men in all, and had their eyes gouged out and their noses and upper lips cut off. One man only was left with a single eye; and Simon gave him the task of leading his blinded comrades to Cabaret, in order to create panic among those defending the château.

It has been pointed out that the same treatment had been previously meted out to a couple of French knights; and that a foreign occupation force, being always numerically inferior, tends to make use of such savage reprisals in order to get itself feared and respected. Simon de Montfort did not invent the rules of warfare; to mutilate prisoners was a sure method of terrifying one's adversary. The dead do not budge, and are soon forgotten; but the sight of a man with his eyes gouged out and his nose slashed off can freeze even the bravest heart. Prisoners also had their hands, feet, or ears lopped: such treatment was most often inflicted on the mercenaries, since no one ever thought of avenging them, and they made as good material as the next man for this sort of warning demonstration. Throughout the war, one of the cruellest known from the Middle Ages, both sides had instances of knights being flayed alive, chopped into pieces, or otherwise mutilated: faith, patriotism and vengeance between them legitimized every kind of savagery. From the sack of Béziers onwards, it looks as though both sides developed a total contempt for their opponents as human beings. This war may have been fought by knights, but it was no knightly conflict: it was a struggle to the death.

Simon de Montfort (who had not been responsible for the massacre of Béziers) was now left almost alone in a hostile country, which nursed all too fresh a memory of the Crusaders' recent military exploits; and he set about making himself worthy, not only of his title of Viscount, but also of the legacy of fear and hatred which he had been left. Yet when we consider his indubitable qualities as a commander, and the admiration that his courage inspired even in his worst enemies, is it not possible that he might have found some means of getting himself less hated than he did? The Occitan nobility did not differ in any essential respect from their peers elsewhere. Popular though he was, Raymond-Roger Trencavel had a fair number of discontented vassals: the lesser feudal barons were peculiarly prone to disaffection. Those who had taken the oath to Simon in 1209 might well have become his faithful allies if their new overlord had contrived to show a little more tact. During the early years of the war there can be no doubt that Simon's brutality produced rather more local patriots than came forward out of sympathy for the young Viscount's bravery and misfortunes.

Simon de Montfort could not, obviously, afford to play the liberal: he was too short of money for that. On the other hand he might at least have exercised a little courtesy; it would appear that he behaved somewhat shortly with his new vassals, who, certainly, were not over-anxious to meet him half-way. For instance, after the defection of one William Cat, a knight from Montréal, he was heard to exclaim: 'I want nothing more to do with any of these damned Provençals!'[5] It is true that at the time he had been in Languedoc for several years already, and had been driven to the limit of his endurance by the endless 'betrayals' and defaultings of those whom he regarded as his vassals. But right from the beginning he seems to have set himself up as the legitimate, unquestioned master of a country over which he held no legal rights whatsoever. He made large distributions among his knights, and to various abbeys and monastic Orders, from property that belonged to the so-called *seigneurs faidits*—those, that is, who chose to abandon their châteaux as fugitives rather than have any truck with the invader. Instead of showing particular consideration to those Occitan *seigneurs* who rallied in support of him (and there were many such) he obviously treated them as inferiors—his remark about 'damned Provençals' proves that—and wounded their pride on countless occasions.

Later he attempted to play the legislator, and tried, by means of the Statutes of Pamiers, to saddle Languedoc with French laws and customs. He never paused to consider how this might infuriate a people who were passionately attached to their traditions, and inclined to regard even the least infraction of their own ways as an intolerable affront. It is possible to wage war without treating one's opponents as though they were a newly-colonized race.

There were numerous instances of such tactlessness; De Montfort further displayed the narrow-mindedness one might expect from a professional soldier, and a degree of personal ambition that finally led him to treat the Crusade as a war of conquest conducted solely for his own profit. Yet it was by his cruelty rather than errors of this sort that Simon de Montfort permanently compromised the cause of the Crusade—inasmuch as it was capable of being compromised any further.

His cruelty was deliberate, necessary, and calculated. All the same, it astonished his contemporaries, and even scandalized that fanatical chronicler Vaux de Cernay: when the latter refers to the hundred prisoners of Bram, he feels he has to excuse 'the noble Count' by saying that he acted thus not for his pleasure but by necessity: his enemies 'must needs drink the cup that they had prepared for others'.[6] Though the principle may be the same, it is obvious that there is a terrible difference between mutilating two men and mutilating a hundred. To behave in such a fashion, De Montfort must have been a deeply cruel man by nature.

In Biron, Martin d'Algais, double traitor to Simon's cause, was exposed in the pillory, with a black cloth draped about him, and exposed to all manner of insults; solemnly stripped of his knightly rank; and finally tied to a horse's tail and dragged through the files on parade, his remains then being strung up on a gibbet. It is true that Martin d'Algais was from Navarre, and a mercenary captain into the bargain; in other words, a person who commanded less respect in the military hierarchy than a local knight. But nevertheless the details of the punishment inflicted on him give a fairly sinister impression of the man who took pleasure in ordering so macabre a ceremony.

During the wars which he subsequently fought in defence of his faith, Simon presided over three mass executions of *perfecti*. At Minerve he even visited the condemned prisoners in gaol, exhorting them to seek conversion. It is true (despite the fact that his victories may have made such executions possible) that final responsibility for these heretical *autos-da-fé* must lie with the Papal Legates. All the same, the Crusader general surely shared that feeling of 'intense joy' which (according to Vaux de Cernay) the soldiers of Christ experienced when confronted with this terrible spectacle.

Rapine, fire, slaughter, systematic destruction of crops, vines, and cattle—such military tactics are as old as time; but Simon de Montfort applied them on a vast scale, and in a country which, theoretically, he regarded as his own domain. The only upshot of his contriving to maintain himself for so long in Languedoc was that his increasing depredations almost wholly wrecked the country's economic life. All in all, Simon de Montfort's principal crime was perhaps being too good a soldier, to the exclusion of all else. In his capacity as a military commander he did all that could possibly be expected of him; he exceeded his spiritual superiors' wildest hopes, and made the extermination of heresy a practical possibility by sapping the physical and moral reserves of the entire country.

It would not be possible, in a work of this size, to narrate the history of Simon de Montfort's campaigns in detail. We must content ourselves by tracing the main stages of their development, together with the parallel activities of Simon's allies and opponents. While he himself (with an energy that deserved some better object) was practising the profession of military conqueror, others were busy too. The Pope, in his anxiety to control events, was launching fresh appeals on behalf of the Crusade. The Legates were manoeuvring to find a way of extending their domination over the entire country. The Count of Toulouse and the great barons of the Midi were drawing up their plan of defence.

As we have already seen, the first few months of the Crusade brought the Church's supporters unlooked-for success; but they also forced them to take the full measure of the task that lay ahead. The most obvious practical result of this campaign was the removal of Raymond-Roger Trencavel, and the accession of a Catholic baron to the Viscountcy of Béziers. But the legitimate incumbent of these domains was still alive: he could not be permitted to survive for long. On 10th November, 1209, after three months' captivity, Raymond-Roger died of dysentery. He may have been poisoned; he may have succumbed as a result of his rigorous imprisonment and the lack of all medical care; but what is quite certain is that he did not die a natural death. His gaolers had done their utmost to cut short his life, and achieved their end in a singularly short space of time. The Viscount was a young man of twenty-four, and at the time of his incarceration full of strength and energy.

He left a son two years old; but, ten days after her husband's death, Agnes de Montpellier, the Viscount's widow, concluded an agreement with Simon by which she renounced both her own rights and those of the child provided she received 25,000 Melgueil *sous* in cash and an annuity of 3,000 *livres*. So now there was no legitimate holder of the Viscountcy of Béziers to contest De Montfort's claim. Despite this, Peter II of Aragon did not confirm this new vassal in his rights, and seemed in no hurry to receive his homage. Numerous vassals of the former Viscount, horrified by the news of his death, now revolted against Simon, and began to launch attacks on those châteaux where he had installed only a skeleton garrison. Giraud de Pépieux, one of the barons who had at first rallied to the occupying forces, now, being anxious to avenge the death of his uncle (a French knight had slain him), made a surprise attack on the Château de Puissergier, garrisoned by Simon with two knights and fifty men-at-arms, and took it. When De Montfort marched on the château, accompanied by the Viscount of Narbonne and his burgher-militia, the latter refused to attack the place, and withdrew. At Castres the burghers revolted and overcame the garrison. In a few months Simon lost more than forty châteaux. His men were dispirited, his coffers empty. The Count of Foix, who had at first preserved an attitude of strict neutrality, now recaptured the Château de Preixan from the Crusaders, and made an attempt to take Fanjeaux.

During this period the Pope solemnly confirmed Simon de Montfort in all his possessions, and bestowed upon him as a gift all goods and lands that he might gain by victory over the heretics.

De Montfort himself saw clearly enough what he had to do. The strongholds commanding the trunk roads had to be reduced. All the great baron-vassals throughout the Viscountcy must be made to do homage. The enemy could not be given time to regroup his forces. Early in 1210 he received some reinforcements: his wife, Alice de Montmorency, arrived during March, bringing several hundred troops with her. Now Simon could recapture his châteaux, hang 'traitors', punish the Bram garrison in a crueller fashion still, and march on Minerve, one of the largest fortified cities in Languedoc and the capital of the Minervois region. It was not difficult to take advantage of the long-standing enmity between William, Viscount of Minerve, and the men of Narbonne; the latter now became firm allies of Simon's.

De Montfort reached Minerve in mid summer (June 1210), and proceeded to reduce its garrison by starving them out and cutting off their water supply. During the surrender negotiations that he conducted with William, it was (a significant point, this) the Papal Legates, Thédise and Arnald-Amalric, who intervened in mid-debate to criticize Simon's over-conciliatory attitude. No doubt, as a hard-headed and practical soldier, Simon reckoned it advisable to be safely established in Languedoc before undertaking a methodical campaign for the suppression of heresy. Be that as it may, at Minerve he would certainly appear to have curbed the Legates' zeal to the the best of his ability. Now the point was this: a large number of *perfecti* and *perfectae* has taken refuge in the city, and Arnald-Amalric knew it. He clearly was afraid that Simon's obtuseness might rob the Church of a fine haul of heretics. Accordingly at some point in the negotiations the Abbot of Cîteaux (irked at appearing more harsh than his pitiless comrade, since 'though he might desire the death of Christ's enemies, he dared not, being priest and monk, condemn them to death himself') had recourse to a piece of trickery which resulted in the truce being broken. Minerve surrendered unconditionally, with a promise that those who submitted to the Church would have their lives spared. The heretics, in other words, had to choose between recantation and death.

On this subject Vaux de Cernay records the sentiments expressed by one of Simon's best captains, Robert de Mauvoisin. This noble knight declared that such a choice could not possibly be offered to *perfecti*; it would simply offer them a chance to escape death by a feigned recantation. He had, he said, taken up the Cross in order to destroy heretics, not to grant them favours. The Abbot of Cîteaux reassured him: '*Don't worry*,' he said. 'I fancy that very few of them will be converted.'[7] Nevertheless the Abbot des Vaux de Cernay (the historian's uncle) and Simon de Montfort himself made every effort to convert these condemned men. But when this proved useless,[8]

he had them brought forth from the château; and a great fire having been got ready, more than one hundred and forty of these heretical *perfecti* were flung thereon at the one time. To tell the truth, there was no need for our men to drag them thither; for they remained obdurate in their wickedness, and with great gaiety of heart cast themselves into the fire. Three women however were spared; being brought down from the stake by Bouchard de Marly's noble lady mother, and reconciled with the Holy Roman Church.

So it was that Minerve witnessed the first great burning of heretics. And yet, though this war was specifically directed against heresy, heretics themselves seemed to play no specific part in it. All we learn is that such-and-such a château contained a great number of them, and that, if taken, they were burnt at the stake. We are clearly only concerned here with *perfecti*—that is, men and women who had already made a solemn abjuration of the Catholic Faith, and who inspired the Crusaders with a sort of religious horror. Nevertheless these mass executions, done with the will and approval of the Church, remained most summary acts of justice, without trial or sentence, and beyond doubt due to the presence of a fanatical and victorious army.

It is hard for us to appreciate the power of these people's beliefs and superstitions, or to understand just how real a thing in their eyes was the Spirit of Evil that dwelt in the Church's enemies. Those who had given themselves over body and soul to this heretical faith were no longer human beings, but limbs of Satan; it is this which explains those crude legends concerning the orgies and abominations which the Cathars were supposed to have practised. Popular imagination outstripped ecclesiastical pronouncement in this matter, distorting and besmirching the outcasts with a will, incapable of explaining their aberrations except in terms of superhuman depravity. Hence the 'joy' of the pilgrims as they gazed on these burnings; it was not the punishment of a criminal they supposed themselves to be witnessing, but the destruction of some diabolical power through the purifying agency of fire.

The *perfecti* were few in number, but the ordinary *credentes* legion. In the end the Crusaders came to regard every person who protected these *perfecti*, even any man who was not their own declared ally, as a potential heretic. The mass of the population were, to all public appearance, Catholics, who had made their submission and sworn loyalty to the Church. Yet they attacked the soldiers of Christ wherever and whenever they could. They perched like eagles in their mountain fastnesses, a constant threat to Crusader patrols. In the cities and towns they rebelled against the authority of the occupying power. It was not, in fact, heretics that Simon had to fight so much as a country that was largely sympathetic towards heresy.

The summer of 1210 was to bring fresh contingents of Crusaders to Languedoc. The bastioned Château de Termes fell at last, after a protracted siege in which there took part the Bishops of Beauvais and Chartres, the Count of Ponthieu, William, Archdeacon of Paris (well-known for his skill as an engineer) and a whole crowd of French and German pilgrims. It was a hard siege. 'If anyone wished to get near the Château,' Vaux de Cernay wrote, 'he was obliged first to plunge into the abyss, and then, as it were, to scale the wall of Heaven.'[9] Raymond, the castellan of Termes, was a valiant warrior; he had a strong garrison, and his troops conducted numerous sorties, which proved lethal to the besiegers. In the Crusaders' camp there was a dearth of food supplies, and De Montfort himself very often had 'nothing to get his teeth into'. It was a burning hot summer, and many of the newly-arrived Crusaders talked of going home even before their forty days were up. When the garrison was forced into negotiations by shortage of water, the Bishop of Beauvais and the Count of Ponthieu decamped at once, and only the Bishop of Chartres (moved by the pleas of De Montfort's wife, the Countess Alice) agreed to stay on a few days longer. Then torrential rains fell, which refilled the cisterns of the Château. The garrison now decided to continue their defence—just when the Crusaders' forces had been reduced by more than half. Only an epidemic, followed by water-pollution, forced Raymond de Termes to abandon the Château with his men, during the night. He was captured and thrown into a dungeon, where he died several years later.

The siege had lasted more than three months. Simon was once more master of the situation, his prestige if anything enhanced; but the number of his troops had again fallen dangerously low. As may be gathered, the pilgrim reinforcements which reached him as a result of Papal propaganda were neither regular nor reliable. According to Vaux de Cernay, it was God's Will that great numbers of sinners should be able to work for their salvation by participating in the labour of the Crusade, and that was why He let this war drag on for so many years: but these sinners cared a good deal more for their salvation than they did for the interests of the Crusade as a whole. They came and went as they pleased, and Simon was forced to adapt his plan of campaign to fit in with the whims of Indulgence-hunters.

These pious characters (such as Philippe de Dreux, the Bishop of Beauvais and future hero of Bouvines, who went into battle wielding a mace, since he had ecclesiastical scruples about using sword or lance) fulfilled their religious obligations according to their lights, but showed no particular concern as to how heresy might be most effectively put down. Perhaps they wanted nothing better than a long, heretic-ridden future to provide them with the opportunity for winning fresh Indulgences. But the authorities of the Church, the Papal Legates in particular, were both clearer-headed and more realistic. They knew that it would require not only feats of arms, but also some extension of Catholic political control over Languedoc if this heresy was to be finally stamped out.

Now the premier baron of Languedoc was still the Count of Toulouse; and it was in his domains, and those of his powerful vassals the Counts of Foix and Comminges, that the biggest centres of heresy were at this period to be found. The result of the policy of terrorization, first implemented at Béziers, was to drive the *perfecti* and their most devoted adherents to seek refuge in those districts which were not directly exposed to the invader. Though in 1210 and even later the territories of the Viscount of Béziers were still sheltering numerous *perfecti* (note that a hundred and forty were captured at Minerve, and four hundred later at Lavaur) it was the area hitherto untouched by the war which now became the centre of a Cathar resistance movement. This movement flourished all the more actively because of the atrocities committed by the Crusaders, which served to increase public sympathy with the persecuted Church.

If this heresy was to be destroyed, then, the first and most overriding essential was to eliminate the Count of Toulouse.

2. *The Count of Toulouse*

In September 1209 the Papal Legates Milo and Hugues, Bishop of Reiz, presented Innocent III with a public indictment against Raymond VI, who, they alleged, had honoured none of the engagements he had entered into with the Church at the time of his reconciliation in Saint-Gilles. Now these engagements, in particular those concerning indemnities to plundered abbeys and the destruction of fortifications, were difficult to fulfil. The Count departed to plead his cause in person. After passing through Paris, where he was received with all marks of honour and granted confirmation of the King's suzerainty over his domains, he finally reached Rome in January 1210, and obtained an audience of the Pope.

Milo (who died soon afterwards, suddenly, in Montpellier) wrote to the Pope as follows about the Count: 'Mistrust his plausible tongue, which is skilled in the distillation of lies and all moral obliquity.' The Count in fact protested to Innocent III that his Catholic Faith remained pure and undefiled, and accused the Legates of persecuting him for motives of personal resentment. 'Raymond, Count of Toulouse,' the Pope wrote to the Archbishops of Narbonne and Arles and the Bishop of Agen, 'has appeared before Us, and made complaint in Our presence against the Legates, who have treated him exceeding ill, though he had already fulfilled the majority of those obligations which our Notary, Master Milo of worthy memory, had imposed upon him. . . .' It is probable that the Pope felt compelled to treat the Count with some circumspection; as De Cernay remarks: 'His Holiness thought that, in an access of despair, the Count might launch a more open and savage attack upon the Church.'[10]

There is no doubt that the Pope was trying to draw Raymond VI, either through fear or self-interest, into the camp of the Church's allies. It may well be that he also felt some personal sympathy for this brilliant and cultured *grand seigneur*. But he was, equally certainly, not the man to orientate his political decisions according to personal likes or dislikes. In his letters both to the Bishops and to the Abbot of Cîteaux he presents his relatively mild treatment of the Count as a ruse, the purpose of which was to lull his enemy's suspicions. As he had previously sent Milo, he now dispatched Master Thédise to act as Arnald-Amalric's assistant; to the latter he wrote: 'He [Thédise] will be the hook you will use to catch the fish in its native water; since this fish has a horror of cold steel [a reference to the Abbot of Cîteaux himself] it is necessary to employ a discreet artifice to conceal it from him. . . .'[11]

Arnald-Amalric did not regard himself as beaten, far from it; since the Pope recommended that he should allow the Count to justify himself in Canon Law, and only condemn him in the event of his refusing to do so, it was essential to leave Raymond no loophole for self-justification:[12]

Master Thédise was a prudent and well-advised man, with great zeal in the pursuit of God's cause. He desired most passionately *to find some lawful means by which the Count could be prevented from demonstrating his innocence.* For he saw very well that if the Count were given authority to exonerate himself—an end which he might achieve by means of fraud or false allegations—the whole work of the Church in this country would be ruined.

This quotation speaks for itself; such a formal admission of bad faith shows how great a danger the Count represented in the Legates' eyes.

So Raymond VI, after three months' delay, was summoned to justify himself before a Council in Saint-Gilles. He had to prove that he was not guilty of heresy, and that he had not had any part in the murder of Peter of Castelnau. Since these two charges would be easily disposed of, he was refused a hearing on the trumpery grounds that he had failed to meet his obligations in other less important matters (e.g. failing to expel heretics from his domains, omitting to disband his mercenaries, not abolishing certain tolls which formed the subject of much complaint against him); and that therefore, since he had shown himself forsworn in these lesser details, he was not to be believed over the main issues. The excuse was shaky, to say the least of it, and in any case mattered little. The Count, however, with a fine display of goodwill, declared his readiness to submit *in toto*, asking only that he should be judged according to the prescribed forms of law. Juridically speaking, he was so completely in the right that the Pope himself—albeit somewhat grudgingly—was compelled to recognize the fact. In a letter to King Philip he wrote: 'We know that the Count has not justified his actions yet; but whether this omission is his fault or not we cannot tell. . . .'

Raymond continued in his efforts to get the case heard, and to reach some understanding with Simon de Montfort. At the end of January 1211 he had a meeting with the new Viscount in Narbonne, in the presence of the King of Aragon and the Bishop of Uzès. Peter II tried to act as mediator in the affair, finally accepting from Simon the homage he had so long postponed. Later still he was to arrange a marriage between his son James (then aged four) and De Montfort's daughter Amicie, entrusting the boy to Simon's care. At the same time he betrothed his sister Sancha to the Count of Toulouse's son Raymond. Since his other sister, Eleanor, was already the wife of Raymond VI, the young Raymond now became his own father's brother-in-law.

Peter II did his best to soften Simon de Montfort, perhaps in the hope of making him realize that it would be to his own best advantage, as Viscount of Béziers, to live on amicable terms with his neighbours. At the same time Peter was displaying his attachment to the House of Toulouse, thinking that by so doing he might shelter Raymond VI from further Papal fulminations. The Albigensian affair was far from being the Pope's sole preoccupation at the time; and the King of Aragon was Christendom's greatest champion in Spain against the Moors.

The negotiations dragged on. The Count had no intention of abandoning his pose as an obedient son of the Church. The Legates could not prevent his proving his innocence *sine die*, besides which they were in a hurry themselves. This adversary of theirs was beginning to look uncommonly like a just man enduring persecution. They had to force his hand before fresh reinforcements arrived for the Crusaders' army.

In the event they did so. A council was held at Arles (only William of Tudela refers to it), at which Raymond was handed a kind of ultimatum by the Legates, specifying the conditions he must fulfil in order to obtain forgiveness for crimes of which he declared himself innocent. These conditions were such that some historians have supposed them to be a romantic fiction invented by the chronicler. The latter tells us, moreover, that Raymond and the King of Aragon had to wait outside in the cold, 'exposed to a high wind', till the document composed by the Legates was delivered to them. Is such calculated disrespect to *seigneurs* of this high eminence really likely? Still, Arnald-Amalric may well have been trying to exasperate his adversary by every means at his disposal. What we know of the Abbot's character shows him to have been a headstrong man with scant respect for lay authority.

The Count read the document aloud to himself, then said to the King: 'Come hither, Sire, and hear what is set down upon this scroll, the strange commandments which these Legates enjoin me to obey.' The King declared: 'Here is a matter that needs mending indeed, by the all-puissant Holy Father himself.'[13] This was an understatement. The document, as might have been expected, ordered the Count to get rid of his mercenaries, to stop giving protection to Jews and heretics, and to surrender the last-named 'in a year or less'. But this was not all. The Count and his barons were forbidden to eat 'more than two kinds of meat'; they were not to wear 'costly garments, but coarse brown homespun'; they were to raze their châteaux and fortresses to the ground, and no longer live in towns but only in the country districts, 'like villeins'; if the Crusaders attacked them they were to offer no resistance. In addition to all this, the Count was to sail to the Holy Land and stay there for as long as the Legates decreed. The conditions of this treaty are such that one could almost suspect the Count of having made them up himself in order to justify his break with the Legates—supposing, that is, that a break was what he wanted; it seems pretty plain, in fact, that the exact opposite was the case, and that he was doing everything in his power to avoid it.

Vaux de Cernay makes no reference to this document, but asserts that the Count, who 'like the Saracens believed in omens derived from the flight and calling of birds, and other such portents',[14] was so alarmed by some unlucky prognostication or other that he hurriedly withdrew from the meeting—an account which squares ill with Raymond's character as we know it. De Cernay, that panegyrist of the Crusade, is anxious to avoid making the Legates responsible for this hurried withdrawal—though in fact it can only be explained in terms of provocation on their part.

After having read the Legates' decree, then, the Count left for Toulouse 'without bidding them adieu', the document still clutched in his hand, and had it read out all along the route, 'that it might be clearly understood of all knights, burghers, and Mass-chanting priests'. This was a declaration of war. The Legates excommunicated the Count and issued a decree declaring his domains forfeit to the first comer (6th February, 1211). They held him responsible for the breakdown of negotiations; and on 17th April the Pope confirmed the sentence of excommunication.

Despite his change of mood, and the publicity he gave to the insult he had suffered, the Count still had no desire to fight. He was beyond doubt a peacefully-minded ruler, and after all, it is hard to blame him for wanting at all costs to spare his subjects the horrors of war. Up to the very last moment he was still trying to achieve a settlement; his inexhaustible fund of goodwill must have exasperated the Legates rather more than a policy of aggression would have done.

Simon de Montfort continued his methodical reduction of the Trencavel domains. The impregnable stronghold of Cabaret surrendered before being besieged. After this triumph Simon marched on to Lavaur, with a new and valuable contingent of Crusaders added to his strength. Lavaur, a fortified town that bore the title of 'château', was taken after a long and bitter siege; the defence was conducted by Aimery de Montréal, the châtelaine's brother. Guiraude de Laurac was the daughter of that renowned *perfecta* Blanche de Laurac, and one of the noblest ladies in the land: a person who commanded great respect, one of those widowed *credentes* who devoted their lives to prayer and good works. She was, indeed, even better known for her charity than her zeal for the Catharist Church.

Lavaur defended itself heroically for over two months, and was finally taken by assault, its walls crumbling under a battering hail of missiles, while sappers undermined the foundations from below. Aimery de Montréal, who had originally rallied to De Montfort's side, was hanged as a traitor, together with eighty of his knights: when the hastily erected gibbet collapsed, some of these unfortunate wretches simply had their throats slit. *Seigneurs* of this sort, whose submission had been extracted by force, and who took the first available opportunity to shake off the invader's yoke, excited a quite special hatred in Simon. He scarcely seemed to see any difference between an oath of loyalty given him by his own petty vassals in Chanteloup or Grosrouvre and a declaration of fealty wrung from defeated men by pure terrorization. Aimery de Montréal was the noblest *seigneur* in Lauraguais, and had twice rallied to Simon's standard. As I have remarked already, the Crusaders were not regarded by the people of the Midi as foes worth their respect; for the most part the Occitan knights only submitted in order to have a

1 Painting by Berruguete (1477–1503) of Saint Dominic at the Tribunal of the Inquisition

2 Painting by Fra Angelico (1387–1455) showing Saint Dominic handing the book containing the profession of faith to an envoy of the Albigensians and, on the right, the book miraculously leaping out of the flames

3 A thirteenth century fresco from the church at Subiaco in Italy portraying Pope Innocent III

4 A drawing of Simon de Montfort taken from a stained glass window in the cathedral at Chartres in France and thought to date from 1231

(a)

(b)

(d)

(e)

(c)

5 Mediaeval knights were often portrayed on their seals. Here are (*a* & *b*) wax impressions of Simon de Montfort and the crest he used on his shield, and enlarged drawings of wax impressions of seals showing (*c*) a Knight from Languedoc, (*d*) Raymond Pelet, Squire of Alais, (*e*) Raymond Trencavel, Viscount Béziers, (*f*) Raymond VI, Count of Toulouse, and (*g*) Raymond VII, Count of Toulouse

(g)

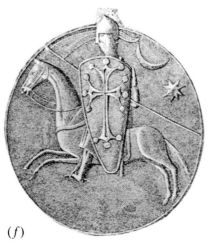

(f)

6 & 7 Manuscript pages from the *Chanson de la Croisade* by William of Tudela showing (6) the taking of the town of Béziers and (7) Count Raymond VII re-entering the town of Toulouse

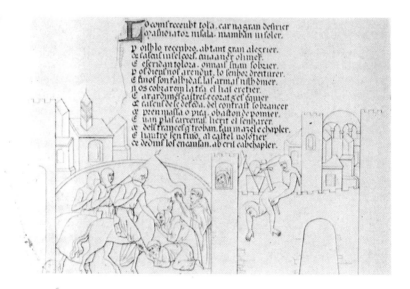

better chance of getting their own back thereafter. But Simon de Montfort had his own interpretation of loyalty. 'Never in the history of Christendom was so noble a baron hanged, and so many other knights beside him.'[15]

In the town of Lavaur there were four hundred *perfecti*, both men and women—at least, so we may assume from the fact that four hundred persons were burnt as heretics when the Crusaders entered the gates. This is a surprising number; it would appear to bear witness, above all, to the generosity and courage of Guiraude, the châtelaine of Lavaur, who had not feared to make her fortress a place of refuge for the *bons hommes*. This great lady was to pay dearly for her devotion. In defiance of every article of war or chivalry, she was turned over to the brutal mercies of the soldiery, who dragged her out of the town gates and threw her down a well. They then stoned her till she was buried. 'This,' the *Chanson* tells us,[16] 'was a great sin and a loss; for never did living soul leave her roof without having eaten well first.'

The four hundred heretics were led into the meadow outside the château, where a zealous crowd of pilgrims had quickly reared a gigantic pyre. These four hundred persons were burnt *cum ingenti gaudio*, displaying a courage which their executioners attributed to their incredible obduracy in crime. This was the largest single holocaust during the entire Crusade. After Lavaur (May 1211) and the capture of Cassès the following month, when sixty heretics were burnt, the *perfecti* sought other refuges than fortresses in their flight from persecution.

We should note that these men, who went to the stake with a serenity that would have shaken the faith of less fanatical adversaries, never sought any kind of martyrdom, and indeed did their utmost to escape death. We do not find them begging their executioners to torture and mutilate them, as St Dominic hoped might happen to him; they were not quixotic hotheads avid for a martyr's crown, but fighters who clung to life that they might continue their apostolate. It was only when they fell into enemy hands, and were called upon to choose between recantation and death, that they kept, steadfastly, the promise they had given on the day of their admission into the Catharist Church. Besides, as we shall see, they were extraordinarily skilful at concealing themselves, and in shaking off pursuers— which suggests that those who have accused them of suicidal tendencies are in the wrong. The Crusade offered them a splendid opportunity for self-destruction, and they entirely ignored it.

F

Those few hundred men and women who were burnt alive in Minerve, Lavaur and Cassès (about six hundred all told, in point of fact) were among the leaders, the guiding spirits of the Catharist Church. Their names are nowhere cited. We know that some of the known personalities who had engaged in controversy with St Dominic and his friends—Sicard Cellerier, Guilhabert de Castres, Benoît de Termes, Pierre Isarn, Raymond Aiguilher and others— survived the first ten years of the Crusade. If there were any bishops among those burnt at Minerve and Lavaur, we have no documentary evidence to show it. It seems likely that the top leaders of this Church (which already possessed a strong organization) looked elsewhere for refuge than in the fortresses and châteaux; these strategic strong-points were a constant target for the enemy, and could all too easily turn into a trap for those within.

We can understand why the Legates reckoned that 'the whole work of the Church in this country would be ruined' if the Count of Toulouse was permitted to exculpate himself; why Milo wrote to the Pope: 'If the Count were to obtain the restitution of his châteaux at Your hands . . . everything we have done to procure peace in Languedoc would be annulled. Better if we had never undertaken such an enterprise at all, rather than to abandon it in this wise.' They knew that the Church against which they fought, galvanized by danger and more defiant than ever, had shifted its centre of operations into the country round Toulouse; and that the blood of its martyrs and the growing unpopularity of the Crusaders had com-bined to raise its prestige to fresh heights, never perhaps hitherto attained.

We have little evidence dealing with the activities of the Catharist Church during these terrible years. Nevertheless, the files of the Inquisition contain testimony taken from those who attended meetings, celebrations of the *consolamentum*, and meals presided over by *perfecti*, in 1211, 1215, and other years; this even in the neighbourhood of Fanjeaux, which was the great centre of St Dominic's preaching. The chroniclers of the period do not inform us (and for very sufficient reasons) in what manner the Catharist bishops maintained contact with their various dioceses, the sort of sermons they preached, and how they kept up the struggle against the Church that was persecuting them. The admissions extracted by the Inquisitors give us only a very vague notion of their activities: they saw the *perfecti*, they listened to them, sometimes they gave them help. That is all. Though in all probability they encouraged their followers to fight in self-defence, there is not one single inflammatory or merely patriotic remark attributed to them; of their much-famed eloquence nothing emerges in the transcripts of the various trials. Either those who heard them knew how to keep silent, or else the judges preferred not to discuss the subject.

We never find a *perfectus* playing even the most unobtrusive part in any of the countless rebellions that constantly flared up all over Languedoc. They never threw up a Joan of Arc or a Savonarola; these fighters whom the Catholic Church found such redoubtable opponents appeared to apply Isaiah's words to the letter: 'He shall not cry, nor lift up, nor cause his voice to be heard in the street. A bruised reed shall he not break. . . .'

Though these men enjoyed such great prestige—their moral authority must have been tremendous—not one of them ever came forward to raise his Church's banner against the universally-hated Catholic hierarchy, or to lead the mob into some retaliatory counter-Crusade. We cannot but be amazed at the self-control which these ultra-pacifists displayed: despite really terrible temptation, they still managed to stick to their vocation in all its purity. It was certainly neither through fear nor inertia that they chose to restrict their participation in the bloody drama of the Crusade to passive martyr-dom. Their strength, they knew, was not of this world.

As sworn foes of all violence they could only fight with spiritual weapons—in sharp contrast to the Catholic Church, where matters spiritual and temporal were so inextricably mingled that even the keenest eye could no longer distinguish them. The struggle was singularly ill-balanced; when an Arnald-Amaury could believe himself a *spiritual* leader, when even St Dominic distributed blows instead of blessings, and became a mere purveyor of human fuel for the bonfires, then the Catharist Church could indeed claim to be the One True Church in the French Midi; and the *bons hommes*, who were venerated as though they were saints, could count on the support of every soul in Languedoc.

So it was that throughout these years of agony Guilhabert de Castres, the Bishop of Toulouse's *filius maior*, and afterwards Bishop himself, continued to visit every part of his diocese, preaching and ordaining new *perfecti*. Less well-known preachers must have enjoyed even greater freedom of movement in the exercise of their apostolic mission. They were never betrayed. The local nobility regarded it as an honour to escort and protect them; burghers concealed them in their houses; working-class men and women served them de-votedly as messengers, maintaining contact between the faithful everywhere.

The Crusade could only triumph once all 'heretical' territories had been completely subjugated: the Legates knew their adversaries too well to have any illusions about this. To win 'peace in Languedoc' a policy of total war was essential; these peace-makers were to reject every attempt at conciliation by the Count of Toulouse, who, even after his excommunication, continued to make proposals for an amicable settlement. In June 1211 Simon de Montfort crossed into the Toulouse region, and this new stage in the Holy War was inaugurated by another *auto-da-fé*, at Cassès. By now the Church was in an irretrievably damaging position, since every victory turned into a moral defeat, which increasingly alienated those whom she wished to win back to the Faith.

The Count had entrenched himself behind the walls of Toulouse. This great city, which lay at the very heart of Languedoc and formed a focal point for every resistance movement in the area, had long been the Legates' major objective. It was not for nothing that when Raymond made them his peace proposals, shortly before this, the offer to surrender all his domains *specifically excluded the city of Toulouse*. As master of Toulouse he remained, ultimately, master of the entire area. While the capital stood intact, with its legitimate overlord still *in situ*, it would still serve as a rallying point for the surrounding districts, even though they might for the time being have to endure enemy occupation. It was on Toulouse, therefore, that Simon de Montfort now marched.

The Crusaders possessed one formidable ally within the walls. Bishop Foulques was not only a fierce partisan of the most thorough-going repressive measures; he was also an ambitious man, determined to occupy that position of extreme eminence—secular no less than episcopal—which the Count, through his excommunication, had forfeited. For the whole of the Crusade, as we shall see, he behaved exactly as though Toulouse were his personal property, and its inhabitants wholly subject to his command, body as well as soul. His fanaticism was notorious. He had given every possible support to St Dominic's mission, and from 1209 onwards he made his diocese a centre of Catholic preaching. He also distinguished himself by the zeal he displayed in hunting down and punishing heretics.

Heretics, however, were still deeply venerated in this great city: so much so that knights were known to get down off their horses in the street if they met a Cathar bishop—as Olivier de Cuc did in 1203 when confronted by Bishop Gaucelm. The population was about equally divided between Cathars and Catholics; so, like the larger

Italian towns about this period, Toulouse was constantly suffering from internal conflicts. These affairs were not really serious; the rival parties would confront each other with shouts of defiance, some standing up for the Count, others for the consuls, and others again for the Bishop. Toulouse, as a capital, fulfilled a similar role in the life of the region as Paris, several centuries later, was to do for the whole of France. It was more than a town: it was a way of life, a symbol, a focal point, the head and heart of the province. Every movement and trend was represented there; all enjoyed the rights of citizenship, and though their freedom may often have been stormy, it was nevertheless genuine. The day that Foulques of Marseilles was proclaimed Bishop, he had some trouble in getting his new parishioners to accept him. But he was an eloquent and energetic man; very soon he had the Catholics behind him in a body, and five years after his nomination he was a force to be reckoned with in Toulouse—through his personal influence rather than his episcopal mandate.

'Bishop Foulques,' we learn from William de Puylaurens, 'was much concerned to prevent the exclusion of all those dwelling in Toulouse from benefits of Indulgence such as were granted to foreigners [i.e. to the Crusaders]. He therefore resolved to attach them to the Church's cause by means of a certain pious institution. . . .'[17] This 'pious institution' was, in point of fact, a brotherhood of militant Catholics who undertook avowedly terrorist activities. The society was known as the White Brotherhood, since its members wore a white cross sewn on their breast; they made attacks on usurers (that is, the Jews) and heretics living in the city, plundering and destroying their homes. The victims of these assaults proceeded to defend themselves by fortifying their houses; and from that time forth, the historian notes, 'the city was split into factions'. A second association was formed, with the purpose of fighting the White Brotherhood; it was known therefore as the Black Brotherhood. 'Daily,' Puylaurens writes, 'the two parties would clash, banners flying, bristling with weapons, even with cavalry in evidence. Through the agency of His servant the Bishop, Our Lord had come to bring them, not a bad peace but a good war.'[18]

This Bishop was, after his fashion, a popular man. He had already succeeded in raising, from among the members of his White Brotherhood, a force of five hundred Toulousain men-at-arms. These he had sent (despite the Count's formal opposition) to fight beside the Crusaders already besieging Lavaur. His troops went into battle singing pious *sirventès* which he had composed for the occasion. His fanatical Brotherhood created an atmosphere in the city very much akin to that of civil war. Right from the start the Bishop had been an avowed enemy of the Count, whose toleration of heretics he roundly condemned. Ever since the Count's second excommunication, he had been openly urging the citizens to rebel against their liege lord. All the evidence suggests that the Bishop considered himself *de jure* master of Toulouse.

With his territory invaded and the threat of a siege hanging over him, the Count could very well do without this enemy within his walls. A day came when Foulques, in his insolence, presumed so far as to suggest that Raymond should take a walk outside the city, since the presence of an excommunicated person precluded him, Foulques, from performing any ordinations. At this the Count ordered Foulques 'to clear out of Toulouse at once, and from all territory dependent thereon'. Foulques at first made a great show of intrepidity:[19]

It is not [he said] the Count of Toulouse who appointed me Bishop; I have not been relegated to this city by him, or for his convenience. Humility I embraced as part of my religious vocation; it is not by some prince's violence that I have attained it; nor shall I abandon it now on his account. Let him come if he dare: I am ready to suffer the assassin's knife if through this cup of sorrow I may win blessed glory in Heaven. Yes, let the tyrant come, with his soldiers and arms; he will find me alone and defenceless. I am ready to pay the price; I have no fear for what this man may do to me.

The leader of the White Brotherhood was very far from being either alone or defenceless; and Count Raymond had no intention of being held responsible for the murder of a bishop. Foulques' speech, in fact, was a gratuitous piece of bravado: he had a shrewd eye for theatrical gestures. After a few days, however, tired of waiting for a martyrdom (or at least some sort of provocation) that never came, and probably feeling that his popularity was no match for the Count's, he left Toulouse and joined the Crusaders' camp.

Now as we have seen, Toulouse was not an heretical city; it contained a large and influential Catholic population. The previous year the consuls had accompanied the Count to Rome, in order to obtain a reversal of the interdict under which their city lay. The men of Toulouse tried to make peace with their Bishop, but Foulques now replied to their overtures with an ultimatum: they must refuse to obey their excommunicate *seigneur*, and must expel him from Toulouse. Unless they did so, the Church would once again place the city under interdict. This proposition was indignantly rejected. Foulques then ordered his clergy to leave the city, barefooted, and bearing the Holy Sacrament. Toulouse passed under interdict again, and became the heretical city *par excellence*, a lawful victim for Crusaders' swords.

Simon de Montfort proceeded to besiege the place, with some newly-arrived Crusaders as reinforcements: among the latter were the Count of Bar, the Count of Châlons, and a large number of German volunteers. The war against Toulouse was already well and truly begun; De Montfort had already captured one or two châteaux in the vicinity of the capital, burnt the sixty heretics at Cassès, and forced the Count's own brother, Baldwin, to capitulate. After putting up a fierce resistance Baldwin went over to the enemy out of spite against his elder brother. Taking into account the fresh troops the Count of Bar had brought him, Simon now felt himself strong enough to lay siege to Toulouse. He soon realized his mistake, and struck camp after only twelve days: the Crusaders' forty-day stint was nearly over, and the army was short of provisions.

This set-back was both foreseeable and, from the strategic viewpoint, had ample excuse. Nevertheless it involved Simon in great loss of prestige. Hitherto he had had an unbroken succession of victories, and now he was forced to fall back before Toulouse: the Occitan knights and the burgher-militiamen began to tell one another that this enemy was not, after all, invincible. A fresh wind of courage and hope blew over the countryside. From this time on Simon was no longer able to pick off one château after another and besiege it. He was attacked himself from all quarters, 'betrayed' daily by his new vassals, simultaneously besieger and besieged, attacking and in flight. He was constantly on the gallop, from Pamiers to Cahors, from Agen to Albi; occasionally beaten off, but never defeated.

Their setback before Toulouse sent the Crusaders off, first of all, into the Count of Foix's territories, where they set about establishing a reign of terror. Auterive was burnt, various châteaux plundered, towns and villages set on fire and vineyards destroyed. Checked at Foix itself, they retreated towards Cahors; the Bishop of Cahors wanted Simon as overlord to replace the excommunicated Count. After receiving the submission of Cahors, Simon learnt that the Count of Foix had taken prisoner two of his, Simon's, most trusty companions: Lambert de Thury (or de Croissy), and Gauthier Langton. He hurried back to Pamiers, where he heard that the folk of Puylaurens had recalled their former *seigneur*, and had the garrison he left behind shut up under siege in the donjon. So he marched again, to Puylaurens this time, and finally retired to Carcassonne.

During this period the Count of Toulouse had regrouped his forces; and now, reinforced by the Count of Foix and two thousand Basque troops sent by the English King, he moved over to the offensive, with every intention of acting as besieger in his turn. Simon, whose own successes in this field left him with no doubts as to the danger of a siege, fled to Castelnaudary—'a very weak château', ill defended, and recently burnt by the Count into the bargain. Too perfect a system of fortifications might stop assailants getting into a fortress, but it also prevented those under siege from getting out. Though the army besieging him in Castelnaudary was far superior in numbers to his own forces, Simon came and went without apparent difficulty. He sent out emissaries to ask for help, fought pitched battles beyond the walls, and, despite the courageous conduct of the Count of Foix, and of his son, Roger-Bernard, routed their troops. Exhausted by Simon's stubborn resistance, the besiegers finally withdrew.

But however brilliant this defensive strategy may have been, it was no real triumph. Those to whom Simon had appealed for reinforcements had ignored his pleas. The men of Narbonne had been unwilling to march except under the command of their own Viscount, Aimery—and Aimery had refused. William Cat, the knight from Montréal, charged with the task of collecting reinforcements, did in fact recruit a body of men—but used them against the Crusaders. Martin d'Algais, the commander of the mercenaries, deserted in mid-campaign, taking his troops with him: he subsequently excused himself for such conduct by blaming the lack of discipline among his men. It was now pretty clear that De Montfort could only rely on his French troops, and such reinforcements as came to him from outside Languedoc. The Counts of Foix and Toulouse, for their part, regarded the Castelnaudary affair as a victory, and so noised it abroad: with the result that all those châteaux which had fallen to the Crusaders now opened their gates to the two Counts, slaughtered their garrisons, and fêted these new 'liberators'. The Counts' forces were less organized, less well-knit than Simon's *garde élite*; but they had numerical superiority, and knew that the local population was on their side. They harassed the enemy, pursued him, retreated before his advance—never victorious, never defeated.

Then in the spring of 1212, with the arrival of new drafts of Crusaders from the North, the situation changed, and Simon de Montfort regained the advantage; from Easter onwards he began to win back the châteaux he had lost, one after the other.

But despite the importance of the 'pilgrim' element (which included, among others, the Archbishop of Rouen, the Bishop of Laon, William the Archdeacon of Paris; Germans from Saxony, Westphalia, and Frisia; the Counts of Berg and Juliers; Englebert, Provost of Cologne Cathedral, and Leopold IV of Austria) this Crusade was coming more and more to look like a war of conquest conducted for Simon de Montfort's benefit. With his 'temporary' forces behind him, Simon set about the reduction of the countryside round Agen. (This land owed allegiance to the King of England; Raymond VI had it *en dot* from his fourth wife Joan, a Plantagenet.) He laid siege to Penne, which capitulated on 25th July, after a month; he captured Marmande, and marched thence against Moissac, which put up a vigorous defence, and then surrendered also. At the close of the summer's campaigning De Montfort's Crusaders, having ravaged the countryside around Toulouse, went into winter quarters at Pamiers.

For Simon (as for the Legates) a new stage of affairs had now been reached. As in preceding years, the commander's military talent, combined with the periodical drafts of warrior-pilgrims which he received from the North, had contrived to triumph over local resistance movements. But this time the resultant gains were so substantial that Simon was able to regard himself as master of all Languedoc: he had swept the country clear of his enemies. The Counts of Foix and Toulouse had retired to the court of the King of Aragon, where they were now planning a retaliatory campaign. Burghers and *seigneurs* had renewed their oaths of allegiance to the conqueror—except, that is, for the *faidits*, whose property now came in very handy for rewarding the French knights for their devoted service. The local bishops were gradually replaced by faithful executors of Papal policy. Toulouse was not yet reduced, but Simon had high hopes of rectifying this situation the following spring. He was, indeed, already thinking how best to put his conquest on an organized basis.

The Statutes of Pamiers show us that De Montfort already regarded himself as the legitimate *seigneur* of Languedoc. He summoned an Assembly in Pamiers, a kind of States General that included Bishops, Nobles and Burghers. At least, it did so in theory; in fact the Bishops dominated the Assembly, and markedly so, while the Legates were conspicuous by their absence. This suggests that while De Montfort was trying to enlist the support of the Church in Languedoc, he was more concerned to free himself from the guidance of the Legates, who were rather too prone to remind him that the whole campaign had been undertaken at the Church's behest and for 'spiritual' ends. Simon had already half-quarrelled with the Abbot of Cîteaux, who, having been elected Archbishop of Narbonne, had also granted himself the title of Duke, and received direct homage from Viscount Aimery.

In the Statutes that he drafted at Pamiers, Simon bestowed upon the Church considerable material advantages: protection of property and privileges, confirmation of tithes and other dues, exemption from certain taxes, such as tallage, and ecclesiastical justice for all the clergy. On the other hand—and this is understandable when we see the annoyance the Abbot of Cîteaux was to cause him—Simon gave the prelates of the Church no part whatsoever in the government of the country. The real power was to be his alone, backed by his troop of French knights.

Simon de Montfort's companions, in fact, were to fill the gap left by the local *seigneurs*, whether the latter were heretics or merely dispossessed by the invader. They were to form a new aristocracy, a ruling class: important fiefs were distributed among them, and in return they agreed to serve the Count [i.e. De Montfort] in all his wars; not to cross the frontier without prior leave; not to prolong their absence beyond an agreed date; for a period of twenty years to enrol none but *French* knights in their service. Their widows, or other female heirs to their châteaux, were not, for a period of six years, to marry other than a Frenchman except with the Count's permission. Finally, *all* heirs were to inherit 'according to the customs and usage obtaining in Paris and that part of France surrounding'. What Simon had in mind, it appears, was a thoroughgoing colonization scheme for the conquered territory—or at least, the gradual elimination of the local nobility, and its replacement by aristocratic blood imported from France. His hostility towards the Occitan aristocracy was persistent and, indeed, well justified. As a soldier his prime aim was, naturally, to eradicate the class which held military power in Languedoc.

He seems not to have been over-troubled about heretics; nor did he set up any special organization for the purpose of hunting them down. In his view this task was the Church's responsibility. Besides, Crusader though he was, De Montfort apparently regarded heresy as a mere excuse for despoiling such *seigneurs* as showed him hostility—or whose property he coveted. Yet till the very end, doubtless in all good faith, he was to proclaim that his battles were fought in Christ's cause.

Finally, the Statutes of Pamiers envisaged a series of measures designed to improve the lot of the common people, and to protect them against the more arbitrary whims of their overlords. These provisions were generous enough, but smacked somewhat of demagoguy, since with the country in a state of war they would tend to become inapplicable. The promise of less crushing taxes and fairer treatment in the courts was small enough compensation for war-levies, increased tithes, and the damage incurred by property during each campaign. Be that as it may, Simon took his legislative functions with the utmost seriousness. Here in this hostile, half-subdued country, where he was hard put to it even to hold his own, he already seemed to be settling in for centuries ahead.

In fact the Count of Toulouse was still the legitimate *seigneur*; indeed, as early as September 1212 the Pope was already writing to his Legates, asking why the Count had not been allowed to lodge a plea in self-justification; whether his guilt had really been established; and if there were any legitimate grounds for deposing him in favour of someone else. This letter, it seems, is not so much a testimonial to Innocent III's taste for equity as the immediate result of some diplomatic work on the part of the Count himself, who had been doing his best, using the King of Aragon as his intermediary, to disparage the Crusade in the Pope's eyes.

Now, after three years' fighting, a certain number of military successes, and the apparent stamping out of all armed resistance in districts affected by heresy, the Pope suddenly seemed to lose interest in the whole affair, well though it had begun. He declared the Crusade over (at least for the time being), criticizing the Legates, and De Montfort in particular, for their excessive and unprofitable zeal. 'Certain foxes,' Innocent wrote, '*were* destroying the Vine of Our Lord in this Province [i.e. Languedoc]. *They have been caught. . . .* Today we have to prepare ourselves against a more formidable danger. . . .'[20]

In fact the Crusade's main enemy was no longer Raymond-Roger Trencavel, or even the Count of Toulouse, but Peter II of Aragon—the leader of the Crusade against the Moors, whose victory over Las Navas de Tolosa (16th July, 1212) was still fresh, who stood as the champion of Christendom against Islam.

So in order to become unquestioned masters in Languedoc Montfort and the Legates still had one decisive obstacle to overcome. The very least we can say is that they were by no means sure of triumphing. If Simon were to be beaten by Peter II (who was a devout Catholic) he would from that moment be a mere adventurer and usurper; the Pope himself, for all his hatred of heresy, would doubtless be forced to bow to the *fait accompli*, leaving the King of Aragon with the task of persecuting heretics in the States that he had thus taken under his protection.

In any case, in January 1213 Peter II had not the slightest intention of taking military action: he assumed that he could impose his will on both De Montfort and the Pope simply by virtue of the high prestige he enjoyed. Still covered with the glory that had followed his brilliant victory over the Moors, this doughty warrior reckoned (not without cause) that the Pope owed him very special consideration; and when he intervened on behalf of his brother-in-law the Count of Toulouse, he doubtless did not expect to have Innocent writing to him, five months later: 'Would God that your wisdom and piety had grown in proportion [to your renown]! You have acted ill, both towards Us and yourself. . . .'[21]

The King of Aragon, who held direct suzerainty over part of the lands belonging to the Viscounts of Trencavel and the Counts of Foix and Comminges, had long regarded this Crusade as an enterprise in direct conflict with his sovereign rights. During the previous century the Counts of Toulouse had, on numerous occasions, been forced to defend their independence against Aragonese claims. Even when the Crusade was at its height, certain of the Viscount of Bézier's vassals, who had sought aid from Peter II, preferred to submit to De Montfort rather than surrender those strongholds which the King of Aragon demanded of them. But the cruel deeds and tyrannical spirit that marked their new *seigneur* must very soon have alienated the sympathies of baron and burgher alike, and made them look towards their powerful neighbour beyond the Pyrenees.

Whatever his claims upon Languedoc, the King of Aragon could scarcely fail to be hailed as a saviour if he drove out the French. 'The people of Carcassonne, of Béziers, and of Toulouse,' as the future King James I was afterwards to write, 'came to my father [Peter II] and told him that if only he would conquer them, he could become Lord of the Realm. . . .'[22] As early as 1211 the consuls of Toulouse had addressed a letter to the King, in which they appealed against the Crusaders' misdeeds, and begged his intervention in defence of a country so close to his own: 'When your neighbour's wall is on fire, your own property burns too. . . .'[23] Peter II was a Catholic; indeed, he had actually persecuted and burnt heretics in his own domains. Barons, consuls and burghers all claimed to be good Catholics, and swore that there were no more heretics left amongst them.

The Count of Toulouse, in agreement with his vassals the Counts of Foix and Comminges, had decided to play his last card. Alliance with the King might place them all in a position of direct dependence upon Aragon, but at least there was a chance of driving the foreign invader from their soil.

Meanwhile King Peter himself took up the cause of ravaged and downtrodden Languedoc. Even if his desire to help his brothers-in-law was not wholly disinterested, we should bear in mind that this feudal monarch felt touched in his honour by the humiliations which his vassals had undergone; and in any case ties of family and nationality might well drive him to defend his sisters' heritage, and uphold a country whose tongue he spoke and whose poets he admired.

His ambassadors, with the Bishop of Segovia at their head, had undertaken to demonstrate to the Pope that heresy as such was defeated, and that the Legates (in league with Simon de Montfort) were now attacking territories that had never been suspected of heresy, and were utilizing the Crusade for their personal advantage and the mere pursuit of new conquests. Furthermore, by attacking vassals of the King of Aragon, they were hindering the latter from prosecuting the Crusade which he had undertaken against the Moors, and which had already yielded such excellent results. Preoccupied as he was by his war against the infidel, the King hoped, by halting this anti-heretical Crusade, to divert into Spain the great hordes of Crusaders who annually filled the French Midi, and whose fighting qualities he had already had occasion to appreciate.

To begin with the Pope was influenced by these emissaries from the King of Aragon, and wrote a really severe letter to Simon de Montfort:[24]

The illustrious King of Aragon has informed Us that . . . not content with taking up arms against the heretics, you also have fought, under the banner of the Crusade, against Catholic peoples; that you have spilt innocent blood, and have invaded, to their detriment, the domains of the Count of Foix and those of the Count of Comminges and of Gaston de Béarn, his vassals, though the population of these said domains was in no way suspect of heresy. . . . Being unwilling, therefore, to deny him [the King) his rights, or to divert him from his praiseworthy intentions, We order you to restore to him and his vassals all those *seigneuries* which you have appropriated by force; lest by retaining them unjustly you cause it to be said that you have laboured for your own advantage, and not for the sake of your faith. . . .

The Indulgences granted to pilgrims who joined in the Crusade against the heretics were cancelled, and 'transferred to wars fought against the paynim, or for the succour of the Holy Land'.

While the Pope was writing his letters, the Legates held a Council at Lavaur. The King, having been invited to speak in defence of the Count of Toulouse, found himself personally threatened with excommunication by Arnald-Amalric. For the sake of the Church in Languedoc it was essential that the Count should be at all costs prevented from regaining his rights, whether in principle or fact: the Legates preferred to run the very serious risk of saddling themselves with a war against the King of Aragon.

To judge from their letters, the minutes of Council meetings, and the account given by Vaux de Cernay, it would look as though the very existence of the Church in the Midi depended on the elimination of the Count of Toulouse. Being better informed on the situation than the Pope or the King of Aragon, they knew that this apparently peaceable and conciliatory person, always so ready to submit, was indeed (so far as the Church was concerned) the 'roaring lion' they spoke of in their letters. Their relentlessness is only comprehensible in terms of the knowledge they had concerning the Count's character; and this they judged rather better than most historians managed to do in the centuries that followed. This 'protector of heretics' was firmly resolved to remain so to the end, come wind come weather; whether his attitude was dictated by personal sympathies, or, as seems more likely, by a genuine sense of justice, Raymond VI represented, in the heretics' eyes, a guarantee of security, a sure prop and stay. From this position he never wavered. This so-called 'weakling' seems in fact to have been a pliable and realistically-minded diplomat, hard to intimidate, and doggedly tenacious of purpose. Raymond realized, perhaps better than anyone, that the Church was a practically invincible Power, against which one could only fight by means of as spectacular a submission as possible. He never abandoned this policy of submission till the day came when his Catholic subjects decided that his cause was also God's cause, the cause of justice and righteousness.

3. *The King of Aragon*

Having successfully drawn the King of Aragon into an enterprise which (to the great scandalization of public opinion) made that devout Catholic monarch a *de facto* protector of heretics, the Count of Toulouse had good grounds for hoping that the campaign being fought against him might now, at last, take on a somewhat different appearance. The so-called Holy War, directed against a heresy about which even the belligerents no longer appeared to care, would be revealed as a war of conquest pure and simple, fought on Christian soil, led by an unscrupulous adventurer, and backed by a handful of ambitious prelates.

The Pope may have hesitated momentarily; but once enlightened by the Legates (who, obviously, did not hesitate to blacken the picture in order to justify their own conduct) he reversed his previous policy and lectured the proud King of Aragon as though the latter were a naughty child. His letter of 21st May, 1213, concluded: 'Such are the orders which your Serene Highness is invited to obey, in every last detail; failing which . . . We should be obliged to threaten you with Divine Wrath, and to take steps against you such as would result in your suffering grave and irreparable harm.'

Peter II, offended (and perhaps worse than offended) by such ingratitude on the part of the Pope, whom he had always served so faithfully, took no notice of this threat. (He was all the more annoyed with Innocent since the latter had refused to sanction the divorce proceedings he had brought against his wife, Marie de Montpellier.) He had already begun his preparations for war, being well aware that there was only one way to reduce De Montfort—by force. He assembled his troops at Toulouse, and it was here that the Pope's letter reached him. He made a purely formal promise of obedience, but never thought for one moment of actually abandoning his allies.

The King of Aragon's forces, when combined with those of the Occitan barons, heavily outweighed De Montfort; as a wise and seasoned warrior Peter II must have reflected that, when all is said and done, right always lies with the victor. 'He summoned all the folk throughout his domains,' the *Chanson* tells us, 'so that there was gathered together a great and a noble host. To all he declared that he would go to Toulouse, to fight this Crusade which was laying waste and destroying the whole country. The Count of Toulouse begged a favour of him, that his lands should be neither burnt or ravaged, since he had done naught wrong, nor harmed anyone in the world.'[25]

Peter II then returned to Barcelona, where he raised an army of a thousand knights; the finest warriors in Aragon and Catalonia were to fight in this campaign. There can be no doubt that the King, who was, in seventeenth century parlance, honour-proud, regarded this war as something more than an opportunity to get his hands on Languedoc. It was the honour of the Occitan nobility, so humiliated by these Northern Frenchmen, that the King and his knights were going to defend: the freedom of their brothers-in-arms, and the cause of *la courtoisie*—or *Parage*, as it was known in the *langue d'oc*. The meaning of this word (like that of so many others) has over the centuries been weakened and narrowed down to a remarkable extent; at this time it evoked the very highest moral values current in secular society. The greatest compliment that the most impassioned lover could pay his lady was to say that she was *courtoise*; and when, in the *Chanson*, William of Tudela's continuator puts speeches into his knights' mouths, they are constantly invoking *Parage*, as they would some divinity.

The songs of the troubadours bear witness to this attitude of mind. Whether he would or no, it was, indeed, for the very existence of a civilization and a national tradition that the King was fighting. 'Then ladies and lovers will recover the joy they have lost,' sang Raymond de Miraval, as he offered vows for Peter's victory. We wonder what these ladies and their lovers were doing in so bloody an adventure; it is clear that we are concerned here with something other than broken families and knights condemned to exile. It was a whole way of life that lay under threat of destruction; a way of life in which *l'amour courtois*, with its ostentation, its affected elegance, its daring mystique and heroic lack of moderation, served as a symbol for a society that avidly craved spiritual freedom.

According to William de Puylaurens, on the eve of the Battle of Muret, Simon de Montfort intercepted a letter from the King of Aragon to a noble lady of Toulouse: a letter in which the King declared that the only reason he had come to drive out the French was for love of her. Moline de Saint-Yon, in his *Histoire des Comtes de Toulouse*, believes that this letter was, in fact, written by Peter to one of his sisters (the King, as a good feudal monarch, would have the interests of his family very much at heart, and would make no mystery of the matter); whether it was or not, a detail of this sort would not on its own constitute a proof of the King of Aragon's frivolity. According to the tenets of the *tradition courtoise*, a knight regarded it as an honour to be able to offer the lady of his heart homage by accomplishing some notable deed in her name. And even if we allow that Peter's private intentions may not have been exclusively chivalrous, what interests us is the atmosphere in which the preparations for this campaign took place. There can be no doubt that the combatants, both in the allied camp and the King's immediate entourage, felt that they were fighting in a noble cause—for *Parage*, for civilization (though the word itself is an anachronism here), against the Northern barbarians. It must be admitted that

Simon de Montfort hardly gave his opponents a very flattering impression of the moral qualities possessed by his French nobility; the significant point is that the Catholic Church now found itself in this barbarian camp.

The bishops who accompanied De Montfort, alarmed by the size of the army preparing to march against them, now tried to negotiate. But the King refused to receive them, declaring that prelates escorted by an army stood in no need of safe-conducts. He could hardly have given them a clearer hint as to the contempt he felt for the way this war was being fought, the continual attempts to turn its equivocally 'sacred' status to profitable advantage. He had not pledged all his possessions and led the flower of his chivalry to the walls of Toulouse merely to be told that by attacking Simon de Montfort he was striking at Christ in person.

Yet this was exactly what his adversaries either believed or wished to believe. De Montfort himself was scared, since at the time—this was September 1213—he had few troops over and above his Old Guard apart from some negligible reinforcements that the Bishops of Orléans and Auxerre had brought him; while Peter's total forces numbered over two thousand knights alone, not to mention about fifty thousand foot-soldiers, mainly recruited in Languedoc (in particular from the regions about Toulouse and Montalban) and consisting of both mercenaries and citizen train-bands.

Peter entered Toulouse in triumph, and was given a tumultuously enthusiastic reception. He now prepared to march against De Montfort, and planted his standard before the walls of Muret, 'a noble but ill-defended château which, for all its paltry fortifications, had a garrison of a mere thirty knights and some of De Montfort's men-at-arms' [Vaux de Cernay]. The siege began on 30th August; as soon as De Montfort heard the news he hurried to the rescue at the head of his troops. He stopped *en route* at the Cistercian Abbey of Bolbonne and, having due regard to the seriousness of his situation, consecrated his sword to God there: 'Lord God,' he prayed, 'Jesus most merciful, You have chosen me, though all unworthy, to fight Your holy war. Today I lay my arms upon Your Altar, that when I join battle on Your behalf I may reap justice in this sacred Cause.'[26] This was a most opportune demonstration of piety: since De Montfort's men could hardly have much confidence in their own numerical strength, they stood badly in need of the moral boost produced by an absolute certainty of fighting for God.

But as we have seen, the bishops (that is, those of Orléans and

Auxerre, together with Foulques, the fugitive Bishop of Toulouse) were not at all optimistic about the possibility of a miracle. They sought rather to dissuade the King from his purpose—having first solemnly re-excommunicated their adversaries, among whom the King himself was not listed by name. It was De Montfort who broke off negotiations, since he knew that they would come to nothing in the end.

The battle took place on 12th September. Simon realized that his army dared not run the risk of being encircled; shut up as he was in the fortress of Muret, his strategy must be to launch a lightning attack in the hope of breaking through the enemy lines. At his council-of-war he declared: 'If we cannot drive them back from their tents, we have no recourse but to retreat instantly.'[27]

The allied armies had established their camp in a strong position on the heights overlooking the plain, a couple of miles from the château, which stood beside the Garonne. Count Raymond, who knew his enemy, proposed that they should sit tight and await the attack, which should be repulsed by concentrated crossbow-fire. Then they should counter-attack, and blockade Simon inside the château; this would force his speedy capitulation. It was sound advice, but it was not followed. The Count of Toulouse was out of luck. This war concerned him, personally, more than anyone else: he was its principal victim. For once he had the chance of retrieving his position; yet he could not obtain a fair hearing for the ideas he proposed. The King's close friends, especially Miguel de Luezia, ridiculed such a plan, and accused him of cowardice. Bitterly hurt, Raymond retired to his tent.

By abandoning his fortified camp Peter lost the initiative, and played right into Simon de Montfort's hands. The warrior-King wanted a fine battle in which his army could test its valour against the invincible French knights, who, he believed, had not hitherto encountered any opponents of their own quality. He wanted to smash them in the field.

When Simon attacked, he was met first of all by the Count of Foix's troops, who very quickly had to retreat before a furious French onslaught. At this point King Peter threw his Aragonese into the battle. Simon, who had only nine hundred knights as against his opponent's two thousand, manoeuvred with great speed so as to prevent the enemy forces from having time to redeploy their positions. By so doing he hoped to preserve a numerical advantage wherever he attacked. He concentrated all his efforts against the

Aragonese, and the two lines engaged with a terrible crash: as the young Raymond VII afterwards recorded, 'it sounded like a whole forest going down under the axe'.[28] It was a hopelessly tangled mêlée. Spears and shields flew asunder, horses were cut down, trampling their riders; everywhere swords rose and fell, while steel helms rang under a rain of blows, skulls were cracked by maces, and the shrieks of the wounded were drowned in the thunderous clamour of arms. Yet this was no full-scale battle, so much as a very brisk engagement between two comparatively small advance guards. The unfortunate thing was that one side should have been led by the King in person.

Simon's aim was to bring down the King at all costs. Two of his knights, Alain de Roucy and Florent de Ville, had taken a solemn oath to kill the King or die in the attempt. Peter of Aragon flung himself headlong into the heart of the battle, which testifies rather more to his courage than his common sense. He had even changed armour with one of his knights before the battle: it was as an ordinary knight, relying on nothing but his strong right arm, that Peter wanted to face Simon de Montfort.

He was thirty-nine years old at the time: a big-built man of herculean strength, and reputedly the finest warrior in his native Aragon. Alain de Roucy hacked his way through to the knight who bore the royal arms, and felled him at a single blow. 'This isn't the King!' he shouted. 'The King is a better fighter.' Observing the incident, Peter called out: 'Here is the King!' and charged to his comrade's rescue.[29] Alain de Roucy and Florent de Ville and their men now hemmed him in on all sides, never giving him an instant's respite. Very soon so desperate a struggle was raging about the King that Peter himself was killed, and all his *maynade* (that is, the knights of the royal House of Aragon) died where they stood rather than retreat and abandon the body of their King.

The news of the King's death spread panic through the rest of the army. The Catalan knights, taken unexpectedly in the flank by De Montfort, broke and fled. The Count of Toulouse's troops had not so far had a chance to intervene; and now, finding themselves swamped by a confused mob of retreating Catalans and Aragonese, they saw that attack was out of the question, and fled themselves.

While the cavalry was being routed in this fashion, the Toulousain train-bands, on foot, were attempting to assault the fortress of Muret. Simultaneously a section of the French cavalry, having abandoned the pursuit of their defeated enemy, returned to the château, fell bodily on this infantry force (which numbered about forty thousand men), cut them to ribbons, and drove the survivors back towards the Garonne. Since the water at this point was deep, and the current rapid, a large proportion of the fugitives died by drowning. Battlefield and river between them accounted for between fifteen and twenty thousand men, or half the entire Toulousain infantry.

De Montfort had won a complete and crushing victory. It was, indeed, something more than a victory: it meant, for the time being at least, the elimination of Aragon as a political power. Peter II's death left the throne occupied by a mere child, whom the conqueror kept as a hostage.

When the battle was over, Simon sent out to find the King's body. Since his troops had already stripped the corpses of all their possessions, this proved no easy task. Having identified his adversary, Simon paid him a final tribute. Then he took off his shoes, bestowed his horse and armour upon the poor, and went to church to give thanks to God. In a few hours' fierce fighting, which his army had survived comparatively unscathed, he had contrived to rid himself of his most powerful opponent; and what was more, he had struck down one of the mightiest monarchs in Christendom without anyone being able to describe his action as a crime. The Battle of Muret had an air of Divine Judgment about it.

The bishops and the clergy, St Dominic among them, had gathered in Muret's church while the battle was raging, and prayed fervently for victory. Now their prayers had been answered in the most striking fashion, and they hastened to spread the good news through the length and breadth of Christendom. The heretics' army had been swept away 'as the wind sweeps dust along the ground' [William de Puylaurens]; a Catholic monarch who had dared to fight for enemies of the Faith had been killed, together with all his knights, and an immense host wiped out in a few hours by a handful of Crusaders whose own losses were, miraculously, restricted to a few sergeants and one single knight. (This is an obvious exaggeration. According to all the evidence the battle was very fiercely contested, and Peter and his *maynade* most certainly did not let themselves be slaughtered like sheep. On the other hand, since only the Count of Foix's troops and the Aragonese were actually engaged, the conflict, numerically speaking, was more or less an even match. Simon's flair for strategy, and above all his courageous if cruel decision to insist on the King's death, had stopped the rest of the army from intervening in time. The two reserve lines of allied troops had quit the battlefield without striking a blow.)

Beyond a doubt the King of Aragon's death came as a depressing shock to the country as a whole. Only yesterday this monarch had ridden through Languedoc at the head of his proud chivalry, arms and armour sparkling, a legend of prowess, acclaimed by all and ready for the fray. Yet now he had shown himself so fragile a reed that De Montfort's first onset destroyed him utterly.

In their consternation the allied princes accused each other freely of treason, and retired without making any effort to reassemble their forces and retrieve the day. The Spaniards went back across the Pyrenees; the Counts of Foix and Comminges returned to their own domains; while the Count of Toulouse and his son fled the country and took refuge in Provence. The victory of Muret had won, for De Montfort and the Church, a country not so much defeated as demoralized by the sudden and brutal shattering of its high hopes.

In the final count it is the city of Toulouse which paid by far the most dearly over this episode, in terms of human lives. The French cavalry's frenzied charge against the men-at-arms of Toulouse was a massacre rather than a battle. If the French had two of their own number to avenge (that is, Pierre de Sissey and Roger des Essarts, old comrades-in-arms of De Montfort's, who were captured at Toulouse and horribly tortured before execution) then Toulouse, 'where scarcely one house had not someone to mourn' would not forget the carnage and drownings of Muret.

The day after his victory Simon did not march on the capital. It would appear that this vast city, even when abandoned by its defenders, distressed and desolate, still was regarded by the conqueror, if not as an actual danger, at least as a potential source of trouble which he did not, as yet, feel strong enough to meet.

But the bishops entered Toulouse, with Foulques at their head, and attempted to negotiate for the city's surrender. The consuls dragged discussions out to an interminable length, argued over the number of hostages to be taken, and finally refused their submission. Meanwhile De Montfort had crossed the Rhône, and was methodically pursuing the conquest and subjugation of the Count's domains. If he waited till the other provinces were in his hands, he argued, then Toulouse would fall to him like a ripe apple.

During the eighteen months following this spectacular defeat of the Southern forces, Simon de Montfort might reasonably suppose that the war, to all practical intents and purposes, was over. Such resistance as he now met was rare, and soon overcome. Despite this he found himself up against a general atmosphere of mulish hostility which can have left him with few illusions as to future prospects. Narbonne and Montpellier both closed their gates against him. Nîmes only admitted him after a threat of reprisals. In Provence, where his scheme for the progressive occupation of the Count of Toulouse's lands was now in operation, the local nobility submitted to him—though with an ill enough grace. Then Narbonne rose against him. Simon, assisted by a body of Crusaders that his step-father, William des Barres, had brought him, succeeded in beating off the rebels' attack; but he was unable to storm the city, since the Cardinal-Legate Peter of Beneventum, acting as intermediary, brought about a truce.

At Moissac there was a burghers' uprising, and Raymond VI laid siege to the town, which was held by a French garrison. But at De Montfort's approach the Count retired. Simon now marched back through the Rouergue and Agenais districts to Périgord, dismantling those châteaux which had offered him any resistance. After a three weeks' siege he took the fortress of Casseneuil, and then those at Montfort and Capdenac. Next he reduced the supposedly impregnable stronghold of Séverac, the seat of one of the oldest families in Rouergue : the Count of Rodez, albeit without any great enthusiasm, now swore allegiance to the victor of Muret, complaining that part of his lands were held in fief from the King of England.

De Montfort had by now received homage from the bulk of the Count of Toulouse's vassals (both direct and indirect) between Périgord and Provence. If all these oaths of allegiance had been regarded seriously by those who swore them, Simon would have wielded a power as great as that of any baron in all Christendom. To read the history of his campaigns one might well suppose that the facts had been embellished by some panegyrist with little regard for the truth. Yet the authors of the *Chanson* (who were far from friendly to him), the correspondence of the Legates, the Pope, and the King of France, all the evidence in fact, combines to attest an *a priori* well-nigh incredible truth—since 1209 Simon de Montfort had not suffered a single real setback, and over a period of five years had gone from one victory to another with almost wearisome regularity. We can well imagine the hopeless exasperation that his unfailing good fortune must have inspired in his opponents. Whether it was God or the Devil who looked after him, De Montfort certainly seemed endowed with *some* sort of superhuman power.

The hatred which he inspired—and which was extended indiscriminately to all Frenchmen—grew apace, but did not seem to diminish his actual power. The massacre of a garrison was followed by such savage reprisals that it soon became an event of some rarity. But while they suffered the occupying forces to impose their will upon them, the people of the Midi must have hoped for a speedy opportunity of taking their revenge: a few hints, one or two facts reported haphazardly by the chroniclers—these suggest just how violent the passions unleashed by this war could be. The official record shows nothing but pacification and submissions: the conquerors were already trying to resolve dissension by diplomatic means, and to share out the country among themselves, even though their occupation of it was on a purely provisional basis. The poet who composed the *Chanson* attributes to Philip II a remark which he may not actually have uttered, but which expresses very clearly the will of the Midi during these dark years: 'My lords, I still have *hope* that, before it prove too late, this Count de Montfort and his brother, Count Guy, may die in harness. . . .'

Meanwhile it was the Papacy, in the person of the new Legate, Peter of Beneventum, that intended to turn this conquest to good administrative account. Faced with De Montfort's growing aspirations, and the implacable hatred he everywhere inspired, the Legate tried, as far as was possible, to shake off the influence of so awkward an agent. On the other hand the local bishops were all in favour of Simon, since his presence guaranteed them not only security, but also material advantages that the Count would never have thought of granting them. Simon was the only man capable of defending the Church's rights by force of arms, and the Legates had to handle him carefully. It was the Cardinal-Legate of France, Robert de Courçon, who confirmed De Montfort in the possession of all lands he had conquered: Albigeois, Agenais, Rouergue and Quercy, these being under Philip II's indirect suzerainty. We may note that the King himself seems to have been wholly ignorant of this development. With the aftermath of Bouvines he had plenty more to worry about; he did not in fact give utterance on the matter until he judged that Simon's position was well and truly consolidated.

Peter of Beneventum, for his part, undertook to win submission to the Church from the legitimate owners of those domains which De Montfort had acquired by right of conquest. Raymond-Roger, Count of Foix; Bernard, Count of Comminges; Aiméry, Viscount of Narbonne; Sanche, Count of Roussillon; the consuls of Toulouse and, finally, the Count of Toulouse himself—all these came and offered their absolute submission to the Church and the Legate in person, swearing that they would do penance, fight heresy in their territories, and refrain from attacking lands conquered by the Crusaders. This ceremony took place in Narbonne, in April 1214. The Count of Toulouse further agreed to quit his fief and abdicate in favour of his son. This was a pure formality, since the young Raymond was wholly devoted to his father, and eager to obey him in all things.

By thus offering multiple evidence of his obedience and readiness to submit, the Count hoped that he might deprive the Church of any excuse for dispossessing him. Moreover, while De Montfort was actually settling in as master of Languedoc, Raymond still regarded himself as the country's legitimate *seigneur*, and wrote placing his domains at the Pope's disposal: '. . . in such wise that all my lands be submitted to the mercy and absolute power of the Sovereign Pontiff of the Roman Church. . . .' Neither he nor the Count of Foix ever diverged from this particular line, which was ingenious if not over-effective—that is, of treating De Montfort as a usurper, but always recognizing the Church's sovereignty.

The Cardinal-Legate accepted this submission—an act which, in the last resort, constituted an implicit denial of De Montfort's claims. Such an acceptance, indeed, seemed to infringe the victor of Muret's rights so flagrantly that his supporters (whose views Vaux de Cernay echoes) could only explain the attitude taken by Peter of Beneventum as pious eyewash, designed to lull the Count's suspicions. '*O legati fraus pia!*' the historian exclaims, without any trace of irony, '*O pietas fraudulenta!*' Vaux de Cernay was indeed a strange Catholic, whose opinions repeatedly hint at:some crude lack of moral principle. But though these ecclesiastical leaders had few remaining scruples (as their behaviour demonstrates) they may well have nursed fears of a different sort. There was, they probably thought, some risk that a man like De Montfort might harm the Church's cause by his excesses, and, through his ambition, put a curb on her temporal powers.

In December 1213 Simon had arranged a marriage between his eldest son, Amaury, and André of Burgundy's only daughter, Beatrix, who stood to inherit all Dauphiné: his political and dynastic intentions were becoming increasingly obvious.

Furthermore, while his adversaries were laying complaints against him at Rome, and asserting (often in the face of all the evidence) that neither they nor their domains had ever incurred the slightest suspicion of heresy, De Montfort himself—and the local bishops who supported him—were finding heresy (or, failing heresy, mercenaries) wherever they wanted to establish their authority.

In January 1215 there was held the Council of Montpellier, with Peter of Beneventum as its President: this gave a provisional ruling on the situation, in anticipation of the Ecumenical Council that was due to meet later the same year at Rome. In the presence of the Archbishops of Narbonne, Auch, Embrun, Arles and Aix, together with twenty-eight bishops and numerous abbots and lesser clergy, the Legate proposed that they should choose the man 'to whom, for the honour of God and our Holy Mother the Church, for the peace of these lands, and for the downfall and extirpation of all vile heresy, we may best and most profitably concede and assign Count Raymond's domain of Toulouse, together with all other lands occupied by the Crusaders' Army'.[31] The prelates, being thus consulted, with one voice chose Simon de Montfort; the only person to reveal any surprise at such unanimity is Vaux de Cernay, who was naturally inclined to discover the hand of God in everything. Now this man who was so eminently 'fitted' to rule Toulouse and the rest of these conquered domains was so unanimously detested that he could not appear in person before the Council: the inhabitants of Montpellier (a Catholic town and, in theory at least, neutral) had forbidden him entry there.* When he attempted to defy this ban, in the Legate's company, he got so hot a reception that he had to withdraw, hurriedly, by a different exit.

The Council's decision dispossessed the Count of Toulouse and his son, but only conferred on Simon the somewhat vague title of *dominus et monarcha*: that is, he was to be as it were a Papal lieutenant, charged with the task of policing conquered territory. This was a good deal less than he wanted. Meanwhile the Count of Toulouse, supported by his brother-in-law (that is, his son's uncle) John Lackland, was waiting for the Ecumenical Council to meet, when he hoped to get his own rights re-established.

While the prelates were busy with their legislation, and Simon equally busy consolidating his authority, a persistent (if muted) campaign of hostility was going on behind their backs. One significant episode in this campaign may be considered here. In February 1214 Baldwin of Toulouse, that brother of Count Raymond's who had come forward on De Montfort's side, was the victim of a conspiracy—or, rather, of a *coup de main*, all the participants in which appear to have been convinced that they were doing no more than their patriotic duty; albeit Baldwin was captured and delivered by *seigneurs* who had duly and properly made their submission to De Montfort.

* Montpellier was a possession of the Kings of Aragon, and its inhabitants could not forgive Simon the murder of their liege lord.

What happened was as follows: Baldwin of Toulouse had received the domains of Quercy from Simon, and was on his way home from taking formal possession of them. He stopped at the Château de l'Olme, near Cahors; the castellan slaughtered his escort and handed him over to Ratier of Castelnau. He was then taken to Montauban, to await his brother's judgment. The latter, being warned of his arrival, at once made his way thither, accompanied by the Count of Foix.

This so-called 'Count' Baldwin, this traitor to his country's cause, had been brought up at the King of France's court and was, in fact, more of a Frenchman than a Toulousain—which, though it does not excuse his behaviour, at least explains it. Baldwin was born in France, at a time when his father was on extremely bad terms with his French wife Constance (from whom he later became separated), and did not come to Toulouse till 1194, after Raymond V's death. Even then his brother received him so coolly that the young man was obliged to go back to Paris and look out letters proving that he really was the Count of Toulouse's son. There was a wide gap in age between the brothers, and they did not get on at all well. Baldwin was treated as a poor relation, and must have felt like a fish out of water at his brother's court. Yet he was a gallant warrior, and had defended the Château de Montferrand against De Montfort in the most brilliant fashion. Having once changed sides, however, he should have kept faith with his new masters to the end.

Be that as it may, though his brother was perhaps as much to be pitied as blamed, Count Raymond showed him no mercy. On his arrival at Montauban he held a council of war, at which the Count of Foix and the Catalan knight Bernard de Portella were also present, and unhesitatingly condemned the traitor to death by hanging. When Baldwin, who was a good Catholic, asked to receive the Sacraments before dying, his brother sent back the reply that a man who had fought so well for his Faith hardly needed any Absolution. He could, however, make his confession, though he was not to receive Holy Communion. So Baldwin was taken out into a meadow close by the château, and hanged from a walnut tree by the Count of Foix in person, while his brother watched. Bernard de Portella acted as assistant executioner; by dispatching this traitor he hoped to be revenged for the King of Aragon's death.

This brutal episode shows that Count Raymond (who two months later was to offer his person and property so humbly to the Church) had not the least intention of giving up the struggle, and was merely biding his time, striking where and as he could. When he had his brother executed in cold blood, simply in order to satisfy the patriotic fury of his vassals, he seems to have been obeying the same political instinct which afterwards led him, in the Pope's presence, to make his protestation of fidelity to the Church. This disconcerting man knew the formula for popularity: he always remained first servant rather than master in his own country.

Baldwin's execution touched off a burst of rejoicing throughout Languedoc, and inspired the troubadours to compose songs of triumph.

Though Simon de Montfort had been chosen by the Council of Montpellier as the man best fitted to rule Toulouse and the rest of the Count's domains, he did not as yet dare to show his face in Toulouse itself. This great city, the key to Languedoc, still affected not to recognize her new overlord. Simon could only enter Toulouse in the company of some personage whose rank and quality might, after a fashion, legitimize the submission which De Montfort alone would have been denied.

Ever since Bouvines Philip II had had nothing more to fear from those 'two lions', John Lackland and the Emperor, who threatened his Northern provinces. Now at last he decided to take an interest in what was going on in the Midi. The lands of the Count of Toulouse formed part of those territories dependent on the French Crown, though his authority there had always been purely nominal. As soon as De Montfort's victory had (as Philip thought) settled the dispute, he became anxious to find out whether the Church had not overstepped her rights in bestowing on one of her own vassals a fief over which *he* had the suzerainty. He took good care not to intervene in person; better not to lend the weight of his authority to this enterprise before finding out more about its potential hazards and advantages. His son had long manifested a pious longing to take part in the Crusade; it was he, accordingly, whom Philip sent—or, rather, permitted to go.

Since Languedoc was theoretically pacified, young Prince Louis's journey came under the heading of 'pilgrimage' rather than 'military expedition'. He took a large number of knights with him, in particular the Counts of Saint-Pol, Ponthieu, Sées, and Alençon. Even though this army had no actively warlike intentions, it was certainly calculated to impress any of the Occitan barons who might feel inclined to challenge the King's authority. But for the time being no one thought of doing so. Compared with De Montfort, the Devil himself would have appeared a good master, let alone the 'gentle and debonair' Louis. There is nothing to suggest that the Prince was ill-received during this peaceful 'Crusade': he was, rather, welcomed as an arbitrator.

The Legate hastened to inform Louis that he 'should not and could not in any way impugn' the Councils' decrees, bearing in mind the fact that the Church's forces had triumphed single-handed, without any help from the King of France—though such help had frequently been solicited.[32] In fact Louis, who was extremely pious, made no attempt to contravene the decisions of the Church; but during subsequent disputes he tended to side with De Montfort.

One instance of this was the quarrel between De Montfort and Arnald-Amalric, Archbishop of Narbonne. The Archbishop sided with the consuls in an attempt to preserve Narbonne's city walls from demolition; the Prince, however, upheld De Montfort, and ordered that the walls be destroyed. In the same way Louis authorized the razing of the walls of Toulouse; though this city was, provisionally at least, free of the Church's jurisdiction, it had to make ready to receive its new master. When the Pope learnt that the French King's son, at the head of an army, had gone off to inspect the territory which the Church had conquered, he hurriedly confirmed Simon de Montfort as 'Warden' of these domains—lest Simon break away from Rome's authority and obtain the title of Count from his lawful suzerain.

Finally, in May 1215, Prince Louis, the Legate, and Simon de Montfort entered Toulouse together. The Count had already departed, being in no mood to grace the conqueror's triumph. It was agreed that the city's moats should be filled in, and its towers, walls, and other fortifications razed to their foundations, 'in such wise that no defender therein might have aught with which to protect himself'. Thus Toulouse was disarmed in advance, and made an open city in the most literal sense of the phrase: it had no alternative but to admit the conqueror. De Montfort moved in immediately, and made the city fortress his headquarters: its fortifications had been spared with this in view. Prince Louis, his forty days' pilgrimage ended, now withdrew: as a memento of this pious expedition he took with him half the jawbone of St Vincent, which had been an object of veneration at Castres. In order to offer the Prince some token of gratitude for his kindness, Simon took steps to obtain this precious relic from the monks of Castres. It was given him 'in consideration of the manner in which he had advanced Christ's cause': he kept the other half himself, and presented it to the church in Laon.

CHAPTER VI

THE CONSECRATION AND FAILURE OF THE CRUSADE

1. *The Lateran Council*

IN NOVEMBER 1215 the Pope's Ecumenical Council was at last assembled as the Fourth Council of the Lateran. It was a veritable international conference, and had entailed upward of two years' solemn preparation. There took part in it two Patriarchs (those of Constantinople and Jerusalem), seventy-one archbishops, four hundred and ten bishops, and eight hundred abbots, representing the Churches of Northern France and the Midi, of East and West alike. There were also ambassadors and delegates from kings and great cities. Its main object was not to settle the Albigensian question; to the Pope's mind this was a matter of secondary importance, as it were a mere administrative problem, which would have to be considered at the end, after the Council had promulgated its resolutions. It was these resolutions that formed the main object of the occasion, and explained why so impressive an array of ecclesiastical dignitaries was now assembled together.

Nevertheless the problem of heresy, and the means by which it was to be fought, possessed a burning immediacy. It was to defend the Church against this danger—and events in Languedoc had made it clear just how grave the danger was—that the Council established its definitions of the Catholic Faith and of orthodoxy. Heretics, whether Cathars or Waldensians, from Languedoc, Italy, the Balkans, and other countries where they had smaller influence, were unconditionally condemned and anathematized. The sanctions to be taken against them were confirmed and redefined; and the Church laid upon secular authority the duty, under pain of excommunication, of fighting heresy.

Those temporal leaders who failed in this duty would be stripped of their rights by the Pope; he would then be free to bestow their domains upon any Catholic *seigneur* that desired them. The Council could hardly have underwritten the work of the Crusade more explicitly, or defined the Church's theocratic attitude with greater clarity. The Pope might not command the actual battalions to unseat kings; but through the decision of the Council he had arrogated to himself the legal right to do so—thus proclaiming the Church's absolute supremacy over secular law.

The Council's inaugural meeting took place on 11th November, 1215, with speeches from the Pope, the Patriarch of Jerusalem, and Thédise, Bishop of Agde, the former Legate in Languedoc. Right from the start the Council regarded itself as presenting an implicit justification of Simon de Montfort's work; though it was not till 30th November that the question of a definitive settlement in Languedoc was officially considered, As this settlement was of high political importance, and vitally concerned both the Occitan clergy and the dispossessed barons, it became the object of intense diplomatic activity, the latter being carried on at the same time as debates in Council. As Vaux de Cernay remarks, 'several of those who sat on the Council, even among the prelates, being against the interests of the Faith, strove for the re-establishment of the Counts [i.e. of Toulouse and Foix] in their domains.'[1]

The Council's decisions, to which we referred above, appeared to offer unqualified approval of the Crusade in principle: but then it had, as they thought, just come to an end. The Count of Toulouse, however, did not consider himself beaten yet. Though he had failed to get the French King's backing, at least he enjoyed that of the King of England, who had recently been reconciled with the Pope. To tell the truth, this was not a very strong trump card: the Pope relied far more on Philip's alliance than on that of the weak and capricious John Lackland, and his English sympathies did Raymond more harm than good. But at least he had one zealous supporter among the English clergy in the Abbot of Beaulieu. He could also count on the backing of the former Legate, Arnald-Amalric, now Archbishop of Narbonne and Primate of all Languedoc: this prelate had all the greater potential value to him through being one of the Crusade's main leaders. Finally, he was also relying on his personal influence, and the juridical weight of his arguments. The Count could also emphasize the fact that he had already gone a good deal further along the path of submission than was required of him. Since—however mistakenly—his own person appeared so suspect in the eyes of the Pope's representatives, he had abdicated and made over all his domains to his son, who, as a mere youth, could not be harbouring a grudge against any living soul. All the Count asked was to be allowed to give the boy a decent Catholic upbringing; for himself, he was only too willing to go abroad—to the Holy Land or anywhere else. Raymond had brought his son over from England for the occasion—the boy was old enough to take part in these discussions, and young enough to charm the assembly with his adolescent grace. It is not beyond the bounds of possibility that the Pope himself was touched by the spectacle of this youthful princeling, the nephew and grandson of kings, whom he must perforce sacrifice to considerations of State. The sympathetic treatment which (according to the *Chanson*) he lavished on the young man was not, in all likelihood, mere hypocrisy.

As his attitude to Raymond VI and his switches of policy over the affair of the King of Aragon suggest, Innocent III would appear to have been, up to a certain point, an impulsive man, and one open to persuasion. It is, nevertheless, very unlikely that he ever genuinely supported the Count of Toulouse, as both William of Tudela's continuator and even Vaux de Cernay (who tactfully criticizes him for it) assert in their respective accounts of the matter.

The author of the *Chanson* was hostile to the Crusade, and appears to have been well informed concerning the debates that preceded the final decision of the Council. He had every reason for crediting the Pope (who was already dead at the time he wrote) with statements condemnatory of Simon de Montfort. In point of fact Innocent's hesitations, whether sentimental or diplomatic, could only have been a piece of bluff, designed to minimize his own responsibility in an affair where (as he knew only too well) ecclesiastical authority was benefiting at the expense of common law. Having, through the Council's vote, established a legal principle, he could hardly now utter a sincere condemnation of that principle's application in practice.

Nevertheless the account which the *Chanson* gives us of these debates must correspond to the truth, in broad outline if not in detail. The episode which it portrays was of vital concern to all the interested parties; there were large numbers of witnesses from both sides; and the whole thing must have received considerable publicity in either camp. Therefore the author must at least have been able to give the speeches a discreet slant in the direction he supposed favourable to his thesis. His description of the Pope being disturbed and worried by the arguments, and going out into his garden for relaxation—where he was followed and harried by the Occitan bishops, all talking at once and accusing Innocent of excessive favouritism to the Counts—this, surely, is drawn from the life; there is no touch of the *chanson de geste* about it. Nor can there be any doubt that the Pope's attitude lent itself to equivocal interpretation.

Simon de Montfort had not come in person to this meeting, judging that he would be better employed in Languedoc; he sent his brother Guy as his representative. Besides, he knew that he had no lack of worthy advocates, since the higher clergy of Languedoc were for him to a man. Since the bulk of the Council members were prelates, the Count's cause could be written off in advance; ecclesiastical solidarity could scarcely fail to swing in favour of the side which the bishops were backing.

The Count of Toulouse, no doubt regarding himself as too great a personage to plead his own cause, left the brief for his defence in the hands of the Count of Foix. Raymond-Roger, whose eloquence was on a par with his gallantry, showed himself, in any case, a good deal more aggressive than his liege lord. But all of them—the Counts of Foix, Toulouse and Béarn alike—loudly proclaimed that they had never tolerated or encouraged heresy:[2]

> I can honestly swear [Raymond-Roger said] that I have never loved heretics; that I shun their company; and that in no respect are my feelings in agreement with theirs. Since Holy Church has in me an obedient son, I am come hither to your [i.e. the Pope's] Court to be faithfully judged, I and the puissant Count my *seigneur*, and his son likewise, a noble and well-favoured youth, who has never wronged any living soul. . . . The Count my *seigneur*, lord of vast domains, has placed himself at your discretion by delivering up to you Provence, Toulouse and Montauban, whose inhabitants were thereafter given over to that most evil and brutal of enemies, Simon de Montfort, to be enslaved, hanged, and exterminated without mercy. . . .

Now the Count of Foix here tampered with the truth at least in one respect, since his sister and his wife had both become *perfectae* in Catharist convents; another sister had turned Waldensian; and the Ariège district was a notorious centre of heresy. All this was pointed out by Foulques, the Bishop of Toulouse; the Count was not, however, disturbed in the least as a result. In order to rouse the indignation of his listeners, Foulques spoke of

> . . . . those pilgrims whom the Count slaughtered and cut to pieces, so many of them indeed that the field of Montgey is still covered with their remains; France still mourns them, and you [*sc.* the Count?] stand dishonoured by their fate! Outside the gates can be heard the fearful cries and lamentations of the blind and mutilated, the outlaws, who can no longer stir abroad without a guide; the man responsible for such butchery, such cripplings, such torture, is no longer worthy to have mastery over his lands!

Foulques was here referring to the massacre, by the Count of Foix, of a detachment of Crusaders near Montgey.

Raymond-Roger protested violently at this, and his answer brought the quarrel back on to its real ground: never, he exclaimed, had he attacked[3]

> ... any worthy pilgrim ... making his pious way to some holy shrine. But as for these thieves, these traitors without either Faith or honour, who wear the Cross that has been our ruin—why, it is true that any one of them who has fallen into the hands of me or mine has lost his eyes, his feet, his hands or his fingers.

It was clearly most audacious of him to attack the Crusade's supreme commander in this way; the Count apparently refused to believe that the 'righteous' Pope to whom he now appealed could conceivably have promised remission of sins to these same 'thieves and traitors'. It was an impressive plea, and probably authentic, since the accusation of cruelty brought against Raymond-Roger figured very largely in this debate. Moreover the Count launched a vigorous counter-attack, the target of which was the Bishop of Toulouse himself, no less: Raymond-Roger accused him of prime responsibility for all the evil done in Languedoc:

> As to this Bishop—for all his vehemence I tell you that through him, in person, both we and God have been betrayed. ... When he was made Bishop of Toulouse, so great a fire swept across this land that never will water suffice to put it out. More than five hundred thousand, old and young, has he destroyed, body and soul. By the faith I owe you, this man's deeds and words and conduct make him appear, not so much a Legate of Rome, but rather Antichrist!

The Count was trying to present the Crusade as a mere exploit in banditry, where the Pope counted for nothing; and the Pope himself felt constrained to remind those present that his followers were supposed to march 'as ones who had seen the Light, bearing fire, water, forgiveness, enlightenment, with mild penance and frank humility', though he also added, 'Let them carry the Cross *and the sword*'. He also recalled that Catholics had fallen in this war; it was not heretics only who were its victims. Then he let other advocates for the defence have their say, in particular Renaud, Archdeacon of Lyons (later excommunicated for heresy), who declared that the Church should protect Count Raymond: 'The Count,' he said, 'was one of the first to join the Crusade; he has defended the Church, and done her bidding; if the Church, who should protect

G

him, instead brings accusations against him, she will be at fault, and
her reputation will sink. . . .' The Archbishop of Narbonne, Arnald-
Amalric, similarly begged the Pope not to let himself be influenced
by the Count's enemies. Coming from a man who had for years
hounded Count Raymond unmercifully, such a remark may strike
us as surprising; but it can easily be explained by the Archbishop's
hatred of De Montfort. We may wonder just how much trust the
Pope still placed in the opinion of this former Legate, who was now
setting the interests of his Narbonne archbishopric above those of
the Church as a whole.

During this debate, in the course of which the Counts of Toulouse
and their vassals were to be dispossessed of their rights for heresy
(or, at least, for a complaisant attitude to heresy), there was never any
argument over heresy as such; everyone rejected it with equal
fervour. The Count of Foix even described his sister, the venerable
and much-revered Esclarmonde, as 'an evil woman and a sinful';
they were all irreproachable Catholics, trusting in the Pope's justice,
a fact which made the latter's position extremely delicate, despite
everything. This is why he made a show of having his hand forced
so as to grant Simon de Montfort the investiture which his supporters
demanded; why he claimed only to be yielding to a majority-vote
of the Church's representatives. It must remain a subject for debate
whether he actually uttered the following words: 'Let Simon hold
this country, and rule it! My lords, since I may not deprive him of it,
let him guard it well if he can, and take care that his claws be not
clipped; for never while I live shall Crusade be preached to go to his
succour.'[4] Innocent himself died the following year; but his successors preached one Crusade after another to help De Montfort,
and later his son. The Pope must have been the first to realize that
heresy, far from having been stamped out, was now attracting the
sympathy (whether avowed or secret) of many who might well have
condemned it before 1209. To ensure that the cause of the Church
triumphed he could only rely upon armed force; and that meant
Simon de Montfort. Compared with the danger that heresy represented in his eyes, the injustice done to the Count of Toulouse was a
very minor matter: for this theocratic theoretician, justice could only
reside in that which furthered the Church's cause.

The Council's decree, promulgated on 14th December, 1215, ran
as follows:

Raymond, Count of Toulouse, having been found guilty on both these
indictments, and his inability to govern these domains according to the

Faith having been long since demonstrated by divers sure tokens, is hereby forever excluded from exercising authority therein, where his hand has all too heavily lain hitherto; and he shall dwell henceforth in a place to be agreed beyond his frontiers, there to do fitting penance for his sins. If he in all humility do obey this decree, he shall receive for his upkeep a yearly sum of four hundred marks. It is further decreed that all those lands which the Crusaders have won from the heretics, their followers, agents or receivers, together with the city of Montauban and also that of Toulouse, where heresy is most rife, shall be bestowed upon the Count de Montfort, that gallant Catholic gentleman, who has done more than any other person in this affair, that he might hold those lands from whom he must needs in right and duty have them. The remainder of the country that is not as yet conquered by the Crusaders will be placed, according to the Church's commandment, under the protection of those best able to maintain and defend the interests of peace and of the Faith; that thus provision may be made for the Count of Toulouse's only son when he comes of age, and that if he show himself worthy he may obtain the whole, or a portion only of his patrimony if that be more fitting.

This decree speaks eloquently enough for itself: never can any victor have imposed conditions on his defeated opponent with haughtier self-assurance. By a species of verbal jugglery of which the Council do not even seem to have been aware, a military victory that was due partly to chance, and partly to the strategical skill of a good general, became instead a victory of Christian truth over error. The way had been prepared for this step by the Crusaders' triumphs in the Holy Land: such campaigns were peculiarly inhumane because the infidel was not entitled to be regarded as a man. But Islam could still inspire that instinctive respect which is due to a Great Power.

The Church's activities on Christian soil were coming to resemble those of a judge who sets about the accused with a big stick, and then forbids him to act in self-defence because the person of a judge is sacrosanct. It is remarkable to find that in the whole of this venerable assembly, which contained prelates from every Catholic country, there were so few people capable of seeing just how odious such an attitude was; or, indeed, of understanding that such a judge puts himself, morally speaking, a good deal lower than the prisoner (even though the latter were guilty) and deserves nothing better than a taste of his own big stick. To explain such an attitude we must needs assume that heresy was at this point a good deal more powerful and widespread than the documents in our possession might suggest.

This Lateran Council took the moral defeat of the Church, sanctified it, and erected it into a law. The Pope had not been unaware of the atrocities committed by the Crusaders: the day after Béziers was taken, the Abbot of Cîteaux had written to him, with appalling frankness: 'Nearly twenty thousand of these people were put to the sword, *without regard for age or sex*'; and yet the Pope's only reaction was to congratulate his Legate. The complaints lodged by the Counts, the consuls, and the King of Aragon; the reports of De Montfort's victories, the burnings, the massacres, the devastation of lands and crops—all these had passed through the chancellery of the Holy See, and neither the Pope nor the cardinals could have been unaware of them. The bishops, sitting in full Council, had heard the accusations which the Occitan barons brought against the Crusaders—accusations that no one had sought to deny. The Bishop of Toulouse might wax sentimental over slaughtered 'pilgrims', but everyone knew perfectly well that these pilgrims had struck the first blow.

Not one Conciliar decision stigmatized the atrocities committed by the Soldiers of Christ, or proscribed such conduct for the future. On the contrary, indeed: Simon de Montfort—'that gallant Catholic gentleman'—was recompensed for having 'done more than any other person in this affray'; and everyone knew just how he had done it. The Pope's scruples, it would seem, derived not so much from an aversion to bloodshed as from a disinclination to take harsh action against someone who might carry weight in political matters. When all was said and done, young Raymond was decidedly less innocent than the new-born infants slaughtered at Béziers.

After the Council's decision it would be unfair to censure the fanaticism of a Foulques or an Arnald-Amalric, the brutality of a Simon de Montfort; the Pope—and the Church through the voice of her prelates—had absolved them of their crimes.

All that remained was for the Count of Toulouse to retire to the place of exile 'beyond his frontiers' that was assigned to him. Innocent III offered him a few polite condolences, and showed himself full of solicitude for the young Raymond, whom he counselled to follow God in all things—even (if we are to credit the *Chanson*) holding out hope to him that he might one day reconquer the lands he had lost. An invention of the chronicler's, or consolatory politenesses spoken by an old man to a child? Whichever it may have been, the young Count learnt by experience: never again did he turn to the Pope's justice in order to defend his rights.

Simon de Montfort, having learnt of the Council's decree confirming him as overlord of the lands he had won, now only needed to receive investiture at the hands of the King of France in order to become Count of Toulouse.

It is significant that his first act of (more or less) sovereign authority should have been aimed against the Archbishop of Narbonne, his former ally and the principal instrument of his elevation. As possessor of the Count of Toulouse's domains, Simon was in fact entitled to be called Duke of Narbonne, as the Counts had always been. Now from 1212 onwards the Legate had arrogated this title to himself; and the hostility between the two men had grown steadily deeper and more venomous. Both had appealed to Rome, and the Pope had given a ruling in favour of the Archbishop (2nd July, 1215). We know that when Arnaud joined the Council he did everything in his power to hinder De Montfort's cause, and the latter was not to forgive him. Doubtless he found the man's arrogance even more insufferable: Arnald-Amalric boasted to all and sundry of having 'loaded De Montfort with honours'. Simon, with some justification, was of the opinion that he owed his good fortune to his own efforts.

So here were these two enemies, facing one another in a conflict that must have filled the Occitans' hearts with joy—though the Archbishop was hardly a match for a man of De Montfort's stature. Still, he marched into Narbonne as though he owned the place, forced Viscount Aimery to render him homage, and gave orders for the rebuilding of the walls, which Simon (with Prince Louis's approval) had had pulled down. When his rival protested, the Archbishop replied: 'If the Count de Montfort is attempting to usurp the Duchy of Narbonne, and in any way hinders the rebuilding of the city walls, I shall excommunicate him, and his followers, and all who proffer him advice or counsel.' How are we to explain this irascible old prelate's complete change of front? He was to defend his city of Narbonne no less passionately than he had once defended the Church against heresy. The day Simon attempted to force his way into the city, the Archbishop rushed off with his troops to bar the way; roughly handled by De Montfort's knights, he fled to the Cathedral, whence he pronounced a solemn sentence of excommunication on the Crusader general, and placed every church in the city under interdict for as long as the 'usurper' violated its territory.

Simon did not let this move intimidate him. He had Mass celebrated in the castle chapel, and rang all the bells furiously during the ceremony. Was the Archbishop's position, then, so uncertain? Could Simon de Montfort thus openly challenge the spiritual leader of a country in which he was no more than secular overlord? At all events, this episode reveals the ageing conqueror as a presumptuous and exceedingly vain man, so drunk with his own power that he struck out blindly at any show of opposition.

Having thus paraded his authority over Narbonne, Simon marched to Toulouse, arriving on 7th March, 1216. He made the consuls swear allegiance both to himself and to his son and heir, Amaury; he also took steps to ensure the city remained harmless for the future. Such walls as still stood were pulled down. The defensive towers on the burghers' town houses were demolished or greatly reduced, and the chain barriers removed from the cross-roads. Then he reinforced the defences of the Château de Narbonne, his personal residence, and isolated it from the town proper by a large moat, which he had filled with water. All these precautions go to show that though he may have regarded this city as his by right, he knew that here more than in most places he stood on hostile soil.

Then, at last, he set off on his journey to Paris, where, garlanded with victory and strong in the Holy See's support, it only remained for him to undergo his solemn investiture at the hands of the French King. Doubtless after so many years of warfare this brief sojourn in his native land, where he was welcomed as a national hero, came like balm to his soul: he must have forgotten what it was like to be admired and acclaimed. De Cernay is probably guilty of slight exaggeration, but he must nevertheless be using solid evidence when he writes: 'What honours were done him in France I could not here set down, nor would the reader believe them if I did. Every city, château and village along his route turned out to greet him in procession, clergy and people together; their devotion reached such heights of holiness and piety that a man reckoned himself blessed if he so much as touched the fringe of De Montfort's cloak.'[5] The common folk, carried away by their priests, would seem to have viewed him as a latter-day St George, who had slain the dragon of heresy.

The King, 'after a pleasant and intimate discussion' [Vaux de Cernay] duly performed the investiture. In a decree given at Melun on 10th April, 1216, the following announcement was made: 'We have taken for Our liegeman Our trusty and well-beloved Simon, Count de Montfort, in respect of the County of Toulouse, the Viscountcies of Béziers and of Carcassonne: to wit, those fiefs and lands which Raymond, formerly Count of Toulouse, held from Us, and which now have been won from heretics and the enemies of Christ's Church.'

Thus did the King docilely submit to the decision of the Church; we may reasonably suppose that he was not exactly displeased at one of his vassals laying hands on territory where his influence had hitherto been negligible. Acclaimed and victorious, by the sovereign decree of Pope and King created one of the premier barons in the Kingdom of France, Simon de Montfort was, nevertheless, to find (on returning to his new domains) that his writ only ran where he stood armed from head to toe, his men behind him; not an inch further.

2. The War of Liberation

In April 1216 the old Count of Toulouse and his son disembarked at Marseilles. Provence, according to the decree of the Lateran Council, formed part of young Raymond's future patrimony; but his father, who instead of remaining abroad to complete his penance had decided to come back with him, clearly was not going to let the youth rest content with 'the remainder of the country that is not as yet conquered by the Crusader'. The Council's sentence, in fact, now gave the signal for a general revolt.

The Counts were given an enthusiastic reception in Marseilles, and the news of their arrival spread throughout the surrounding countryside. Avignon sent messengers to them, and as soon as they appeared outside the walls, a delegation of barons and burghers received them on bended knees, and offered them the town. 'Sir Count of Saint-Gilles,' said the leader of this delegation (as we read in the *Chanson*), 'we humbly beg you and your well-beloved son, being of our own blood and lineage, to accept this our honourable pledge: all Avignon greets you as *seigneur*, and each of us delivers into your keeping his person and his possessions, the city elders, the public gardens and town gates', etc. The Count lauded the men of Avignon for the way they had welcomed him, and promised them 'the high esteem of *all Christendom* and of your own country; for you are bringing back chivalry, and Joy, and *Parage*.'[6]

Father and son now entered the city:

There was neither greybeard nor stripling who did not run through the streets for joy, and he who ran the fastest held himself fortunate. Some cried 'Toulouse!' in honour of the Count and his son, while others exclaimed 'Ah Joy! Henceforth God is with us!' With hearts resolved and eyes all wet with tears they gathered and knelt before the Count, and cried with one voice: 'Jesus Christ, Saviour most glorious, grant us the power and the strength to bring them both back to their inheritance!' So thick was the press round the procession that recourse was had to threats, and sticks and clubs were freely used.

Avignon had not been made to suffer either the ravages of war or the tyranny of French domination. The burst of enthusiasm which set the whole town at the feet of its despoiled and exiled *seigneur* was but one manifestation of that burning patriotism unleashed by war throughout the Southern province.

The larger part of Provence evinced the same sort of enthusiasm, the same urge to free their oppressed neighbours. Raymond VI assembled his forces in Avignon, where he also received homage from other towns and castellans, and held a council of war. The old Count decided to go over into Aragon, recruit troops there, and attack the enemy in the South: his aim was to liberate Toulouse. Meanwhile his son would besiege the town of Beaucaire, which was held by a garrison of De Montfort's.

This was to be a war without quarter, without any attempts at reconciliation; there were no more appeals to the Pope and the Legates. It was a war of liberation, pure and simple, a new sort of 'Holy War' fought in the name of Mercy and *Parage*, for Christ and for Toulouse. Because he had gone as far as any man could go in his policy of submission, his confidence in Papal Justice, the dispossessed Count returned home wearing a martyr's halo, as one who had been sacrificed to the Church's tyranny. To the population of Languedoc, be they Catholic or heretic, the Church was by now an enemy no less heartily detested than De Montfort himself. The Count—defeated, mocked, humiliated—had only to show his face to be borne off in triumph, with tears of joy being shed all around him and shouts of welcome ringing in his ears. He did not as yet dare to plunge into the fray himself, preferring to reserve this moment for Toulouse. It was his son, the real Count (since his father had abdicated in the boy's favour) who now set about the task of reconquest.

Young Raymond first led his Avignon troops against Beaucaire; the inhabitants of the town welcomed him with an offer to hand over their French garrison. Though he entered Beaucaire as a liberator, the young Count did not manage to capture the garrison. This body, under the command of Marshal Lambert de Croissy (or de Limoux, from the name of the lands granted him in Languedoc), now retreated into the fortress, where it prepared to stand siege. Guy de Montfort, Simon's brother, together with Amaury de Montfort, hurried to Beaucaire to relieve the garrison, and sent messengers to Simon, who was on his way back from France. On 6th June De Montfort arrived before the town in person.

He first tried to take Beaucaire by assault, and failed. Since the town's supply lines were linked with its port, there was no danger of a shortage of food or water. Supplies came in constantly, by the Rhône, from Avignon, Marseilles, and other towns in Provence. 'Thus the Crusaders found themselves besieging, in a manner of speaking, every city which dispatched supplies—that is, the whole of Provence.'[7] Simon de Montfort had with him only his personal troops, together with some mercenaries and indigent knights who had accompanied him from France in the hope of enriching themselves. To besiege Beaucaire required siege-engines and a properly fortified camp, and there simply was not enough manpower for the job. The beleaguered garrison was in sore straits, and Lambert de Limoux had the black flag hoisted to show his leader he could not hold out much longer.

Every one of De Montfort's attacks was beaten off. 'There were few local men-at-arms, and those that there were lacked enthusiasm, and were of little use to the Army of Christ; whereas their adversaries were both bold and staunch.'[8] Frenchmen taken prisoner were hanged or mutilated, and their severed feet used as missiles. The garrison, though starving and decimated, continued to hold out; but every attempt by the Crusaders to break into the town was a failure. For three months Simon de Montfort persisted in these assaults; all of them, to the growing delight of his adversaries, were repulsed. His army was immobilized, and his officers' energy (not to mention their patience) seriously depleted. Here was a general whose chief outstanding virtue was never to abandon his men in the hour of peril; though the siege might be condemned to failure, he could not permit himself to raise it. And Lambert, in dire extremities, now once more hoisted the black flag.

Hearing that the old Count had recrossed the Pyrenees at the head of an army, and was advancing on Toulouse, Simon decided to negotiate. He asked for his men's lives to be spared; granted this condition, he would raise the siege. Raymond accepted these terms, though since he held the upper hand all round he was in no way obliged to do so. The garrison which had held out so valiantly capitulated on 24th August, and was handed over intact to De Montfort.

Having thus with great difficulty saved his honour and considerably damaged his prestige, the invincible Simon de Montfort was now obliged to beat a retreat. He had been baulked by a youth of nineteen, whose experience in the profession of arms was nil. Now he marched towards the Pyrenees to meet the old Count. The latter, however, carefully avoided an encounter by withdrawing into Spain once more; he knew his opponent too well, and had no intention of prejudicing his chances by a defeat—especially when his son's success had filled the whole conquered country with fresh hope. So Simon fell back on Toulouse. He knew all about the city's unshakeable loyalty to its Counts, and calculated that he could damage them most by striking at their seat.

This new 'legitimate suzerain', in fact, intended to requite the city for what he regarded as its treachery: he spoke of destroying it utterly. This scheme was as impractical as it was monstrous, but up to a point we can understand it. Experience and intuition had taught Simon just how much power resided in a major city, and the vast part it could play in a country's resistance. While Toulouse stood, the Counts would never be defeated, since the whole organic life of the area was centred and orientated on its capital.

The men of Toulouse, terrified at De Montfort's approach, hurriedly sent off a delegation to him with protestations of loyalty. But in the face of the new Count's frankly hostile attitude, and the excesses committed by the troops who formed his advance guard, the burghers revolted. Simon stormed into the unfortified city, sword in hand, and set fire to three of Toulouse's main quarters: Saint-Remésy, Joux-Aigues, and St Stephen's Square. But the burghers 'opposed force by force. They laid barricades of beams and barrels across the open squares to block their assailants' advance; they repelled every attack, labouring the whole night through without respite, fighting not only the enemy, but also spreading fires.'[9] The new Count's first entry into his capital after his investiture could hardly have taken place more inauspiciously.

Toulouse welcomed the master thus set over them with such an explosion of wrath that the French knights were held, beaten off in fierce hand-to-hand street fighting, and finally forced to take refuge in the Cathedral. The burghers surged forward to the barricades, brandishing improvised weapons, 'sharpened hatchets, bill-hooks or pestles, clutching longbow or crossbow. . . .'[10] While the fire raged on, Simon rode hither and thither through the city, in an endeavour to regroup his forces. He organized a charge down the street called Straight—'a furious charge which made the earth tremble'; he tried to force the Cerdan Gate and open a way to the faubourg. When his attack finally failed, he withdrew to the Château Narbonnais, that residence which, as a wise precaution, he had so strongly fortified several months earlier.

The rioters had, indeed, won; but De Montfort still disposed of sufficient troops in the area to avenge this set-back. The burghers possessed neither fortresses nor a regular army, and could not rely on any rapid reinforcements. Bishop Foulques undertook to restore peace between the new Count and the rebels.

The author of the *Chanson* presents the Bishop's conduct at this juncture in a particularly odious light. Foulques, in an unctuous and ingratiating speech, protested his utter devotion to his flock, and guaranteed them, under oath, and with the Church as surety, De Montfort's pardon together with protection for their persons and property, which were to remain inviolate. But once the burghers were disarmed and in Simon's power, it appears, Foulques encouraged him to treat them with great severity. In fact, the Bishop acted with conscious and deliberate perfidy; and it has been suggested that the writer (whose distaste for Foulques is only too obvious) has blackened the picture somewhat. But all that we know concerning the behaviour of this redoubtable bishop during the Crusade, and the hatred which he inspired throughout his life in the folk of Toulouse, would appear to indicate that the chronicler was hardly exaggerating. Foulques felt personal resentment against the city for daring to go counter to his own expressed wishes.

The consuls agreed to discussions, and Simon appeared in person at the City Hall to sign the truce agreement; but no sooner had the burghers been disarmed than French troops moved into all the better fortified houses, and the more notable citizens were arrested. Simon confiscated their possessions and expelled them from Toulouse. 'Forth from the gates went the banished ones: knights, burghers, bankers, the flower of the citizenry, escorted by a troop of armed and angry soldiers, who belaboured them with blows, threats, curses and insults, and forced them to move at the double. . . .'[11] Having thus rid himself of the richest and most influential burghers, Simon next published an edict throughout the area, calling upon all persons capable of handling a pick and shovel to come to Toulouse and set about the city's demolition:

Then might you have seen houses and towers, walls, rooms, fortifications, all collapsing together. They demolished living quarters and workshops, colonnades, frescoed chambers, vaultings and portals and lofty pillars. So great a noise came from every quarter, such dust and fracas and hammering and banging, that all was mingled in one, and the sound was as of an earthquake, or a roll of thunder, or beaten drums.

The agony of Toulouse now reached its apogee:[11]

All through the city rose the sound of wailing and lamentation: husbands, wives, children, sons, fathers, mothers, sisters, uncles, brothers and many persons of substance, all weeping. 'Ah God,' they cried, one to the other, 'what cruel masters! O Lord, see how you have delivered us into the hands of brigands! Either give us back our lawful *seigneurs*, or let us die!'

In fact Simon did not want to destroy the whole city, but only the more heavily fortified quarters. Nevertheless, despite the advice of certain of his friends, including his own brother, he now decided to show no mercy. Since he could clearly expect nothing else from the men of Toulouse, his one concern now was to use his advantage in order to plunder the city itself: he needed money badly. He gave out that he would issue a pardon in return for thirty thousand silver marks: so vast a sum was this that it led Puylaurens to suppose that De Montfort was egged on to demand it by treacherous counsellors who desired the relief of the town and the return of the Counts. We need not look so far afield: the inhabitants of Toulouse could hardly have been exasperated any more than they already were. Simon, then, had nothing to lose. He was relying on his soldiers to bleed the city white, and thought he had nothing more to fear from the citizen body, now both disarmed and deprived of their leaders.

So Simon left Toulouse, where the inhabitants were 'unhappy, sad, afflicted, miserable, weeping and suffering, eyes brimming with hot tears . . . for they were left neither flour, nor cheese, nor ciclatoun [i.e. cloth-of-gold] nor purple nor any fine raiment. . . .'[12] He made his way to Bigorre, to negotiate a new agreement that carried both political and financial implications: he wanted to obtain, for his second son Guy, the hand of Petronilla, who was Bernard de Comminges' daughter and heir to Bigorre through her mother's line. Petronilla, already married *en secondes noces* to Nuno Sanche, the Count of Roussillon's son, was separated from her husband and given in marriage to young Guy, who wed her at Tarbes on 7th November, 1216, and thus came into possession of the County of Bigorre. After these hastily celebrated nuptials, and another setback at the fortress of Lourdes, which he failed to storm, Simon—being by now once more short of cash—went back to Toulouse to demand something more in the way of taxes. This time there was a levy on absentees—that is to say, on those persons whom he had expelled himself.

De Montfort was not yet strong enough to undertake a campaign against the Counts of Toulouse, who were themselves at present preparing for a new offensive in Provence—an area so far untouched by the war, and solidly devoted to their cause. He therefore decided to set about his most implacable enemy Raymond-Roger, the Count of Foix, and attempt to crush him, at least, into obedience. He began by laying siege to the château of Montgaillard (or Montgrenier) which was held by that doughty warrior's son. The château capitulated on 25th March. It seemed as though the whole business was beginning all over again, and Simon must needs besiege every stronghold in the country, one by one. In May he took Pierrepertuse, in the Termenès area, after which he made for Saint-Gilles, whose inhabitants had risen in revolt, driven out their abbot, and were now refusing him entry to their town.

The wind had changed now, beyond a shadow of doubt. Simon was no longer the Crusader general, but a man trying to hold on to what he had won. Innocent III died on 15th July, 1216; his successor, Honorius III, had not yet had time to appreciate how the situation in Languedoc was changed. The new Legate, Bertrand, cardinal-priest of SS. John and Paul, met everywhere with such flat hostility that the towns actually shut their gates on him. The Counts of Toulouse were masters of Provence; young Raymond now styled himself 'young Count of Toulouse, son of Lord Raymond by the Grace of God Duke of Narbonne, Count of Toulouse, and Marquis of all Provence', openly rejecting the decisions of the Lateran Council, and the authority of the King of France.

Simon de Montfort's failure before Beaucaire had meanwhile produced a vigorous reaction from the ecclesiastical authorities. The year 1217 was to see a fresh contingent of Crusaders descending on Languedoc, the Council having now made a general, unlimited grant of Indulgences (exactly similar to those enjoyed by Holy Land Crusaders) to any person who henceforth took up the Cross against heretics, in any land whatsoever. With the aid of these fresh reinforcements (led respectively by the Archbishop of Bourges and the Bishop of Clermont) Simon now captured the fortresses of Vauvert and Bernis, and crossed the Rhône at Viviers. If he could not undertake the conquest of Provence, at least he intended to intimidate his opponent. The arrival of the new Crusaders, and the military aid which the troops of the local bishops provided, had some slight effect: Adhémar de Poitiers, Count of Valentinois, made his submission, even offering to betroth his son to one of Simon's daughters. But the latter had no more time to waste on Provence; he was hastily summoned back to Toulouse.

'The citizens of Tolosa' [i.e. Toulouse], wrote Vaux de Cernay, 'or rather, Dolosa [i.e. the city of trickery: the pun cannot be reproduced in English], impelled by a diabolical instinct, and being apostate from God and his church,'[13] received within their walls Count Raymond himself, at the head of an army of Aragonese troops and *faidits*. Now Simon's entire family was inside the Château de Narbonnais—his wife, his brother's wife, not to mention those of his sons, and grandchildren of both the De Montfort brothers.

The château itself was held by De Montfort's garrison; but the Count's army had approached the walls and, taking advantage of a heavy mist, forded the Garonne by the Bazacle mill and entered Toulouse on 13th September, 1217. The Count was given a triumphal welcome:[14]

When those in the town recognized the banners [of the Count], they approached him as though he were risen from the grave. And when he came into the city through the postern gate, all the inhabitants ran to meet him, young and old, knights and ladies, men and women of the commonalty, and knelt before him, and kissed his garments, his feet, legs, arms, and several fingers. He was acclaimed with tears of joy, for this was the return of prosperity, rich in flowers and fruit!

It was not yet prosperity; but there was, now, a chance of fighting. Raymond VI had assembled all his vassals—the Counts of Foix and Comminges, the exiled *seigneurs* of Toulouse, and those from Gascony, Quercy, and the Albi district; the *faidit* knights, who had taken to the woods or lived in exile in Spain, and for whom this return to Toulouse was the very symbol of liberation. ' . . . And when they saw the city, none was so lacking in feeling that his eyes did not fill with tears; and each man said to himself, Holy Mary, give me back the place where I was bred! Better to live and die there than wander through the world in want and shame.'[15]

Every Frenchman who had not taken refuge inside the fortress was slaughtered; but the citadel itself, being well-defended, could hold out for a considerable time. All Guy de Montfort's efforts to relieve it, however, were unsuccessful. This explained Simon's hurried arrival at the head of his troops, eager to launch an assault upon this rebellious city. But he was welcomed by such a hail of arrows and quarrels that his cavalry fell back in disorder, and his brother and younger son were both wounded. The men of Toulouse counter-attacked; the French were forced to beat a retreat, and resigned themselves to laying the city under siege.

Now if the Crusaders had previously been forced to reduce fortresses—and even towns such as Lavaur and Carcassonne—by starvation and the use of siege-artillery, then it follows that a city like Toulouse, being of considerable dimensions and set on a large river, was practically impossible to isolate. To do so would have demanded a far larger army even than that of the 1209 Crusade. The city no longer had its ramparts, but its inhabitants had wasted very little time. Hardly was the Count inside the limits before he had given orders to dig moats, build barricades of stakes and beams, and erect wooden barbicans. Despite their apparent fragility, these improvised fortifications held up well enough—so long as there were good defenders to man them, and not too overwhelming a superiority of numbers among the assailants. But not only were the military resources of the besieged superior to those of De Montfort; the entire civilian population, from the oldest man to the youngest boy, from the lady-chatelaine to the meanest maidservant, had transformed itself into a fighting militia, an auxiliary force:[16]

> Never in any city were such wealthy workers seen; for here they all set to, Counts and knights, burghers and their ladies, merchants both male and female, gentleman-bankers, boys, girls, sergeants and soldiers, each with a pick or a shovel . . . and each with his heart in this urgent task. At night all were on the alert: lamps and torches were set up in the streets, and there was a loud noise of drums, gongs, and fifes. Women and girls bore witness to the general rejoicing by dancing and singing gay ballads.

And during this siege the larger part of the demolished ramparts rose again, while the enemy looked on helplessly.

It was an unequal struggle. When Simon de Montfort left Provence he had forbidden the messenger who brought the letter from his wife, under pain of death, to mention the relief of Toulouse, or the Count's presence in the city; but the news had already spread throughout the entire country. The Provençal troops he intended to take with him now deserted. The forces that the Archbishop of Auch had mustered at Guy de Montfort's behest disbanded themselves *en route* and refused to march on the capital. The French soldiers and knights, the only men on whom Simon could rely, were immobilized in the various towns they had been required to garrison.

De Montfort launched an appeal to Catholic Christendom: Foulques once more quit Toulouse and, at the Cardinal-Legate's request, went into France to preach a Crusade against his own city as being a nest of rebels and heretics. De Montfort's wife, the Countess Alice, went in person to make her plea to the French King: perhaps she was relying on her personal connections (her brother was Constable of the King's army) rather than on the support of the King himself, who only appears to have favoured causes that were already won. Besides, De Montfort's reverses followed too soon upon his investiture for the King to concern himself with a vassal who had so weak a grasp upon his own domains.

It was, once again, the Pope who made an effort to save the situation. Honorius III started a new propaganda campaign against heresy, and did his best to bring down a new Crusade upon Languedoc. Just when it looked as though the first Christian country to turn against the Church had had its business settled once and for all, the whole task (it now transpired) was to do all over again—and under far harder conditions than had prevailed in 1208. The ardour of the Northern Crusaders had long ago evaporated; while the Church's adversaries were no longer a few pacifist heretics who abhorred all violence, and barons who were always ready to swear fidelity to her cause, but a whole people, who quite consciously and openly rejected her authority.

Toulouse continued to improve both her fortifications and provisioning, by land and water, under the eyes of a besieging force too weak to do anything except shut itself up in a fortified camp and await reinforcements. The engagements that continued throughout the winter were little more than brief skirmishes; but both camps vied with one another in their cruelty towards prisoners. Inside Toulouse hatred for the French rose to such a pitch that the wretches who were taken alive, after being paraded in triumph through the streets, had their eyes and their tongues gouged out; others were hacked to pieces while still alive, burnt, or dragged at a horse's crupper. In De Montfort's camp hatred was beginning to give way to despair.

The real conflict was resumed in the spring. All Simon de Montfort's attacks were beaten off so vigorously that his knights (according to the *Chanson*) displayed their exasperation quite openly. The author did not, in all probability, actually take part in Simon's conferences with his lieutenants; and the speeches he puts into the mouth of a Gervais de Champigny or an Alain de Roucy are doubtless imaginary. On the other hand there is nothing to show that the historian could not have drawn his inspiration from rumours actually current at the time in the French camp. One might well suspect him either of prudence or opportunism when one finds him attributing highly moderate proposals to Guy de Lévis or Guy de Montfort, whose sons (at the time when he wrote) were very firmly established in Languedoc; such would not be the case with regard to Foucaut de Berzy, a knightly brigand executed in 1221 by Raymond VII. During the long discussions which the French knights held with their leader, we can sense that they were at the end of their tether, nearly driven mad, and sorely tempted to put the responsibility for their failures squarely on Simon's shoulders; yet they remained loyal to the end, as much through their personal devotion to Simon as on account of that unity created between them by the atmosphere of hatred in which they moved. 'Pride and harshness have the mastery of you,' Alain de Roucy told his commander. 'You love what is cheerless and fainthearted.'[17]

At last the reinforcements of Crusaders from the North arrived: a contingent of Flemish troops, led by Michel de Harnes and Amaury de Craon. After a series of fierce engagements, Simon succeeded in occupying the Saint-Cyprian quarter, on the left bank of the river, and thence launched an assault on the bridges that gave access to the town proper; but the French failed to gain a footing on them, and were forced to retreat.

The siege had now been going on for eight months. At Pentecost the young Count arrived, bringing fresh reinforcements with him, and rode into the town under the besiegers' very noses. The populace welcomed him in positive transports of delight: people pressed forward to catch a glimpse of him, and gazed 'as though he were a blossom of the rose'. 'The Son of the Virgin, to comfort them [i.e. the people of Toulouse] sent joy upon them with an olive-branch, and a bright star, the morning star above the mountain-top. This brightness was the gallant young Count, the lawful heir, who crossed his threshold bearing the Cross and cold steel.'[18] The author here catches an echo of that impassioned affection which the people felt for their young hero of Beaucaire; and these lines alone enable us to gauge the great gulf which divided the two camps. One side knew exactly why they were fighting, and for whom; the other was merely trying to hold on to half-conquered loot that had already begun to slip through their grasp. Their anger and their pugnaciousness (both amply illustrated by the chronicler) stemmed from the humiliation of being held in check by men whom they deemed inferior to themselves, 'mere unarmed burghers'.

Despite the arrival of a sizeable troop of Crusaders commanded by the Count of Soissons, Simon had still scarcely begun to mount any adequate defence against the sallies of those under siege; and meanwhile Bertrand, the Legate, was reproaching him for his lack of ardour:[19]

Now the Count [i.e. De Montfort] was full of weariness and anxiety, being worn down by his losses and sore exhausted; nor could he bear with any patience the daily pin-pricks of the Legate, saying that he was an idle fellow, and grown cowardly. Whence it came, men say, that he prayed God to send him peace, and heal his grievous sufferings in death.

The Legate had an excellent case for pressing home his attack on the old warrior: a man who had won so many victories, and attributed them all to Divine Protection, must needs now, through his defeats, incur the suspicion of having committed some crime which had brought down God's wrath upon him. The gallant Catholic gentleman whom the Church had honoured so highly (granting him domains larger even than those of the King of France) and who enjoyed the aid of troops that the Church had been sending him for years, now suddenly revealed himself to be incapable of storming an ill-fortified town, defended by men whom he had whipped many times before.

In June—the ninth month of this catastrophic siege—De Montfort decided to construct a gigantic *chatte*, a mobile tower that could gradually be moved nearer and nearer to the enemy's ramparts. From the top of this erection his men would be able to overlook the besieged garrison's quarters, and plaster them with concentrated fire. The men of Toulouse, however, damaged the tower with shots from their stone-guns; and then, when it had been repaired and was ready to go into action once more, they made a dawn sortie and attacked the French camp from two sides. Simon was hearing Mass when a messenger told him that the men of Toulouse were already within the camp, and his Frenchmen falling back. After concluding his devotions Simon rushed into battle, and managed to drive the enemy back as far as the moat.

Guy de Montfort, who was busy guarding the siege-engines, was wounded by an arrow fired from the ramparts. As Simon hurried across to him, lamenting loudly, he was struck on the head by a stone from a stone-gun, which (the *Chanson* tells us) was served and fired by women and young girls. 'A stone flew straight to its proper mark, and smote Count Simon upon his helm of steel, in such wise that his eyeballs, brains, teeth, skull and jawbone all flew into pieces, and he fell down upon the ground stark dead, blackened and bloody.'[20]

This violent, instantaneous death, which took place at the height of the battle and in full sight of both camps, was greeted by the men of Toulouse with a great outburst of joy: 'The town and the very paving-stones rang to the sound of horns, trumpets, church bells ringing and hammering in glad carillons, drums, gongs, and bugles.'[21] This enormous clamour of relief was answered by a murmur of consternation from the French camp. The army had already lost enough heart over the setbacks endured during the siege, and the death of their commander produced total demoralization. De Montfort's son, having got the Legate to confirm him in his father's former titles, made an abortive attempt to set the town on fire, and then retired inside the Château Narbonnais. A month after his father's death he raised the siege.

Toulouse had triumphed. Amaury returned to Carcassonne, where he buried his father in great pomp; now he was to see the young Count win back from him, bit by bit, all the domains that Simon had held, and this despite the Pope's appeals and the intervention of the King of France in the person of his son. It was to take seven years of warfare to do it; but the invader had already suffered the *coup de grâce*. He slowly became less and less anxious to fight, abandoning towns and strongholds one after the other till he found himself, one fine day, with no troops and no money for his homeward journey.

With Simon de Montfort gone, the Crusade found itself, so to speak, decapitated. Besides, despite the efforts of the Pope and the Legates, this war had long ceased to be a Crusade. Amaury was struggling for his inheritance; and like all dictators' sons, he inspired neither terror in his foes nor yet trust in his putative supporters. When the Church, by the decision of the Council, dispossessed the Count of Toulouse, it seems to have escaped everyone's notice that Simon de Montfort was not immortal, and that though he himself could, in fact, 'hold' this country, he was the only man who could. After Simon's death the Pope found himself in the wholly ridiculous position which befalls someone who entrusts a crushing responsibility to a man obviously incapable of sustaining it. So very soon he turned away from the unfortunate Amaury, and disposed of his rights in favour of another ally, who possessed far greater power, and was endowed with prestige enough to influence every country in Western Christendom. It was the King of France who was to complete Simon de Montfort's work.

The author of the *Canzon de la Crozada* [*Chanson de la Croisade*] greets Simon's death with the following words:

Straightway they bore him to burial in Carcassonne, and celebrated the funeral service at the monastery of Saint-Nazaire. And those who can read may learn from his epitaph that he is a saint and a martyr; that he is bound to rise again to share the heritage, to flourish in that state of unparalleled felicity, to wear a crown and have his place in the Kingdom. But for my part I have heard tell that the matter must stand thus: if one may seek Christ Jesus in this world by killing men and shedding blood; by the destruction of human souls; by compounding murder and hearkening to perverse counsel; by setting the torch to great fires; by destroying the barons and dishonouring *Parage*; by winning lands through violence, and working for the triumph of vain pride; by fostering evil and snuffing out good; by slaughtering women and slitting children's throats—why, then he must needs wear a crown, and shine resplendent in Heaven.[22]

Whatever fate may be reserved to all eternity for Simon de Montfort's soul, those who admire Napoleon, Caesar, Alexander and their like will not be able, in all fairness, to withhold their admiration from this Great Captain. The rest will be at liberty to observe that he was, taken all in all, a somewhat mediocre sort of person, chosen to perform a brutal task, and acquitting himself in it about as well as he could have done. The moral responsibility for his acts lies less heavily upon him than it does on those who had the power to bless and to absolve them, in the name of Jesus Christ.

CHAPTER VII

THE KING OF FRANCE

1. *Raymond VII's Victory*

SIMON DE MONTFORT'S DEATH was received in Languedoc with quite extraordinary demonstrations of joy. This joyous atmosphere spread through the whole country like wildfire, bringing fresh strength to those who had long since despaired of the implacable tyrant's luck ever failing him, anywhere. De Montfort's death came like the end of a long nightmare; it was the miracle they had yearned for so long. A popular ballad of the period runs:

> *Montfort*
> *Es mort*
> *Es mort*
> *Es mort!*
> *Viva Tolosa*
> *Ciotat gloriosa*
> *Et poderosa!*
> *Tornan lo paratge et l'onor!*
> *Montfort*
> *Es mort!*
> *Es mort!*
> *Es mort!*

Honour and *Parage* were coming back; the tyrant—the folk of the Midi made themselves believe that every ill they now suffered from was De Montfort's doing—now lay in a rich vault in Carcassonne, a corpse merely. His friends made out that he was a martyr, comparing him to Judas Maccabaeus and St Stephen; by his death all the labour of the Crusade was undone. The relatives and comrades-in-arms whom he left in Languedoc were brave enough, a force to to be reckoned with—as long as they had their leader. But now they were useless: they had lost all faith in themselves.

Amaury de Montfort appealed for help to the King of France, while the Pope himself preached a new Crusade, and likewise pressed Philip to send an army into Languedoc. While this was going on

Raymond VII reconquered the Agenais and Rouergue regions, and won a clear victory in the field over his French opponents, outside Baziège.

So Prince Louis appeared a second time in the French Midi; and on this occasion his father raised no objections to his joining a Crusade. He brought with him twenty bishops, thirty Counts, six hundred knights and ten thousand archers: a formidable force, which should, on the face of it, have struck terror into the hearts of a population already exhausted by ten years' warfare. He joined up with Amaury de Montfort's troops before Marmande, and captured the town. A frightful massacre took place. The garrison and its leader, Centulle, Count of Astarac, were spared (with the intention of exchanging them against French prisoners) but the victors slaked their fury on the ordinary townsfolk:

. . . They hurried into the town, waving sharp swords, and it was now that the massacre and fearful butchery began. Men and women, barons, ladies, babes in arms, were all stripped and despoiled and put to the sword. The ground was littered with blood, brains, fragments of flesh, limbless trunks, hacked-off arms and legs, bodies ripped up or stove in, livers and hearts that had been chopped to pieces or ground into mash. It was as though they had rained down from the sky. The whole place ran with blood—streets, fields, river-bank. Neither man nor woman, young or old, survived; not a single person escaped unless they remained in hiding. The town was destroyed also; fire consumed it.[1]

The author of the *Chanson* reckons that the majority of the inhabitants were massacred. William the Breton records that there were slain at Marmande 'all the burghers, with their wives and children; every inhabitant, to the number of five thousand souls'.[2]

The slaughter was executed in cold blood—a long preliminary discussion took place as to how the garrison should be treated. It has been regarded as a symptom of Amaury's angry desire to avenge his father. But it is more likely that it was a conscious repetition of the massacre at Béziers, which had terrorized the inhabitants of Languedoc to such profitable effect. It is strange to find bishops and barons discussing the 'dishonour' they would bring upon themselves by putting soldiers to death, and subsequently unleashing their troops upon defenceless civilians, women and children included. It would appear that (for the Northern knights rather more than those of the Midi) burghers were beings who belonged to a lesser breed, and whose murder was a matter of little consequence. That pious prince, Louis, took no action to prevent this revolting piece of intimidation from being carried out. But ten years' warfare had seasoned the people of Languedoc, and they took care not to react (as they had done after Béziers) with a series of mass capitulations. The country had long since become inured to terrorism.

After this bloody exploit the King's army marched on Toulouse, and found the city well fortified and organized for resistance. Raymond VII had shut himself up there with a thousand of his knights. In the face of Prince Louis's threat he appealed to the townsfolk, and had the relics of St Exupère* exposed in the Cathedral crypt. For the third time, and with considerable enthusiasm, the people of Toulouse prepared to stand a siege.

The siege began on 16th June, 1219, and was raised on 1st August. The powerful forces of Prince Louis, having completely invested and cut off the city, launched several vigorous assaults against it— only to find that the besieged had not the slightest intention of capitulating. The Prince, who had come into Languedoc for the purpose of installing fear among its inhabitants—fear due to the prestige and might of his royal person—now realized that he had to do with a really tough opponent. He decided to act as those other Crusaders had done in the early years of the war, and leave Amaury de Montfort to maintain his position in the country as best he might, at his own risk and peril. Scarcely had his statutory forty days elapsed when Louis raised the siege, leaving his siege-engines behind.

This abrupt departure surprised his contemporaries: they attributed it variously to treachery on the part of the French knights, or a secret agreement between the Prince and Raymond, or even to mere base calculation on Louis's part: he coveted Toulouse and the surrounding countryside for himself, and was not in the least anxious to reconquer them for Amaury's benefit. Whatever the reason, however, this fresh triumph gained by the men of Toulouse represented a tremendous setback for their adversaries—which meant for the French Crown. The young Count's reputation continued to burgeon; and now it was the turn of the Midi nobility to drive out the usurping Northern barons who had occupied their lands, to strip them of *their* domains, and to wrest back from them the titles they had wrongfully assumed.

These barons had been settled by Simon de Montfort in the various châteaux and other fortresses which had fallen to him. The object of this was to ensure their loyalty. They were not, we may take it,

---

* A Bishop of Toulouse who defended the city against the Vandals in the fifth century. He died *c.* 411 A.D., and his feast-day is observed on 28th September, together with that of St Wenceslaus of Bohemia. (Trs.)

zealous upholders of the Faith, since the Catholic chronicler William
de Puylaurens describes them thus:[3]

> Howbeit one should not, nay, one could not recount the infamous
> conduct in which they [*sc.* 'the servants of God'] indulged. Most of them
> had concubines, whom they acknowledged publicly; they carried off
> other men's wives by force, and shamelessly committed both these and
> other similar outrages. Truly it was not in the spirit that had brought them
> hither they now acted thus: the end of the business was very different from
> its beginning.

Two of these knights, the brothers Foucaut and Jean de Berzy, were
little more than professional brigands, notorious for their greed and
their cruelty. Though, according to the *Chanson*, Amaury and
Prince Louis had such a high regard for them that they spared the
whole Marmande garrison simply to set them free, nevertheless
Puylaurens asserts that they killed all prisoners who could not pay
them the exorbitant sum of a hundred gold *sous*, and had, on one
occasion, forced a father to hang his own son. After being taken
prisoner by Raymond they were both beheaded.

The French garrison of Lavaur was massacred. Amaury's brother
Guy was wounded and died in captivity; and despite all efforts by the
Pope, who called upon the Counts—that is, young Raymond and
the Count of Foix—to make their submission, the French now
suffered one defeat after another. Alain de Roucy, the King of
Aragon's murderer, was killed in that same fortress of Montréal
which De Montfort had bestowed upon him. The reinforcements
which Amaury received from the Bishops of Clermont and Limoges
and the Archbishop of Bourges could not stop Raymond gaining
complete control of the Agenais and Quercy districts. Amaury now
held the South alone, where Narbonne and Carcassonne still
remained loyal to him.

Despite reiterated demands from the Pope, the King of France
refused to intervene in this affair. His son's defeat had discouraged
not only him but the great French barons as well; all those who
might otherwise have been drawn to Languedoc in the hope of
conquest were now, with Simon de Montfort's example before them,
having second thoughts on the matter. The young Count was going
from strength to strength; people once more remembered that he
was either cousin or nephew to most Western monarchs (crowned or
uncrowned), and their equal in birth. Now he made approaches to
the French King with a view to effecting his reconciliation with the
Church; he offered Philip his oath of allegiance in return for a fief

which the King had, five years before, bestowed upon Simon de Montfort.

We cannot tell what decision Philip II would finally have made in respect of this vassal whom the Church had dispossessed. Amaury de Montfort, seeing that the game was up, had offered him his domains, but the King had declined the offer: no doubt he preferred to let the two rivals exhaust each other in a struggle which involved him, personally, in no expense.

In August 1222 the old Count of Toulouse died, at the age of sixty-six. He had been the excuse for the Crusade if not its actual cause. He had been hunted, despoiled, humiliated, and made the object of every sort of calumny. He had been hated by the Church and revered by his own subjects. After an utter and crushing defeat he had returned in triumph, to be greeted as a saviour by his countrymen at a moment when he no longer had a possession to his name. He had been stripped of his rights by King and Church, and reconfirmed in them by the will of the people; and he died in the belief that his cause had triumphed. His son, to whom (officially, at any rate) he had had the good sense to make over his office, was already the national leader, and could carry on his work. The elimination of Amaury de Montfort was only a question of time. Languedoc had acquired, together with its freedom, the sort of national unity it had never known before the Crusade; and the Counts of Toulouse now enjoyed such popularity as they had never dreamed of.

Nevertheless the Count died excommunicate; and despite his wishes and prayers, he was deprived of the Last Sacraments when on his death-bed. Both his will and all the witnesses who came forward at the inquest (held on his son's orders) attested that he died in the Catholic Faith. He was affiliated to the Order of Knights Hospitallers, and had expressed a wish to be buried in the Hospital of St John of Jerusalem, which belonged to this Order.

His death was darkened by the misery of being debarred from the succour of religion; and after his death his body had to endure every indignity reserved for the excommunicate. Being forbidden burial in consecrated ground, the corpse lay for years in a coffin outside the cemetery, quite neglected, in a nearby garden. For a quarter of a century his son made vain petitions to the Holy See, but got no satisfaction for all his enquiries and diplomacy. Since little care was taken of the body it was eaten by rats, and its bones subsequently scattered. Later the skull was extracted from the coffin and kept by the Hospitallers.

After his father's death the young Count (he was by now twenty-six) went on with his methodical reconquest of the country. The French were now not even the hated tyrants of yesteryear, but simply undesirable aliens, who had to be put beyond the frontier with all dispatch. Both sides were exhausted by the war, and neither any longer regarded it as a vital necessity. In May 1223 a truce was concluded between the young Count and Amaury de Montfort: this truce served as preliminary to a Peace Conference, held at Saint-Flour. And though the two adversaries did not reach complete agreement at Saint-Flour, they at least contrived to ease the tension somewhat. Raymond, indeed, displayed enough goodwill towards Amaury to put away Sancha of Aragon and marry Amaury's sister.

Williams de Puylaurens[4] recounts how, during this truce, the Count made a joke in somewhat doubtful taste: one day when he was in Carcassonne as Amaury de Montfort's guest, he made it appear that he had been arrested. At this his followers fled in terror, and the two Counts had a good laugh together. We are told that Raymond VII was 'fond of laughter': was the same true of Amaury? Could the war in which their fathers had exhausted their resources and, finally, lost their lives be so soon treated as a joking-matter by these boys of twenty-five? Raymond's triumph carried no hatred with it; Amaury, though on the defensive, did not give way to despair. The two of them had known each other since adolescence; from the age of fifteen onwards they had lived in an atmosphere of bloodshed, cruelty, treachery and vengeance. By now they must have been heartily sick of hatred; and they were, in all likelihood, not the only ones.

When the truce failed to produce terms for peace, both sides appealed to the King of France, and a Council was held at Sens. But King Philip, who was already gravely ill, died before he could get there, on 14th July, 1223; and his son, being preoccupied with the more urgent tasks which his accession to his father's throne imposed upon him, failed to come to any decision in the matter. He contented himself with sending Amaury a subsidy of ten thousand silver marks; and the war continued.

Amaury's position became so critical that, despite the support given him by the aged Bishop of Narbonne, Arnald-Amalric, he could only keep on about twenty knights, for the most part old companions-in-arms of his father's. (Arnald-Amalric had by now quite forgotten his former hatred of De Montfort; he had even pledged some of his Church property to enable young Amaury to pay his troops.) In vain did Amaury offer his French estates in pawn; no one was any longer willing to advance him money. Yet the one thought he now had in mind was to organize his departure.

The Counts of Toulouse and of Foix, only too glad to be rid of him at last, signed a pact with Amaury on 14th January, 1224. They promised to respect the persons and property of those who had sided with De Montfort during the war, and to keep their hands off the garrisons that Amaury was leaving in Narbonne, Agde, Penne d'Albigeois, Valzergues and Termes. Carcassonne, Minerve and Penne d'Agenais remained, in theory at least, De Montfort's.

Amaury now left Carcassonne, taking the bodies of his father and brother with him. He was so hard pressed for money that he had to pledge his uncle Guy and several other knights to some Amiens merchants *en route*, for the sum of four thousand *livres*. Immediately after his departure Carcassonne was recaptured by the Counts, and handed over to young Raymond Trencavel, son of Viscount Raymond-Roger. The youthful prince returned to his rightful domains with the cheers of the inhabitants ringing in his ears; and fifteen years after the massacre of Béziers, Languedoc had its own former *seigneurs* (or at least their sons) restored to it. The people could, for a brief moment, fancy themselves back in the good old days of their independence.

2. *King Louis's Crusade*

But it all meant nothing. This independence was a mere phantom. From a juridical viewpoint it was challenged both by the Church and the Capetian dynasty of France. Practically, it was at the mercy of a new war—a thing which, in a country already exhausted and bled white, could no longer be endured.

To make good her losses Languedoc would have needed twenty or thirty years of peace; the respite given her in fact was barely two. Nor was it even a genuine respite; the prospect of yet another Crusade hung permanently above her head, and from the beginning of 1225 (less than a year, that is, after Amaury's departure) Pope Honorius III was energetically pressing the King of France to undertake it. The negotiations that took place between King and Pope meant a certain delay in the preparations for this Crusade, but were essentially a process of bargaining, by which the two allies sought to delimit their respective spheres of influence, and to extract promises and guarantees from one another for the future. But both of them knew that the work which had begun so well must now be brought, and quickly, to a successful conclusion, before their adversary had time to gather fresh strength.

The King answered the Pope's appeals by posing certain conditions. He demanded Plenary Indulgences for his Crusaders, together with excommunication for any who attacked his domains in his absence—and, indeed, even for all those who refused to march with him or give him financial aid. He also asked the Church for an annual subsidy of sixty thousand *livres*, over a ten-year period. The Pope was to nominate the Archbishop of Bourges as Legate and, finally, to dispossess, solemnly and definitively, the Counts of Toulouse and the House of Trencavel; the King to be confirmed in possession of their domains.

The Pope hesitated, no doubt reflecting that the King's only thought was to enlarge his domains at the Church's expense. A weakened Count of Toulouse, excommunicate into the bargain and constantly threatened both by the King and the Church, might possibly follow the Papacy's lead rather better than an awkwardly powerful King of France. In this calculation the Pope was quite right; if a French King such as St Louis came as an unlooked-for blessing to the Church, his grandson, Philip the Fair, was to make it very clear at Anagni that an over-powerful, over-centralized France would not choose to fight for ever under the banner of Christ. Such a danger, supposing that Honorius foresaw it, was, however, less imminent than that of recrudescent heresy. Besides, the Pope was concerned with the situation in the Holy Land, and did not want to risk immobilizing all the available French chivalry in Languedoc; he never lost sight of the Albigensian Crusade's true purpose. So he attempted to force Count Raymond to persecute the heretics himself, by holding over him the threat of a second French invasion.

The King, for his part, seeing the Pope disposed to treat with Raymond, declared that things being as they were, this matter of heresy was no longer his concern. The Count gratefully did his best to prove his good intentions to the Holy See, and at the Council of Montpellier, in August 1224, swore to hunt down heretics, expel mercenaries, and recompense both the despoiled churches and the Count de Montfort—provided the latter undertook to renounce his claims to the title.

The Pope, no doubt little satisfied by Raymond's promises, and fearful of annoying the King of France, dragged the discussions out to great length; finally he summoned another Council at Bourges, where the arguments of the two would-be Counts of Toulouse would be heard by an assembly of the Church's representatives. On

30th November, 1225, forty archbishops, a hundred and thirteen bishops, and a hundred and fifty abbots from every province of Northern France and the Midi met in Bourges. It is obvious that a jury composed of such prelates could not possibly find in favour of Raymond, who was both excommunicate and suspected of sympathizing with heresy. His case was lost before it even came to a hearing.

The Council, under its President Romanus of S. Angelo, the new Cardinal-Legate, contented itself with receiving the depositions of both parties; after which it sent the Count of Toulouse on his way, and put off its verdict till a later date. As had happened on that previous occasion, when the Legates refused to hear Raymond VI's plea in self-justification, the prelates who composed the Council of Bourges were only looking for a legal method of condemning the Count without giving him a hearing. He could not be permitted to give, in public, those guarantees which the Church demanded of him, and which he was perfectly willing to supply. The bishops doubted his good faith, while the King had no wish to lose his own rights over Languedoc along with Amaury's.

Thus both interested parties were absent when sentence of excommunication was passed—or rather reaffirmed—against Raymond VII, Count of Foix and Viscount of Béziers, on 28th January, 1226. At the same time Amaury de Montfort sold his rights and titles to the King; and, with the Church's approval, the King now became, at last, legitimate overlord of Languedoc, to the exclusion of the country's true suzerains.

This time there was no question of a Crusade preached from church steps and Cathedral pulpits; this was a Crusade in name only. The King of France was going forth to do battle and win a province, after a series of more or less cumbersome diplomatic manoeuvres designed to furnish his conquest with some sort of legal excuse. It is quite obvious that all this traffic in homage—received, offered, refused, sold, or accepted—had no value *per se*; that even when sanctioned by the Church its sole justification was the might-is-right principle. It was not his hatred of heresy that drove the King to enlist the support of the Church, financial no less than moral; and to refuse to go on a Crusade before he had wrung from the Papacy a formal recognition of his rights to complete an unrestricted suzerainty over the lands of the Midi. He made use of the Church, just as the Church made use of him.

Though this was to be purely a war of conquest, Louis VIII intended to benefit fully from all the advantages which the Church bestowed upon her 'soldiers of Christ', and indeed to get financial subsidies from her. With such powerful trumps in his hand the King contrived to raise a very considerable army. But despite its sheer size, not to mention the valour of its knights and the splendid equipment it could boast, this army (as we shall see) was far from united, and had no great enthusiasm for the task before it. The 'Languedoc affair' had turned into a personal enterprise of the King's, and doubtless carried little appeal now for the fanatic—let alone the baron with ambitions. Indeed, in order to get his barons to join the Crusade at all, the King was obliged to impose severe penalties on those who refused to come. Even the clergy were grumbling; they had to surrender the tenth part of their income to finance the Crusade, and this sum was mulcted from them with great regularity.

The King announced his Crusade in January 1226, and the army was on the march in June. It would appear to have been stronger in mere numbers than that which came down the Rhône in 1209 and marched on Béziers; though in all probability it was rather less formidable. Nevertheless, its approach spread such a wave of panic through the Midi that the Count of Toulouse (though determined to defend himself) must have realized that the game was lost in advance.

As the man responsible for the massacre of Marmande, Louis VIII could hardly hope to inspire either confidence or respect in the South. For all his piety and kindliness, he must have had a great reputation for brutality throughout the area since, at the news of his impending departure, in the spring of 1226, numerous *seigneurs* in the Midi hastened to make their act of submission to .he King. Such was the case with Héracle de Montlaur and Pierre Bermond de Sauve (the late Count Raymond's son-in-law) who actually set off post-haste for Paris; the list also included Pons de Thézan, Bérenger de Puisserguier, Pons and Frotard d'Olargues, Pierre-Raymond de Corneilhan, Bernard-Otho de Laurac, Raymond de Roquefeuil, Pierre de Villeneuve, Guillaume Méchin, and others. Now these *seigneurs* came from a group of nobles which was loyal to the Counts of Toulouse by tradition. We find their names among those who accompanied Raymond VI to the Lateran Council, and who afterwards rebelled against French authority under Raymond VII. Bernard-Otho de Laurac (or de Niort) was a heretic destined, a few years later, to suffer constant persecution because of his beliefs; and yet it was he who wrote, or caused to be written, these words to Louis VIII: 'We are zealous to place ourselves beneath the shadow of your wings, and under your wise dominion.' To believe in the sincerity of such loyalist protestations would demand considerable naïvety.

When the cities learnt that the King's army was actually on the march they sent deputations to the King himself, assuring him of *their* fidelity. Béziers was the first to do so, followed by Nîmes, Puylaurens, and Castres. Later, during the siege of Avignon, envoys came from Carcassonne, Albi, Saint-Gilles, Marseilles, Beaucaire, Narbonne, Termes, Arles, Tarascon and Orange. This catalogue speaks eloquently enough for itself: nothing but terrorism could have produced such a flood of spontaneous submissions. These townships actively loathed the French, and were fiercely jealous of their independence; they could not have the slightest desire to place themselves beneath the shadow of the King's wings. No: what they were remembering was the fate of Béziers and Marmande.

But the Count of Toulouse on the contrary had no intention of submitting. He gathered together the most faithful of his vassals, in particular Roger-Bernard of Foix and Raymond Trencavel; he also appealed for help to his cousin-german Henry III of England, and to Hugues X of Lusignan, the Count of the Marches, to whose son he planned to marry his only daughter. But Hugues dared not march against the King of France, while Henry III, threatened with excommunication by the Pope, contented himself with merely sketching out a plan of alliance. In point of fact there was hardly anyone on whom Raymond VII could rely apart from an army much weakened by the defection of numerous barons, and the city of Toulouse itself. He was also putting his trust in time: when the first moment of terror had spent itself, his subjects would return to him.

The royal army halted before Avignon: its citizens first protested themselves the King's obedient servants, and then refused to grant the army free passage. On 10th June the King, 'to avenge the insult done to Christ's army', took an oath that he would not budge till the town was taken, and had his siege-engines set up. After the first panic had subsided, Avignon decided to hold out. Besides, she was a city of the Empire, and had no intention of allowing a King of France to lay down the law for her benefit. The walls were thick, with a strong mercenary garrison and a large citizen-militia to defend them. In fact Avignon fought back with such vigour that for two months the outcome of the war hung in the balance. The King's troops were exposed, not only to hunger, epidemics, and the arrows and quarrels of the besieged, but also to attacks by the forces of the Count of Toulouse, who harried and raided their rear. But while this was going on the King was receiving deputations from various *seigneurs* and towns in the Midi, who had been impelled to submission both by the presence of the Crusaders and the fear of fresh massacres. The prelates, in particular Foulques and the new Archbishop of Narbonne, Peter Amiel, were busy negotiating these capitulations in advance, promising peace and clemency on the King's behalf.

At Carcassonne consuls and townsfolk were terrified enough to drive out Viscount Raymond and the Count of Foix. The Count of Provence appeared outside beleaguered Avignon to solicit the King's protection. Narbonne (where the Catholic element was still powerful), Castres, and Albi all offered to surrender even before the approach of the royal army. Yet Avignon held out successfully, and its defenders even went so far as to make attacks on the King's camp. Amongst the Crusaders themselves there was a growing feeling of discontent, and barons such as the Count of Champagne and the Duke of Brittany evinced a desire to return home.

Thibaut of Champagne did, in fact, abandon the King before the end of the siege, as soon as his forty days had expired. But the blockaded city was now beginning to suffer from famine, and the Legate, Romanus of S. Angelo, negotiated its surrender. After a three months' siege Avignon capitulated, and was obliged to accept the terms her conqueror imposed: the surrender of hostages, the destruction of her ramparts and fortified houses, heavy financial levies. Never before had this great free city—vassal to the Emperor, and reputedly impregnable—undergone such harsh treatment. Frederick II, indeed, protested to the Pope against this violation of his rights: but in vain. The King disregarded the Emperor's objections, and left a French garrison in the city. The surrender of Avignon was a stroke of luck for the King's army, coming when it did: a few days afterwards the Durance overflowed its banks and flooded the site of their encampment.

It was no less a piece of good fortune that the cities of Albi and Carcassonne—whose submission, with the King held down before Avignon, had been somewhat theoretical—now opened their gates to him and accepted all his conditions without demur. The fall of Avignon—one of the biggest Gallic cities in the country—impressed people almost as much as the fall of Toulouse would have done.

The King occupied Beaucaire, and indeed all the major towns along the road to Toulouse, from Béziers to Puylaurens, without having to strike a blow. But before Toulouse he halted his advance. The capital of all Languedoc had sent him neither message nor deputation; and the Count's troops, despite their being greatly inferior in numbers to those of the King, were nevertheless harrying the royal army, conducting a guerilla campaign of ambush and skirmish, picking off scouts and laggards. Moreover, those same *seigneurs* who, a few months earlier, had sent the King letters greeting him as a saviour, 'bedewing his feet with tears and tearful prayers', as Sicard de Puylaurens put it, were now very far from tendering him homage; instead they had taken to the mountains and were getting ready to fight back.

The King re-established De Montfort's old comrades in their fiefs; as well as Guy de Montfort, to whom he gave (or gave back) the town of Castres. He left seneschals behind in every place he had occupied; from the Pyrenees to Quercy, from the Rhône to the Garonne, town after town submitted in advance, and surrendered its keys to him. His army was demoralized and decimated through sickness, but he kept it going; it drew fresh strength from the vast distress of this country, now exhausted by fifteen years of continuous warfare. In October 1226 the royal forces had neither the strength nor the desire to undertake the siege of Toulouse: contemporary chroniclers are unanimous in their accounts of the situation— discouragement, exhaustion, and crippling losses both from disease and battle casualties. The King was ill himself, and in fact died on the road a few days after quitting Languedoc.

If every town had put up the same sort of resistance as Avignon, this royal Crusade would have resulted in total disaster. But the King and the Legate had calculated their move well. They were, so to speak, attacking a wounded man, who was barely convalescent and still incapable of standing on his own feet. Avignon, on the other hand, had not suffered the ravages of war in De Montfort's time. Once again the half-victorious were to withdraw in a state of exhaustion themselves: local passive resistance was still powerful enough to make their march a gruelling and ambush-ridden experience. Home the Crusaders came, bearing the body of their pious King sewn up in an oxhide; but there was no hint of triumph about their return.

Louis VIII was thirty-seven when he died. Thus the throne passed to a boy of eleven, and the regency to Louis's widow, who was forced to cope with a revolt by his major vassals. Unluckily for Languedoc, this widow happened to be Blanche of Castille, a woman endowed with more energy and ambition than either her husband or her son ever possessed. The men of the South who rejoiced at Louis's

H

death soon realized that they had exchanged Charybdis for Scylla; and later we find the troubadours actually regretting 'good King Louis'.[5]

The army which the King left in Languedoc to guard his conquered territories was rather larger than that possessed by Simon de Montfort in September 1209. His position was far less precarious. A royal seneschal such as Humbert de Beaujeu was not dependent upon the goodwill of transient Crusaders; the King of France was under an obligation to send him help at need. Nevertheless, during the winter of 1226–7, the Counts of Toulouse and Foix recaptured Auterive, La Bessède, and Limoux; the Southern nobility rallied once more, and the population rose against the French. Humbert de Beaujeu asked for reinforcements from France: he might be solidly established in Carcassonne (it was only natural that the city which had served as De Montfort's headquarters for fifteen years should now fulfil the same function for the royal army), but the neighbouring townships and châteaux had reverted to their original *seigneurs*.

The Lady Regent, faced with a coalition between these great vassals—the Counts of Champagne, Boulogne, Brittany and the Marches—stood in need of money; she had the idea of financing her feudal war with the tithe granted by the Church for the Albigensian Crusade. But despite the fury of the Legate, Romanus of S. Angelo, who on this occasion backed the Queen against the Church, the prelates refused to pay. Moreover, since the bishops appealed to the Pope, Blanche of Castille could only get her money by providing Humbert de Beaujeu with reinforcements. Even supposing that, either by threats or promises, she won a speedy victory over this consort of vassals, the 'Languedoc affair' would still be a source of considerable trouble to her. It was her husband who had begun the conquest of this province, and now the French Crown could not abandon it without losing face; yet it seemed as though it could only be subdued by a series of major military expeditions, renewed annually. With England as a permanent threat to France, the Queen could not allow her forces to be immobilized in the Midi; and yet the Pope was constantly urging her to renew the Holy War against heresy.

Blanche of Castille had no intention of using the fact that she was a woman, and a widow, to shrug off her responsibilities. Despite the dangers threatening her in the North, she managed to keep enough troops in Languedoc to harry and weaken the enemy, if not to defeat him. With the reinforcements which he received in the spring of 1227, Humbert de Beaujeu recaptured the château of La Bessède, massacred the garrison, and ravaged the countryside in the Tarn district. The next year he advanced into the County of Foix (where

Guy de Montfort was killed before Varilles) and though he lost Castelsarrasin, he retook the fortress of Montech. Then, with fresh reinforcements led by the Archbishops of Auch, Narbonne, Bordeaux and Bourges, he marched on the still impregnable Toulouse. The French plan of campaign was no longer to win military victories, but to lay the country waste, in such a way that it gradually became incapable of defending itself.

Puylaurens reveals this in a very explicit fashion while describing the havoc wreaked by Humbert de Beaujeu's army before Toulouse. Under the leadership and inspiration of Foulques (the refugee Bishop who, being unable to return to his diocesan city, was filled with holy fury against his flock there) the Crusaders set about the systematic destruction of the area immediately surrounding Toulouse. In the summer of 1227 the French set up their camp to the east of the city; and from this base they organized daily expeditions against the vineyards, cornfields and orchards. Turning themselves into what might be termed anti-husbandmen, they scythed the fields flat, uprooted the vines, and demolished the farms and fortified villas.

The Crusaders heard Mass at dawn [William de Puylaurens wrote];[6] then they broke their fast in sober wise and marched away, with an advance guard of archers leading them. . . . They began their work of destruction on the vineyards nearest to the town, at an hour when the inhabitants were barely awake; then they would retire in the direction of their camp, followed step by step by the fighting troops, still pursuing their work of destruction. They repeated this manoeuvre daily for something like three months, till the devastation was more or less complete.

The historian, a great admirer of Foulques, adds: 'I recall the pious Bishop saying, as he watched these havoc-makers returning, for all the world like fugitives: "By fleeing thus we triumph in marvellous wise over our enemies." And indeed, this was a way of inviting the men of Toulouse to be converted and learn humility, by taking from them the source of their pride. Thus it is with a sick person: we keep beyond his reach all that might harm him if taken in excess. The pious Bishop acted like a father, who will only chastise his children out of the love he bears them.' A cynical remark, this, if we recall that the source of their 'pride', the thing they risked taking 'to excess', was nothing more nor less than their daily bread.

The Count was preoccupied with the conduct of the war, and anxious to recapture strongholds and strategic centres from the French; he did not have sufficient forces at his disposal to oppose this devastation of his domains. Besides, it was not some band of vagabonds he had to deal with, but a powerful and well-organized army, that was methodically pursuing its special brand of warfare sans fighting, in which the enemy consisted of cornfields, vineyards, and cattle.

Despite this the struggle had regained its erstwhile bitterness; in retaliation for the slaughter of the La Bessède garrison, the Counts horribly mutilated all prisoners (knights excepted) that they took in a battle near Montech, and turned them loose in the forest without eyes or hands. Humbert de Beaujeu, together with the Crusaders and archbishops who accompanied him, knew now that the country would never submit with a good grace to the King's authority; these domains would never realize what was 'in their own best interests', as William de Puylaurens put it, till the day that their inhabitants ceased altogether to exist as a separate nation.

The time was now approaching when the Count of Toulouse had begun to appreciate the need for some sort of respite—though this might be at the price of his capitulation. A respite, that is, which would allow the country to heal its wounds and prepare for another round in the conflict. But if, by agreeing to discussions aimed at effecting a peace treaty with the King, Count Raymond hoped to procure for his subjects the chance of regaining—at least temporarily —both peace and a basic standard of prosperity, he under-estimated both the intelligence and, above all, the unscrupulousness of his adversaries. This peace treaty he signed was to stand revealed, in the event, as harsher than any war; and though he had never been truly conquered, he was to find himself saddled with conditions that no monarch would dream of imposing on his enemy—even after the most shattering victory.

Though a perusal of this treaty's clauses is still a stupefying experience, and may tempt us to explain it by the crude *mores* current during the period, we should not forget that contemporary opinion was equally stupefied by it; nor that this naked triumph of might-is-right ran flat contrary to the whole feudal code. We may well ask ourselves what strange misapprehension led the Count (who clearly lacked neither courage nor common sense) to sign such a treaty; and the answer must be sought in the condition of absolute misery to which his subjects had been reduced by the war.

The King's Crusade had merely served to exasperate hatred yet further: what good could be expected of a sovereign who concentrated all his energy upon ravaging the countryside and uprooting trees? In 1229 the Count was still resisting, but his most loyal vassals, such as the De Termes brothers and Centulle d'Astarac, laid down their arms through fear of seeing their domains subjected to the same treatment as the Toulouse district. The capital was threatened with famine. The defeats inflicted upon the enemy's troops, who were not fighting upon their own soil, and were free to return home whenever they so desired, seemed derisory in comparison with the havoc wreaked on Languedoc by twenty years' campaigning.

In three years the French had lost the King himself, the Archbishop of Rheims, the Counts of Namur and Saint-Pol, Bouchard de Marly, and Guy de Montfort—to look no further than the summit of command. The losses in men-at-arms for the campaign of 1226 alone were reckoned at twenty thousand; and though the historians of the time knew nothing of precise statistics, and doubtless exaggerated their figures, it seems clear that the French army's losses were indeed extremely heavy. Yet the Queen and the Legate (whose energy could scarcely be called in question) found themselves upbraided by the Pope for their dilatoriness in persecuting heresy.

Pope Gregory IX, elected to succeed Honorius III after the latter's death in 1227, was none other than Ugolino, the Cardinal-Archbishop of Ostia and a great friend of St Dominic. This old man (who was related to Innocent III) possessed a more domineering and intransigent temper even than his cousin and predecessor in office had done; while the Lady Regent, whatever her political ambitions may have been, and however strong her zeal for the Faith, could hardly help being embittered by the demands and threats of this new Pope—especially when she was at such pains to have the rights of her son, who was still a minor, respected in France.

It was from the French side that the proposals for peace originated; they were addressed to Raymond VII through the mediation of Elie Guérin, the Abbot of Grandselve. Naturally it was the heretics who had to pay the cost of this peace: on this point neither the Count nor his friends could be under any illusions. But they did not foresee a treaty that would mean, quite simply, the annexation of their country; a treaty of which each several clause (as William de Puylaurens remarks in amazement) would have sufficed to pay the Count's ransom in the event of his being taken prisoner. But though he was an ecclesiastic, our historian still thought in strictly feudal terms, and his judgments were formed according to notions of law which the totalitarian trends of the great monarchies and the Church were to render increasingly fragile. 'This treaty,' he concluded (with rather more depression, one feels, than he cared to admit), 'must be ascribed to God's hand rather than man's.'[7]

CHAPTER VIII

THE FINAL YEARS OF OCCITAN INDEPENDENCE

1. *The Consequences of the War*

BEFORE EXAMINING the antecedents and consequences of this disastrous treaty, we should try to get some idea of what life in Languedoc was like, during the troubled yet optimistic years that followed Simon de Montfort's death.

The horns and trumpets and peals of bells that rang out in Toulouse to acclaim the conqueror's death had their counterpart in dozens of towns and literally hundreds of châteaux: these, being reconquered by the Counts and returned to their traditional *seigneurs*, were celebrating the recovery of their liberty.

The poet of the *Chanson* breaks off his narrative abruptly in the midst of Prince Louis's preparations for the siege of Toulouse; he tells us nothing concerning the epic of those tragic years during which the Midi only raised its head to be ground back into the dust once more. He is, nevertheless, the only source to give us any picture of the atmosphere—feverish joy, violent enthusiasm, hatred, anguish, and hope—in which the population of Languedoc lived through the hours of their uneasy freedom.

He alone shows us Toulouse making ready to repulse De Montfort: men toiling at the barricades while torches and flambeaux flared in the streets and on the ramparts, and the whole place rang to the sound of gongs and drums and bugles, and girls and wives danced in the public squares, chanting ballads. The poet translates and partakes of that elated affection which the people felt for their Counts, both the old and the young one; he shows us men down on their knees, kissing the hem of old Count Raymond's robe, weeping for joy, and then hurrying off to snatch up their improvised weapons and join in the hunt for Frenchmen, who were hunted down through the streets and slaughtered. He describes the terrible, almost joyous fierceness of these engagements; the constant ebb and flow of soldiers, victorious or defeated, over the bridges and ramparts, through the ditches and across the outlying quarters of the city. He sketches an arresting picture of bright-polished armour, of lacquered or enamelled helms and shields all glittering in the sunlight, mingled (amid the noise and clash of battle) with a mess of severed limbs and smashed skulls, that drenched the ground with torrents of blood.

As a witness of those terrible days he experienced, while describing them, a joy and pride that must belong to the people as a whole; it would be hard to question the authenticity of his testimony, since its very partiality brings it nearer to the truth, and from it we can see what freedom means to a people threatened with the loss of freedom. During those first years after Simon de Montfort's death, the country must have lived through an extension of those early hours, with the same intoxication of spirit—and the same pattern of blood and misery, bonfires and salvoes, celebrations and the settling of old scores.

Though the country's leaders knew what danger still lay in the King's ambitions and the anathemas of the Church, the common people, now rid of their oppressors, were able to believe that the bad days were over. But the Counts and legitimate *seigneurs* now re-established in their rights brought home '*parage* and honour'— and nothing else. Provence and Aragon had supplied them with considerable reinforcements both in arms and men; but it was still the people of Languedoc who had to bear the greater part of the war's expenses.

The burghers of Toulouse had given unstintingly of their wealth and lives, believing that it was better to die than to live in shame. But after their triumph over De Montfort and Prince Louis, Toulouse itself—one of the first cities in Europe—was left with its houses in ruins, its coffers empty, its trade destroyed, and its male population literally decimated—it was not for nothing that the stone-gun which fired that fatal shot at Simon de Montfort was manned by women. A large part of the Toulouse citizen-militia had perished at Muret; we do not know how many burghers were killed in the street fighting during the revolt of Toulouse, but it must have been a considerable number, since the crusading knights had fought for two full days, in an unfortified town, against ill-armed inhabitants. During the eight-month period of siege the citizens who made up the infantry, artillery, and auxiliary arms must (as always happened in mediaeval warfare) have suffered infinitely greater losses than the knights, who had their armour to protect them. But quite apart from the actual combatants, the civilian population must have suffered severely from starvation, cold, and disease: contributory factors being the destruction of whole quarters of the city, the monstrous taxation exacted by De Montfort, and privations due to the siege itself. Afterwards Count Raymond had billeted his knights and troops of mercenaries inside the walls; and during the siege, even with supplies coming in from outside, it was Toulouse that had to foot the bill for this army. Though the war benefited some trades, it paralysed others altogether; during the years of the Crusade Toulouse (like the other large cities of the Midi) had ceased to be the major industrial and commercial centre which it was before 1209. Cut off from the great trade fairs, her stocks of merchandise exhausted, Toulouse needed well over a year of peace to repair her losses.

If Narbonne had been left more or less untouched, Carcassonne —despite the requisitioning of all the city's assets in 1209 by the Crusaders—also managed to regain at least the semblance of prosperity in a comparatively short time. Since De Montfort's headquarters had been in Carcassonne, he had every reason to encourage trade there; and the local burghers consequently included a large number of war-profiteers. Béziers, which had been sacked and burnt to the ground, nevertheless rose again almost at once; no doubt it was repopulated by a mixture of displaced persons, hangers-on of the Crusaders' army, and those burghers who had left town before the disaster, but who now came back to find what was left of their homes. Yet it remained henceforth a ruined city, that could not attempt to win back its former power and prosperity. Towns such as Limoux, Castres and Pamiers had been given in fief to De Montfort's companions, who did not scruple to exploit their resources to the ultimate profit of the Crusade—and their own pockets. The towns in the Quercy and Agenais districts had suffered less than most; yet even so, Moissac had stood siege, Marmande had been plundered, and its inhabitants massacred, while Montauban, being loyal to the Counts of Toulouse, had played an active part in the war, and lost a good number of its troops at the Battle of Muret. Even when they avoided such strictly military hazards, the big cities of the Midi, being saddled with crushing taxes both by their bishops and the Crusaders, and having lost (on account of the war) a good proportion of their trading facilities, found themselves considerably impoverished.

The big châteaux, such as Lavaur, Fanjeaux, Termes, Minerve and others, which were centres of a flourishing culture—social, intellectual and spiritual—had suffered rather worse than the towns. They had been taken by assault, depopulated, razed to the ground, or subjected to a harsh occupation by the victorious foe. They still mourned their slaughtered defenders, whose families, scattered during the campaign, now regathered after the liberation to count the dead and the missing. The holocausts of Minerve and Lavaur, the well where Lady Guiraude was buried under a hail of stones, the hanging of Aimery de Montréal and his eighty knights, the hundred mutilated prisoners of Bram—all these and many other tragic memories, unknown to us but doubtless stamped unforgettably on men's minds at the time, must have filled Languedoc with thoughts of hatred and revenge rather than joy.

In the *Chanson de la Croisade* the Count of Foix is made to speak of all those Crusaders—'traitors without honour or faith'—whom he had the chance to kill or mutilate: 'All those that I slew or destroyed filled my heart with joy; but those that fled or escaped caused me great agony of mind.'[1] Such was popular sentiment at the time. Shortly before the fall of Lavaur a detachment of German Crusaders, who were unarmed (or at all events taken by surprise),* had been massacred by the Count of Foix and his son: the Crusader was not regarded so much as an adversary as a maleficent beast that must be destroyed by any and every means. And though Baudouin of Toulouse was merely hanged, prisoners of lesser rank—even including knights—were drawn and quartered in the public squares, to the joyous acclaim of waiting crowds. Raymond VII displayed his chivalry to the vanquished on several occasions, however: at Puylaurens he spared the lives of the garrison, and treated the widow of that brigand Foucart de Berzy with punctilious respect. When Guy, De Montfort's son, died as a prisoner, the Count returned his body to Amaury with full military honours. But neither the common people, nor the *faidit* knights, nor even the Count of Foix had such scruples; the Crusade had kindled an implacable hatred of the French throughout Languedoc, and this hatred was very far from being extinguished.

The Occitan chivalry indeed suffered heavily during this war; but their losses, as we have seen, were nothing in comparison with those sustained by the infantry—burghers or professional soldiers, not to mention the brigand-mercenaries, whose death was no loss to anyone, but who formed a powerful fighting force—and indeed by the civilian population. To the twenty thousand or more civilians

---

* The Montgey affair was the only definite occasion when Crusaders and 'pilgrims' were slaughtered *en masse*. According to Catel (cited by Dom Vaissette, 1879 ed., Vol. 6, p. 355) 'there were thousands slain'. As a measure of reprisal the town and château of Montgey were razed to the ground.

massacred at Béziers, and the five or six thousand who died at
Marmande, there must be added the countless victims who fell
during sieges or forays; the armed forces, which always contained
a proportion of brigands (even the permanent hard core being itself
composed of professional soldiers and strong-minded regulars),
never showed any great tenderness for the ordinary citizen. This
hatred and contempt of the soldier for the civilian, which was
allowed a free rein during the great massacres, must have cropped
up frequently upon other occasions too. The Crusaders' troops were
universally hated and hunted; they risked their lives in every deserted
back street, on every lonely path. They could hardly be expected
to make a point of protecting widows and orphans.

Napoléon Peyrat is surely exaggerating when he talks of a million
Occitans having died during the fifteen years' campaign; yet there
can be no doubt that the country must have undergone such losses
in terms of human life as no chronicler or document reveals, and far
greater than any figure to be obtained from a bare perusal of the
available evidence. This was a period when there was neither a
regular census nor any kind of statistics. Though the death of a
knight would be noted, the bulk of anonymous corpses are only
referred to, here and there, in terms of gouting brains or ripped-out
lungs dragging in the mud. Even in their moments of agony the
common people have no history.

With its cities impoverished, its commerce ruined, and its population
decimated, post-liberation Languedoc was, on top of all this, further
threatened by that permanent scourge of the Middle Ages, famine.
Its country districts—fertile in the parts round Toulouse and Albi,
but poor-soiled up in the more mountainous regions—had suffered
for years on end from the destructive attentions of the enemy. No
doubt these were less methodical than the campaign which Humbert
de Beaujeu carried out in 1228, but they were equally violent. From
1211 to 1217 Simon de Montfort had annually ravaged the valleys
around Ariège, in the hope of thus defeating the Count of Foix; we
may well ask ourselves how these already poor districts survived
through such a period. Round Toulouse and Carcassonne vineyards
were uprooted and crops burnt on several occasions; and we can
gauge just how highly the semi-urban, semi-agricultural population
of the Midi valued their vines from the fact that the inhabitants of
Moissac capitulated in 1212 'because vintaging-time was at hand'.
Vines could be replanted, and corn resown; but so many men had
been killed, or driven by their wretched lot out on to the highways,

as beggars or footpads or vagabond soldiers; and many more were worn out with hunger and disease, and could not summon up the energy required to bring their ravaged lands under cultivation again. The job would have taken years; and however devoted a peasant may be to his soil, the permanent threat of invasion will tend to make the axe drop from his hands, out of sheer discouragement.

Despite Simon de Montfort's omnipresent shadow, we cannot suppose that every field and vineyard in the whole of Languedoc was affected by the war; besides, the folk of the Midi had been accustomed to disasters of this nature for centuries past—although upon a somewhat smaller scale. This does not alter the fact that the devastation of the countryside in the Toulouse area seems to have produced terror of a sort that one associates with the sack of a major city.

Despite all this it would appear, when we turn once more to the author of the *Chanson*, that the Occitan leaders' policy was geared to expenditure rather than economy. At the outset of the reconquest, the men of Avignon told Raymond VI: 'Do not hesitate to bestow gifts or incur expenses',[2] while the Count and his friends talked of little but 'arms, amours, and gifts'. The Count frequently promised to enrich those who had supported him, and De Montfort himself was irritated at finding his adversaries 'so proud and brave and indifferent to expenses'. Not the least of De Montfort's qualities was his practical streak; he was no spendthrift, and only showed generosity when disposing of those territories he had conquered. For the Count of Toulouse, on the other hand, there was no greater glory than this giving of rewards; yet at the very best all he could do was to recover from the French the domains they had occupied, and return them to their rightful owners. Furthermore, these domains would have to be won back by force of arms, and were liable to be in a sorry condition when he did get them. In order to make really generous gifts he would have had to fleece his own lands, which were impoverished enough already; and however great a spirit of sacrifice existed among the great cities of Provence, their patriotic enthusiasm could not last for ever.

It is clear that the upkeep of these lawful *seigneurs* constituted a less onerous burden for the population than that of an occupying army would have done; they had an interest in husbanding their country's resources. But we should not assume that Raymond VII and his knightly entourage intended, after their initial victories, to adopt that mode of life prescribed for the Languedoc nobility by the

Council of Arles' famous charter, which provoked Raymond VI to rebellion: that they should wear nothing but ill-favoured dark home-spun, and live in the country only, not in towns. A parade of wealth was closely linked to notions of honour and freedom: the return of *Parage* had to be celebrated with proper festivities. The common people might be content with dancing and singing and ringing the church bells; but the nobility organized banquets and presented their ladies and friends with jewellery or race-horses. Bishop Foulques receives praise from William de Puylaurens for the splendid hospitality which he bestowed upon the prelates assembled at the Council of Toulouse—'even though he had not received any sizeable benefices that summer'.[3] And if the bishops contrived to wring enough good cheer from their ravaged dioceses to astonish visiting guests, the *seigneurs* could hardly do less for their friends and allies: it was a matter of prestige.

The troubadours sang of the return of springtime and freedom, and glorified Count Raymond. Various princely marriages were celebrated. After the years of dispersal during the French ascendancy the Southern nobility now tried to re-establish its cohesion by a series of such alliances, together with exchanges of gifts and the renewal and strengthening of bonds of vassalage. With a majority of the native knights forced into exile or a mountain retreat, the French *seigneurs* who had settled on their estates had often married Occitan widows or heiresses. Bernard de Comminges' daughter Petronilla had been forced to marry Guy de Montfort; the old man shot at, and wounded, his son-in-law from the ramparts of Toulouse. This policy of intermarriage advocated by De Montfort had borne little good fruit. Most of these undesirable sons- or brothers-in-law had either been killed or driven from the country. The first concern of this proud, aristocratic society was to restore *Parage* and the *tradition courtoise*; for them the Crusade had been not only a national affront but a matter of personal dishonour as well.

In this war pride of caste and pride of country went hand-in-hand. The burghers were fighting for their privileges, the nobility for their honour and their lands, the common people for their freedom; while all of them strove to preserve their own tongue and their independence as a nation. The nobility, strengthened by several military victories and their position as the ruling class, had recovered rather more rapidly than the middle and lower classes; besides, they were still fighting and constantly needed more money to continue the war. Yet in sober truth the country had long since overdrawn its real capacity for resistance.

2. *Catharism as a National Religion*

Since the time of De Montfort's victories, the Church had benefited from the conqueror's protection, and had been enriched by a variety of gifts—in particular the goods of dispossessed heretics. But now she found herself in a more critical position even than before 1209; for the Counts and the *faidit* knights were not only trying to get back this confiscated property, but also to lay hands on those domains which Raymond VI had been compelled to give up to the Church. Encouraged by his military successes, Raymond VII had even repossessed himself of the County of Melgueil, which had been made a direct fief of the Papacy, and held by the Bishop of Mague-lonne. Such bishops as were enthroned during the Crusade now had perforce to fly from their sees; Guy des Vaux de Cernay, Bishop of Carcassonne, had gone back to die in France, and was replaced by his predecessor, Bernard-Raymond de Roquefort, who had been evicted from office and was therefore a popular choice. Foulques, the excommunicate Bishop of Toulouse, did not dare show his face there, since he was held responsible for all the city's misfortunes. Thédise, Bishop of Agde (the former Legate and one of the principal instigators of the Crusade), together with the Bishops of Nîmes and Maguelonne, and the Primate of All Languedoc (that aged figure Arnald-Amalric, Archbishop of Narbonne), had been forced to take refuge in Catholic Montpellier. Here, where the riotous populace could not touch them, they pursued a vigorous diplomatic campaign, in which excommunication notices alternated with appeals to the Pope. At times they tried to conciliate the Counts; at others they did their best to bring down royal or pontifical thunderbolts on their heads.

After a period spent backing Amaury de Montfort, the former Abbot of Cîteaux was now betting on local nationalism; he seems at last to have grasped just how great a danger the French threat represented to his country—and perhaps for the very political independence of the Church in Languedoc. Having realized that the King would never undertake this Crusade except on condition of annexing the Midi provinces, Arnald-Amalric now definitely swung over to Raymond VII, and was working to get him recognized by the Church as legitimate *seigneur* of his own domains. It is an odd fact that this former Crusader general should have been practically alone among the Bishops of Languedoc in having some end in view beyond the extirpation of heresy and the Church's immediate material interests. At least, he may have done so. But this turbulent, bellicose prelate died in 1225, bequeathing to the Abbey of Fontfroide his books, his arms, and his warhorse. In him the nationalist movement lost an ally who may not have had much influence, but at least never lacked energy. Arnald-Amalric was replaced by Peter Amiel, a declared partisan both of the Crusade and the French Crown. The Occitan clergy was now identified with a political party as aggressive as it was unpopular, and all the more dangerous in that its every setback was regarded in Rome as a defeat for the Church.

That the Church *was* excessively unpopular in Languedoc is not at all surprising. By openly and wholeheartedly approving the Crusade, these bishops and abbots merely alienated confidence— even that of loyal Catholics. The troubadours bracketed Frenchmen and clerics as targets for their maledictions—*Francès et clergia*—and on several occasions the *Chanson* credits Occitan *seigneurs* with remarks such as: 'We should never have been defeated *if it had not been for the Church.* . . .' The Church, even for those who invoked the Saints and venerated relics, was the enemy by definition. Must we assume from this that she had no local supporters at all?

Every major city had its Bishop, who was a most puissant *seigneur*: frequently co-suzerain of the community, and on occasion its sole overlord. Béziers and Toulouse both owed homage simultaneously to the Count (or Viscount) and the Bishop; and the pretensions of an Arnald-Amalric, *qua* Archbishop, to the Duchy of Narbonne were contestable but by no means extravagant. Even in a situation—such as that of Toulouse before Foulques' arrival—when episcopal authority was virtually in abeyance, the bishopric still disposed of a vast administrative organization, complete with fiscal and judiciary branches; this afforded employment to numerous persons, clerks for the most part, who served the Bishop and derived their livelihood from him. Before the Crusade, when the Church was both weakened and little regarded, there were plenty of powerful and prosperous abbeys in Languedoc; Cistercian reforms had produced a revival of Catholicism, and Foulques of Marseilles the troubadour, far from turning Cathar, had become a monk at Fontfroide. The monasteries were not all mouldering or emptied by mass desertions. Abbeys such as Grandselve or Fontfroide were centres of deeply sincere religious life, and the monks who spent their days there in prayer and fasting rivalled the *perfecti* when it came to austerity. The number, and the great wealth, of these abbeys makes it plain that, despite the lamentations of Popes and bishops, the Church in Languedoc was very far from being reduced to a mere cypher. The very hatred she aroused bears witness to her relative power; and even if she had no other supporters apart from the clergy themselves, these constituted a permanent minority—small, indeed, but far from negligible—in the very heart of the community.

The mere fact that they led a comparatively easy life, and were in any case hardly ever bothered by real hardship, conferred a kind of superior status on them *ab initio*. They were also literate, and therefore very often indispensable adjuncts to the smooth functioning of civic life. They were secretaries, accountants, translators, notaries; and very often scholars, engineers, architects, economists, jurists, and heaven knows what else. Even in a country which was almost visibly acquiring a secular culture, they still formed an absolutely essential intellectual élite.

There can be no doubt that many such clerics, during the misfortunes which befell their country, must have thrown in their lot with the nationalist cause. But this was a dangerous choice to make: as Churchmen they could not break openly with the Church. It is true that before the Crusade we find cases of priests and even of abbots who favoured heresy (or at any rate, did not fanatically oppose it); it is equally true that later there were monasteries that sheltered heretics, and clerics who attended sermons by the *perfecti*. But such tolerant views cannot be representative of the majority; certainly not of the more active missionary element.

Besides, these abbots and bishops—apart from the ones appointed during the Crusade—had friends and relations in the country, not to mention all the persons bound to them by motives of self-interest— the merchants, whose best clients they were; the contractors who carried out commissions for them, and many others. Doubtless among all these adherents there must have been at least some loyal supporters. Finally, the Church's party could count on the allegiance of all those who had too openly favoured the occupying Power while the Crusade was being fought; those who had cemented bonds of marriage or friendship with the French; and also those sincere or fanatical Catholics of the sort who had formed Bishop Foulques' White Brotherhood in Toulouse. As we shall see, the Crusade bred a strong Catholic reform movement, which in a few years achieved international status; it won over the Church, and had hopes of winning the masses as well.

In a country where hatred of the foreign invader seems to have been well-nigh universal, these various elements could only form a minority; but the very violence of feeling unleashed by the war must have sharpened their desire for revenge. We should bear in mind that Southern patriotism was a relatively recent phenomenon, and that fifty years earlier the burghers of Toulouse had themselves called in the Kings of France and England to protect them against their own Count.

So despite the national coalition that formed in Languedoc after Simon's death and Amaury's withdrawal, the country had no chance of internal peace while the Church continued to hold the threat of its thunderbolts over such legitimate suzerains as had reconquered their own lands. Peace with the Church was vital to Raymond VII. Quite apart from considerations of foreign policy, it would help to stabilize the situation at home. We cannot tell whether he would have bargained over the fate of the heretics or not, since the Church never gave him a chance to furnish proof of his good intentions. By the time Raymond received her absolution, he was tied hand and foot.

A study of what contemporary historians had to say about the war in Languedoc might well lead one to ask *why* the Church was so fiercely determined to crush a country that had no reserves of strength left, and was, when all is said and done, only fighting to retain its independence. In the texts as they stand there is no real question of heresy. True, the spread of this 'adversary' is deplored on occasion; but the thing itself remains so elusive and anonymous that it might well be taken for some mysterious epidemic rather than what it was—a vast religious and nationalistic movement. The Catholic sources observe that heresy continued to exist, that it was growing, and that the authorities refused to fight it. The Occitan writers do not refer to it at all.

In this respect nothing could be more characteristic than the *Chanson de la Croisade*. The poet of Occitan freedom only mentions the heretics in order to state that the Count of Foix, the Count of Toulouse, and others had never favoured them or sought their company. The accusations of heresy brought against them and their peoples are the purely slanderous invention of their enemies. The princes and knights fighting to win freedom for their country are as good Christians as any, if not better. They are constantly invoking God, Christ, and Our Lady. If these knights are more inclined to cry 'Toulouse!' than 'God with us!', the Crusaders for their part cry 'Montfort!' Both sides claim, with an equal show of conviction, that they cannot be vanquished since they have Christ Jesus fighting on their behalf. The barons who speak of restoring *Parage et Merci* do not, it is true, stint their criticism of the Church; yet the impression they give is of sincere and steadfast Catholics who are deeply shocked by the Pope's political tyranny. They do not sound like men fighting for a rival creed. Their enemies certainly asserted that they would exterminate 'all heretics and *ensabatés*', i.e. the Cathars and the Waldensians or Vaudois; but no one in the Occitan camp regarded himself as being either. On both sides, in fact, heresy seems to have served as a mere excuse.

This was certainly so in the heat of combat, and it is, above all, with battles and sieges that the poet-chronicler is concerned. Both his account and such troubadour ballads as have survived were composed and, invariably, copied out at a period when the merest suspicion of heresy was enough to put one in danger of life imprisonment, exile, or ruin. If a profane literature existed at the time which openly favoured heresy it has, for obvious reasons, been destroyed. If the centuries had preserved the work of some Catharist Vaux de Cernay, telling the deeds and *gestes* of his spiritual leaders, the miracles God had wrought on their behalf, and describing the grandeur of their work, then no doubt the Crusade would present a radically different appearance to us. History only exists through the evidence; and though one might have the imagination of a Peyrat, there would still only be a few names and shadowy figures to set against such terrible but intensely alive characters as De Montfort, St Dominic, Innocent III, Foulques, or Arnald-Amaury.

Yet fifteen years of war and terrorization had not sufficed to quell these faceless giants. In a weakened and bankrupt country they still represented so great a danger to the Church that the Pope continued to send out appeals to all Christendom, to harass the King of France, and to heap every imaginable sort of curse upon the leading statesmen of Languedoc—in short, to act as though the Church's very salvation depended on the Albigensian heresy being crushed. Obviously it was not just to further the ambitions of the French King, his most faithful ally, that the Pope deemed it necessary to destroy Languedoc as an independent nation. He did so because heresy (whether despite the Crusade or as a result of it) was making such progress there that an indigenous ruler, good Catholic though he might be, could no longer struggle against its diffusion; and because there was a danger that it might finally induce the country as a whole to break away from the Church.

Morally speaking, this separation had already taken place. The population would have needed considerable spiritual courage and positively heroic patience to persevere in the faith of a Church which presented itself in the guise of a hated foreign conqueror—especially when another Church already existed in the country, which, as a persecuted body, had by force of circumstance become identified with nationalism.

It is commonly stated that the Middle Ages were an Age of Faith. Generalizations of this sort are often misleading, and it would be more exact to say that the evidence left us by mediaeval civilization is, more often than not, imbued with profound religious feeling. Like every culture, that of the Middle Ages was the product of its religion; but already by the twelfth century culture and religion had become separated, and the secular literature of the period, poetry included, displays an almost complete indifference to religion as such. The political machinations of kings and princes (sometimes even of Church dignitaries) followed those eternal laws which had no point of contact with faith, and of which Machiavelli was to become the theoretical exponent. The common people venerated the Saints as in olden times they had venerated their gods of sun and wind and rain. The Church was frequently hated and mocked, even in those areas where men would cross themselves in horror at the very mention of heresy. Yet the Middle Ages *were* a great Age of Faith, in the sense that there existed no values, or system of values, which could fitly be set up in opposition to the Christian faith. Every human aspiration or genuinely profound experience led back to that faith, as rivers flow seawards. And though the chivalrous ideal and the social stirrings of the common people had, in point of fact, little to do with religion, few men considered the possibility of discarding the whole concept of the Church *in toto*.

Though there may have existed various groups of sceptics or agnostics—it would appear that Languedoc, being wide open to all intellectual currents, and partly emancipated from the Church's domination, contained more unbelievers than other areas—nevertheless scepticism seldom sufficed as a faith by which to live, let alone to die. The evils of the Crusade had bred a strain of fiery patriotism throughout the country; but these men who were going out to die for their fatherland shouted 'Christ with us!' as a battle-cry. By accusing the Church of responsibility for their misfortunes, they were led willy-nilly to identify themselves, in their heart of hearts, with that other Church, which for so long now had been telling them that Rome was the very embodiment of Satan.

Here we are faced with an underlying ambiguity of belief; and because of it we can never be quite certain just to what extent Languedoc was really converted to Catharism after Simon de Montfort's death—or, indeed, to Waldensianism, which, to judge from the evidence, gained many adherents during these years. When the Count of Toulouse's supporters (or even the author of the *Chanson* himself, or the troubadours) mention God and Jesus

Christ, it is very probable that they are speaking as Cathars, and that their Deity is the 'Good God' of the Manichaean faith. But we have no certain knowledge about this. On the other hand, these people also went to church, and venerated relics and the Cross; we do not know whether they did so out of any profound conviction, or merely in a spirit of easy-going traditionalism.

When disaster struck the country, it is likely that the Cathar *perfecti* came to some sort of agreement with those Catholic elements sympathetic towards them, and decided to admit a national, patriotic creed which could be adapted equally well both to the observances of the Catharist cult, and to Catholicism's more traditional ritual. The country had its own saints and sanctuaries, even its own national Catholic bishops—as, for instance, Bernard-Raymond de Roquefort, mentioned above, whose mother and brother were both well-known Cathars. As a concession to human frailty the Cathars (who honoured the memory of the Apostles and Evangelists) could perfectly well authorize their followers to invoke these particular saints.

Though we possess no firm evidence on this subject, it is a fair presumption that Catharism during the decade 1220–30 often displayed such modified characteristics as might tend, outwardly at least, to bring it back into line with Catholic practice. There is a phrase in the Catharist Ritual—though this, it is true, was only composed towards the close of the thirteenth century—which appears to indicate as much. It reads: 'Yet let none of you suppose that this baptism [the *consolamentum*] should lead you to despise *the other baptism*, or anything good or Christian said or done by you hitherto.'[4] Now these words were addressed to the postulant already deemed worthy of becoming a *perfectus*. It follows, then, that those who did not aspire to this dignity could be good Cathar believers while still remaining attached to Catholic observances. The only requirements for a *credens* were that he should hate Rome and the French.

It would be rash to assert that the whole of Languedoc went over to Catharism. What seems more probable is that those who were sincerely seeking God (and in these troubled times there must have been many of them) turned towards the Cathar rather than the Catholic Church.

When the Pope, the bishops and the King spoke of driving out *heretics*, it was well understood that this term did not include all persons whatsoever adhering to an unorthodox sect. The *credentes*, even when tried and condemned for heresy, were never described as heretics: in the phraseology of the period this word was equivalent to *perfectus*—in particular a Cathar *perfectus*. It was so well understood in this sense that the Inquisition referred to Catharist bishops as 'heresiarchs', to distinguish them from ordinary *perfecti*. We know next to nothing about the main body of ordinary believers: those persons interrogated by the Inquisition were, in their several ways, active members of the sect, and thus a minority. But our information concerning the *perfecti* is somewhat fuller.

Nevertheless, even this testimony is both dry and monotonous in the extreme; it can be more or less boiled down to some such statement as: In such a year, at such a place, so-and-so (whether deacon or *perfectus*) preached before such-and-such, or administered the *consolamentum* to such-and-such other persons. He was harboured in the house of X, a believer, and received gifts from Y, another believer. Nothing but names, places and dates. Even the Inquisition's records have not come down to us intact. A large number of transcripts were destroyed at the time, by those parties most concerned to do so. Others fell to bits or vanished in libraries and archives. But even in their fragmentary state these documents alone give a most impressive picture of the Catharist Church's activities, both during the Crusade and in the years that followed.

The first fact we should note is that, despite the war which devastated the entire countryside, and despite the massacres of Minerve and Lavaur, the various Cathar churches had kept up their activities, and were as well organized in 1225 as they had been before the Crusade. In that year there were four such churches (or rather, dioceses) in Languedoc—those of Albi, Toulouse, Carcassonne, and Agen. In 1225, at the Council of Pieusse, a new diocese, that of Razès, was created, and Benoît de Termes appointed its Bishop. The circumstances in which this bishopric came into existence show to what an extent the Catharist Church had already become an organic element of Languedoc life. The inhabitants of Razès complained of the difficulties occasioned by the fact that part of their district came under the Bishopric of Toulouse, and part under that of Carcassonne. The Council decided to satisfy the demands of these members of its flock; it was agreed that the Bishop of Carcassonne should select the new Bishop from among his deacons, and that the one chosen should then be consecrated by the Bishop of Toulouse. It would be hard to imagine a situation of this sort arising if the Catharist Church was composed of men who perforce lived in hiding, and trembled at possible accusations of heresy.

After Simon de Montfort's death heresy had come out into the open again; and in 1225, the year of the Council of Pieusse, it was preoccupied with administrative and hierarchical problems, just as though it were an officially recognized body. In 1223 the Legate Conrad of Oporto, when summoning the French prelates to the Council of Sens, wrote that the Cathars of Bulgaria, Croatia, Dalmatia and Hungary had just elected a new Pope; and that an emissary of this heretical Pope, Barthélémy Cartès, had arrived in the Albigeois district, where he was ordaining bishops and attracting great crowds of the faithful. The existence of a Bulgar 'Pope' is most improbable; but it is significant to find the Cathars of Languedoc renewing their ties with the most ancient and revered of all the Manichaean Churches, and drawing fresh sustenance from the contact. They too needed to feel themselves members of a universal brotherhood. About this time many heretics, fearing that the persecutions might return, began to arrange places of refuge for themselves in less disturbed provinces, where their Church remained comparatively untouched—Lombardy, for instance, or countries still further East. Moreover there are various signs which suggest that the Eastern Cathars had not forgotten their persecuted brethren.

If the official authorities remained, to all appearances, unaware of the Catharist Church, and, indeed, denied its very existence, this was done for easily understandable political motives. But the reason they did nothing to combat it, at a time when their most vital interests and the very independence of the country were at stake, is because heresy was far too popular and too powerful: the triumph of the nationalist cause was heresy's triumph also.

According to certain Catholic historians, the Cathars were very skilful at confounding their own cause with that of the country as a whole. But this did not require much skill in the event, and we may well wonder what else they could have done, short of surrendering *en masse* to the Crusaders and declaring that their religion deserved to be destroyed. The reason why their cause was mixed up with that of the resistance movement was that the people chose to defend them rather than stamp them out. As far as we can tell, popular resentment never credited the *bons hommes* with the responsibility for involving the country in war: at least there is no suggestion of the sort in the documents known to us.

For fifteen years Languedoc was engaged in a struggle to the death. On both sides there were many instances of atrocity, treason, cowardice, revenge and injustice; yet never, either then or later, was the name of even one *perfectus* associated with episodes of this sort, which render even the most legitimate warfare so horrible. Even the heretics' worst enemies never accused them of anything other than their refusal to recant. It is easy to see how, to that hard-pressed society, such hunted, indomitable pacifists must have appeared as the only true fathers in religion and sources of spiritual consolation, the one genuine moral authority which men could obey.

The Catharist deacons and *perfecti* continued to exercise their ministry in the very midst of the Crusade. The diocese of Toulouse even had two bishops; in 1215, when Gaulcelm was already fufilling this office, Bernard de la Mothe was likewise raised to episcopal status, doubtless because the threatened Church needed as many pastors as possible. The deacon, William Salomon, held secret meetings in Toulouse while De Montfort was still master of the city. In 1215 we find a deacon called Bofils preaching at Saint-Félix, while earlier, in 1210, another deacon, Mercier, had all the nobility of Mirepoix attending his sermons. But it was from 1220 onwards in particular that the Cathar ministers' activities achieved a new intensity—or at least become easier to detect in the documents at our disposal. The evidence concerning their meetings, and the various stages of their ministry, increases considerably. Since they were no longer obliged to operate underground, they now visited the houses of their followers without any fear that they might compromise them; they preached in public, ordained new *perfecti*, consoled the dying, and presided over liturgical feasts. Their activities may still have been semiclandestine, but they were no longer secret. Great *seigneurs* received the *consolamentum* on their deathbeds, while rich burghers bequeathed large sums to the Church in their wills.

During the years of Raymond's reconquest of Languedoc, we can find traces of about fifty deacons. These deacons were lower than the bishops, and held powers the precise nature of which, for lack of detailed evidence, is somewhat difficult to determine. At all events they acted as leaders of the community, and the fact that there were fifty of them may lead us to infer the existence of at least several hundred *perfecti*, both male and female. The great burnings of 1210–11 had destroyed something like six hundred of them—though not even this is a firm figure: the victims may well have included some *credentes* who received the *consolamentum* at the eleventh hour rather than recant, such as that G. de Cadro who was 'burnt [*combustus*] at Minerve by the Count de Montfort'.[5] But the Catharist Church must have recovered from this terrible blow with fair rapidity, since it kept both its organization and its hierarchy, and a considerable number of *perfecti* as well.

A bare thousand apostles, probably not so many, could present no danger apart from the ascendancy they exercised over the population. This, however, must have been enormous; everyone in Languedoc knew them, yet it took the Inquisition whole decades of pitiless policing and terrorization to achieve their final suppression. We can best judge the extent of the devotion they inspired from the rigorous measures devised against all who gave them aid.

They were everywhere. As we have seen, they even organized meetings in Toulouse during De Montfort's occupation; and after the reconquest of the country by its own legitimate *seigneurs*— almost all of whom were themselves *credentes*—there was no longer anything to check the spread of the movement. It does not look, however, as though they enjoyed quite the same freedom as they had done before the Crusade. The Counts might be able to favour heresy with impunity (Roger Bernard of Foix did so openly, and Raymond VII in a discreeter fashion); but the very perils to which they were exposing their country ensured that the *perfecti* behaved with rather more circumspection. It was during this period that there was founded a series of ostensible weavers' workshops which actually functioned as Catharist seminaries, or something very like them—such as that at Cordes, which was run by Sicard de Figueiras, and visited by all the nobility of the area. Guilhabert de Castres (who was promoted from *filius maior* to be Bishop of Toulouse about 1223) had a similar house and hospice at Fanjeaux; this was near Prouille, the site of the first Dominican monastery. (The Pope openly supported the new Order of Preaching Friars, whose illustrious founder had died in 1221.) This indefatigable Cathar Bishop spent his life on pastoral visits; he was in charge of communities at Fanjeaux, Laurac, Castelnaudary, Montségur and Mirepoix, not to mention Toulouse itself, which was reckoned fortunate in having him as Bishop. At this period he must have been rising sixty, since he was already in charge of the 'seminary' at Fanjeaux some thirty years earlier, and it was to be twenty years more before he died. In 1207 he had held his own with St Dominic and the Papal Legates during the debate at Montréal. Between 1220 and 1240 traces of his comings and goings can be found in most of the towns and châteaux around Toulouse, Carcassonne, and the County of Foix. He was in Castelnadaury during Amaury de Montfort's siege of the town in 1222; and later, when the Cathars were again the victims of persecution, it was he who asked Raymond de Perella, the *seigneur* of Montségur, to place his fortress at their Church's disposal, and to organize the Cathar resistance movement's headquarters there. The date and circumstances of his death remain unknown.

It is a little disconcerting to find history telling us so little about this man, and indeed about the other leaders of the movement, such as Bernard de Simorre, Sicard Cellerier, the Bishop of Albi, Pierre Isarn, the Bishop of Carcassonne who was burnt in 1226, Bernard de la Mothe, Guilhabert's successor Bertrand Marty, and many more besides. Yet Guilhabert himself seems to have been one of the greatest personalities in thirteenth-century France. (On the other hand we know all about, say, Innocent III's correspondence, or Simon de Montfort's pious outbursts.) The history of the deeds and actions of these persecuted apostles might well have proved as rich in inspiration and instruction as that of a Francis of Assisi: they too were messengers of God's love. It is not immaterial to recall that these torches were put out for ever, their faces obliterated and their example lost to all those whose lives they might have guided during the centuries that followed.

Nothing can make reparation for this crime against the Spirit. But at least, by confessing our ignorance, we can recognize that something important was destroyed. Mediaeval history as we know it would present a false picture if we omitted this great blank.

Confronted with such an increasingly powerful heretical movement, the Church in Languedoc would appear to have lacked any adequate weapon of intimidation. If the very bishops had been obliged to seek refuge in Montpellier, what could mere ordinary priests and clerics do? Despite the oft-iterated promises of the Count of Toulouse to expel all heretics, the clergy could only feel secure under the authority of the King of France. Even had he possessed the most burning desire to be rid of his heretics, the Count could only have achieved this end with the help of a foreign army—something which he manifestly did not want.

The Church may have been practically powerless during the years of liberation, but she did not remain inactive. The Order of Preaching Friars, created by St Dominic and recognized on 11th February, 1218, by Honorius III, had taken root in the Toulouse area under Foulques' patronage. It was not as yet an independent monastic Order, but simply a community of monks whose particular object was to fight against heresy.

We have already examined the origins of St Dominic's activities in Languedoc. To found a monastery at Prouille, a few miles only from the great Cathar centre of Fanjeaux, required some courage at a time when the heretics controlled this area. Three years later the Crusade reversed the situation, and St Dominic's enemies were themselves persecuted and deprived of their lands. Simon de Montfort, who had considerable respect for the erstwhile Canon of Osma, bestowed upon the new monastery a part of the domains confiscated from the De Laurac family, the lords of Fanjeaux. These same *seigneurs* regained their property once more after Raymond VII's victory. But by then the monks of Prouille had already come under the special protection of the Papacy, and their brethren had founded similar communities not only in the rest of Languedoc, but throughout all Europe.

Beyond any question St Dominic was one of the leaders in the struggle against heresy in Languedoc, perhaps even *the* supreme spiritual leader. During the Crusade, the Legates were too busy with warfare and diplomacy to have any time to think about heretics; the only bishop who showed real energy in the anti-heresy campaign was Foulques of Toulouse, and even he had St Dominic's help at first, and perhaps derived inspiration from his example. So eminent a historian as Jean Guiraud even suggests that Dominic may have had some part in the creation of the White Brotherhood of Toulouse; the Bishop and the Canon from Prouille were fired by the same zeal for their Faith, and shared the same pugnacious temperament.

For ten years St Dominic had pursued his evangelical mission in Languedoc, and as the Crusade wore on this mission became both equivocal and morally dubious: we may presume that the Preaching Friars were recruited from among fanatical Catholics rather than converted heretics. At all events, Dominic left Brothers Claret and Noël in charge at Prouille, and moved to Toulouse itself, where he became the Bishop's most loyal assistant. In July 1214 Foulques passed a decree by which 'to extirpate heresy and eliminate vice, and promote the teachings of the Faith . . . we do hereby appoint as preachers in our diocese Brother Dominic and his companions'.[6]

Dominic was a member of the Bishop's retinue during his enforced exile: we have already had occasion to observe him at Muret, where he distinguished himself by the vehemence of his prayers on the Crusaders' behalf, invoking God with clamorous supplications. This fiery preacher, whom his mother had seen during a prophetic dream in the form of a barking dog (barking against God's enemies, naturally), could not sit idle and wait for Christ's armies to triumph. He went on with his preaching mission, and laid the foundations for his future Order, gathering round him a group of fearless and ardent men, devoted body and soul to the task of preaching and exterminating heresy.

Besides being protected by the Bishop of Toulouse, who conferred these highly unusual preaching privileges upon him, Dominic was also invested by the Legate, Arnald, with Inquisitorial powers—that is to say, he was recognized as a competent authority in matters of orthodox belief. It was his duty to 'convince' heretics, to pronounce converts absolved and reconciled with the Church, to impose penances upon them, and to issue them with certificates proving their return to the Church's bosom. We only possess one such certificate (surely there must have been more?) but we do have the evidence of various persons converted during the Crusade, in 1211 and 1214, especially in the Fanjeaux area. His biographers, Thierry d'Apolda and Constantine d'Orvieto, record another fact which shows St Dominic to have been in direct contact with the ecclesiastical courts, and to have interrogated persons charged with heresy. The story goes that several heretics, for all the Saint's objurgations, persisted in their errors, and were to be consigned to the secular arm; whereat Dominic, staring at one of them, realized that he could be brought back to God, and intervened to save his life. Twenty years later this hardened heretic was, in fact, converted. (Constantine of Orvieto tells us that the man's name was Raymond Gros. In 1236 a *perfectus* of this name turned Catholic and denounced a large number of *credentes* to the Inquisition. But it may not be the same person.) This act of mercy on St Dominic's part leads one to suppose that he could, if he had so desired, have saved the other condemned men from the stake, in the hope that one day—five, ten, even twenty years later—they might also be converted. Considering his fearless character, it seems unlikely that he refused to intervene in favour of these wretches through terror of the Legate, or fear lest he might weaken the Church's authority. There are three possible excuses for a man who has the power to save his neighbour from a ghastly death, and fails to use this power to its uttermost limits: cowardice, great hardness of heart, or extreme fanaticism. It is hard to forgive such a person, and harder still to admire him.

It was in him, nevertheless, that the Catholic resistance movement against heresy was to be embodied, and it was his spirit that was to dominate the Order of Preaching Friars that he had created, and which was to make such fantastically rapid progress during the next few years. By the time of Dominic's death in 1221 his Order possessed numerous monasteries, and enjoyed most marked favour from the Holy See. We shall frequently have occasion to come back to this Order: to the spirit which animated it and the history of its development. One thing is certain: it was born of the Crusade, and was long to remain impregnated with memories of those bloody years; it had not been created to bring peace to troubled souls, and it preached neither charity nor forgiveness.

King Louis's Crusade had caught Languedoc as the country was struggling back to normality, and still badly crippled. It plunged the population into a state of desperation which can only be guessed at from the countless defections and mass surrenders which, in the course of a few months, put half the country into the hands of the King's army. This despair, however, must have been of short duration, since the resistance movement was rapidly reorganized, and the King's death sent hopes soaring once more. The French occupying forces now only managed to maintain their position with great effort, aided by reinforcements from the North. But during the course of the brief campaign in 1226, that legalistic character Romanus of S. Angelo found time to reorganize the King's conquest along the lines of the Statutes of Pamiers, by decreeing yet sterner reprisals against heretics. Where the French could not enforce their authority these new laws remained a dead letter; but after 1226 the heretical witch-hunt began again. The Catharist Bishop of Carcassonne, Pierre Isarn, was burnt at Caunes, as was the deacon Gérard de la Mothe after the capture of La Bessède. The Crusade had begun once more; and though the country might be more stubbornly determined to resist than it had been in 1209, it was too exhausted to hold out for long.

Thanks to the Crusade, Languedoc had become more 'heretical' than ever; but at least the war had reduced her to that point of weakness at which the genuine suppression of heresy at last became feasible. The King (or rather, the Lady Regent) was no doubt concentrating on the idea of annexing a fresh province with the Church's assistance. To the Church heresy represented such a danger that she recked little of the incalculable moral and material harm which such an annexation might do to the country. The ills of the times had meant that (to borrow Dante's dolorous remarks concerning Foulques) the shepherds were transformed into wolves.

But there can be little doubt that the Inquisition was a worse disaster for Languedoc than this annexation by the French Crown.

3. *The Treaty of Meaux*

After twenty years of warfare, Languedoc was united to France in the most traditional and (on the face of it) most legitimate fashion in the world: that is, by the marriage of the King of France's brother to the woman who stood to inherit the County of Toulouse. If Raymond VII had had a son instead of a daughter, the French conquest might have been withstood for much longer yet, and the House of Toulouse, given time, have succeeded in recovering part at least of its independence. The Saint-Gilles line was too popular in the country, and the right of inheritance too universally acknowledged as sacred, for plain, unvarnished spoliation of the Counts of Toulouse to be possible. Simon de Montfort's adventure had proved that beyond any doubt.

Raymond VII had only one daughter, and the Countess Sancha had given no further child to her husband for the past nine years. If in 1223 the Count was already thinking of repudiating the Infanta of Aragon in order to marry Amaury de Montfort's sister, this was doubtless because he knew that his wife would never give him an heir. The Church would not agree to a divorce that might support Raymond's dynastic ambitions: princely marriages during this period were made and unmade at the requirements of political interests, but only the Church had the authority to annul them, and restricted her approval to such repudiations as might serve her cause, or at least did not interfere with it.

It followed that the little princess, Jeanne, was destined in advance to become the instrument of royal conquest. Her father, anxious to provide himself with a son-in-law who might prove a likely ally, had betrothed her to the son of Hugues de Lusignan, Count of the Marches, the most-puissant *seigneur* of Poitou, and the King of France's declared enemy. At the instigation (and threats) of Louis VIII, the Count of the Marches was obliged, in 1225, to return to her father the child that had already been entrusted to his care.

So it was a matrimonial alliance which formed the basis of the peace treaty which the Lady Regent proposed to the Count, through the mediation of the Abbot of Grandselve. It was to Blanche's second son, Alphonse of Poitiers, that the little Countess of Toulouse was to be wed; in 1229 both children were nine years old.

To make this marriage possible a Papal dispensation was required. Raymond VII was related both to Louis VIII (his paternal grandmother, Constance, was Louis VII's sister), and to Blanche of Castille (his mother, Joanna of England, was sister to Eleanor, Blanche's mother: both were daughters of Eleanor of Aquitaine). Though this relationship was near enough to constitute—in theory at least—a canonical bar to marriage, it nevertheless appeared, at first sight, a guarantee for the future. The settlement of the Languedoc question took on the aspect of a family affair; and when she sought the hand of the Princess Jeanne on her son's behalf, Blanche of Castille seemed to be treating Raymond as a relative rather than as an adversary.

Notwithstanding this, the conditions proposed by the Queen, and passed on to Raymond through the good offices of the Abbot of Grandselve, were quite exceptionally harsh. Over and above this forced marriage, by which the French Crown acquired Languedoc *en dot*, the Count was also required to furnish various guarantees and indemnities which would have the immediate effect of making the province a dependency of the Royal House.

It was at Baziège, towards the end of 1228, that Raymond had his meeting with Elie Guérin, the Abbot of Grandselve, and received these peace terms from him. At all events, there is an instrument dated 10th December, and signed by the Count, in which he agrees to accept the Abbot as mediator, and promises to 'ratify all things done by him and with him in the presence of our well-beloved cousin Thibaut, Count of Champagne'. This communication adds that the decision has been approved by the barons and consuls of Toulouse. Guérin, whose good offices and—in a way—whose arbitration the Count now sought was, through his grandmother Marie of France (another of Eleanor of Aquitaine's daughters), related both to the Queen and to Raymond himself. Thibaut of Champagne, despite the rumour that he was in love with the Queen, was a somewhat recalcitrant vassal of the French Crown. He was one of those great feudal lords who constantly wavered between loyalty to their monarch and intermittent impulses towards independence. A versatile, brilliant, cultivated man, a practising poet with a passion for literature and the *tradition courtoise*, Thibaut was well known for his liberal views, which verged on the anti-clerical. (Among his verses we find some which openly castigate the conduct of the Church in 'forsaking sermons to make war and slaughter folk', while 'Our Head [i.e. the Pope] makes all the members suffer'.[7]) It is plain that he had every reason to feel sympathy for Raymond VII; in 1226 his participation in the Crusade had been very half-hearted. But, doubtless for this very reason, he was not in very good odour at the moment with Blanche of Castille. At all events his mediation would seem to have served absolutely no purpose, apart perhaps from giving Raymond false hope.

Though Thibaut of Champagne, as we shall see, accomplished very little, the Queen must by this time have become most anxious to conclude a peace treaty with the Count: for already, by January

1229, despite the rigours of winter and the difficulties of the journey, the Abbot of Grandselve was on his way back to Toulouse, bearing the draft of the treaty which Legate and Lady Regent had worked out between them.

According to the terms of this draft the King of France (in the person of his mother) laid claim to complete and undisputed ownership of the ancient domain called Trencavel—that is, the Razès, Carcassès and Albigeois districts, together with the town of Cahors and those lands in Provence, beyond the Rhône, appertaining to the Count of Toulouse. The King 'left' to the Count the Bishopric of Toulouse, and 'ceded' to him those of Agen and Rodez (meaning the Agenais district and the southern part of Rouergue); yet even in these domains Raymond was required to dismantle thirty fortresses in all, of which twenty-five were expressly named (amongst them being important towns such as Montauban, Moissac, Agen, Lavaur and Fanjeaux), while the five not so designated were left in the King's discretion. The property of those persons 'dispossessed' by the reconquest (i.e. De Montfort's Crusaders) was to be restored. The Count was to surrender to the King nine fortresses (including Penne d'Agenais and Penne d'Albigeois) for a period of ten years.

Furthermore, the Count was to 'deliver up' his daughter, who would be given in marriage to an (undesignated) brother of the King, and would become sole heiress to the domains of Toulouse, thus excluding any further issue which her father might have at a later date—except in the case of her predeceasing him, if he at the time had legitimate offspring.

Only if he accepted these terms could he be reconciled with the Church, and this was an essential preliminary condition of the treaty. A clause noted that 'if the Church does not grant us pardon . . . the King shall not be bound to observe this peace, and if the King does not observe it, our own obligation to keep it will thereby become void'. This draft treaty, which was made known by heralds throughout the towns of the Midi, scarcely made any mention of heretics. The obligation to persecute them was doubtless implied by the very fact of reconciliation with the Church, but there was no specific mention of the measures to be taken against them, and these would seem to have been left to the Count's initiative.

Hard though its terms were, this treaty was not deemed absolutely unacceptable by the barons and consuls whom Raymond summoned to the Capitol in Toulouse, in order to put the French Crown's proposals before them. It was ultimately decided that the Count should go in person to Paris, accompanied by a delegation of barons and other dignitaries from all the principal cities, and try to negotiate a more advantageous peace, still on the basis of this draft treaty. The Abbot of Grandselve conveyed the Count's response to the Queen, and she decided to call a meeting at the end of March, its purpose being to reach final agreement concerning the conditions of the peace treaty. The place chosen for this meeting was Meaux— a more or less neutral town, since it belonged to the County of Champagne.

The treaty was not yet signed. The very fact that it was the other side who were now demanding negotiations, and treating the matter with uncommon urgency, doubtless led the barons of the Midi to suppose that this proposal was simply a manoeuvre. The North had decided to bargain over terms, and had deliberately pitched their demands exorbitantly high to start with; then they had room for subsequent adjustment. Given the frightful economic position of Languedoc, it would have been rash to reject any peace offer out of hand; we may be sure, then, that the Count went to Meaux ready to negotiate and argue the case, but not to surrender unconditionally.

We may well ask what considerations could possibly have made Raymond VII sign a treaty far harsher than that originally proposed to him—especially when even the latter had only been accepted with some reservations by his vassals and counsellors. If even a well-informed contemporary such as William de Puylaurens (who cannot be suspected of anti-French fanaticism) confesses his ignorance on this matter, we are even more in the dark today. The logic of history requires that the victor should reduce the vanquished as far as is humanly possible. We can only infer that, despite some appreciable military successes, Languedoc's condition was really desperate— far worse than we could ever guess from the surviving evidence. It nevertheless remains true that this was an outrageous treaty, harsher (if that were possible) than the simple dispossession of Raymond enforced by the Lateran Council.

The Count of Toulouse arrived in France at the head of a large delegation, in which the Occitan nobility, clergy, and burghers were all represented. Among these persons of note were a score of distinguished citizens of Toulouse, all either consuls or barons: they included, amongst others, Bernard VI, Count of Comminges; Hugues d'Alfaro, the Count's (bastard) brother-in-law; Raymond Maurand, the son of that Pierre Maurand who was scourged and sent into exile in 1173; Guy de Cavaillon, Hugues de Roaix, Bernard de Villeneuve, and various others. The Count of Foix, Roger Bernard, did not accompany his liege lord. No doubt his heretical inclinations were too notorious: he probably feared lest his presence in person might wreck the negotiations. Thus the delegation was deprived of the one man who (even more than the Count of Toulouse himself) represented the very spirit of resistance in Languedoc. On the other hand the clergy were well represented. The energetic newly-appointed Archbishop of Narbonne, Peter Amiel; the old Bishop of Toulouse; the Bishops of Carcassonne and Maguelonne; the Abbots of La Grasse, Fontfroide, Belleperche and (naturally) Grandselve all accompanied the Count, determined to defend the Church's rights at the Council of Meaux. The retinue also included the new *seigneurs* of the Albigeois district, De Montfort's former comrades (or the heirs of such as had meanwhile died), Guy de Lévis, the so-called 'Marshal of the Faith', Philippe de Montfort, Jean de Bruyère, Lambert de Croissy's sons, and others, all of whom had come to receive official investiture at the King's hands, and confirmation in their new possessions.

The Queen had indeed summoned a Great Council at Meaux, with bishops and abbots aplenty from the North to match those of the Midi. The assembly was presided over by the Archbishop of Sens, assisted by the Archbishops of Bourges and Narbonne; but the *de facto* leader of the ecclesiastical delegation was the Cardinal-Legate Romanus of S. Angelo, in his capacity as Gallic Legate, who had with him the Legates of England and Poland also. Heading the Crown's representatives were Mathieu de Montmorency the Constable, and Mathieu de Marly, both of whom were related to De Montfort, together with Count Thibaut of Champagne, the official mediator of the peace that was about to be concluded.

The Count of Champagne apart, then, Raymond VII found himself, on his arrival in Meaux, faced with an assembly consisting either of his worst enemies, or else of ecclesiastical dignitaries who could not possibly argue with him as an equal, but at best might regard him as a repentant criminal. He had come to treat with the King of France, and now found himself being, so to speak, haled before an ecclesiastical tribunal. It is true, on the other hand, that the secular powers were represented by a Lady Regent who was worth ten bishops on her own.

Blanche of Castille's zeal for the Catholic Faith is too well-known to need insisting upon here. Far from copying her grandmother, Eleanor of Aquitaine (who presided over Courts of Love and led a brilliant, worldly existence), Blanche devoted all the time she had left from her family duties as a mother to study and prayer.

She had eleven children; and though the legend that she nursed them all herself is probably untrue (we know that St Louis had several wet-nurses) it nevertheless remains a fact that she took personal control of their education, and maintained a profound influence over them till the end of her life. A highly autocratic woman, she remained the *de facto* ruler of the realm even after her son's majority. It is she, rather than the Cardinal-Legate, who must be held responsible for the Treaty of Meaux; but she in her turn was driven by a higher Power, which she served with blind (though not wholly disinterested) devotion. Owing to an alignment of exceptionally favourable circumstances, her piety turned out to run parallel with her private interests in the matter of Languedoc.

It was undoubtedly bad luck for Raymond VII that, in an affair which was liable to decide his country's whole future, he was obliged to deal with a woman. A man, were he King Philip II in person, might have blushed to commit so gross an abuse of power; he would in all probability have been restrained by respect for feudal traditions, fear of public censure, and the need to handle his opponent carefully in the hope of making an ally out of him. In Blanche's attitude we can sense the toughness of a widowed mother, still with infants in arms to care for, and obliged to 'protect herself'. The fact that she was a woman, a member of the weaker sex, placed her outside those unspoken conventions which regulate men's dealings with one another. In political matters she had the (frequently lucky) audacity of the amateur, whose daring decisions tend to be based on ignorance and contempt for the rules rather than any deep calculation. But she remained a woman, and was therefore liable to let herself be dominated by her emotions. An aggressive Catholic, she saw no harm in paying more attention to priestly than lay counsel when affairs of State were under discussion. Her attachment to the Legate Romanus of S. Angelo shows just how far she identified herself, body and soul, with the Church party.

It is unimportant to know whether that guilty relationship which contemporary opinion attributed to the two of them did or did not in fact exist. (Certainly the Legate was still a young man, and the affection which the Queen showed him was only too much in evidence.) Proud, pious, the mother of eleven children, bowed down by the weight of her crushing responsibilities—had the Lady Regent either the time or the passion to waste upon amorous adventures? Public hearsay accused her, just as she herself was later to accuse Anne of Austria—another Regent who was obliged to lean on a priest in order to rule. The important and indisputable thing is that Romanus of S. Angelo had great influence; that the Queen backed her Legate wholeheartedly, and gave him a free hand whatever the circumstances.

The programme for systematically repressing heresy (which transformed the Treaty of Meaux into an instrument of absolute police control, and gave the Church a stranglehold upon Languedoc) was worked out under the Legate's direction. But the Queen herself also professed such a horror of heresy that some time later St Louis, her son and her ardent disciple, actually advised his friends to run their swords through anyone whose arguments, in their presence, smacked of heresy or atheism. She could hardly help giving her wholehearted approval to any measure that the Legate might take against the Church's enemies.

The whole basis of the negotiations proposed to Count Raymond contained one quite deliberate solecism. Looked at in one way, he was the head of a belligerent country that had decided to conclude peace terms. But from another viewpoint he was an excommunicate, without rights or titles, who had committed the crime of contesting the King's claim to lands which a decision of the Church had specifically bestowed upon the French Crown. It was to the Count of Toulouse that the Abbot of Grandselve had addressed his mission; but once arrived in Meaux, Raymond VII was no more than a common excommunicate, and even to accept his unconditional submission would be doing him too great an honour. It follows that all the preliminary negotiations had been a mere blind, designed to draw the Count into the trap.

When he was actually in Meaux he could either accept the conditions his judges laid down, or else break off negotiations altogether; there were no other alternatives. Anyway, it is by no means certain that in the event of an open rupture the Count would have been allowed to depart freely, and begin the war again. After the peace treaty was signed he remained a prisoner in the Louvre; there is nothing which suggests that in the event of his refusing his signature to the document he would have been treated with greater consideration.

The modifications made by the Legate to the preliminary draft were very considerable. To begin with, Toulouse was once again to be deprived of its walls, five hundred fathoms of which—over half a mile—were to be razed to the ground, while the Count's residence, the Château Narbonnais, was to become the property of the French King. Furthermore, the indemnities to be paid for war-damage to churches and abbeys (even those of Cîteaux and Clairvaux, which were not in Languedoc at all and had sustained no damage in consequence) ran into enormous sums, and so did the upkeep of the royal garrison in the Château Narbonnais—twenty thousand marks in all, payable over a period of four years. Over and above this, the treaty laid down that a theological college should be established in Toulouse, for the maintenance of which the Count was likewise to pay an annual sum of four thousand marks: its staff would be chosen by King and Church in consultation. Finally, the Count formally agreed to combat heretics, and have them hunted out by his bailiffs; to pay two silver marks to any person responsible for the capture of a heretic; to confiscate the goods of all excommunicate persons who had not made their peace with the Church after a year's delay; to refrain from giving public office to any Jew or person suspected of heresy; and to fight all those who refused to submit to this treaty, the Count of Foix in particular.

The Count's daughter and heir was to pass (as arranged) into the hands of the French King, and the Count's heritage with her. Even supposing the King's brother (who was to be her actual husband) died without issue, and the Count sired other legitimate children, the King still stood to inherit. This was both contrary to precedent and somewhat illogical: to ensure his possession of the County of Toulouse the King still required a legal excuse such as this proposed marriage. We must assume that Raymond, too, was relying upon the laws of inheritance being observed. He was only thirty-two, and had plenty of time in which to remarry and so upset the Lady Regent's over-ambitious plans.

Various historians, beginning with Dom Vaissette, have criticized Raymond over this treaty. We do not know what pressure was put upon him to sign it; but it is clear that in his eyes, and those of all his contemporaries, this was a 'forced peace',[8] and hence a provisional one only, which could be renounced as soon as circumstances became more favourable. The precedent of the Council of Lateran was still fresh in all men's minds. Throughout history it is the defeated who have always practised a political morality based on the 'scrap of paper'; treaties are only binding for the conqueror.

Now that the conditions of this treaty had been finally fixed by the Synod of Meaux, it only remained to have them solemnly confirmed by the young King and the Lady Regent. The ceremony was arranged for Maundy Thursday, which fell on 12th April. Only then, standing on the steps of Notre-Dame, in the presence of the Queen, the barons, the Legates and the bishops, and the Parliament and people of Paris, was the Count finally to win absolution and be reconciled with the Church.

Since this day was to celebrate the restoration of peace between the King of France and a great vassal of the Midi, it had to be marked by such pomp and ceremony as would be worthy of so notable an event. The act of diplomacy must also be high spectacle. There were stands and seats erected all round the forecourt of the Cathedral; Notre-Dame itself was still brand-new, glittering with gold and bright colours, though rivalled in splendour by the sumptuous garments of barons, ladies and prelates, banners and canopies and carpets, the armour of the King's Guard, and the splendidly caparisoned horses. The Queen and her son, young King Louis IX, were seated on their thrones, with the prelates on their right and the barons on their left; before the King there was placed a desk, with a copy of the Gospels upon it. It was on this Bible that the Count had to swear to observe the peace treaty.

To be quite blunt, the Count had to figure in this ceremony not as a prince coming to sign a treaty, but as a defeated victim led in triumph behind his conquerors' chariot. Fourteen years earlier far more shameful treatment was meted out to Ferdinand Count of Flanders: he was dragged through Paris on a cart, shackled hand and foot, and exposed to the insults of the crowd; and the populace, always glad to see a *grand seigneur* humiliated, regarded the Count of Toulouse as a sworn enemy of the King of France, justly punished for his perfidy. But Raymond VII had neither been defeated in battle nor taken prisoner, and was not guilty of any breach of his sworn word: he had come of his own free will to conclude a peace that offered more advantages to France than it did to his native land. If it was necessary at all costs to present him as a defeated foe who was only being shown mercy as a mere generous gesture, this (apart from the rôle which the Church played in the whole affair) was because the Capetian Royal House was gradually becoming powerful enough to believe in its own Divine Rights.

The King's Scrivener now stood out before the King and the Lady Regent, and the assembled prelates and barons, and read the text of the treaty aloud. This treaty was drafted in the name of the Count of Toulouse, since he, as it happened, was the only party to it obliged to give any undertakings whatsoever. Neither King nor Church promised *him* anything at all—apart from the release of the people of Toulouse from their obligations to the King and the De Montfort family: obligations which in any case no longer possessed a real or binding force. In this treaty the Count made the following declaration:

Let the whole world know that, having for long waged war against the Holy Roman Church and our well-beloved liege lord, Louis King of the French; and desiring with all our heart to be reconciled in the communion of the said Holy Roman Church, and to live henceforth as a loyal servant of our liege lord, the aforesaid King of the French, we have made what efforts we could, either in our own person or through the mediation of others, to conclude a peace. And that, with the aid of Divine Grace, such peace has been concluded, between the Church of Rome and the King of France on the one hand, and ourselves on the other, as follows—

There is something rather odd about a treaty in which the Church officially lowers herself to the level of a belligerent party, to be bracketed with the French King; never can the equivocal confusion of spiritual and temporal authority have been pushed quite so far. The entire manoeuvre made it appear as though the Church, in order to absolve an excommunicate person, was first obliged to have him dispossessed by a third party. The antecedents of this anomalous situation go back to the Lateran Treaty. From the Church's viewpoint the King, as inheritor of De Montfort's rights, was the legitimate *seigneur* in this case, and had every right to make what disposals he wished.

Though these arguments were based on a piece of pure legal fiction, the Count and his delegation had no way of answering them, short of coming out openly against the Church. It was the Church's terms that were read out first: the extermination of heretics by all possible means, restitution of Church property, compensation to be paid for damage to churches or injuries suffered by the clergy, the foundation of a theological college, penitential journeys to the Holy Land, and so forth.

The King's part in this peace treaty was only mentioned afterwards, apropos the marriage of the Count's daughter to one of the King's brothers. Never was a more magnificent gift received in so grudging and peevish a spirit:

In the hope [the treaty ran] that we shall persevere in our devotion to the Church and our loyalty to his person, the King has *graciously consented* to receive from us our daughter, whom we shall deliver into his care to be given in marriage to one of his brothers; and to leave us Toulouse and the diocese thereof, save for those domains that are the Marshal's, which the Marshal shall hold of the King; in such wise that after our death the city and County of Toulouse shall pass to our son-in-law, or in default of that, to the King . . .

Thus the classic law of inheritance was transformed into a royal favour, an excuse invented by the King for leaving the future father-in-law of one of his brothers with the usufruct of his former domains. Yet Raymond VII, himself the grandson of a daughter of France and an English King, hardly needed to regard his own daughter's marriage to one of the King's brothers as a gracious favour on that monarch's part.

So the public reading of this equivocal treaty continued, with an enumeration of towns to be dismantled and indemnities to be paid, of oaths of loyalty to be extracted from vassals, right on to the final clause, the only one which mentioned the King's obligations. (The King released the citizens of Toulouse, and all the inhabitants of the surrounding countryside, from obligations contracted either to him, or to his predecessor, or to Count Simon de Montfort.) When all had been read out, the Count and the King appended their signatures at the bottom of the treaty.

Once the treaty was duly signed, and after the Count had promised to leave twenty hostages behind (these to be selected from among the members of his suite) as a pledge of his loyalty, Raymond VII was, at long last, reconciled with the Church. But first he still had to undergo the same public humiliation that had been inflicted twenty years before on his father, in the forecourt of the Church of Saint-Gilles. He was stripped of his robes, and a cord was placed about his neck; thus attired he was brought into the cathedral by the Legate, Romanus of S. Angelo, together with his fellow-Legates of Poland and England, and led up to the High Altar. Here he had to go down on his knees while the Cardinal-Legate scourged him. 'It was great shame,' wrote William de Puylaurens, 'to see so noble a prince, who had long held his own against powers both mighty and many, thus haled to the altar bare-footed, clad only in shirt and breeches.'[9] The chronicler himself belonged to the diocese of Toulouse, and was personally attached to its princes; but it seems clear that his anguish was not shared by the majority of those present, for whom the Count of Toulouse was a foreigner, France's enemy, another Ferrand of Portugal.

The question has been raised why Blanche of Castille ever consented to expose her kinsman (who had already received sufficiently unjust treatment) to so bloody and utterly uncalled-for an affront. When Raymond VI was scourged at Saint-Gilles he stood under suspicion of a capital crime, committed within his domains, for which as Head of State he had in any case to bear final responsibility. He was punished by the Legate on his own soil; this was an ecclesiastical matter, and no foreign sovereign was present to witness his humiliation. Paris was not the only place where the Church of Rome could, in theory at any rate, display her authority.

Now Raymond VII, on the other hand, had never been charged with the murder of a Papal Legate, nor had his Catholicism ever been called in question. Though he had taken up arms against Simon de Montfort, his claims were so clearly legitimate that, even when they crushed him, his adversaries could not deny him the title of Count of Toulouse. Furthermore, he had submitted of his own free will, in response to the urgent solicitations of his enemies. It looks as though the Church, far from chastising him, should have paid homage to his conciliatory spirit. This public humiliation of a Southern prince in the forecourt of Notre-Dame seems to have been primarily a political triumph for the French Crown, which had contrived—by using the Church as its instrument—to pull down a powerful feudal baron.

Blanche of Castille, with rather more audacity than her father-in-law Philip II had ever displayed, was now steering the Capetian dynasty towards nothing less than a personal cult of the monarch, and thus to that absolutism which, four centuries later, was to produce the quasi-deification of a Louis XIV. Taking the Papacy as her model, the Queen acted as though the mere fact of opposition to the royal will constituted a sacrilege. She had good cause to behave as she did. For nearly a century the kingdom had been exposed to the threat of English encroachment, and was constantly placed in jeopardy by the insubordination and intrigues of the great barons. The young Louis IX was still a mere child, incapable of making himself feared. The Count of Toulouse, that rebellious vassal, that ever-dangerous adversary, must therefore not only be reduced to a state of obedience, but also *humiliated*, as a striking object-lesson and demonstration of royal power. The rods that Romanus of S. Angelo wielded symbolized the coming triumph of the monarchy over the feudal system.

After the wretched ceremony that took place on Maundy Thursday 1229, the Count of Toulouse remained imprisoned in the Louvre for a further six months—which shows how greatly he was distrusted, and how much it was feared that his presence might prevent the various clauses of the treaty from being implemented. He was not allowed back to his own city till its ramparts had been pulled down, and the King's emissaries were in occupation.

From April till September, then, Raymond VII remained incarcerated in the Louvre, together with the distinguished citizens and barons of Toulouse that he had brought with him. There is a letter of the King's which claims that he 'stayed in prison at his own request'. In fact we may assume that the Queen and the Legate thought otherwise: once set at liberty, would not the Count have straightway denounced the treaty and shut the gates of Toulouse against them, thus risking a war to the death? Though the treaty made provision for the surrender of hostages, it contained no stipulation that the Count should himself be numbered among them.

While the Count remained shut up in a tower of the Louvre, the commissioners appointed by the Queen and the Legate (Mathieu de Marly and Peter of Collemezzo, the Gallic vice-Legate) departed for Languedoc, to take possession of those territories ceded to the King. They also set in train the demolition of the walls of Toulouse, and organized the garrisoning of the Château Narbonnais. This done, they proceeded to the dismantling of fortifications in such strongholds as the treaty indicated. They encountered no resistance. The peace treaty was signed, the Count held as a hostage, and his signature was there as a guarantee of the Royal Commissioners' good faith. The two Infantas of Aragon, Eleonora and Sancha, Raymond's mother-in-law and wife respectively, were expelled from their quarters in the Château Narbonnais to make way for the King's Seneschal; while the little Princess Jeanne was taken from her mother—whom she was never to see again—and conducted back to France.

The great vassals of the Count of Toulouse came and paid homage to the King's emissaries. At first the Count of Foix refused his submission, on the grounds that the treaty which had been signed was not the one to which he had, in principle, given his assent. However, in July he consented to a meeting at Saint-Jean-des-Verges, about a league to the north of Foix: his own vassals were urging him to make peace. At least this great Southern leader was allowed to make his submission on his own soil, with his vassals and troops about him—and to do so with all the honours of war. He promised all that was required of him: the freedom of the Church, the restitution of tithes, the persecution of excommunicate persons, the expulsion of mercenaries and so on. On the matter of suppressing heretics, no one dared to ask him for too precise an undertaking, since his adherence to the Cathar faith was notorious: his courage won respect for his beliefs. After the signing of this agreement he journeyed to France in person, and was received by the Queen.

Meanwhile the Count of Toulouse—a prisoner still—accompanied

Blanche of Castille and the young King when they went to receive little Princess Jeanne from the hands of the Seneschal of Carcassonne. Henceforth the Count's daughter was to know no mother except for the stern Lady Regent; and in twenty years her father only saw her twice again. Once this precious hostage had been delivered, the Count was granted a certain measure of liberty, even receiving the arms of a knight from young King Louis. (His excommunication was doubtless deemed to have in some sense disqualified him from holding knightly rank.) The seasoned warrior, the hero of Beaucaire and Toulouse, must have found it an odd sort of favour to have the ritual accolade bestowed on him now, and by a boy of fourteen into the bargain. According to the laws of chivalry, the reverse process would have been more appropriate, since the lowest knight was reckoned superior to an inexperienced youth, though the latter were a king. Were persons of the blood royal already in the process of becoming those 'sons of the gods' of whom La Bruyère speaks? Be that as it may, the Count accepted this dubious honour with a good enough grace. He had, after all, seen many more such in his time.

When the Count of Foix arrived in Paris to ratify the agreement signed at Saint-Jean-des-Verges, he must have realized that it is harder to negotiate on enemy soil than at home; certainly the Queen managed to get the castle of Foix from him, for a five-year period, to house the King's troops. She then proceeded to allot him a pension of a thousand Tours *livres*—this to be raised from the revenues of land in the Carcassès area, which formed part of the Count's own heritage, but had now been confiscated.

Having thus received the homage of the last rebellious baron in Languedoc, the Queen allowed both Counts to depart home.

CHAPTER IX

THE CHURCH'S PEACE

1. *The Church and Heresy*

AT THE END OF THE TWELFTH and the beginning of the thirteenth centuries, the Catholic Church could only claim to be *catholic*, i.e. universal, on the plane of abstraction or mysticism; in point of fact she was one only among the various religions of the Western world, and by her pretensions to hold a unique monopoly of faith she was now tending, more and more, towards the status of a powerfully organized sect, rather than that spiritual home of all mankind which she claimed to be.

The great heresies of earlier centuries had already implanted a deeply intolerant spirit in her. Large-scale invasions and mass conversion of the barbarian peoples (some of them very late, as in the case of the Saxons, Scandinavians, and Slavs) had enriched Christendom with a heterogeneous collection of new adherents, still semi-pagan in outlook, who, when they adored Christ and the Saints, could scarce distinguish them from their own ancient deities. Islam had overrun North Africa, the Eastern Mediterranean, and a large part of Spain, and seemed less inclined than ever to give up its conquests. Its aggressiveness and proselytizing spirit were at least as strongly developed as in the case of Christianity; the Crusades in the Holy Land were defensive campaigns fought by Christians against an adversary who, quite unequivocally, was seeking to impose his own faith by force of arms. The Greek Church, which had long been divided from Rome both in fact and spiritual outlook, now dominated those countries in Eastern Europe which were subject to Byzantium or influenced by her culture, such as Bulgaria and Russia. She also contested Rome's authority in the other Slav states, which preferred their various national tongues to the barely comprehensible Latin that the Papacy imposed upon them as an ecclesiastical language.

Italy, Spain (though partly dominated still by the Moors), France, England, Germany, Poland, the Scandinavian countries, Hungary, Bohemia and Bosnia were all Catholic—to varying degrees according to their distance from Rome and the date of their conversion to Christianity. Countries like Bosnia or Hungary were still half-pagan, and the Jews—indeed, even the Moslems—had no less influence there than did the Catholics. South Russia was pagan still, and the chief of one Crimean tribe had been baptized as recently as 1227.

The Baltic states remained pagan despite the joint efforts of Poles, Germans and Scandinavians to convert them willy-nilly. In Germany and England Catholicism was the state religion, and accepted by the people as a whole, though the authorities were in constant conflict with Rome. The Pope's most redoubtable political enemy was the Emperor; and the latter's influence in Northern Italy was so great that this area long remained one of those most resistant to the Church's authority. Spain, being obliged to defend the Faith against Islam, was a country where Catholicism gained in fervour through its status as the national religion, set up against that of a foreign oppressor. But though Spain was winning back her independence, she was still constantly threatened by Islam.

The one powerful and trustworthy ally that Rome possessed was the Capetian dynasty in France; yet Philip II's conduct had shown the Papacy that a King of France was not invariably or by definition the Church's paladin. What an ambitious Pope such as Gregory VII or Innocent III longed for was the foundation of a Christian Empire with the Pope at its head, and crowned heads to serve as his lieutenants. This fitted in well enough with the authoritarian temperament of these two great Popes; but it had no connection with reality.

While Islam and even the Greek Church—despite the setback it had received as a result of the 1204 Crusade—still constituted a permanent exterior threat to Rome, the officially Catholic countries also found themselves confronted with an increasing amount of open opposition to the Church: one thing all the heresies had in common was an absolute and violent rejection of Rome.

The Balkans, Northern Italy and Languedoc were the areas where heresy flourished most; and of these heresies Catharism was, during the twelfth and thirteenth centuries, by far the most influential. Even so the centres of heresy in France and Germany and Spain were just as numerous and active.

At the beginning of the thirteenth century the Roman Church had become a major political power, and was in danger of losing her influence over the secular *élite* even in those countries where no one thought to query her orthodoxy. In a fair number of Catholic countries heresy had won over whole crowds of adherents, and already possessed traditions and an organized administration, not to mention its own ministers and martyrs.

About 1160 the Cathar Church of Cologne had adepts in several South German towns, especially Bonn. Despite the condemnation and martyrdom of its leaders, this movement caused Canon Eckbert of Schönau the liveliest fears as regards the numbers of his Catholic flock. In England the Cathars seem to have been comparatively unsuccessful; yet a missionary group that went across from Flanders, in 1159, made quite enough conversions to disturb the local clergy. The latter did not condemn them to the stake, however; instead they branded them with red-hot irons and drove them out into the country-side, where, since the people were hostile and would not succour them, they died of cold. Yet there were still Cathars in England as late as 1210, for in that year one of them was burnt in London, and there was a Crusade preached against them.

In Flanders Cathars were very numerous, and the Catharist Church of Arras was so powerful that in 1163 Bishop Frumoald, much as he might deplore the situation, could do nothing to combat it. It was only in 1182 that the actual leaders of this Church who were brought to trial and burnt. Right up to the time of the Inquisition, Flanders remained a centre of heresy.

In Champagne, during the second half of the twelfth century and the first part of the thirteenth, the Cathars possessed several clandestine communities which were actively sought by the clerical authorities. We have already noted the anecdote of the young girl from Rheims, whose devotion to her virginity cost her her life: though she, and the old lady who gave her instruction, may have been the only heretics actually discovered in Rheims, this does not necessarily mean that there were no others. Such women were courageous enough to keep a secret. But the most important Cathar community seems to have been that at Montwimer [Mont-Aimé]. This group existed from about 1140 onwards, and was not discovered till the time of the Inquisition; its importance can be judged from the fact that no less than a hundred and eighty-three heretics were burnt there by an Inquisitor named Robert the Bulgar.

In 1154 a Southerner, Hugues de Saint-Pierre, founded a heretical community near Vézelay, in the County of Nevers. This had socialist tendencies, but was undoubtedly Cathar-inspired: it gathered together those inhabitants of the district who wanted to shake off the tyrannical authority of the local clergy. Despite the support of the

Count himself, these men were convicted of heresy, and their leaders condemned to the stake in 1167. This, however, did not prevent their doctrines spreading throughout the region surrounding Nevers, and into Burgundy as well. Here, especially in the neighbourhood of Besançon, they drew people's sympathies to such a degree that priests who argued against them were liable to be stoned. The two leaders of the movement were convicted of heresy by the bishop, and burnt.

In 1198 the Bishop of Auxerre, Hugues de Noyers, uncovered a regular nest of heresy at Charité-sur-Loire. The Nevers Dean of Chapter was himself lending support to Catharist doctrines, and heresy was rampant even among the clergy. Terric, the leader of the local community, was burnt in 1199, but the development of the sect remained such that Pope Innocent III was compelled to send a Legate on a special mission of enquiry in the Nevers area. In 1201 a knight named Evrard de Châteauneuf, a follower of Terric's, was burnt at Nevers; his nephew William, the Dean of Chapter, managed to escape, and took refuge in the Narbonne district, where he was afterwards to become one of the Catharist Church's leaders, under the name of Theodoric, or Thierry. Despite these persecutions, Catharism was far from being put out of action: in 1207 the Cathar sect at Charité was still provoking fulminations from the Bishops of Troyes and Auxerre. In 1223 that famous Inquisitor Robert the Bulgar was still receiving Papal injunctions to stamp out heresy in this area.

In Northern France there were comparatively few heretical communities; and since the bulk of the population was hostile to heresy, such heretics as there were had perforce to shroud their activities with a veil of secrecy. Nevertheless, the success achieved by the movements in Vézelay and Arras, besides the existence of such flourishing colonies as those of Montwimer and Charité, all goes to suggest that the Cathars were more numerous than either the Church or the secular authorities suspected. At the beginning of the thirteenth century Catharism did not as yet represent a serious challenge to the Church in France; the members of the various communities could only form a secret league, which by its very nature lacked aggressiveness. It is by no means certain that this movement might not have grown more powerful, and emerged into the open—as had happened in Italy and Languedoc half a century earlier—if the Church had not concentrated all the resources of its foreign diplomacy and internal organization on the struggle against heresy. If France, the most Catholic of all Christian countries, harboured heretical cells that were

sufficiently well-established for the Catharist bishops of Bulgaria and
Languedoc to consider a French Catharist Church a necessity, then
in other lands Catharism must have already been aspiring to challenge
Rome's supremacy.

Though in numbers it was far inferior, the Catharist Church had
already, by the close of the twelfth century, begun to credit itself
with the prestige and prerogatives of a universal Church. Wherever
it possessed any influence its moral credit was good. It had its own
doctrine; and despite one or two variations of detail this proves on
examination to have been remarkably stable and coherent—always
the same, from the eleventh century to the fourteenth, in Bulgaria
and Toulouse and Flanders alike. This unity of thought alone
bears witness to the Catharist Church's strength. The Cathars
had their own immutable ritual, their own hierarchy and traditions,
their own literature and theology. They were already in a position to
set up their own organization against that of the Established Church.

We have already seen the prestige that Catharism enjoyed in
Languedoc. At this point it would be appropriate, and by no means
irrelevant, to sketch, very briefly, the history of the Catharist
Churches in those other countries where heresy was now powerful
enough to be officially—or unofficially—recognized. Rome's attitude, from the Crusade and the Lateran Council up to the establishment of the Inquisition, can only be explained in terms of a very
real, indeed a most formidable, threat to her position. We cannot
say that the policy of tyranny and oppression which the Church
adopted was mere wanton abuse of power; if it proved, in the long
run, disastrous for the Church herself, it nevertheless corresponded
to a most urgent necessity. When Rome burnt heretics, she was not
trampling on a disarmed adversary. She was defending herself
against a redoubtable foe, who moreover enjoyed the immense
advantage over her of being regarded as the champion of spiritual
liberty. However scanty its organization and fighting resources, a
persecuted Church always has a moral advantage over an Established Church. In the process of destroying the Cathars, Rome
found herself obliged to destroy something vital in the Catholic
Church too, a large part of its *raison d'être*. There can be no doubt
that she would have defended the Faith better by giving way to her
enemy and returning to the catacombs. But for a long while now the
Catholic Church had not been a Church merely, but a caste, a social
class, and a political power as well.

The Cathar Church was not, as yet, any of these things; the only interests it had to defend were spiritual ones. In attacking Rome the Cathars were on excellent ground, since in many Catholic countries the Church of Rome represented neither a civilizing influence nor a national tradition nor even a guarantee of protection against feudal anarchy, but was simply a foreign religion, forcibly imposed by governmental authority.

Thanks to the labours of two Bulgars, Cyril and Methodius (who had translated the Liturgy and the Scriptures into vernacular speech) the Greek rite had already spread among the Slav population of Hungary and the Balkans. They remained profoundly hostile to the Catholic clergy, who forced Latin upon them; and the monks of the numerous religious houses that existed in these parts, far from supporting the Church, were her most dangerous opponents. Being despised and oppressed by the Latinate clergy, and nearer to popular tradition than to the culture which Rome imposed, they tended to embrace heretical doctrines, which, thanks to their authority as Christian ministers, they then proceeded to disseminate. In contrast to this the Catholic bishops and priests in the Slav countries were very few, had no influence over the people, and set a most scandalous and corrupt example.

During Innocent III's Papacy Hungary, Croatia, Slavonia, Bosnia, Istria, Dalmatia and Albania (together with Bulgaria, Macedon and Thrace, which came under the Greek rite) were all countries where the Catharist faith enjoyed exceptional freedom and, in many cases, official State protection. Towards the end of the twelfth century, in Bosnia, the governor of the province, ban [Prince] Kulin, together with his entire family, was notoriously devoted to heresy. In Dalmatia the diocese of Trugurium was one of the great centres of Catharism, known not only locally but throughout Western Europe as well. In the towns of Split, Ragusa and Zara, almost the whole of the nobility were Cathars. Not only in Bulgaria (the original home of Catharism) was there an important Catharist bishopric, but also in Constantinople itself. In these countries even the Catholic bishops—such as Daniel of Bosnia or Arrenger of Ragusa—evinced some sympathy for Catharist doctrines.

Since Innocent III's accession the bishops of the Slav countries, scared by the progress which heresy was making, had done their best to intimidate these adversaries: first by means of persecutions, and then with appeals to secular princes. The King of Hungary, who was loyal to the Pope, attempted to put pressure on the ban of Bosnia, and the latter made several seeming concessions; but his successor, Ninoslas, supported the Cathars even more openly, and actually nominated a heretic to the episcopal see which fell vacant at Daniel's death. Bosnia now became officially heretical: no Catholic services were celebrated there, and from 1221 onwards the province became one of the most important centres of Catharism, offering help and asylum to persecuted Cathars from other countries.

Meanwhile Innocent III was making great efforts to convert the Bulgars. These people were at present subject to the Byzantine Church, and had an extremely large number of Cathars (or Bogomils) amongst them. The Pope crowned as Czar of Bulgaria a certain Kalojan, who had made his submission to Rome in order to obtain Papal aid against the Greeks. Innocent soon found, however, that his protégé was protecting the heretical *seigneurs* in his province; while John Azen, who was Czar of Bulgaria from 1218, gave the Cathars complete freedom of worship, and allowed them to preach as they would.

In Hungary, King Emeric, and after him Andrew II, both of them sincere Catholics, yielded to the exhortations of Innocent and his successor, Honorius III, and made several attempts to stamp out heresy in their country. With their support the bishops and Legates fought a bitter struggle against the Bosnian Cathars; and in 1221 a Hungarian monk named Paul established a convent of Preaching Friars at Raab—though during their first mission in Bosnia thirty-two Dominicans so exasperated the crowds with their preaching that they were flung into a river, and drowned. And despite the apparent submission of *ban* Ninoslas, heresy remained so powerful in the province that by 1225 Honorius III felt called to preach a Crusade—without result. The Archbishop of Colocza offered John, the *seigneur* of Sirmie, two hundred marks if he would agree to join a Crusade, and even so failed to persuade him. The only person who fought a military action (in 1227, and to very little purpose) was the King of Hungary, Andrew II's son Coloman.

In Bosnia the Pope instituted a second bishopric, to counter-balance the influence of the bishop already *in situ*, who had himself gone over to heresy. In this new see he placed a German Dominican, John of Wildeshusen, whose violent measures quickly made him unpopular. In order to reduce the *ban* of Bosnia to submission, the Pope appealed to Duke Coloman of Slavonia, as he had previously appealed to the King of France over Languedoc. Coloman, at the head of a fresh Crusading army, won—or claimed to have won—some successes (1238), but the heretics seemed none the worse for his activities. The Pope sent out a new Dominican bishop: after two years he resigned his post in despair.

In the Slav countries, then, heresy was powerful enough to be accepted as an official religion—though this depended upon political circumstance and the convictions of each individual ruler. Its success may be explained in several ways. There was the Slavs' natural antipathy to the ascendancy of Rome; there was the weakened authority of the Greek Church, which, though as strict as Rome in matters of orthodoxy, was less powerfully organized (being simultaneously threatened by Islam in the East and Rome in the West) and in a sense rather nearer to the spirit of Manichaeism than its Catholic counterpart. It is not, therefore, altogether surprising that these barely Christian countries, which were open to so many rival influences, should have supplied such a favourable soil for the growth of heresy.

Rather more extraordinary is the fact that Italy, long a Catholic nation and the home of the Popes themselves, should for some time now have been as tainted with heresy as Languedoc. There were even Cathar communities in Rome. In the twelfth century we hear of flourishing heretical colonies in Milan, Florence, Verona, Orvieto, Ferrara, Modena, and as far south as Calabria. While the Crusade against heresy was laying waste the French Midi, the Italian Cathars enjoyed a quasi-official freedom, and formed most powerful clans in the various towns—powerful enough to unseat Catholic bishops and *seigneurs* on occasion.

Lombardy was a veritable hotbed of heresy. Territorially, it belonged to the Empire, and formed a battleground for endless sanguinary struggles between the Emperor's and the Pope's supporters. Both these great Powers, of which the province was perforce a dependency, alternately wooed and threatened it. Its great commercial cities were virtually autonomous republics, and extremely jealous of their freedom. For the Lombards more than any other Christian country the Church represented a political power-group; the subsequent struggles between Guelfs and Ghibellines were to demonstrate that in Italy religious passions often took second place to their political equivalent. It was this particular aspect of the overall struggle for national independence and social emancipation which the Catharist movement in Italy took up. The bishops, who as powerful feudal overlords were always ready to fight for their privileges, met with a stubborn resistance in the cities—a resistance which very often paid no more than lip-service to the motive of religious zeal. The Catholics, for their part, were fighting less for the Faith than on behalf of family clan or political party.

Paradoxically enough, it was just this state of permanent civil war which for long preserved a climate of comparative religious tolerance in Italy. So long as local Catholics continued to take up arms in person against their heretical fellow-countrymen, a certain balance of power was maintained, which forced both sides to exercise some moderation; while the Pope, who had no intention of losing his stake in Lombardy, could hardly appeal to the Emperor to launch a Crusade from which the latter would have profited all too well. Indeed, in 1236, when the newly-formed Inquisition was ramping through every Catholic country with somewhat excessive zeal, the Emperor could actually accuse the Pope of supporting heresy, and of allowing himself to be corrupted by the gold of Lombard heretics. Gregory IX was the last person one could suspect of venality; but the Italian Cathars, being equally detested by Pope and Emperor alike, in fact owed their relative security to the accident of these two great personages being at political loggerheads.

The Church was unpopular in Italy, where the clergy were exceptionally aggressive, bellicose even, and threw themselves with enthusiasm into various civil wars. The higher prelates were anxious above all to preserve those rights which the increasing power of the commons tended to challenge—often by violent means. Every sort of religious sect flourished in Italy: Arnaldists, who were followers of the reformer Arnaldus of Brescia, Waldensians, or the Judaising Pasagians; but the Cathars were the most numerous and influential. A large proportion of the nobility had joined them, and they felt strengthened by the support of their fellow-Cathars in Languedoc and the Slav countries. They had their own schools, taught in the public squares, and took part in controversies with the Catholic clergy. At the beginning of the thirteenth century Lombardy was regarded, more or less, as a centre of pilgrimage for all Western Cathars, who travelled thither to consult the learned theologians of their sect, and to receive the sacrament of the *consolamentum*—or to have it renewed—at the hands of some particularly revered *perfectus*.

In the time of Innocent III the Cathar Churches were well represented in Italy. They had bishops at Sorano, Vicenza and Brescia, while their *filii maiores* ruled the communities in other towns. Milan was an official centre of all heretical Churches: the magistrates of this city, being anti-clerical in their views, openly protected every sect, and gave asylum within their walls to all heretics exiled from their own countries. In towns such as Viterbo, Verona, Florence, Ferrara, Prato, and Orvieto the Cathars were dominant, and the Catholic bishops powerless to make strictures upon them. In Faenza, Rimini, Como, Parma, Cremona and Piacenza they had flourishing groups, while the little town of Desenzano possessed a particularly large and influential Cathar community. In Treviso the heretics were protected by the official authorities, and even at Rome they had schools where they expounded the Gospels.

At the beginning of the century the Italian Cathars enjoyed such security that they could permit themselves some theological divergence and schism within the body of their own Church. Thus the Bishops of Sorano and Vicenza followed the school of Trugurium, or Albania, while the Bishop of Brescia embraced the doctrine held by the Bulgarian Cathars—the first asserting that the Principle of Evil was eternal, and the second, that in the beginning only the Good God had existed. The two sects indulged in the most furious theological squabbling amongst themselves. About 1226 the first of them split into two separate halves, one being represented by Bishop Belismansa, and the other by his *filius maior*, John of Lugio.

Innocent III was most alarmed by the rapid spread of heresy throughout the peninsula. He began by making threats of an administrative nature, such as banning heretics from public office; but these instructions were seldom carried out in the event. Excommunication, too, proved ineffectual. Direct action by the Pope's emissaries was hardly more successful: at Orvieto the governor sent out by Innocent, Pietro Parentio, was murdered by heretics in the city, who objected to his acts of violence. At Viterbo heretics were promoted to consular rank in defiance of the Papal veto: in 1207 the Pope was obliged to visit the town in person to ensure that the leading members of the sect had their goods confiscated and their houses destroyed. After 1215, when the Lateran Council confirmed all measures practised by Church and State against heretics, and elevated them to the status of unalterable laws, persecution became fiercer, but scarcely any more efficient—and this despite the support which Frederick II, the Emperor, gave to the new policy of repression. At Brescia, in 1225, Catholics and heretics came to open warfare; the Catholics were beaten, and the heretics set fire to their churches and pronounced anathemas over Rome. Despite the fulminations of Honorius III, these Brescian Cathars remained in power. At Milan, in 1228, positively Draconian measures were laid down by the bishops, and sworn to by all citizens of note: expulsion of all heretics, demolition of houses, fines, and so on. But these decrees were never implemented: the richest burghers and other notabilities quite openly gave refuge to Cathars, and endowed schools and hospices on their behalf. At Florence, despite the arrest and recantation of the Catharist Bishop Paternon, in 1226, the community continued to flourish, and its membership included a good number of priests, artisans, and common folk—not to mention the nobility. At Rome the Cathars were so numerous that their influence in the city remained very great indeed, despite threats of fines, loss of civil rights, and other reprisals—and the creation of a body known as 'Christ's Militia', the object of which was, specifically, to fight heresy.

When the Pope had recourse to the Order of Preaching Friars, and gave them the particular task of countering heresy, several Dominicans possessed of great energy and remarkable eloquence—such as Peter of Verona, Moneta of Cremona, and John of Vicenza —went travelling through the towns of Lombardy, whipping up Catholic enthusiasm for the fray, sowing terror among heretics, and even going so far as to put themselves at the head of armed troops. Peter of Verona, a converted Cathar, was assassinated in 1252, which earned him his canonization and the title of St Peter the Martyr. Everywhere Catholics began to fight back. In Parma there was founded a society of the 'Knights of Jesus'. At Florence a Community of Our Lady was formed, and men enrolled in militant religious groups, with the object of preaching anti-Catharist propaganda. Nevertheless the heretics in this town could count on some most zealous support from the ranks of the local aristocracy—and, indeed, from the common people: despite the efforts of the Inquisitors, the local clergy dared not taken any action against them. In Milan things were different: here the Emperor's threats forced the inhabitants to make proof of their orthodoxy, and in 1240 the *podesta* Oldrado of Tresseno had a large number of Cathars burnt at the stake. In 1233 John of Vicenza burnt sixty persons at Verona; two years later the Cathar bishop, John of Beneventum, was burnt at Viterbo, together with several of his companions; at Pisa, two *perfecti* went to the stake in 1240.

But the Inquisition found an increasing resistance to its activities in most of the towns as time went on. At Bergamo the city magistrates remained deaf to all the Legates' threats; at Piacenza an Inquisitor named Roland was manhandled and sent packing by the mob; at Mantua, in 1235, the Bishop was assassinated, while at Naples the heretics sacked the Dominican monastery.

At the death of Gregory IX, in 1241, the Cathars were as powerful in Italy as they had been half a century earlier. About this period, it has been estimated, there were over two thousand *perfecti* in Lombardy, not counting the one hundred and fifty belonging to the Church of Verona. The death of Frederick II in 1250 freed the Pope's hands, and allowed him to concentrate all his efforts on stamping out heresy in Northern Italy; but till the beginning of the fourteenth century the Lombard towns were to remain obstinate centres of Catharism. The struggle between magistrates and bishops went on with the same intensity of violence, fuelled by political passions and inter-clan rivalry. An increasing number of *autos-da-fé* decimated the ranks of the *perfecti*; Inquisitors were assassinated. As Catharism began to lose ground, new heresies sprang up to replace it; and the French heretics still sought refuge in Lombardy, with the object of reorganizing their persecuted Churches there.

In the French Midi, as we have seen, the spread of heresy did not give rise to any social disturbances. Only a few privately inspired movements, such as the White Brotherhood organized by Foulques, recalled that atmosphere of civil war which was a permanent feature of the times in the Lombard towns. Italian Catholics were ready to take up arms for the Pope, since they saw in him a champion against the Emperor who was oppressing them. But in Languedoc the situation was such that, even before the Crusade, almost everyone apart from the clergy was against the Pope. The Southern cities had little sympathy with a Power that exploited them without offering any compensation at a social or political level. The bishops themselves were worldly and rapacious, only serving the Pope insofar as the Pope's aims furthered theirs. They preferred, on the whole, to leave the heretics in peace, since the latter were very often their personal friends or relations. The Crusade had succeeded in strengthening those deep ties of internal solidarity which bound almost the whole country together; but it had also set up an ever-increasing opposition between the Church and lay society.

As the enemy and rival of the Papacy, Frederick II would have asked nothing better than an excuse to crush the Lombard heretics by force of arms, and then to occupy the province; and the Pope took great care not to furnish him with any such opportunity. On the other hand the King of France could occupy Languedoc with the Pope's encouragement and solemn blessing: in this latter instance His Holiness did not hesitate to identify God's cause with that of French advancement. The crusade had managed to produce a state of affairs which was exceedingly rare in the Middle Ages: a country where commons, nobles and burghers, far from squabbling amongst themselves—or even co-existing in an atmosphere of mutual distrust—formed a genuine and close-knit national party, under their legitimate sovereign. Moreover, though misfortune alone may produce a special situation of this sort, it can never, even so,

come about save amongst a people who are already deeply unified
and consciously aware of their own national greatness.

It is unlikely in the extreme that the whole population of Languedoc turned heretic; but what does seem certain is that it was, by
1229, solidly anti-Catholic, since by then the Church had become a
national enemy. The treaty of Paris put the Church and the French
King on exactly the same footing: who, then, could show reverence
for the Pope (without being regarded as a traitor) in a country
where, for twenty years now, the word 'Frenchmen' had been
synonymous with 'brigand' or 'bandit'? The King had shown himself
no more magnanimous than Simon de Montfort; and he was a good
deal harder to get rid of.

When Raymond VII signed the treaty that handed his country
over to France, he did not thereby lose any popularity; he was
regarded as having been victimized. A ravaged and war-torn land
was now controlled by various seneschals and foreign officials, who
tore down the walls of its fortresses, occupied the capital (with the
intention of forestalling any hankering after independence on the
Count's part), and exacted from these already bankrupt domains
taxes exorbitant enough to paralyse the entire economic life of the
area. All this was done in the Church's name, and at her behest.
A large proportion of the revenues to be collected—a half, in fact—
was earmarked for the churches and abbeys; and the bishops, now
more powerful than ever, would have a free hand to collect their
tithes and other dues. The King's administrators would see to it that
the sums were paid. The Carcassès, Razès and Albigeois districts,
together with Narbonne and its domains, became the property of
the French Crown—as indeed they had been since 1226, but this time
the annexation seemed final and definitive. The regions around
Toulouse, Quercy and Agen, were still in fief to the Count of Toulouse, though the latter had a French garrison sitting in his capital to
keep an eye on him. When the Count re-entered Toulouse—still
unconquered, this city, though its walls were about to be razed yet
again—he was accompanied by the Cardinal-Legate, Romanus of
S. Angelo in person. The Legate intended to make the men of Toulouse—indeed, all Languedoc—realize once and for all that this
peace treaty had been made, primarily, by and for the Church.

But the Church was not in fact a victorious Church, moving in to
lord it over a conquered nation: she had been defeated. The real
conquerors—the Crusaders, the French King, above all the wretched
condition of the people of Languedoc—had furthered the heretics'
cause in the most amazing way. The Church as such was so utterly

beaten that it took an armed occupation force to make even a show of saving her face. Now she had to set about the reconquest of this country in earnest, and by some other method than the coercive strength of the secular arm; and unless she devised a new system of control, more effective than that represented by armed violence, she ran a considerable risk of being reduced to mere empty threats.

Her task was no easy one. However, ever since 1209 a far-reaching reformation movement had been developing inside the body of the Church: this had meant that she could recruit a large number of energetic campaigners, who were ready to do anything to ensure the triumph of their Faith. If their activities called the policeman to mind rather than the missionary, that was because they were fighting against over-heavy odds, and no longer had much choice in the weapons they could use. In order to allay the hatred which the people of Languedoc felt for them, neither generosity, justice nor moderation would have sufficed; they would have been obliged, quite simply, to disappear themselves. Charity could hardly reach *that* far.

2. The Council of Toulouse

In November 1209 the Cardinal-Legate, Romanus of S. Angelo, arrived in Toulouse to inaugurate—with all due pomp and ceremony —the new era of peace and prosperity which was now beginning for Languedoc: the prosperity being that of the Catholic Church, under the aegis of the powerful and most happy protection afforded her by the French King, while the peace was to be manifested in unity of Faith, and the loyalty of *seigneurs* and commons to Church and King alike.

A solemn ceremony took place in Toulouse itself. The Count was obliged to make a second act of public submission before the Legate; and though the latter did not insist on another scourging, he nevertheless behaved as though he were some absolute monarch who, out of his pure bounty, had chosen to accord pardon and partial restitution of property to some rebellious subject, now properly repentant. The text of the treaty was read aloud and made public before the bishops and local nobility there assembled: the latter swore to observe all its clauses faithfully.

Here was a brilliant conclusion to Romanus's career in France. The Legate did not, however, quit Languedoc—or, indeed, Toulouse —until he had placed the Church's new policy with regard to this country on a sound and stable footing. The Count's various undertakings, and the oaths sworn by his vassals, were not, this time, to suffer the fate of all the many agreements previously entered upon by the rulers of Languedoc: good intentions which were never fulfilled in the event, and the fulfilment of which was declared an utter impossibility. Determined to strike while the iron was hot, the Legate, with characteristic energy, set about assembling a Council of all the Midi prelates. This was to be held in Toulouse, and had two main points on the agenda: firstly, the foundation, or rather the complete renovation, of a university in Toulouse (the Legate Conrad of Oporto having already laid the foundations of this Catholic university during the Crusade); and secondly, a solid and effective organization for stamping out heresy.

It is curious to read the circular letter drawn up at this Council by the new university's theological faculty, and intended for distribution to every major centre of scholarship in the West, with the object of attracting new students to Toulouse. Romanus of S. Angelo had brought with him various Parisian professors of theology and philosophy, who had quit the university there after the quarrel that split the Schoolmen and the Notre-Dame chapter. The new university had no lack of funds, since the Count was obliged to pay an annual sum of four thousand silver marks for its maintenance. To read the manifesto drafted by these freshly-appointed professors, one might suppose that the country to which they were seeking to attract students was a haven of peace amidst the tumult and war raging throughout the rest of Europe. The local population, it was claimed, had mild manners and welcomed strangers; the cost of living was by no means expensive, there were plenty of lodging houses, the climate was agreeable, and so on. Finally, the new university was going to 'exalt to the skies the cedar-tree of the Catholic Faith' in a place where 'the thorny brushwood of heresy had spread like a forest'. Wartime slaughter was to be replaced by the more pacific battles of controversy.[1] In short, the Count of Toulouse being reconciled to the Church had brought his country peace, the victory of the Faith, and promises of future prosperity and well-being.

This, indeed, was what the country wanted: the whole country, not just the Catholic element. The people, and the Count himself, were weary of war. Peace—even a cruel and forced peace—would give Languedoc a breathing space. At least the peasantry could sow their corn without being afraid of having the land ravaged every year.

Over a period of twenty years Toulouse had seen quite a few conquerors ride through her gates: Simon de Montfort and Prince

Louis, Foulques and the Legates. There was at least a hope that the reign of the new masters would last no longer than those of their predecessors. The Count retained some of his powers, and the Legate would soon return to Rome.

Romanus of S. Angelo was not, quite clearly, under the illusion that he had abolished heresy by a stroke of the pen, or that the era for 'more pacific battles of controversy' was at hand. On the contrary: never again in Languedoc were debates to be held between the supporters of heresy and Catholic truth. Heretics were certainly not allowed to set out their arguments for refutation from a Chair of Theology (or anywhere else, indeed, except in prison); the 'pacific battles' were reduced to monologues. Emboldened by the terms of the Treaty of Paris, the Legate drafted a series of regulations. Though these did not, on the whole, introduce any innovations in respect of ecclesiastical legislation, it was the first time that they had been so systematically or permanently enforced.

The suppression of heresy now became obligatory by common law. Like the civil or criminal codes, it applied to all alike; indeed, it was even more rigorous, since every single inhabitant was affected by it, without any exceptions whatsoever. Under these new regulations a girl of twelve who (because of illness or prolonged absence, say) had failed to take the oath to fight heresy—or even had not been able, for some reason, to make her Easter confession—was liable to incur suspicion of heresy, and have legal sanctions enforced against her.

The most striking thing about these regulations is their methodical, not to say bureaucratic, thoroughness. They would seem—on paper, at any rate—to have set up a system of virtual police control over the entire population; and we may well query whether the Church possessed the physical means to enforce such articles to the letter. Certainly she could only have attained this end after long years of unremitting effort.

The main articles of Romanus's decree are as follows:

In each parish the archbishops and bishops are to nominate a priest, and two or three lay persons of good repute, to visit each house, and all suspect localities such as caves, barns, and so on—anywhere, in fact, that might serve as a hiding place for heretics. If they find any heretics during their search, they are to notify the Bishop, the *seigneur* of the area, and the bailiffs, that the law may take its course. Similar searches are to be carried out by *seigneurs* and abbots, in houses, towns, and especially forests.

Whosoever shall be convicted of having allowed a heretic to live within his domain shall lose the said domain, and himself be handed over for summary justice to his own *seigneur*. If any heretics shall be found on his land, he is still liable under this law, even though his connivance with the said heretics remain unproven. The house in which a heretic is discovered shall be burnt, and the property upon which it stands shall be forfeit.

Any bailiff who shows himself negligent in the pursuit of heretics shall lose both his goods and the post he holds.

No man shall be punished as a heretic or heretical believer save by the bishop of the area or a judge of the Church, and then only after due judgment.

Any person is entitled to hunt heretics upon another man's land, and that man's bailiffs shall be obliged to give him assistance. Thus the King's bailiffs may search out heretics upon the Count of Toulouse's domains, and *vice versa*.

When a heretic of his own will abandons heresy, he shall change his place of residence, and be pronounced free of all suspicion; he shall wear two crosses sewn upon either side of his breast, they to be different in colour from the garment he wears; he shall discharge no public office, nor shall he be permitted to draft any manner of public record, unless reinstated in his rights by a letter from the Pope or the Legate. Any heretic who returns to the Catholic Faith, not spontaneously, but through fear of death or some such reason, shall be cast into prison by the bishop; and those who receive his property shall be liable for his maintenance. If, however. he be destitute, the bishop shall provide for him.

Every male aged fourteen and upwards, and every female over twelve years, shall abjure heresy, swear loyalty to the orthodox Faith, and promise both to search out heretics, and to denounce any such that are known to them. The names of every person dwelling in the parish shall be recorded, and they shall all swear this oath before the Bishop or his deputy; absentees shall do so within fifteen days of their return. Those failing to take the oath (and their names will be easily ascertained from an inspection of the lists) shall be treated as heretical suspects. The oath must be renewed every two years.

Every person, of either sex, once having attained the age of reason, must confess to their parish priest (or to some other priest if their own *curé* permits it) thrice yearly. They are to make their Communion at Christmas, Easter, and Pentecost, providing that they are not counselled to abstain, on any particular occasion, by their parish priest. Priests are to seek out any who fail to attend

Holy Communion, and who thereby incur suspicion of heretical beliefs.

All heads of households are obliged to attend Mass on Sundays and feast days, on pain of a twelve-denier fine, unless they are excused by illness or some other legitimate cause.

No person shall possess either an Old or a New Testament; exception may be made in the cases of the Psalter, the Breviary, or Our Lady's Book of Hours, though these shall be in Latin only.

No person under suspicion of heresy shall practise as a doctor. A sick person who has received Holy Communion shall be kept under watch to prevent any heretic, or suspected heretic, from coming near him.

Wills shall be made in the presence of the parish priest, or, if he be absent, in that of some person of good repute, clerical or lay: if not, they shall be null and void.

It is forbidden for any *seigneur*, baron, knight, castellan, or other such person to entrust the administration of his estates to a heretic or heretical believer.

Any person denounced by public opinion, and whose ill reputation is known to the Bishop or other trustworthy individuals, shall properly be regarded as a heretic. [See Appendix D.]

As can be seen, these decrees, to be adequately enforced, would have needed large numbers of personnel supervising their execution. Doubtless each parish priest could draw up a list of his parishioners, and even mark off those who had failed to take the oath or make their Communion, and pronounce them suspect of heresy. It was already difficult enough to bring all such to trial, simply on the grounds of sheer numbers. The fear of getting oneself into trouble might drive many of the faithful to conform to the rules; but it was still essential, in the long run, that this fear should be justified by the effective authority of the Church.

It was not, perhaps, difficult to find two or three lay persons in each parish anxious to hunt out heretics; but these two or three had also to be backed up by the majority of the local population. Without such support it would be hard to lay hands on the heretics once they were tracked down.

Self-interest might drive the *seigneurs* to confiscate land that belonged to those who sheltered heretics; while fear of losing property or position, and of seeing their houses demolished, might force people to deny heretics the right of asylum. But there still had to be an authority strong enough to take charge of this heretic-hunt, to demolish houses and confiscate lands. Quite apart from the inevitable disorders which such a system of repression was liable to provoke throughout the country, it was doubtful how far the Count and his vassals could be relied upon in the execution of these measures; and even the King's own officers were already fully occupied with their existing duties. The bishops had their own armed posses available; but in order to capture a heretic one first had to find him, and all heretics were highly skilled at throwing pursuers off their tracks. Moreover, among those proscribed were large numbers of powerful *seigneurs* whom it would be very awkward to attack, and who had in any case taken an oath to prove their religious orthodoxy.

Romanus of S. Angelo was not content merely to promulgate these decrees of his. Before he left Toulouse he was determined to impress public opinion by holding a really spectacular trial, something that would intimidate those who regarded his regulations as non-enforceable. Now he had in his hands at the time two heretics who had recently been discovered and arrested by men in the service of the Count of Toulouse. (The Count had tried to inspire confidence in the Legate by giving him this proof of his, the Count's, goodwill.) These two were both *perfecti*. One of them, William, is even referred to by Albéric des Trois Fontaines[2] as the Albigensian 'Pope' [*apostolicus*]; he may in fact have been Bishop of the Albi diocese, or at all events an especially revered old man whom his captors (in order to make their catch sound more important) dubbed with the title of 'Pope'. The other *perfectus*, also called William (his surname being de Solier), was likewise a heretic of note, well known throughout the Toulouse diocese.

The so-called 'Albigensian Pope' went to his death with that firm composure characteristic of all Cathar ministers, and was solemnly burnt in Toulouse, while the Cardinal-Legate looked on. But William de Solier was converted to Catholicism, and thus became an extremely valuable supporter of the Church. So that it could legally receive his deposition, the Council gave him full rehabilitation; whereupon he denounced a great many persons whom he knew to be members of the Catharist Church. He was excellently placed to give information concerning their identities, their hide-outs, and their meeting places. He does not, however, appear to have denounced or exposed very many *perfecti*, for the persons mentioned by him in his testimony were ordinary *credentes*.

The Bishop of Toulouse next summoned a number of witnesses whose religious orthodoxy was well known, and caused them to give evidence against such heretics as they knew. In combination with William de Solier's statements, this formed an impressive list of suspects. Those accused were cited to appear before an ecclesiastical tribunal.

But this initial inquiry gave few solid results: when they were interrogated the suspects simply refused to talk. Some, who were either bolder or more knowledgeable than the rest, demanded to know the names of the witnesses who had laid evidence against them. This was their most basic right; unless an accused person was confronted with the witnesses to his offence, there could be no regular trial in law. But it is plain that special circumstances applied in this case: the judges could not reveal the names of their informants, since this would expose such persons to public reprisals, and discourage similar acts of delation in the future. So the Cardinal-Legate refused to furnish those charged with the names of their accusers; whereupon they followed him as far as Montpellier, and repeated their request there.

Romanus of S. Angelo prevaricated his way out of this dilemma. He showed them the list of all those who had been cited to give evidence at the preliminary enquiry, without saying if they had yet made their depositions, or identifying those against whom they had testified. Instead he asked the accused whether they could pick out, from this list, the names of their personal enemies. This threw the accused off balance; they could not tell if the witnesses listed might not have testified in their favour, or even have made no personal accusations whatsoever. The result was that they dared not impugn a single one of them, and threw themselves on the Legate's mercy. This trick of Romanus's was later to be widely employed by the ecclesiastical tribunals.

It was not even in Toulouse itself that the Legate conducted the trial of these heretics, but Orange; and it was likewise in Orange that he held a Council to promulgate—throughout those States of Languedoc which were now vassal to the French Crown—the regulations which he had already instituted back in Toulouse. The Bishop of Toulouse, Foulques, had gone with him; and it was Foulques who, on his return to the capital, was responsible for imposing on the accused such penances as the Legate had prescribed. Romanus of S. Angelo now left the Midi and returned to Rome, where shortly afterwards the Pope nominated him Bishop of Oporto.

3. *The Church's Dilemma and the Dominican Reform Movement*

At this point the Legate was convinced that 'the Church had at last found peace in Languedoc' [Pelhisson]. But his Inquisitorial decree, despite the burning of William the *perfectus* and the mass arraignment of suspects, seems not to have made any great impression on the people of Toulouse. Bishop Foulques, who had been made responsible for the suppression of heresy, was so unpopular that he dared not stir abroad without an armed escort, and had great difficulty in collecting the tithes due to him. The Count, as is quite understandable, did nothing whatsoever to defend his Bishop's rights; the aged prelate complained bitterly about this, saying, with involuntary cynicism: 'I have lived nowhere better than in exile, and I am ready for exile once more.'³ In any case Foulques was not to occupy the episcopal see of Toulouse much longer. Overcome by age and weariness, and above all disheartened by the invincible hatred shown him by the inhabitants of his diocese, he soon retired to the monastery of Grandselve, where he prepared himself for death by composing hymns. He finally died in 1231.

The systematic suppression of heresy laid down by the Treaty of Meaux and solemnly inaugurated by Romanus of S. Angelo was then, to all practical intents and purposes, unworkable. The ecclesiastical authorities were morally separated from the rest of Languedoc; and the punitive measures taken by them against heresy had, it would appear, achieved little except to create a conscious, well-organized spirit of dissimulation among the heretics and their partisans. The new laws remained a dead letter, because anyone who had the slightest connection with the ecclesiastical authorities made firm protestations of his orthodox beliefs; and since the Church vigilantes were few in number, and consequently little feared, life went on regardless of them.

'The heretics and their followers,' declared William Pelhisson the Dominican, referring to the period immediately after the Treaty of Meaux, 'armed themselves ever more strongly, and multiplied their wiles and stratagems against the Church and the Catholics. In Toulouse and its environs they did more harm than was occasioned by the war.'⁴ We know nothing of the Cathars' activities during these years except such facts as can be gleaned from the records of trials or other investigations, or those that were of public notoriety; even in this latter category there must have been much that the judges missed. They were not omniscient, and no one was inclined to supply them with information.

The *seigneurs* of Niort (who played leading rôles in a long and spectacular trial to which we shall have occasion to return later) openly gave refuge to five *perfecti*, whom they refused to surrender even on the Archbishop of Narbonne's injunction. They also arranged meetings of heretics, and took in numerous suspects; their mother Esclarmonde was a *perfecta* famous throughout the area, and so zealous and influential that her spiritual superiors had given her a special dispensation allowing her both to eat meat and to tell lies (concerning her faith and her co-religionists) when she found it necessary.

In 1233 a large gathering of heretics and their followers was held in the castle of Roquefort: they had come from miles around to hear William Vidal preach. Fanjeaux was still an official centre of the Catharist Church; all the knights and gentry in the district would attend meetings presided over by Bishop Guilhabert de Castres. In 1229 Cavaers, the Dame of Fanjeaux, had solemnly summoned all the nobility of the region to her château at Mongradail for the admission of her nephew, Arnald de Castelverdun, to the ranks of the *perfecti*. In Toulouse, the house of Alaman de Roaix (who belonged to that same Roaix family which had sheltered the Count of Toulouse when he was driven out of his own palace by the Bishop) was no more nor less than a regular 'heretical establishment', where travelling *perfecti* of either sex were lodged, and religious meetings were held. At Cabaret, the deacon Arnald Hot was in residence at the château; in 1229 this château had been occupied by French troops, yet two years later it was already a meeting place for all the heretics in the area. The Cathars, deacons and *perfecti* alike, travelled the countryside without even attempting to conceal themselves: bestowing the *consolamentum*, preaching, and, indeed, exercising their ministry in a more or less normal fashion. We find the *perfectus* Vigoros de Baconia covering the whole of the Toulouse and Ariège regions in this way: indeed, he obviously had no need to hide himself, since at the news of his arrival, the faithful flocked in from all the surrounding villages to listen to his preaching and good counsel.

The religious fervour of the Cathars and their adherents had not been in the least shaken by the decrees passed at the Council of Toulouse. On the contrary: there was a steadily increasing mood of exasperation abroad, provoked by a combination of factors—the presence of French troops, the obligation to return to the Church those properties impounded during the war, the obligation on the people to pay tithes regularly, the obligation to make over once more to De Montfort's Crusaders, or their heirs, the châteaux which had since reverted to those with more legitimate claims upon them. The Peace of Paris was a despoiler's peace, a one-sided imposition upon the country, from which the Church alone derived any benefit, and which could not be regarded as final or binding.

The nobles, in particular those who belonged to the former House of Trencavel, had been stripped of their possessions and humiliated in their pride. They were, in any case, naturally pugnacious men, and inured to the struggle by twenty years of warfare; so their one thought was to hatch plots together while awaiting the chance to get their revenge. Languedoc had only laid down its arms because it lacked the money with which to carry on the war. Despite his solemn undertakings, the Count's only aim was to hamper any advance that the Church and the French forces might make in the country thanks to the special facilities granted them under the peace treaty. The *seigneurs* who had made their submission still remained lords of their own domains, and were all the less inclined to renounce such rights now that their oaths of loyalty should (in theory, at least) put them beyond the Church's suspicions. Local officials, such as the *seigneurs'* bailiffs or justices of the peace, openly opposed any efforts to hunt down or arrest heretics, and made no attempt to stop those who took up arms against the King's officers.

For instance, the seneschal André Chauvet, or Calvet, was assassinated in 1230, during a round-up he had organized to trap the heretics of La Bessède[5]; this murder went unpunished, though the local *seigneurs* (the Lords of Niort) and even the Count of Toulouse himself were accused of complicity in it. These same Lords of Niort, who came under the diocesan authority of the Archbishop of Narbonne, had, in 1233, made an armed assault on the grounds of the archbishopric itself. Not content with driving off cattle and taking a group of servants prisoner, they forced their way into the Archbishop's house, wounded him, manhandled his clerks, removed the *pallium* (that symbol of archiepiscopal authority) together with many other valuables, and finally set fire to the surrounding countryside. The Archbishop, Peter Amiel, lodged a complaint with the Pope, denouncing the said *seigneurs* as heretics and rebels, which indeed was the least he could have said in the circumstances. But though he might protest to the Pope, he could not obtain justice in his own diocese—and that despite the presence of French authorities on Occitan soil.

In the Toulouse area public reaction against the Church was all the more violent since the Count supported it more or less openly. When a Dominican, Roland of Cremona, preached *ex cathedra* in the new university against heretics, and made accusations of heresy against the inhabitants of Toulouse, the consuls protested vehemently, and demanded that the Prior of the Dominican monastery should silence this impetuous preacher of his. But Brother Roland

8 Drawing from a bas-relief in the thirteenth century St Nazaire Church in Carcassonne showing an episode in the siege of Toulouse and believed to depict the death of Simon de Montfort on 25th June, 1218

9 An engraving by Nicolas Cochin (1688–1754) taken from a painting by Pierre-Jacques Cazes (1676–1754) showing Count Raymond VI of Toulouse receiving absolution at Saint-Gilles

10 Glazed terra-cotta relief from the door of the Cathedral in Florence by Andrea della Robbia (1435–1525) showing a meeting between Saint Dominic and Saint Francis

11 & 12   View and town plan of Toulouse, both from seventeenth century engravings

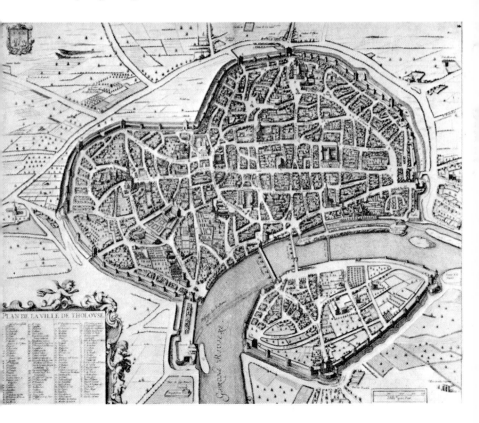

13 The fortified church at Albi

14 & 15 A view of the Cathedral and the town of Béziers from the river; (**14**) a nineteenth century lithograph print, and (**15**) a modern photograph

16   The street behind the St Nazaire Church in Carcassonne

17 The castle at Carcassonne

18 The castle of Montségur on its hilltop seen from the south-west

19 A view of the town of Carcassonne

continued to attack the conduct of the citizen body with all his previous vigour, and provoked a scandal by having the bodies of two recently dead persons exhumed and burnt: A. Peyre, an official benefactor of the Saint-Sernin Chapter, and Galvanus, a Waldensian minister buried in the cemetery at Villeneuve. Both these men, though heretics, or at least under suspicion of heresy, had been very highly regarded in Catholic circles. These acts, performed 'for the greater glory of our Lord Jesus Christ and Blessed Dominic, and in honour of our Holy Mother the Church of Rome' [Pelhisson], shocked public opinion and resulted in the consuls making a second protest to the Dominican Prior. This time Brother Roland was sent packing. The same writer, Pelhisson, criticizes both knights and burghers in Toulouse for their incessant and outrageous attacks on those whose business it was to hunt out heretics. The job of heretic-hunting became so dangerous, in fact, that the Church authorities required considerable courage to go on with it in the face of such opposition, and to bring captured suspects safely to ecclesiastical prisons for subsequent interrogation and trial.

The difficulty was not so much discovering heretics as contriving to secure their persons. The tribunals were very often reduced to passing sentence *in absentia* or arresting people who lay under no particular suspicion and against whom nothing serious could be proved—such as the twelve-year-old girl from Montauban, Peryon-nelle, who had been brought up in a convent of *perfectae* and was reconciled to the Church by Bishop Foulques. But better even than this, the burghers sometimes went over to the offensive themselves, using their adversaries' own weapons. For instance, during the course of a dispute, Peter Peytavi described one Bernard de Solaro, a buckle-maker, as a 'heretic' (and rightly so, it would seem); whereupon the buckle-maker brought suit against him for slander. Peytavi was summoned before the city Council and condemned by the consuls to several years in exile, besides having to pay a fine to the court and damages to the plaintiff. Peytavi's real crime was not so much questioning the buckle-maker's orthodoxy as making too public a display of his Catholic sentiments. He lodged a protest against the verdict with the Toulouse Dominicans, and appealed from them to the Bishop. Before an ecclesiastical tribunal, with two Dominicans, Peter Seila and William Arnald, acting on his behalf, he won his appeal hands down, and his opponent was forced to flee into Lombardy. Apropos this incident Pelhisson wrote: 'Blessed be God and His servant Dominic, who defended their own so well.'[6] The importance attached by the Church to so insignificant an affair (the two

K

Dominicans who supported Peytavi were none other than the future
Inquisitors of Toulouse) shows in itself how bitter and fruitless a
struggle the ecclesiastical authorities were now waging against the
civic power wielded by the consuls. They were reduced to thanking
God because they had contrived to reverse a judgment in favour of
a man under suspicion of heresy; and even so they had not convinced the consuls, but only their own Bishop.

This Bishop, enthroned on the death of Foulques, was Raymond
du Fauga, or de Falgar, who belonged to the Miramont family,
from the neighbourhood of Toulouse. He was a hard and fanatical
Dominican, who, according to William de Puylaurens, 'began as his
predecessor had ended—pursuing heretics, defending the rights of
the Church, and urging the Count (sometimes gently, sometimes
more forcibly) into the paths of righteousness'.[7] It is true that the
Bishop must have had a decidedly forcible way with him, since he
had managed to drag the Count (whose 'crass negligence' in the
persecution of heretics all Catholics deplored) into a special round-
up, at the head of an armed posse—and during this round-up a
nocturnal gathering was surprised in a wood near Castelnaudary.
Nineteen heretics were captured on this occasion, among them
Pagan or Payen de La Bessède, a *faidit* and one of the leading
Cathar nobles, a knight whose valour was a by-word. Pagan and his
eighteen companions were straightway condemned to death and
burnt, on the Count's orders. We may well ask ourselves what
arguments the Bishop could have deployed in order to force the
Count into so harsh an act, which was completely out of character,
and which constituted a species of treachery towards a vassal: the
faidit nobility had always been Raymond's most loyal supporters.
At all events, having given Raymond du Fauga this indubitable
proof of his good intentions, the Count clearly regarded himself as
quit for the time being, and took no steps to prevent *seigneurs* and
consuls alike from defying the Church's authority more or less
openly.

The restlessness throughout the country was so marked that the
Pope himself, through fear of a general rebellion, adopted a comparatively mild policy towards the Count of Toulouse. In 1230 he
advised the new Legate, Peter of Colmieu, to treat the Count
carefully, 'in order to increase his zeal towards God and the Church'.
He granted the Count a delay of payment over the ten thousand
marks of compensation he owed the Church, a sum imposed by
the Treaty of Meaux. He even authorized him to help discharge

the debt by imposing contributions on the local clergy. Finally, on 18th September, 1230, he agreed to re-examine the judgment condemning the late Raymond VI, since his son was deeply distressed at not being able to bury the old Count in consecrated Christian ground according to his dying wishes. This blackmailing attitude to Raymond VII's filial piety went on for a long time: in fact the old Count was never to be granted Christian burial. But the Pope nevertheless continued—to all appearances, at least—to treat Raymond with some circumspection, since 'in order to increase his piety, he may profitably be watered like a young plant, and nourished with the milk of the Church'.[8] This indulgent attitude, which the Count's behaviour only partially justified, can hardly be explained by a desire to curb the ambitions of the French King: the King was a fifteen-year-old boy, and his mother for all her energy had enough trouble with her ever-rebellious Northern vassals. Through the Count's person the Pope sought to soothe over-inflamed public opinion, and to afford the Church some protection in a country that had become increasingly hostile to her.

It seems almost certain that in those areas which were subject to French *seigneurs* or royal seneschals rather than the Count of Toulouse, the Church's position was worse still—as is demonstrated by the way the Lords of Niort treated the Archbishop of Narbonne. But in 1233 this same Archbishop, whose safety had been so seriously threatened, decided to take legal action in person against his attackers, who could count on zealous support even among the ranks of the local clergy. However, he still could not act until he obtained the express approval of Gregory IX, who appointed as judges the Bishop of Toulouse, the Provost of Toulouse Cathedral, and the Archbishop of Carcassonne. In order to have these *seigneurs* actually brought to trial, the Archbishop was first obliged to consult the Pope at Anagni (where Gregory spent 1232) and subsequently to go to Rome. On 8th March, 1233, a Papal Bull was sent to the Bishop of Toulouse, bidding him 'execute the sentences passed upon the Lords of Niort by the Council of Toulouse'.

The Lords of Niort were among the most powerful feudal barons in the whole of Languedoc, possessing domains in the Laurac, Razès, and Sault districts. They had already been excommunicated by the Council of Toulouse, and the excommunication was reiterated in 1233. Notorious heretics, despite all their avowals to the contrary, these men had little fear of the Church's spiritual thunderbolts; and in order to reduce them by force the agreement, indeed the aid, of the Count of Toulouse was essential. The Count, however, drew the line at arresting his own vassals; so the Pope had recourse to the King of France, or, more accurately, to the Lady Regent. Faced with the double threat of Papal wrath and renewed hostilities with France, the Count gave way, and summoned a Council of bishops and barons, before whom he promulgated a decree against heresy, on 20th April, 1233. He took the same line as the Council of Toulouse had done in 1229; the result was that these regulations, hitherto restricted to the domain of *ecclesiastical* justice, now became part of the penal code, coming under the Count's own juridical authority.

The Lords of Niort (or two of them at any rate, Bernard-Otho and William) were summoned before a tribunal by William Arnald, refused to answer questions, and walked out. Next day they were arrested and imprisoned by the seneschal, John de Friscamps. The truth was that the only way in which the Church could impose her will was by force of arms, with the Count, however reluctantly, supporting the occupying power. The trial of these secular leaders of the Catharist resistance movement was only possible thanks to a French seneschal's intervention.

The trial itself was long and inconclusive. A large number of witnesses testified against Bernard-Otho and William de Niort—something easier to arrange in Toulouse than in their own part of the country, where they were so powerful that their mother, Esclarmonde, had been able to defy the Archbishop himself openly, and more or less show him the door. Various priests and clerks came forward and declared that Bernard-Otho de Niort not only publicly entertained heretics in his house, but also debarred from his lands those persons who came to seek out such heretics; that he had, on one occasion, gone into a church, stopped the priest's sermon, and put up a *perfectus* to preach in his stead; that he had taken part in the murder of André Chauvet, and so on. Oddly enough, there were just as many witnesses who testified to the Niort brothers' religious orthodoxy—particularly with regard to this same Bernard-Otho, who would seem to have adopted a double-bluff policy of the most thoroughgoing sort. According to William de Solier (who, it must be said, showed great reluctance to denounce his former friends) the accused was regarded in Catharist circles as a 'notorious traitor', a man in the King of France's pay. Some Brothers of St John of Jerusalem, from the Order's house at Pexiora, spoke of the accused as a sincere Catholic who, in his zeal for the Faith, had actually been responsible for the deaths of about a thousand heretics. The Archbishop of Vielmores, Raymond the Scrivener, came forward and declared that Bernard-Otho was a most loyal supporter both of King and Church, and that the trial as a whole had been activated 'by hatred rather than charity'.

Despite such cumulative testimony in his favour, Bernard-Otho was pronounced a heretic, and condemned to death for his stubborn persistence in refusing to confess anything throughout the proceedings. His brother William and his son Bernard, who had in the end confessed, were condemned to life imprisonment. The sentence of death was not carried out: the French barons settled in the Midi (with the single exception of Guy de Lévis, the son of Simon de Montfort's companion-in-arms) opposed this execution, which, they asserted, was liable to provoke serious disturbances throughout the country. In any case Bernard-Otho and William regained their freedom shortly afterwards, since three years later they were condemned all over again, Bernard-Otho *in absentia*. The third of the Niort brothers, Guiraud, had, very sensibly, not put in an appearance at Toulouse. Instead he had gone to ground on his estates, where he and his mother continued to serve the Catharist faith as zealously as ever.

Though Bernard-Otho de Niort had on several occasions come to terms with the French, and had even fought beside Simon de Montfort, he still, even after his condemnation, remained a loyal servant of the Catharist Church. His equivocal behaviour can be explained by the urgent need there was to deceive the enemy, and give more effective help to his own side by so doing. Yet on the day when, grievously wounded, he asked for the *consolamentum*, Bishop Guilhabert de Castres bitterly reproached him for 'all he had taken from the [Catharist] Church', and demanded a fine of twelve hundred Melgorian *sous* in recompense. The Catharist Church too could show as hard an authoritarian side when required, and instilled great fear into her followers, even though the chastisements she had at her disposal were of a strictly spiritual sort. The persecutions had made her more flexible and tolerant over various points of doctrine (as we can see from the permission granted certain *perfecti* to eat meat and conceal their convictions in circumstances that might otherwise imperil the Church's interests); but in some ways, too, her discipline must have hardened. The *perfecti* now found themselves obliged to demand greater sacrifices from the faithful. They could no longer trust everybody; the gifts and legacies which provided them with the means of subsistance had been rendered illegal by these newly-established laws. The moral influence which they exerted upon their followers must have been very different from that employed by the Catholic Church but when we recall that for many people in

Languedoc these men were the sole custodians of truth, and the *consolamentum* the one essential condition for salvation, there can be no doubt that this influence was a force to be reckoned with.

The all-prevailing discontent in Languedoc was primarily due to the devastations wreaked by twenty years of warfare, which had changed a free and flourishing country into a poverty-stricken area, its freedom forfeit to a foreign power. The poet Sicard de Marvejols mourned over what was lost:

> *Ai! Tolosa et Provensa!*
> *E la terra d'Argensa!*
> *Bezers et Carcassey!*
> *Quo vos vi! quo vos vei!*

It is true that no one banned the Courts of Love or other more popular amusements; that marriages and baptisms were still performed; and that the commercial cities continued as far as was practicable to attract customers and foreign trade. But the nobles were ruined, and had no more money to spend on festivals than they did on warfare; while the presence in the towns of a foreign authority, and the vastly increased activity of the ecclesiastical vigilantes, tended to create an atmosphere of resentment and suspicion. Throughout the ravaged countryside there wandered bands of famished brigands, against whom it was becoming steadily harder to maintain order. By compelling the Count and his vassals to dismiss their mercenaries the treaty had achieved two results: it had deprived the Occitan *seigneurs* of an instrument for their own protection and the policing of their domains, and it had turned loose on the countryside a series of armed bands which, since no one was paying them any longer, proceeded to collect for themselves.

For years now the people of Languedoc had fought in the hope of seeing better times; and now they found themselves saddled with a peace which left them not only poorer than ever, but still under foreign domination. They were becoming increasingly bitter as time went on, and held the Church, rather than the French, responsible for their misfortunes. The clergy were more intimately connected with the country's life than were the King's officials and those *seigneurs* who held their lands by virtue of De Montfort's conquests. The clergy were everywhere. Each village had its priest, and every town its quota of monasteries, chancelleries, and ecclesiastical militiamen. The larger part of this clerical body consisted of Southerners, whom many of their fellow-countrymen tended to regard as traitors—though some of them, it is true, opposed the Church's policy on patriotic grounds.

Here were men who dwelt in an impoverished country, yet who now claimed even greater benefices than they had previously done; men who were wealthy, or at least comfortably off, yet who had recourse to French arms or threats of reprisals whenever anyone refused to pay their taxes. In a war which had seen so many human lives, so much energy and enthusiasm squandered to no purpose, these men had figured in the public mind as profiteers *par excellence*. As a result they had incurred such hostility that Pelhisson was almost certainly mistaken in accusing heretics alone when he referred to their causing more harm in Toulouse and its environs than ever the war had done. In any case, the Pope's attempts to conciliate the Count had proved useless: in this country a policy of moderation and tolerance could do the Church nothing but harm.

Since Languedoc was already in part the direct property of the French Crown, and in part the heritage-to-be of a brother of the King, the Pope could hardly launch an appeal for a fresh Crusade. Nor was the Lady Regent anxious to resume a long and costly war which would have compromised the agreements reached in the Treaty of Paris: she contented herself with an occasional threat to Raymond, who always made haste to offer her new pledges of his submission.

The suppression of heresy—and, indeed, not only heresy as such but naked anti-clericalism—was a difficult business. It was not properly organized, and more than one authority was responsible for it, with differing systems of legislation. The Bishop's diocesan writ lacked sufficient armed men to enforce it, while the Count was lax in his duties and suspected of sympathy with the heretics. Even the French *seigneurs*, it seems, had something better to do than carry on endless guerilla skirmishing under the pretext of looking for heretics.

When the Pope decided to entrust the suppression of heresy to a special organization, consisting of men who were professional 'Inquisitors' and nothing else, it was not his intention merely to provide the bishops with yet another assistant, whose purpose would be to relieve them of a part of their responsibilities. It was, indeed, true that the bishops already had such a load of diverse worries and duties that they could hardly devote their time to chasing heretics; yet neither Raymond du Fauga, the Bishop of Toulouse, nor his predecessor Foulques, nor indeed Peter Amiel of Narbonne, had lacked either zeal or energy in the defence of their Faith. No; the special Inquisition which Gregory IX instituted in his round letter of 20th April, 1233, was to be, as the Pope saw it, an instrument of terrorization. Otherwise it had no reason to exist.

There was nothing new about the term 'Inquisition' in itself. It had long been used to describe that process at law which consisted in tracking down heretics in any given country, and making them recognize the error of their ways. All bishops held periodical Inquisitions, when they questioned and tried persons suspected of heresy. The decrees passed by the Councils of Verona, Lateran, and Toulouse set up what might be described as permanent Inquisitions, since they made not only the bishops but also the civil authorities responsible for hunting down and punishing heretics. For the first time, however, Gregory IX now envisaged the creation of Church dignitaries whose sole function should be to conduct Inquisitions, who should have the official title of 'Inquisitor', and who, in their Inquisitorial capacity, should be responsible to the Pope personally, and not subject to the Bishop's authority. This in itself was a revolutionary step, since it placed an ordinary monk—at least as regards his official actions—on an equal footing with the Bishop, and even in a way above him. As we shall see, an Inquisitor's prerogatives were such that the Bishop concerned could neither excommunicate nor suspend him—nor even counter his decisions without a formal order from the Pope.

The power granted to these Papal High Commissioners was, to all intents and purposes, unlimited. It still remained to select men capable of justifying such trust. This new institution would scarcely have been possible if the Pope had not had, ready to hand, a brand-new religious fighting force, a fiercely aggressive body whose strength and potential he had gauged well.

St Dominic (he was not yet a saint at this period, but his canonization followed very shortly afterwards) had died in 1221, at the age of fifty-one. He had pursued his ministry in the Midi for over a decade (1205–17), fighting heresy first with a mixture of patience and preaching, then with more violent methods, and gathering the Catholic elements of the population about him; in 1218 Honorius III had granted his preaching-and-poverty movement official recogtion, under the title of 'The Order of Preaching Friars'. The sheer power of Dominic's personality, combined with the urgent need that existed for change and reform in Catholicism, had been such that at the time of his death there were already sixty convents of Preaching Friars established up and down Europe. When his successor, Jordanus of Saxony, died in 1237, the number had risen to three hundred. These monasteries had sprung up not only in France, Italy and Spain, but as far afield as Poland, Greece, Scandinavia, Greenland and Iceland.

The Preaching or Mendicant Friars, then, already constituted a vast missionary movement, composed of men ready to go out and fight for their Catholic Faith. They led incredibly bleak and austere lives, these heroic vagabonds who devoted themselves, with inexhaustible fervour, to the business of preaching. Their activities drew many young and energetic men to join them, men eager to give themselves to God's service; the Dominicans' mission was not only to set an example of voluntary poverty and prayer, but also, and especially, to convert souls for God—whether by fighting heresy, or the pagan creeds, or Islam.

An Order that had come into existence in mid-Crusade, at a time when battle, slaughter, and the *auto-da-fé* were commonplaces, could not—in the heretical countries at least—be anything but fiercely fanatical. This, at all events, is what emerges from the behaviour of those Dominicans resident in Languedoc, the Inquisitors especially. Yet before the official setting up of the Inquisition, it would not appear that they suffered any kind of martyrdom. St Dominic himself went, more or less on his own, through districts where the heretics were in control, and suffered nothing worse than a few jeering insults, a few stones flung at him by peasants. The Crusade had made the heretics' supporters abandon that attitude of comparative tolerance which their enemies, even so, regarded as the very height of anti-Catholic bigotry. Yet religious fanaticism in the South was not a genuinely murderous emotion. Even during the most violent popular uprisings Dominicans might be beaten up or sworn at, but they were very seldom killed, except in certain special instances to which we shall refer later. Compared with their adversaries, those Dominicans whose names have survived the passage of time appear to have been men of a very rare and special temper. It is clear that when he turned to the Prior of the Provincial Dominicans (that is, those in the South of France), the Pope was counting on this dignitary to choose men with an exceptional passion for the Faith. Bishop Raymond du Fauga, who was to prove so remarkable a fanatic, may not have been an Inquisitor; but he was a Dominican.

If the Pope entrusted this Order with the suppression of heresy, that was, surely, because he knew he could find men in it who would, within very wide limits, stop at nothing.

CHAPTER X

THE INQUISITION

1. *Early Activities*

ON 27TH JULY 1233 Gregory IX nominated Stephen de Burnin, Archbishop of Vienne, as Apostolic Legate for the provinces of Narbonne, Arles, Aix and Vienne, and the dioceses of Clermont, Agen, Albi, Rodez, Cahors, Mende, Périgueux, Comminges, Lectoure and Le Puy, with the special mission of extirpating heresy in the French Midi. He widened the Legate's plenipotentiary authority to embrace the provinces of Auch, Bordeaux, Embrun, Catalonia and Tarragon; and it was through the Legate as intermediary that, in the name of the Holy See, the two Brothers chosen by the Dominican Provincial of Toulouse, Peter Seila and William Arnald, had their powers confirmed. They were the first Inquisitors.

Peter Seila was a wealthy burgher of Toulouse, one of St Dominic's first companions. As a fervent disciple of the Spanish monk's, he had given one of his houses to provide shelter for the growing Dominican community. William Arnald was a native of Montpellier, and enjoyed considerable authority among the Dominicans in Toulouse. These men were granted full authority to proceed against heresy, without being responsible to either episcopal or civil justice; and the powers they held were valid throughout the dioceses of Albi and Toulouse.

The first action taken by the two Dominicans in their Inquisitorial capacity was the capture of Vigoros de Baconia, regarded as the leading heretic in Toulouse. Vigoros was tried, condemned, and executed almost immediately. By depriving the Catharist Church of one of its most dynamic leaders, the new Inquisitors had inaugurated their campaign with a masterly gambit.

While Peter Seila stayed behind in Toulouse, William Arnald left on a grand Inquisitorial tour of the entire province. He visited Castelnaudary, Laurac, Saint-Martin-la-Lande, Gaja, Villefranche, La Bessède, Avignonet, Saint-Félix, and Fanjeaux, in each place rallying the ecclesiastical authorities to his support in hunting down heretics and investigating suspects. He must have acted with quite uncommon vigour, since that same year the Count wrote to the Pope, complaining of these plenipotentiaries sent out by the Holy See, and accusing them of charges such as he had never laid against the diocesan judges in the Bishop's court. These Inquisitors, he alleged, ignored all proper legal procedure, interrogated suspects behind closed doors, denied accused persons the assistance of a lawyer, and generally provoked the most acute terror. Some of those summoned before them were so scared that they denounced innocent people, while others took advantage of the secret conditions under which testimony was given, and charged their private enemies with heretical beliefs.

The Count further accused them of instituting proceedings against persons long since reconciled to the Church, and of punishing as rebels others who were attempting to lodge an appeal with the Holy See. 'Indeed,' he wrote, 'they would appear to be toiling to lead men into error rather than towards the truth, since they are causing great disturbance in the country, and by their excesses are stirring up the people against clergy and monastics alike.'

It would seem, then, that from 1233 onwards the suppression of heresy in Languedoc changed its nature and became a good deal more vigorous. Yet the two Dominicans had no greater physical resources at their disposal than the Bishop. Later they were authorized to travel with an armed escort that formed, as it were, their bodyguard, and which included, over and above men-at-arms, various gaolers, notaries, assessors and counsellors. These Inquisitorial assistants were never very numerous; in 1249 Pope Innocent IV complained that there were too many of them, and limited them to twenty-four per Inquisitor—which suggests that they had not, even so, run into hundreds. At the very beginning, the Inquisitors did not even have these special auxiliaries, but called upon the local authorities, both lay and ecclesiastical, to provide them.

The strength of these men, then, lay above all in their dynamic energy; in the knowledge that they would not be hampered in the performance of their duties by any kind of officialdom; and in the arbitrary, not to say illegal, trials which they were enabled to hold. Beyond any doubt they succeeded in spreading a genuine wave of panic throughout the country.

The Count's protest indicates that the whirlwind activities of these two monks were provoking general resentment—which at least bears witness to their efficiency. The Pope, as a pure formality, advised his Inquisitors to proceed more circumspectly; he also wrote to the Legate, Stephen de Burnin, and to the Bishops, asking if they would intervene in case of necessity to protect the innocent. But it does not appear that these pious exhortations by Gregory IX curbed the Inquisitors' zeal in the slightest degree. On the contrary: from Toulouse to Quercy public agitation grew steadily greater.

The Inquisitors came up against an unexpected adversary in Toulouse, in the person of one Jean Tisseyre, who dwelt in an outlying part of the city. He was a working-class man who went through the streets haranguing the crowds in some such terms as these:[1]

> Listen to me, citizens! I am no heretic: I have a wife, and sleep with her, and she has borne me sons. I eat meat, I tell lies and swear,* and I am a good Christian. So don't believe it when they say I'm an atheist, not a word of it! They'll very likely accuse you too, as they have me: these accursed villains want to put down honest folk and take the town from its lawful master.

Such subversive comments naturally attracted the attention of the Inquisitors. They arrested Tisseyre on suspicion, and condemned him to the stake, though he persisted in declaring himself a good Christian and a Catholic. When Durand de Saint-Bars the magistrate tried to carry out the sentence, the people rioted, and there was such a noisy demonstration by the crowd against monks and magistrate that the condemned man had to be taken back to his cell. But the wrath of the Toulouse burghers was not appeased yet: they demanded Tisseyre's release, and tried to destroy the city Friary of these Dominicans, who condemned decent married men as heretics.

It is very probable, in point of fact, that Tisseyre was not, strictly speaking, a heretic, and that his conduct was provoked by genuine altruistic fury at the excesses of Inquisitorial procedure. He was a patriotic citizen, horrified to see these 'accursed villains' attempting to wrest the town from its lawful master. No doubt he sympathized with the heretics, as did many other people, through hatred of the Church. He was a martyr to the freedom of Toulouse; and there is one very significant fact about his story. When in prison, he met several *perfecti*, who had just been brought in by Denense, the bailiff of Lavaur. He became an immediate convert to their faith, embracing it with such ardour that he received the *consolamentum* from them; despite the Bishop's adjurations, he made an open confession of his allegiance to the Catharist Church, and his wish to share the fate of these *perfecti*. He was burnt with them, and, as Pelhisson writes,[2]

---

* This refers to accusations regularly brought against the *haeretici* who were, of course, specifically forbidden by their creed either to lie or to swear.

'all those who had hitherto supported him were now covered with confusion, and cursed and reviled him', a fact which demonstrates pretty clearly that he was not previously regarded as a heretic.

Tisseyre's defenders might be covered with confusion, but the Inquisitors must have had red faces too. The voluntary martyrdom of a Jean Tisseyre constituted no less serious a charge against them than the execution of a doubtful heretic would have done. Though few citizens of Toulouse brought themselves to follow Tisseyre's example, his stand must have strengthened the faith of many luke-warm or hesitant Catharist sympathizers; for here was a man, notoriously not a *credens*, who had embraced Catharism precisely when, as he knew, his conversion would entail certain death for him. He must, too, have achieved some popularity not only among the heretics, but also with those Catholics who remained loyal to their Count, and objected to the Church's policies rather than her doctrine.

For two years Arnald and Seila established a veritable reign of terror in Toulouse and throughout the County. For fear of prose-cution people flocked forward to accuse themselves, and in such great numbers that the Dominicans could not interrogate them all, but were obliged to co-opt the Friars Minor [Franciscans] and Toulouse parish priests. This would generally happen after a public sermon, during which one of the Inquisitors had fixed a 'period of grace'—varying from a week to a fortnight—for all those who came and confessed their errors spontaneously. Those who failed to present themselves were, once the time allotted had expired, prose-cuted according to law. They were arrested and jailed by the Domini-cans, with the assistance of the civil magistrates. For the most part such voluntary depositions concerned events long since past; but it is plain that only those whose testimony led to the arrest of *perfecti*, or seriously compromised important *credentes*, benefited by the plenary indulgence of their judges.

Many of these people found themselves undergoing penances of a canonical sort, which ranged from carrying a cross to going on a pilgrimage, or paying a fine. This meant they escaped prison; but they remained permanently under the threat of a fresh decision on the Inquisitor's part. He could summon them before him again and impose a harsher sentence: judgments pronounced by the Inquisition were never final—except, of course, in the case of a death sentence.

For instance, just such a General Inquisition took place in Tou-louse after Good Friday of 1235, with voluntary mass confessions and many arrests. One man named Doumenge, who omitted to come forward, was seized and threatened with execution. He only won his freedom by personally taking the city magistrate and the Abbot of Saint-Sernin to Cassès, where ten *perfecti* were hidden, in a place known to him. Of these ten, three managed to escape, but the rest were captured and condemned to the stake.

Seila and Arnald made a joint expedition into the Quercy district. At Cahors they held a series of posthumous trials, and exhumed and burnt numerous corpses as a result. In Moissac there must have been an ultra-Catholic local administration, since here it was that the Inquisitors found two hundred and ten persons guilty of heresy, and burnt them, too. The panic that this monstrous holocaust stirred up in the area was so great that, when one of those accused contrived to escape, he was given asylum in Belleperche monastery, and disguised himself as a monk. It was not the only occasion (and there must have been other instances unknown to us) upon which local monasteries took in a heretic and protected him. Other religious Orders did not approve the ruthless severity of the Dominicans. The Count's continual protests forced the Pope to send the two Inquisitors out of Toulouse from time to time: on such occasions they withdrew to the Quercy region. Though at Moissac their success would seem to have been complete—an *auto-da-fé* involving two hundred and ten victims is, indeed, a unique event in the annals of this period—numerous complaints reached the Pope from Cahors, all of them denouncing the arbitrary manner in which these new judges conducted hearings. To soothe public feeling the Pope reinforced the two Dominicans with a Franciscan, Brother Stephen de Saint-Thibéry: this addition changed matters not a whit. Their travels in the Quercy district completed, Seila and Arnald returned to Toulouse, where—thanks to the presence of the Count and the considerable powers enjoyed by the consuls—there was a more than usually strong opposition awaiting them.

On 4th August 1235, St Dominic's feast day—the first time it was ever celebrated, the Saint having been canonized a few months before—solemn Masses were sung in every church in Toulouse (especially those of the Dominicans) to mark the occasion with all due ceremony, and glorify this new Saint. The day was also conspicuous for a tragic incident—which the Dominicans, however, regarded as meritorious, and attributed to their saintly Founder. Just as Bishop Raymond du Fauga was washing his hands after Mass, prior to entering the refectory, he received information that a certain *grande dame* had been granted the *consolamentum* in a house down a nearby street. No doubt infuriated and repelled by so provocative an act, the Bishop, together with the Prior of the convent and several of his monks, went to the address given. This old lady was the mother-in-law of Peytavi Borsier, a notorious *credens* who acted as a liaison officer with the 'heretics' proper.

The old lady was seriously ill, perhaps actually dying; no doubt either her vision was impaired, or else she failed to grasp what was going on. At all events, she fell victim to a singularly grim misunderstanding. When she was told that 'my lord Bishop' was coming to see her, she thought this person must be the *Cathar* bishop. Raymond du Fauga, moreover, made no attempt to cure her of this misapprehension: on the contrary, he prolonged it by deliberate ambiguity, and his interrogation of the dying woman on matters of faith elicited a full confession of heretical doctrines held by her. He even took his perfidious behaviour so far as to encourage her to remain steadfast in her beliefs; for, said he, 'the fear of death should not make you confess aught else than that which you hold firmly and with your whole heart'. Then, when the old lady protested her steadfastness, saying she would not renounce her faith for that little portion of life yet remaining to her, the Bishop revealed his true identity, pronounced her a heretic, and adjured her to recant and embrace the Catholic Faith. The dying woman, horrified no doubt but in no way intimidated, 'persevered with increasing stubbornness in her heretical allegiance'. This scene took place before numerous witnesses, of whom its narrator Pelhisson was one.

Convinced now of the woman's irredeemable obstinacy, the Bishop summoned the magistrate. Summary judgment was passed upon the old woman, who was then carried in her bed (being unable to walk) as far as the Pré-du-Comte, or Count's Field, put to the stake, and burnt forthwith. 'This done,' Pelhisson tells us, 'the Bishop, together with the monks and their attendants, returned to the refectory and, after giving thanks to God and St Dominic, fell cheerfully upon the food set before them.'[3]

This story might well have passed for a piece of slander invented by those who disliked the Inquisition. Yet it cannot be doubted, for Pelhisson, as a Dominican, could have had no possible motive for inventing it. All the same, it is so odd that it might have come from a madhouse. The harshness of contemporary ethics cannot wholly explain it, and in any case the principal actor was not a brigand-knight, but a bishop. Not even fanaticism can account for a whole group of monks and clergy behaving quite so savagely towards a helpless old woman. Surely, despite her condemnation, she could at least have been left to die in peace, and burnt after her death? The most surprising thing of all is the farce enacted by Raymond du Fauga, in the presence of the Prior and a large number of Dominicans, who thus (whether willingly or not) became accessories to his deception—a trick that was utterly beneath the dignity of the episcopal office, and reduced Raymond to the level of a common spy. Yet the chronicler rather congratulates the Bishop for his craftiness, and is not, one feels, lying when he refers to the monks' *cheerfulness*—as they returned to the refectory to consume the meal so providentially interrupted. Such an attitude suggests some sort of militant Brotherhood, or legal Klu Klux Klan, which was, nevertheless, itself hunted and persecuted, and determined to win at all.costs. At least a proportion of the Dominicans in Languedoc must, at this period, have resembled such a Brotherhood. This was why the Office of the Inquisition had been entrusted to them, rather than to anyone else; it was also why the complaints and indeed the systematic hostility of Count and consuls was primarily directed against the Dominicans.

The execution of Peytavi Borsier's mother-in-law provoked rather more terror than indignation in Toulouse. It was followed by a public sermon from the Prior of the Dominicans, Pons de Saint-Gilles, who described the bonfire that had calcined the poor old woman's mortal remains as being akin to the fire which the prophet Elijah called down from Heaven to confound the priests of Baal,[4] and solemnly defied both the heretics themselves and any who sheltered them. Finally he exhorted Catholics to 'put away all fear and bear witness to the truth'. During the next week crowds of 'Catholics' did in fact come forward and 'bear witness to the truth'—either repenting of their own past sins or purging their consciences by denouncing other suspects. 'Among these crowds,' Pelhisson wrote,[5] 'there were many who abjured heresy; while others confessed that they had relapsed, but now returned to the unity of the Church; and others, again, denounced heretics, and swore always to do so betimes.' The chronicler was no optimist; though praising God for the efficiency of the Inquisitors' methods of research, he added: 'And being thus begun, they will continue till the end of the world.'

More and more heretics were now being exhumed and condemned posthumously, a practice which provoked continual disorders in the city. The consuls and the Count's officers used their official position to help many persons condemned either to the stake or life imprisonment to escape. In order to stop this virtually open opposition on the part of the civil authorities, the Inquisitors decided to arraign several of the town's more notable figures on charges of heresy. These included some well-known *credentes*, and even members of the clergy suspected of favouring heretical beliefs; while three of them—Bernard Séguier, Maurand, and Raymond Roger— were consuls. They flatly refused to appear, and demanded that William Arnald should, forthwith, suspend all Inquisitorial investigations or leave Toulouse. When the Inquisitor took no notice of this warning, the consuls, accompanied by their men-at-arms, turned up at the Dominican monastery in person. Arnald was forcibly expelled from Toulouse, and commanded to leave the Count's territories. He accordingly betook himself to Carcassonne, which lay in the French King's fief, and from there pronounced sentence of excommunication against the consuls, on 5th November, 1235.

Meanwhile the Dominicans, to avoid any appearance of yielding to constraint, were determined to indict the accused—and this despite the express veto of the consuls, who had threatened to execute anyone serving these summonses. The Prior chose four of this Brethren to perform this mission, and they undertook it as an earnest of martyrdom. Among them was Pelhisson himself. Their adversaries proved less fierce than these courageous monks had supposed, and made no attempt on their lives; but when they came to Maurand the Elder's house, the messengers were at least beaten up, and had the dogs set on them.

The following day the consuls appeared outside the Dominican convent with their sergeants-at-arms, and followed by a large crowd of citizens. They ordered the monks to quit Toulouse, and when they refused, had them seized and flung out into the street. The Dominicans marched out of the city chanting the *Te Deum* and the *Salve Regina*, symbolic witness of the Faith. They were soon obliged to disperse, since the consuls had forbidden citizens to succour them in any way. The Prior made his way to Rome, where he informed Gregory IX of the attack which the Dominicans had suffered—with the approval, indeed on the orders of, the Count of Toulouse. Bishop Raymond du Fauga was now, in his turn, also expelled from the city.

Raymond VII can hardly have hoped that the Pope would approve such an act of rebellion. Yet the abuses of which the Dominicans in Toulouse had been guilty were so flagrant, it seems, that he reckoned on being able to justify his conduct even before the Holy See. Though he continually declared his fidelity to the Church, he begged the Pope at the same time not to saddle him any longer with these Dominicans—or at the very least, to strip them of their Inquisitorial powers.

When the Pope learnt what had happened in Toulouse, he wrote an extremely severe letter to Raymond. In it he listed (among other lesser matters) various things he had heard. The consuls had forbidden the citizens of Toulouse to sell or give anything whatsoever to the Bishop—or, indeed, to his clergy. They had seized the Bishop's house, inflicted injuries on sundry canons and other clerics, and debarred Bishop and priests from preaching in public. The Count was no longer paying the professors in the new university their salaries, and as a result studies there had come to a halt. The Count and the consuls had forbidden anyone to answer a summons served by the Inquisitors, on pain of corporal punishment and loss of property. After listing all these and many other facts—the charges being infinitely more serious than any ever preferred against Raymond VI, who had nevertheless died excommunicate—the Pope threatened to excommunicate the present Count once again, if he persisted in his hostile attitude to the Church.[6]

Now Raymond VII intended to remain on peaceable terms with the Church, as he had already demonstrated by arresting Pagan de la Bessède in person, and agreeing to the trial of the Niort brothers. He behaved like any Head of State who finds himself obliged to meet his subjects' demands, if only in a token fashion. Since he was scared of war with France no less than of excommunication, he could not support heresy; at the same time he was anxious to avoid rioting or any other serious trouble. It looks very much as though he succeeded, partially at least, in winning over the Pope and the King. The latter—or rather, his mother—wrote to the Pope, passing on the Count's complaints against the Inquisitors, and on 3rd February, 1236, the Pope himself wrote to the Archbishop of Vienne, the Provincial Legate, with instructions that the latter should curb the Inquisitors' powers. Finally, 'with the consent and active agreement of the Count of Toulouse', the Inquisitors resumed their duties. But though the Pope had advised them to moderate their behaviour, it does not seem that they paid any heed to this recommendation, or, indeed, that their effective powers were in any way reduced.

As soon as the Inquisitors were back in Toulouse the trials began again, with increased violence. A large number of people were denounced by a former *perfectus*, Raymond Gros, who had of his own free will become a Catholic convert. His revelations caused a good many posthumous trials to be held: many of the corpses that were dug up and committed to the flames had belonged to the nobility or higher bourgeoisie. In September 1237, too, the cemeteries were subjected to a most thorough official search; the graves of twenty or so of the most highly respected people in Toulouse were violated, and their bones or decomposing carcasses dragged through the streets on hurdles, while the public crier recited the names of the deceased, adding: *Qui atal fara, atal pendra* [Whoso does the like, will suffer a like fate].

As for the living, Pelhisson names something like a dozen who were burnt at the stake; but it was easier to condemn a man to death than to execute him. Several prospective victims belonged to noble or consular families; and it would seem that the Inquisitors never had a chance to lay hands on them, since the city magistrate and the consuls refused to arrest such persons—which earned them yet another excommunication. The most notorious heretics in Toulouse now left the country under the protection of the authorities, seeking refuge either in secret hiding places unknown to the Inquisitors, or else in the fortress of Montségur. This last was a more or less impregnable retreat, which became the official headquarters of the Catharist resistance movement.

The Inquisition fared much as it had done in Toulouse when it began to operate in territory belonging to the French Crown. It met with resistance—sometimes violent, sometimes merely stubborn—but obtained a certain measure of success as a result of the terror it inspired. Very early on, in 1233, it acquired a couple of martyrs—two Inquisitors who had come to conduct an enquiry in Cordes, and were murdered there during an uprising. After this they never ventured into the country districts without an armed escort. But in 1234, at Albi, an Inquisitor named Arnald Cathala decided to go and dig up a dead woman heretic himself, the magistrate having refused to do so; a crowd assembled, dragged Cathala out of the cemetery, gave him a severe beating, and threatened to kill him.

The appearance of the Inquisition in Narbonne—a town which had escaped the horrors of the Crusade, and was reputedly Catholic —again stirred up considerable trouble. The borough would appear to have been somewhat more tainted with heresy than the city proper, and in any case hostile both to the Dominicans and the Archbishop. Here the riot took on a more political character, with the consuls for the outer wards accusing the Inquisitors and the Archbishop of an attempt to reduce their municipal franchise. Following the precedent set by Italian towns, Narbonne split into two parties, city and borough: the former supported the Archbishop and Brother Ferrier, the Inquisitor, while the latter demanded the removal of both. As happened elsewhere, the Preaching Friars suffered most from these internal squabbles, because of their unpopularity. In 1234 their convent was invaded by a party of rebellious burghers, who sacked and plundered it. With even greater audacity, the consuls of the borough summoned the Count of Toulouse to their aid; and the Count came out in person to restore the peace, albeit Narbonne owed allegiance to the French Crown. He set up a local bailiwick under his own authority, and nominated to it Olivier de Termes and Guiraud de Niort, both of them powerful heretical *seigneurs* and declared enemies of the Archbishop.

The episode ended in a victory for the city, thanks to some exercise of royal authority by the King's seneschal, De Friscamps. But the city consuls were long obliged to beg Brother Ferrier to come back to Narbonne and perform his Inquisitorial duties there, simply as a means of protecting themselves against the permanent hostility which those in the outer borough felt for them.

Though they appeared, in the Count's words, 'to be toiling to lead men into error rather than towards the truth', in five years the Inquisitors managed to establish such an atmosphere of terror in Languedoc that they obtained a large number of voluntary submissions—mostly from people who had done no more than display some sympathy with heretical beliefs. For instance, we know that Peter Seila imposed two hundred and forty-three canonical penances at Montauban in 1241, during the week before Ascension Day. The following week he dispensed a hundred and ten penances of various sorts at Moissac; there were two hundred and twenty at Gourdon in Advent Week, and eighty more at Moncuq. Not all the Inquisitorial tours of duty bore such plentiful fruit; many sets of records and trial transcripts have not survived. The figures we derive from existing documents only tell a fraction of the truth. At the same time it must be said that the Inquisitors did not practise the kind of summary justice which the Crusade had made possible at Lavaur and Minerve: on the contrary, they took great care to keep a record of all their investigations. They were all the more concerned to do so since the main object of such interrogations was to obtain names, and the minutes taken during each case could be utilized as damning evidence against thousands of suspects. The Inquisition's files, which were guarded with great care, constituted a source of alarm for the larger part of the population: no one could be sure that they had not been the subject of at least one denunciation for harbouring or abetting heretics. It was enough if they had greeted such-and-such a *perfectus* in the street, twenty years before, or taken part in a meal where heretics were fellow guests, or done any other similar thing. Sometimes a wholly fictitious accusation did the trick: after all, it was impossible to refute. Who could prove that, at some time and place which was never (deliberately) made too clear to him, he had *not* been met in the company of a *perfectus*, by some person whose name was never revealed?

One of the main reasons for the terror which these Inquisitors inspired was their omniscience. For some decades the bishops had shown themselves powerless to fight against adversaries, the vast majority of whom claimed to be Catholics, and to number none but Catholics among their acquaintances. The Inquisitors, on the other hand, had in some miraculous fashion managed to make literally thousands of people come forward *of their own volition*, and admit that they either were or had been heretics themselves, and that they had associated with other heretics. Now though some bishops had shown themselves careless in the matter of suppressing heresy, those who ruled the Languedoc dioceses in 1229 could certainly not be accused of tepidity on this score; nor did they lack subordinates or confidential agents to whom they might entrust Inquisitorial duties. Episcopal justice had always been extremely severe upon heretics. But Inquisitorial justice was no longer justice at all, in the strict meaning of the word: this is what made it so formidable.

It shook public confidence and undermined public morale; it bred an atmosphere of permanent anxiety throughout the country. The *perfecti* and the more steadfast among the *credentes* might know the risks they were running, and *why* they exposed themselves to such dangers; but the bulk of the population, heretical though it might be, was nevertheless made up of folk who wanted to go on living. The constant threat of arbitrary, unpredictable prosecutions terrified and exasperated them. A people can fight for its liberty; but a man who is always wondering whether his neighbour across the way has denounced him, and whether he might not do better to go and accuse himself rather than wait for a summons, is disarmed in advance. If he is to fight, he must have the support not only of his neighbour, but of all the inhabitants in the quarter. There were one or two popular riots; but a riot could not go on for long, and if it failed, it brought yet worse terrors in its wake. The authority of the Count and the consuls had succeeded in driving the Dominicans out of Toulouse; but external pressure brought to bear by the King and the Pope had seen to it that they came back more powerful than ever. The Pope in all likelihood had neither the power nor the inclination to curb his Inquisitors' zeal. The Dominican Inquisition was an instrument of terrorization, and could not give up its main function. For centuries to come various Popes continually upheld and defended the Dominicans against all the attacks of common people or civil authorities alike.

2. *The Inquisition at Work*

Before observing how the Catharist Church reacted when faced with this new danger, we must try to understand exactly how the Inquisition went about its work in Languedoc; what its real power was, and what repercussions it had upon the life of the country.

The whole idea of suppressing heresy systematically, and entrusting the task to a special organization, showed very clearly that Pope Gregory envisaged changes in those traditional methods and principles according to which such suppression had hitherto been conducted. For almost a century now heretics had fought ecclesiastical justice, and long practice had taught them how to hold their adversary in check. But the new procedure, which enjoyed the Pope's advocacy and encouragement, broke away entirely from legality—or what had till then been commonly regarded as lawful practice. At this period criminal proceedings were governed by Justinian's Code, which laid down various measures, in respect of such a prosecution, that were designed to guarantee the rights of the accused person. Every prosecution had to be initiated in one of three ways. Either an individual must lay the indictment, in which case he was obliged to produce proof of guilt; or else a denuciation could be made before a judge, with witnesses to support it; or, finally, there was provision for cases in which public notoriety or obvious scandal could by themselves secure an indictment. Only in this last instance could the judge proceed alone, without any accusation or denunciation on the part of a private individual; and even so the truth of such 'public notoriety' had to be confirmed by a sufficient number of witnesses.

In the matter of heresy examples of denunciation and, *a fortiori*, personal indictment were rare; and after the Treaty of Paris, instances of 'public notoriety' also became infrequent. We have already seen how, during the trial of the Lords of Niort, there were plenty of witnesses ready to swear to the brothers' devoted Catholicism—and this though they were open heretics. Now if such powerful *seigneurs*, who openly protected heresy and fought on its behalf, could pass as Catholics in the eyes of the clergy, it follows that the common run of *credentes* must have been even more adept at disguising their sentiments. Plenty of people were able to practise their religion in peace, so long as they did not flaunt it before those suspected of being on the side of the clergy. In a country which had just survived twenty years of warfare and oppression, this mood of collective dissimulation must have been developed to a remarkable degree. Dissimulation which is practised, not out of hypocrisy, but as a legitimate method of self-defence, can go to considerable lengths: for instance there was that official benefactor of the Saint-Sernin chapter, Peyre, who despite his professions of heresy was buried in the church cloister [see above, p. 277].

In the last resort, the only 'notorious heretics' known as such, and continuing to perform their ministry, were the *perfecti*; and they were hard to catch. There were hundreds of them in existence, yet the records covering the years 1229–33 only refer to a few isolated cases when a *perfectus* was captured: and these were more or less accidental. In order to become effective, the machinery of the law needed some overhauling.

The only way in which this could be brought about was by ignoring certain legal provisions. Hitherto, before any suspect could be brought to trial, he had to be indicted by some impartial person of good reputation; and even so he had the right to be confronted with the witnesses who had testified against him. Further, three categories of witness were debarred from giving evidence against any accused person: (1) all those whom he might fairly regard as his 'deadly enemies'—and the definition of 'deadly enemy' could in fact be stretched to include any person who, at any time, had been prejudiced against the accused, or even made slighting remarks concerning him; (2) members of his family, his servants, and, in the broadest sense, all who were in any way dependent upon him; (3) the excommunicate, heretics, and other infamous persons.

In certain especially serious cases, known as 'crimes extraordinary', such as high treason, lèse-majesté, sacrilege and heresy, kinsmen and servants were allowed to appear as witnesses. The Inquisition extended this right to all other categories of debarred witnesses, except 'deadly enemies'. As has been noted above, before William de Solier could testify against his former co-religionists, Cardinal Romanus of S. Angelo had been obliged to reconcile the ex-*perfectus* to the Church, and indeed to rehabilitate him. The Inquisitors did away with this formality, which would have forced them to 'reconcile' a good many people whom they had no wish to treat as good Catholics. The testimony of heretics was deemed valid if it tended to incriminate other heretics, invalid only if the witness were favourable to the accused. The evidence of infamous persons—thieves, crooks, prostitutes and the like—was likewise admissible. As for 'deadly enemies', granted that the accused was unaware of witnesses' identities, and that the judge was quite at liberty to ignore any connection there might be between the witnesses and the accused, this restriction now became almost meaningless.

Furthermore, accused persons could not enjoy the benefit of legal representation, even though they had a right to it in theory: the mere fact of wishing to defend a heretic, or supposed heretic, meant that the lawyer himself became suspect of heresy. His arguments then became inadmissible, and he exposed himself to considerable risks. Few lawyers had the courage to undertake so hopeless and unrewarding a brief.

It seems as though the hearing of evidence *in camera* was the Dominican Inquisition's major innovation—although Romanus of S. Angelo had already employed it, more or less, after the Council of Toulouse, without, however, elevating it into a system. It was the first and almost the only reason for the terror which the Inquisitors inspired, and a prime factor in their ultimate success. By creating an atmosphere of suspicion and distrust in even the most united communities, this technique contributed significantly to their moral disintegration, and in the end made organized resistance quite impossible—there was henceforth scarcely any resistance at all except where the civil authorities were directly behind it. We have observed the activities of the Toulouse consuls, and those representing the borough of Narbonne. We have seen how the Niorts' bailiffs barred heretic-hunting posses from setting foot in any township belonging to their masters. In 1240 the Count of Toulouse's bailiffs took a similar stand (either by threats or armed force) in Montauriol and Caraman, against Brother Ferrier's commission. Though such incidents were doubtless more frequent than might be inferred from a study of the available documents, they remained, despite everything, exceptions. Such officers and administrators as made themselves responsible for these acts of rebellion against the Church were courting the most severe penalties, and could only act upon the formal commands of their masters; while the Count himself, continually harassed and threatened, and too weak to allow himself the gesture of open defiance, only intervened when the execution of his orders might, at a pinch, be interpreted as spontaneous insubordination on the part of some local authority.

The Inquisitors themselves were utterly fearless. Though several of them paid with their lives for their excessive zeal, the vigour and proud self-assurance which they possessed enabled them to have their way with the population of Languedoc. In any case the latter had already become accustomed to seeing the Church as a vast potential menace. It was the clergy who had brought about the Crusade, and, ultimately, triumphed: they might be few in number, but behind them stood the formidable might of Rome, ever prepared to bring down fresh catastrophe upon their heads.

An Inquisitor would arrive in a town or borough accompanied by notaries, clerks, gaolers and, sometimes, a small escort of men-at-arms. He would take up residence either in the Bishop's Palace, or the Dominican monastery if there was one in the area, or any other religious establishment in the town. This done, he would deliver a public sermon, attacking heresy and announcing a 'period of grace', which was normally a week and no more. Those who failed to come forward of their own free will during this 'period of grace' were liable, once the week was up, to have proceedings taken against them. Those who *did* come forward voluntarily were safe from such serious punishments as confiscation of goods or imprisonment: they did not risk losing their lives. Even though they might have been gravely compromised, they were still only liable to canonical penances.

So even in a town where heresy flourished, a certain number of *credentes*—the most nervous, or those who knew they had enemies— would hasten to bring accusations against themselves: sometimes, perhaps, in the hope of masking more serious sins, they would confess trifling or even wholly imaginary faults. (A good example is the miller of Belcaire who accused himself of the following misdemeanour: during a visit to him, he said, certain women had invoked God and St Martin to look after his mill: whereupon he replied that it was he who had built the mill, not God, and he would see it was kept in good running order.)

The judges, it goes without saying, were not interested in admissions of this nature; in order to prove his good faith, the repentant sinner was required, above all, to denounce persons whom he knew to be suspected heretics. If he revealed such information, his anonymity was guaranteed. Naturally at first he was likely to name his personal enemies, or those whom he hardly knew, or knew to be little involved with the Cathars. However, the penance to be imposed on him was decided, not according to the gravity of his sins, but in proportion to the sincerity of his repentance; and his sincerity was calculated from the number and, above all, the *importance* of the heretics whom he denounced.

On the face of it, then, those who made voluntary self-accusations were not exactly heroes. Though canonical penances (even though they might not involve loss of liberty) were, as we shall see later, liable to be quite severe, still the guarantee of secrecy protected the interrogated suspect against any possible reprisals. The cowardice of so many of these voluntary converts formed the Inquisition's first, and greatest, supporting factor: the denunciations of two witnesses sufficed to authorize official action against any presumed heretic.

Thus a large number of persons who had not been prosecuted by the local authorities were now denounced. They still had a chance to come forward of their own accord during the 'period of grace'; and many of them, knowing that they were compromised whatever happened, took this way out. Those who did so could not be officially prosecuted. These prosecutions began with a written summons, which had to be served upon the person of the accused, and on reception of which he was required to appear before the Tribunal. He was questioned without any witnesses being present, and without being told the precise nature of the charges brought against him. Under such conditions he frequently admitted more than he was asked, assuming that the judges were better informed than in fact was the case. If the charges were serious ones, he was held in prison while awaiting trial; and this was almost always done if he refused to confess. This happened even more frequently in that confession also carried with it the obligation to compromise one's co-religionists: a thing which honourable persons refused to do, even when they were not in fact heretics. If he was not put in prison, the accused was released on bail, the recognizances being extremely high. He was kept under observation, and forbidden to leave town. But once he was in prison he lay entirely at the mercy of his judges, and cut off from any sort of guarantee or external help.

The Inquisitor himself was judge, prosecutor and examining magistrate rolled into one. The other monks who assisted him could only act as witnesses; the same applied to the clerk who transcribed evidence. It followed that there was no discussion of the case, no opportunity for advice to be taken. The guilt of the accused, and the punishment that he merited, were determined by the Inquisitor's will alone. Though they had no effective power, the Inquisitor's aides were given the task of extracting confessions, the Inquisitor alone being unable to deal with all suspects. Those who refused to confess were subjected to relentless questioning, in the course of which they very often betrayed themselves. If this failed they were imprisoned, under such unpleasant conditions that, after a shorter or longer spell inside, even the most obdurate were forced to submit. The cells where these recalcitrant suspects were kept were sometimes so small that their inmates could neither stand up nor lie down; or entirely unlit, as in the prisons of Carcassonne, or the Château des Allemans at Toulouse. The toughest prisoners were shackled hand and foot, and systematically starved of food and drink. Certainly those who, rather than talk, underwent this kind of treatment for months, sometimes for years, formed a very tiny minority. For a large number, threats alone sufficed.

Nevertheless, when confronted with accused persons who were capable of giving them information, but strong-minded enough to ignore threats, the Inquisitors could not always afford the time to let them 'rot away' in gaol. Such prisoners might lawfully be tortured— a procedure admitted by the civil code for the unmasking of serious crimes, but from which, in theory, the ecclesiastical courts were supposed to abstain. In point of fact they too employed torture, but with the reservation that neither death, mutilation, nor bloodshed should be produced by it: for the clergy the shedding of blood constituted an irregularity in Canon Law. Since very ancient times the Church had employed scourging both to punish the guilty and to obtain confessions: birch-rods or leather thongs were the instruments used, and if they were scientifically applied they had as much effect as the most exquisite torture. In any case, torture was doubtless employed by the Inquisition well before 1252, (the year in which its use for this purpose was given official sanction[7])—just as it had been by episcopal tribunals in the eleventh and twelfth centuries. There is no reason to think that judges who had so swiftly terrorized an entire province would baulk at methods of persuasion already being practised by regular tribunals.

If the accused person gave in and talked after being put to the torture, he was made to repeat his declaration outside the torture-chamber, and in the presence of a clerk; he had at the same time to state formally that his declaration was voluntary, and not obtained by force. If he refused—and only one instance of this is on record, cited by Bernard Gui in the 'Sentences of the Inquisition at Toulouse' —he fell under greater suspicion than before, being treated as a relapsed heretic and put to the torture afresh. If he still would not talk after being tortured, the Inquisitor was at liberty to repeat the treatment next day, and for as many times as might prove necessary.

It is true that in the majority of cases 'immurement', or incar- ceration in gaol under the harshest possible conditions, was regarded as torture enough. But there are one or two very rare cases on record of *perfecti* who tried to put an end to themselves in prison by going on hunger-strike. This was afterwards used against the sect, being regarded as a proof of their heretical convictions: it served to enhance the legend of their permissive attitude towards suicide.

Though the Inquisitor strove at all costs to obtain an admission of guilt, this was not, strictly speaking, essential to justify a conviction. To prove any man a heretic it was sufficient for him to be denounced as such by two witnesses. But in practice the Inquisitors nearly always wrung a confession out of the accused before sentencing him. We are forced to assume that, appearances to the contrary notwithstanding, evidence was somewhat hard to come by, especially at first. Those who came forward and confessed tended to incriminate either the dead or people whom they knew to be well out of reach—which explains the large numbers of condemnations recorded posthumously or *in absentia*. As time went by, evidence became increasingly plentiful. Denunciations snowballed, delivering up to the Inquisition in turn the neighbours, friends and relations of suspected persons. These in their turn were asked for yet more names and details, yet more information concerning heretics' hiding-places and the like. Yet the capture of heretics proper, the *perfecti* that is, was never an easy matter. Doumenge, the man who, to save his own life, had in 1234 been responsible for the arrest of seven *perfecti* at Cassès, was shortly afterwards murdered in his bed. At Laurac, a sergeant who had arrested six *perfectae*, including the mother of a knight named Raymond Barthe, was subsequently hanged by the knight himself. The capture of a *perfectus* spelt danger for his betrayer, since only those who had been initiated knew where the *perfecti* could seek refuge. Mere denunciation by name weighed most heavily upon the mass of the Catharist Church's followers, those *credentes* who took little active part in their faith; but for them life was fast becoming quite intolerable.

Those who were brave enough to face all such tests and hazards had to lead a clandestine existence. They sought refuge in impregnable retreats such as Montségur or Quéribus, or in districts like the Laurac region or the County of Foix, where heresy remained powerful enough to hold its own against the Church. If they were caught, they suffered martyrdom. The gaols of Carcassonne, Toulouse and Albi were all full—in Carcassonne, indeed, they had to build new ones—and when a prisoner was sentenced to solitary confinement, it was generally for life.

The difference between the situation now and in 1229 was that now others beside the *perfecti* ran a risk of being condemned to death. We have seen how enraged the folk of Toulouse were after Jean Tisseyre's first condemnation, and how they tried to prevent the judges from burning a *married man*. It was not only the *perfecti* who were executed but also particularly obdurate *credentes*; and this increased the terror which the Inquisition inspired. Any man now could, with a little imagination, convince himself that he was destined for the stake.

In fact the vast majority of suspects incurred canonical penances and no more—though these penances seriously disrupted the lives, not only of those on whom they were inflicted, but of their families as well. They were of three kinds: (1) the wearing of the 'heretic's cross', a penance invented or at least first brought into general usage by St Dominic; (2) an obligation to go on a pilgrimage; and (3) the performance of some charitable work, e.g. the support of a poor person for several years, or even for the rest of the penitent's life.

There was nothing unusual about these penances *per se*; they were amongst those commonly dispensed in ecclesiastical courts. But when they were imposed in great numbers, often for the most trifling faults, they threatened to become a real scourge.

The wearing of the cross was regarded as a shameful punishment, and was mainly—see the decrees of the Council of Toulouse—aimed at *perfecti* who had become voluntary converts. But in practice *perfecti* seldom got off with so mild a penance, which tended to be reserved for ordinary *credentes*. During the early years of the Inquisition it would not appear that this penalty was among the most frequently imposed: the truth was that to have been a heretic carried no stigma of shame in a country where heresy inspired neither loathing nor contempt. If, moreover, this light punishment was the price paid for an act of gross betrayal, it served also to identify, and expose to the hostility of heretics at large, those converts whom the Church had a strong interest in protecting, and might even employ as spies. Later, however, towards the close of the century, the same punishment was to become a greatly dreaded one; those who 'wore the cross of heresy' were outcast pariahs, boycotted by their fellow-citizens. As a result the penalty was more frequently employed.

Pilgrimages, on the other hand, like monetary fines, were imposed upon almost all suspects who appeared before the Tribunal of their own volition. They had the advantage of removing the presumed heretic from his native land for a shorter or longer period; but it is not hard to imagine the difficulties that must have arisen for the victim's family and business affairs because of them—not to mention the fact that for people of modest means such journeys meant greater expenses than they could well afford. So many penitents were sent no further afield than Puy or Saint-Gilles; but the majority still had to make their way to St James of Compostella or Canterbury, Paris or Rome. Some, indeed, were sent on a route that took in Puy, Saint-Gilles, St James of Compostella *and* Canterbury: this meant that they had to cross the Pyrenees, make their way through Catalonia, return to Languedoc, travel the length of France, cross the Channel, and so come to Canterbury. Such a pilgrimage, counting the return journey, would take several months at least. The penitant took with him a letter from the judge, which had to be endorsed by the ecclesiastical authorities at his destination. Other pilgrims again, especially soldiers, were sent either to the Holy Land or to Constantinople, where they were obliged to serve in the Crusading armies for a certain number of years: two or three on the average, but sometimes as many as five.

By thus dispersing thousands upon thousands of *credentes* along every road in Europe, and dispatching them to the armed forces overseas, the Inquisitors rid themselves of a certain number of potential adversaries: it is easy enough to see the prejudicial effect this move might have on a country that was impoverished and disorganized enough already. What is more, the 'involuntary pilgrims' themselves might well reckon that they had been lucky to get off so lightly. And yet this type of penance was imposed on people (for instance) who were guilty of—what? Speaking to some heretics during a sea voyage, or kneeling in 'adoration' before a *perfectus* at the age of eleven, on parental orders. These cases are quoted by Bernard Gui, and therefore took place somewhat later; but right from the beginning the Inquisitors did not neglect anything, however small, that might justify a penance. Most of the suspects had nothing to reproach themselves with apart from listening to heretics preach, or attending their meetings.

In this way an entire population, or the greater part of it, was systematically watched, spied upon, and harrassed by every kind of irksome restriction. Attendance at Mass and partaking of the Blessed Sacrament became duties imposed by an omniscient network of police spies, and failure to conform brought down completely arbitrary official sanctions upon the offender. Decisions concerning heretical offences were entirely at the Inquisitor's discretion: a man under suspicion of the merest peccadillo, if he refused to confess, was punished far more severely than a *perfectus* who voluntarily denounced his fellows. There was not (as in the civil or criminal codes) a list of established penalties for such or such an infraction of the law; there was merely a system of competitive bidding in the art of delation.

This explains the deadly monotony of those Inquisitorial records which deal with the interrogation of heretics. Such persons were asked where, when, at whose house and in whose company they had seen heretics—and very little else. Bernard Gui's *Practica Inquisitionis* informs us further that not all an accused person's testimony was suitable for the record; thus anything they might have said to present their faith and their leaders in a favourable light was probably deleted by the clerk of the court. Apart from this, the *Practica Inquisitionis* preserves for us a model of the sort of interrogation which was practised upon the Cathars:

'. . . The accused shall be asked if he has anywhere seen or been acquainted with one or more heretics, knowing or believing them to be such by name or repute: where he has seen them, on how many occasions, with whom, and when;

'item, whether he has had any familiar intercourse with them, when and how, and by whom introduced;

'item, whether he has received in his own home one or more heretics; if so, who and what they were; who brought them; how many times they stayed with the accused; what visitors they had; who escorted them thence; and where they went;

'item, whether he heard them preach, and if so, what was the substance of their discourse;

'item, whether he did adoration before them, or saw other persons adore them or do them reverence after the heretical manner;

'item, did he eat bread that had been blessed with them, and if so, what was the manner of its blessing;

'item, whether he made with them the pact known as *convenensa* . . .;

'item, whether he greeted them, or saw any other person greet them, after the heretical fashion;

'item, whether he was present at the initiation of any amongst them; if so, what was the manner of the initiation; what was the name of the heretic or heretics; who were present at the ceremony, and where was the house in which the sick person lay; . . . whether the person initiated made any bequest to the heretics, and if so what and how much, and who drew up the deed; whether adoration was done before the heretic who performed the initiation; whether the person initiated succumbed to his illness, and if so where he was buried; who brought the heretic or heretics thither, and conducted them thence;

'item, whether he believed that a person initiated into the heretical faith could attain salvation . . .', and so on. Other items had to do with the accused person's own conversion and past life, the other *credentes* he knew, his relatives, and similar subjects.[8] The answers and revelations of those *credentes* interrogated by the earliest Inquisitors show that the judges practised this pattern of questioning right from the first, and never sought to vary their methods.

Whether the questions were posed to the timorous folk who rushed round to the Tribunal on the first day of the 'period of grace', or those unfortunate wretches who had been exhausted by months of torture or imprisonment, their answers were almost invariably the same: nothing but names, places, dates:[9]

At Fanjeaux, there were present at the *consolamentum* of Auger Isarn the following: Bec de Fanjeaux, William of La Ilhe, Gaillard de Feste, Arnaud de Ovo, Jourdain de Roquefort, Aymeric de Sergent (*milites*): [deposition of R. de Perella, 1243]. Atho Arnaud of Castelverdun demanded the *consolamentum* while in the house of his relative Cavaers at Mongradail: Hugues and Sicart de Durfort went to find William Tournier and his companion. The deacons Bernard Coldefi and Arnald Guiraud resided in Montréal, and to meetings held by them there came: Raymond de Sanchas, Rateria, the wife of Maur de Montréal, Ermengaude de Rebenty, widow of Peter de Rebenty; Berengeria de Villacorbier, widow of Bernard Hugues de Rebenty, Saurina, widow of Isarn Garin de Montréal, and her sister Dulcia; Guiraude de Montréal, and Pontia Rigaude, wife of Rigaud de Montréal. . . . This took place in 1204.

This means that the deposition relates to events over thirty years old. But be they dead or alive, persons convicted of participation in a heretical ceremony, though it might have taken place thirty, forty, or even fifty years earlier, must still be punished: the dead by exhumation and the confiscation of their heirs' estates, the living by canonical penances or imprisonment.

We can understand the feeling of hopelessness, of creeping suffocation, that must have overwhelmed people subjected to such a régime. Other later epochs were to experience the pressure of similar police-state terrorization; but it is the Dominican Inquisition which must take the credit for having actually invented the system. Once the trail had been blazed, there were plenty of imitators ready to follow them along it and perfect their methods: though it would seem that, apart from purely technical improvements, there was very little left for them to discover.

But during those first few years the Inquisition was bitterly resisted; and yet, because of the unconditional backing which the Papacy throughout gave to its new militant arm, that resistance was doomed to failure from the beginning.

L

CHAPTER XI

THE CATHAR RESISTANCE

1. *The Organization of the Resistance*

THE CATHARS WERE ALL the less inclined to disarm in that this persecution supplied them with first-rate arguments for their own propaganda—a tangible proof, if one may put it like that, of the diabolical nature of the Church which they were fighting. In any case, they did not regard their cause as lost. The Churches of Bosnia, Bulgaria and Lombardy were powerful bodies that disputed territory —sometimes with success—against the Church of Rome. The same applied to the Slavic countries. These sister-Churches sent emissaries, encouraging letters, and more concrete assistance into Languedoc. In 1243, while the battle for Montségur was raging, the Catharist Bishop of Cremona sent a messenger to Bishop Bertrand Marty, saying that the Church in Cremona was enjoying profound peace, and could he, Bertrand, send them two *perfecti*? Those countries where the Cathar Church *was* 'enjoying profound peace' (a situation which was not to last) drew, like some Promised Land, very many heretics and *credentes* who were sick of persecution. In the decade between 1230 and 1240 very many Cathars emigrated to Lombardy.

The bravest and most militant among them, however, stayed at their posts, preferring to risk death rather than abandon their faithful followers. They organized their lives on a clandestine basis, and waited for better days. Pelhisson's statement that, during this period, the heretics did more damage than at the time of the Crusade is probably to be explained by the *perfecti* having discarded their attitude of 'passive resistance' (if not their pacifism): now they were ready to encourage and excuse acts of violence. Though their religion forbade bloodshed, and would not allow its ministers to kill a chicken or even a mouse, it too had now made shift to justify violence: since certain beings were not fallen souls expiating their penance, but direct incarnations of the Power of Evil, it was no crime to eliminate them. It went without saying that the Inquisitors and their accomplices were included among such diabolical creatures. Besides, the *perfecti* had no need to incite their fellow-countrymen to violence; the natural instinct was only too pronounced among them already. The *perfecti* could, however, play a political rôle, and use their influence on the Catharist *seigneurs* to make them join in the struggle, by causing them to realize the spiritual benefits they would derive from such an act.

It was at this period that there was instituted the pact of the *convenensa*, which does not appear to have been practised before. If he was bound by this pact, the *credens* could still receive the *consolamentum* in his dying moments, even though, because of wounds or some other cause, he found himself deprived of the power of speech. Later the custom was, for fairly obvious reasons, to become more widespread. Since they could not undertake to administer the sacrament to unknown persons, through fear of a trap, the *perfecti* hit on this method of counting their own flock. The very fact of being bound by the *convenensa* meant that a man could impose a moral obligation upon the *perfecti*: they must, if it were physically possible, give him the *consolamentum* on his death-bed.

The more Catharist life was driven underground, the greater its intensity and enthusiasm. Lukewarm believers, or those who had become heretics out of self-interest, or in conformity with the prevalent fashion (as was the case before 1209, and even after the reconquest of Languedoc by the Count) were gradually weeded out of the community. But the numbers who attended heretical religious meetings did not shrink: their ranks were swelled by all those who disliked the new régime, and saw that the heretical Churches offered the only genuine, organized resistance movement. The Waldensians were now more active and powerful than they had been during the Crusade; the Churches, formerly rivals, now made a common front, and we find from the records that many Waldensian *perfecti* came to preach in Languedoc, especially in the Ariège district.

These men's apostolic mission was a hard and perilous one. They pursued it steadfastly: it was not fear of danger that compelled them to live in charcoal-burners' huts, or rough lean-tos of branches, deep in the forests, or on abandoned farmsteads. At Montségur, Quéribus, or indeed in Lombardy, they could have found far greater security than in these precarious retreats. The reason they led a hunted and wandering existence was in order to be able to continue with their activities—to remain in close touch with those who were still faithful to them, or whom they hoped to win back to their faith.

The first thing a *perfectus* and his *socius* did on reaching the outskirts of a village or borough was to find a safe place of lodging for the night. This was sometimes in a Cathar's house, supposing the district to be one not too strictly patrolled by the ecclesiastical authorities. Such areas were quite common: to begin with there were the châteaux of the Lords of Niort, or other lesser feudal barons such as Lanta Jourda, Lord of Calhavel, and the greater part of the nobility of Fanjeaux, Laurac, Miramont, and so on. On occasion the Count's bailiffs themselves pointed out 'safe' houses to the *perfecti*, where they could be sure of a good reception. Boroughs such as Sorèze, Avignonet or Saint-Félix had priests who were sympathetically disposed towards heresy if not actual heretics themselves. As a rule these wandering preachers would stop at some retreat outside the town: thus they ran less risk of being recognized, and were not liable to compromise those who offered them hospitality. Their presence was only revealed to the most trustworthy *credentes*; and the Cathars maintained a vast network of secret agents who would act as messengers or guides for them. If the district was controlled by a priest or bailiff of notoriously Catholic sympathies, the *credentes* were obliged to find various excuses for going out of town. Poorer folk would make expeditions to collect firewood, women would go in search of mushrooms or berries; the nobility would go hunting. Even so it was essential that there should not be too massive an exodus from any one parish; so the faithful went in small groups, and at several days' interval.

Generally the *perfecti* would assemble their congregation in some clearing, deep in the forest. In the vicinity of a town these meetings would take place at night, so that the inhabitants could take advantage of the darkness to slip out unobserved. Quite a few of these meetings were surprised by raiding patrols of men-at-arms, or by means of spies [*exploratores*] in the pay of the Inquisitors. The most notable of these raids was the one during which the Count of Toulouse arrested Pagan de La Bessède and eighteen other heretics.

Mostly those who hunted down the heretics in this way had few troops at their disposal, and took their lives in their hands if they ventured into the forest. The *credentes*, amongst whom there was a good sprinkling of soldiers, mounted guards during all sermons or other ceremonies held in the open; and if a meeting was raided, in most cases the heretics managed to get away. For instance, the Dominican Raoul, acting on information received from a spy, arrived with an escort in a wood near Fanjeaux, but only succeeded in capturing one prisoner. In 1234 a certain priest called Peter was out looking for heretics, and fell into an ambush planned by the local bailiff; he managed to get away himself, but his companion was killed. In 1237 two *perfectae* were captured and burnt at Montgradail, two more at Saint-Martin-la-Lande, and two at Villeneuve, near Montréal. Women, either because their activities in fact exceeded those of their male brethren, or else because they felt less threatened, and therefore took fewer precautions, tended to be captured more frequently. Once the Abbot of Sorèze sent an agent [*nuncius*] to arrest two *perfectae* staying in the town, and the local women set on this fellow with sticks and stones to prevent the arrest being carried out. When the Abbot came and reproached them for their behaviour, they made the *nuncius* look a fool by asserting that he had mistaken two perfectly respectable married women for heretics. But *perfectae* who were caught by themselves in the forest, or in a town where the inhabitants were less resolute—or less hostile to Catholicism— appear to have passed fairly quickly from prison to the stake : we can only assume that the Inquisitors knew in advance there was nothing to be got out of them.

In his study of the Inquisition Jean Guiraud records the story of a woman named Guillelme de La Mothe. Before she was burnt she contrived to pass on at least a partial account of her prior tribulations. From 1230 onwards she and her *socia* lived in a wood that was the property of one Peter Belloc. They then moved on for three weeks to another wood, known as Le Bosc-Blanc. After this some *credentes* escorted them to the Salabose Forest, and later to that of Avellanet, where they spent a year. Next they had some time on the move, going from forest to forest in the Lanta district, and finally being led by a *perfectus*, G. Roger, to the Garrigue woodlands, after which they lived for a few months with various *credentes*, latterly spending nine months all told in the house of a certain Pons Rivière. By 1240 they were flitting from house to house, never spending more than a day or two in any one place; and next we find them back in a forest hut again. So they went on, shifted from forest to farm, from town to forest, by *credentes* anxious to keep them from harm and *perfecti* who always had fresh instructions for them. They were caught at last in the forest, near Gratiafides in the Lantarès district. It was only after she had been imprisoned for a year that Guillelme de La Mothe told this story. Every person she named was thereby set in the category of *receptatores haereticorum*, liable to trial and imprisonment. This woman and her companion had led a life of danger in order to serve their Church's cause : and it was not to get mercy from her judges that Guillelme talked, since she was burnt in any case.[1]

However great the devotion and loyalty of the *credentes* to their *perfecti*, they knew that torture might lead even the bravest among them to betray their whereabouts. This is the reason why, in doubtful areas—and even in the neighbourhood of Toulouse itself—the heretics would build themselves huts in the woods. Their presence was known to most of their followers, who could come and find them if a dying person needed the *consolamentum*, or there was any other ceremony to be performed.

Since they could not obtain provisions for themselves, the *perfecti* lived off the charity of their followers and indeed this charity was well organized and amply sufficient, if we are to believe the testimony of those who admitted having taken food, clothes or money to the heretics. We hear of bread, flour, honey, vegetables, raisins, figs, nuts, apples, hazels, strawberries; fish, either fresh or, sometimes, baked or stewed; wine, loaves, cakes, and various cooked dishes, some plain, some positively luxurious. The latter were prepared by local peasant women, who could, without arousing suspicion, either go into the forest themselves, or send their children instead. The richer *credentes* would supply the heretics' hide-outs with bushels of wheat and kegs of wine—and the best wine in their cellars, too.

Other women would take up collections to buy wool, with which these involuntary hermits would weave clothes for themselves or their poorer brethren; cloth merchants would give them material, while others supplied ready-made garments, gloves or hats. Others again made them presents of water-jugs, plates, razors, or similar miscellaneous objects. We know about such gifts only because the donors were brought before the Tribunal as a result.

Occasionally, not only to camouflage their religious calling but to earn themselves a living, the *perfecti* would practise a trade. We hear of *perfecti* who were cobblers or bakers, of *perfectae* employed to spin wool, or as housekeepers for rich *credentes*. The Waldensian *perfecti* in particular reckoned on living by their own labours, and they turn up as coopers, hairdressers, saddlers or masons. From 1229 onwards heretics were rather less prone to practise the craft of weaving, since this guild was particularly suspect of heresy; yet some did continue as weavers even under the Inquisition.

Many Cathar and Waldensian *perfecti* enjoyed a high reputation as doctors, and could in this way make some return to the *credentes* who gave them lodging or supplies. Their adversaries were not slow to suggest that this was an excellent device for winning people's confidence, and extracting legacies for the Catharist Church from those who were sick of a mortal disease. It was, indeed, one way of winning confidence. To further this end many practitioners, especially among the Waldensians, took no fees and supplied their own drugs. A Waldensian named De Vaux and William of Ayros, a Cathar, travelled from village to village and château to château, spending as much of their time healing the sick as preaching sermons. It looks as though we have to do here not with a mere propaganda device, but with genuine medical vocations—which would arise naturally enough in men who consecrated their entire lives to the practice of charity. The profession of medicine was one from which they were, as we might expect, officially debarred; and the mere fact of their continuing to tend the sick meant that suspicion was bound to fall on them.

In his *Summa*, written about 1250, Raynier Sacchoni criticizes the Cathars for their love of money, though he adds, honestly enough, that because of the persecution they suffered they were obliged to have considerable sums in cash at their disposal. Since the Catharist Church was forbidden to own land or property, or to take any part in business activities, and thus little by little was reduced to a state of total illegality, the only way it could keep up its activities was through financial gifts. The money was required not so much for the maintenance of its ministers (being great fasters, they spent little on themselves) as for the purchase and distribution of its sacred texts and apologetic or polemical literature; the organization of meetings and liaison work—success frequently depended on some official keeping his mouth shut; and for travel expenses, journey money, or the support of needy *credentes*. Everywhere and at all times money has been an effective way of getting things done—especially in the case of people with a price on their heads. In 1237, for instance, the bailiff of Fanjeaux arrested Bishop Bertrand Marty in person, together with three *perfecti*; but released them again on payment of three hundred *sous tolsas*, which the faithful had collected at once by means of an on-the-spot whip round. For every one known case of bribery there must have been dozens which never came to light. Men who were constantly at the mercy of any blackmailer who threatened to denounce them would not be over-scrupulous about buying their lives with gold.

The *perfecti* were wealthy, and reputedly so. They paid generously for services rendered. Since they could not carry large sums about with them (a difficult matter when banknotes were non-existent) they entrusted their money to reliable persons, who in turn buried it in secret caches known to themselves alone. Such treasure would be at the Catharist Church's disposal in cases of urgent need. The large sums which the Cathars possessed in every area where they conducted their apostolic mission came from several sources. First and foremost there were the bequests which the faithful made on their deathbeds after receiving the *consolamentum*: such legacies were more or less obligatory for the rich *credens*, and even people of modest means would bequeath the *perfecti* their clothes, a bed, or some other household utensil. Another source of income consisted of collections taken up on the Church's behalf by trustworthy agents, who went round soliciting gifts both in cash and kind.

The Cathars' underground activities seem to have been well organized during the first years of the Inquisition: official records divide up those *credentes* who gave aid to heretics into various categories. There were the *receptatores* (these were the most common offenders) who gave hospitality to *perfecti*; the *nuncii*, who acted as liaison agents, guides or messengers; *quaestores*, or fund-raisers; *depositarii*, or those selected to conceal and guard treasure. Obviously these various offices were not kept in watertight compartments, and the names given to such *credentes* were mainly a convenient means of identifying their offence. No *credens*—and with good reason— himself affected the title of *quaestor* or *nuncius haereticorum*. Never- theless, such an organization did exist; and the fiercer the perse- cution became, the closer were drawn those bonds that linked the Catharist *perfecti* and their flock. Though danger might discourage the weaker brethren, more generous natures found it a positive stimulus; and even those whose faith was a lukewarm affair must have hesitated when the only alternatives possible for them were to keep faith or betray it. Rather than stoop to treachery they, too, preferred to risk the perils of prosecution.

2. *The Sanctuary of Montségur*

One place which the Cathars possessed was the fortress of Mont- ségur. Montségur, as everyone knew, was the Catharist Church's open and official headquarters in Languedoc. Knights and their families would make pilgrimages thither; ordinary folk would go there secretly, alone or in groups, in order to participate freely in their Church's ceremonies. They also went to receive a blessing from the *bons hommes*, and to ask their advice or instruction apropos the struggle against the enemy.

The fortress stood on land belonging to Guy de Lévis, the 'Marshal of the Faith' and the new suzerain of Mirepoix. It had, apparently, formed part of Esclarmonde's inheritance (she being Raymond-Roger of Foix's sister), and was held by Raymond de Perella, vassal to the Counts of Foix. No one contested the claim of this puissant *seigneur* to his domains, since Montségur was regarded as an utterly impregnable eyrie, being situated high among the mountains, well away from any major road, in a district notoriously addicted to heresy. Neither the Crusaders nor the King's troops had considered the capture of this fortress a feasible proposition. Strategically it was of little value, and to besiege it would have presented immense difficulties.*

The mountain or peak of Montségur is about 3,500 ft. high, a gigantic rounded outcrop shaped like a sugar-loaf, and inaccessible except on its west flank. Even here the path down into the valley is both steep and exposed. The rock lies on the northern slopes of the Pyrenees, dwarfed by other surrounding peaks from six to nine thousand feet high, and flanked on three sides by deep valleys. The fortress built on its summit was very small, and could not hold even a large garrison; still less could it house a large community in times of peace. The heretics who fled for refuge to Montségur lived in the village at the foot of the mountain, or in numerous huts constructed on the west side of the rock itself. Since Guy de Montfort's raid, no enemy troops had invaded these well-guarded and inhospitable domains. After the Crusade a veritable Catharist colony had formed around Montségur; it was so sizeable that merchants flocked in from neighbouring towns, always certain of finding customers there. Like every centre of pilgrimage—and this, beyond any doubt, was what Montségur was—the sleepy little town was well on the way to becoming a busy trading-community.

In 1204 the fortress, which had long been regarded by the Cathars as an especially propitious focal point for their faith, collapsed in ruins. The *perfecti* asked their *seigneur*, Raymond de Perella, to rebuild it and strengthen its fortifications. Though at this point the Cathars had no urgent need to protect themselves, their request was met. The mere fact of their making such a demand shows that Montségur represented something rather more to these heretics than a potential place of refuge from their enemies. From the beginning

---

* Despite the assertion made by the anonymous translator of the *Chanson* that the fortress was taken by the Crusaders, the truth seems to be otherwise. In 1212 Guy de Montfort occupied Lavelanet and laid waste the surrounding countryside: he may have burnt the *village* of Montségur.

of the century Catharist bishops, Guilhabert de Castres in particular, had come to preach there. Esclarmonde of Foix, whose rights over Montségur seem to have been somewhat ill-defined, and whose personality remains a decided mystery, must nevertheless have exercised great influence in the area, since Foulques pays her an oblique compliment by asserting that 'through her evil doctrines she succeeded in making a number of conversions'.[2] Whether or not this great lady—who in 1206 became a *perfecta*—played any part in the resuscitation of Montségur's fame, it is certainly true that the Cathars' particular obsession with the fortress dates from the beginning of the thirteenth century. In 1232 Raymond de Perella was Montségur's sole *seigneur*, and it was from him that Guilhabert de Castres asked permission to turn the place into an official asylum for the Catharist Church.

At the time Guilhabert was the uncontested spiritual leader in these parts, and made frequent visits to Montségur. He did not, however, remain long there on any one occasion, and continued to lead the wandering life characteristic of all Cathar ministers. But the convents of many *perfectae* had been broken up during the troubles —establishments which formerly offered a way of retreat to aristocratic widows, and served as places of education for pious young girls. These women now flocked in great numbers to the neighbourhood of Montségur, and built themselves huts on the rock. Those of the *perfecti* who led a contemplative life, or were called upon to instruct apostolic candidates in their faith, also found themselves compelled to seek out a retreat where they could devote their lives to prayer and study. Below the walls of the fortress there gradually grew up a village of these huts, their foundations half scooped out of the rock, half suspended in the void with a sheer drop below them. So inaccessible and inconvenient a refuge cannot have been altogether uncongenial to the ascetic temper which characterized these seekers after God.

This village was plastered against the rock-wall under the fortress like a group of swallows' nests, and had a strong palisade of stakes surrounding it. Taking the fortress's position into account, even the most primitive fortifications would suffice to repulse any assailant. But it is plain that only people prepared to make every sort of sacrifice could survive in such cramped quarters and primitive conditions.

Numerous *perfecti* and *credentes* lived in the village below the mountain: this formed a sort of transit camp, where visitors of every age and condition came to stay for shorter or longer periods, while they made expeditions up to the fortress, took part in services, paid their respects to the *perfecti*, and finally went back home to live as 'good Catholics' once more. By pressure of circumstances Montségur was to become in a sense not only the headquarters of Catharist resistance, but of all resistance whatsoever. That class of the population which showed greatest devotion to heresy was also best fitted to organize rebellion.

Despite decimation, ruin and exile, the aristocracy of Languedoc was still powerful in 1240. Most of the Count of Toulouse's vassals had hung on to their domains; so had those of the Count of Foix, and some of the former vassals to the House of Trencavel. Any collaboration between them and the occupation authorities had been highly reluctant on their part: their main ambition was to remain masters of their own lands, and they found the Inquisition a source of countless annoyances. The Count of Toulouse himself might be powerful enough to protest openly at this; but his vassals most often contented themselves with a show of veiled but stubborn hostility. At first the more powerful amongst them, such as the Niort brothers, could indulge in open warfare against the Church. Others, without going quite so far as to invade the Archbishop's palace, raided convents and churches—a fine old feudal tradition. The Count of Toulouse could not, on political grounds, allow his vassals to indulge in excessive acts of violence; but in the territories belonging to the Count of Foix, the *seigneurs* were still more or less masters of their own estates. It was from the Pyrenees that the Occitan nobility now organized their armed resistance movement.

The domains of the Count of Foix straddled the Pyrenees. On the French side, in Languedoc, they included the Ariège Valley and the land adjacent thereto; while in Spain there was the Viscountcy of Castelbon, which Roger Bernard possessed by virtue of his marriage to the heiress concerned. The noble families on the Spanish side of the Pyrenees had close ties both of kinship and vassaldom linking them to their cousins in southern Languedoc. The two countries might be divided by a mountain range, but there were profound similarities of race, language, and tradition to unite them. The Roussillon region has remained Catalan into our own times; similarly, in the Middle Ages the Carcassès, Ariège and Comminges districts stood closer to Catalonia and Aragon than they did to Provence or Aquitaine. Moreover, during the Crusade very many noblemen from the mountain country of Languedoc had crossed the passes and found a natural refuge among their fellow-aristocrats in Catalonia or the Cerdagne Valley. We have already seen how Peter II of Aragon regarded the attack on the Counties of Foix and Comminges as a personal affront: as far as his knights were concerned, the defence of Languedoc had been a matter of *patriotism*. Dispossessed and driven from their estates, the *faidits* formed a powerful group in Spain, despite the Catholic sympathies of young King James I. Raymond Trencavel spent his time at the court of the King of Aragon, surrounded by friends and vassals, actively planning his revenge.

After ruling over Carcassonne and the surrounding territories for two years, this young man (he was born in 1207) was driven out by Louis VIII's troops in 1226. He benefited a good deal from the prestige enjoyed by his father, whose courage, and tragic death, were still living memories for the men of Languedoc. In the eyes of all fief-holders formerly vassal to the House of Trencavel, Raymond was the legitimate *seigneur;* and his return was all the more fervently desired in that the situation created by the Treaty of Paris stimulated a discontent which only increased as time went on.

Raymond Trencavel could not rely on any support from the King of Aragon. Neither the Count of Toulouse nor the Count of Foix could risk openly supporting a *seigneur* who laid claim to lands that were French Crown property. He could rely, to the last man, on the *faidits*—though these landless knights had nothing to offer but their swords and their strong right arms—and upon the secret support of those *seigneurs* who had made submission to the King, but were ready to rebel at the first opportunity. Olivier of Termes, in the district of Les Corbières, possessed several strong fortresses which had never submitted to the French King, and could be utilized as arms depots and assembly points. It was in the mountains of Les Corbières, in the Sault district and the Cerdagne Valley that the rising of these native *seigneurs* was planned. They could only rely upon the great princes if their *coup* succeeded; they were forced to rely solely on their own resources. Because of this they clung with redoubled ardour to the Catharist faith: for most of them it was already the faith of their fathers, and, above all, the symbol of their liberty.

In 1216 they had fought for the Count of Toulouse. Now they had Raymond VII, who was a signatory to the Treaty of Meaux, constantly harried by King and Pope alike, and always on the look-out for fresh allies: a teetering tightrope-walker and a far less certain source of aid. Though he might still be the one man capable of uniting all the forces of resistance behind him, and getting the entire country into the battle, it was still impossible to fight in his name against his express wishes. But every man was free to do battle for his faith.

This is the reason why for ten years Montségur was the very heart and centre of the Resistance in Languedoc. The *faidits* came over the mountains from Spain, and gathered in that high and holy place, where Catharism was practised with a solemnity that equalled, indeed surpassed, that of the pre-war period. Those knights who were secretly conspiring in Languedoc itself went up to Montségur to meet their friends, hold meetings, and receive instructions. Many of these pilgrimages must have been of a political rather than a religious nature; and though we know nothing for certain about their activities, it is unlikely that the *perfecti* (themselves drawn for the most part from the lesser nobility) were wholly ignorant of this patriotic movement. Perhaps while holding forth to their followers on the vain nature of a world created by the Prince of Evil, they also found time to mention the liberation of Languedoc.

Oddly enough, our actual knowledge here is practically nil. We do know that Guilhabert de Castres, Jean Cambiaire, Raymond Aiguilher, Bertrand Marty and others were familiar with a great many knights who played a preponderant rôle in the struggle for independence. Guilhabert de Castres, who must have been extremely old by now, would come down from Montségur and travel, under heavy escort, to various châteaux in the area, where he made brief stays. All these trips were planned in advance with great care, and in absolute secrecy. It is plain that this indefatigable bishop had no intention of ceasing to visit his flock merely through fear of danger; but it also seems reasonable to assume that he played an active and personal part in the revolt that was being planned, and that he encouraged his followers to fight rather than to adopt a policy of non-resistance.

The surviving evidence merely states that such-and-such a *perfectus* came to such-and-such a place, that he broke bread there, and that sundry persons cited 'adored' him. If we follow the activities of score upon score of knights, noble ladies, and men-at-arms, in all their comings and goings and various sojourns upon Montségur, and so on, we learn precisely nothing, apart from the one fact that they listened to sermons. For instance, early on in the siege of Montségur (13th May, 1243) we find two men-at-arms, three *perfecti*, and a deacon named Clamens all coming down from the fortress and breaking through the enemy lines to go to Causson. Now the entire object of this expedition was to bless bread and break it with two other heretics in Causson. There is a possibility that the conduct of *perfecti* and *credentes* in the neighbourhood of Montségur was controlled by strict religious and ritual canons, the importance of which we cannot evaluate for lack of detailed evidence. But the opposite, too, might well be true.

It is, perhaps, a little difficult to picture the *perfecti* organizing terrorist activities. But after all, we have seen Catholic bishops, and even Catholic Saints, flinging themselves frenziedly into the fray: the danger in which the Church stood justified every means of action. If they had behaved likewise the Catharist ministers would have had an even better excuse, since their religion was being subjected to more violent persecutions. It was the men of Montségur who took part in the most notorious act of terrorism that the whole history of the Inquisition has to show us. Though the *perfecti* did not inspire it, they may well have approved of it. At a point when the defence of their Church coincided with that of their native land, the holy men on Montségur (who were, after all, made of flesh and blood) could be no less patriotic than the *faidit* knights.

Raymond de Perella and his son-in-law Pierre-Roger of Mirepoix were among the most active leaders of the aristocratic resistance. It is virtually certain that they were in secret communication with the Count of Toulouse—not to mention Raymond Trencavel, the Count of Foix, and the larger part of the Catharist nobility.

Great *seigneurs* such as the Lords of Niort were among those who gave substantial assistance in kind to the *bons hommes* on Montségur after the winter of 1234, when all the standing crops were killed by frost. Bernard-Otho of Niort personally saw to the collection of the sixty hogsheads of corn which were sent up the mountain. Twenty hogsheads were contributed by the nobles of Laruac, ten came from Bernard-Otho himself, while the remainder was made up from gifts provided by *seigneurs* and citizens in the neighbourhoods of Carcassonne and Toulouse. A large number of other collections were taken up, both in cash and kind, for the replenishing of the fortress's funds and supplies.

Montségur, in fact, was turned into an arsenal. An arms depot was set up there, the size and importance of which can be gauged from subsequent events. It seems probable that the knights who came there to pray also used their pilgrimage as an occasion to deposit some contribution in the shape of spears, arrows, crossbows or armour. Vaissette[3] even conjectures that Montségur may have served as an arms cache for Trencavel, but the facts do not confirm such a supposition: there is no evidence linking Trencavel with Montségur. In any case the vast hoard of weapons that was accumulated in the fortress could just as easily have been destined for the defence of Montségur itself as for the eventual use of an army of liberation.

Furthermore, Montségur, as the 'capital' of the Catharist Church in Languedoc, afforded protection not only to a large proportion of the sect's ministers, but also to its 'treasure'. This treasure consisted, in the first place, of money: the defence of the fortress and the maintenance of a considerable number of *perfecti* required substantial cash backing; Montségur was under an obligation to assist those Brethren campaigning in areas where they were exposed to persecution. But the 'treasure' certainly included other things as well: sacred books, possibly manuscripts of great antiquity composed by learned doctors for whom the Cathars felt especial reverence. Catharist literature was abundant, and when the *perfecti* came to instruct the faithful, or Cathar neophytes, they did not stick solely to the New Testament. They were no less passionately addicted to theological study than the Catholics, and determined to preserve their own doctrine in its original purity. Thus they attached very great importance to those books which helped to keep them in the orthodox tradition. Did the 'treasure' perhaps include anything else—relics, or objects regarded as sacred in some way? Certainly no witness ever refers to such things; but it is also a fact that the scheme of questioning employed by Inquisitors makes no provision for enquiry along these lines. It is possible that a special manuscript copy of the Gospels, or some other object connected with the Catharist cult, may have been regarded with special veneration (the Cathars were, after all, only human) and kept on Montségur because of its peculiar sanctity. But whatever the nature of the 'treasure of Montségur', the place itself was beginning to take on exceptional importance in the minds of all *credentes* throughout Languedoc. It became their holy place *par excellence*.

Did it have this status earlier than 1232, or before the Crusade? Apparently not. During the period when the Cathars were free to practise their religion where they pleased, Montségur was a sacred spot only for the heretics in the Foix area: the spirit of local independence operated here as elsewhere. Yet its position and ground-plan show that it could have been a temple as well as a fortress. It seems very likely that Montségur was adapted for the celebration of Catharist rites, perhaps at a time when the Cathar Church felt strongly enough established to erect and consecrate its own sanctuaries, after the fashion of the Catholic Church. In 1204 Catharism was virtually the official religion throughout the Foix region.

It was between 1232 and 1242 that the fortress became a holy place; the dying were carried to Montségur on mule-back, up along mountain paths, anxious to receive the *consolamentum* there, followed by burial in the shadow of its walls. Thus the knight Jordan Calvent—though he had already received the *consolamentum* —still had himself taken up to die on Montségur. Peter William of Fogart made the journey in the company of two *bons hommes*; but he was in such a weak state that he could not get as far as Montségur itself, and died while resting at Montferrier. Noble ladies from the surrounding districts retired thither to receive the *consolamentum* and spend the rest of their lives in prayer: in 1234 Marquesia de Lantar, Raymond de Perella's mother-in-law, was made a *perfecta* here by Bertrand Marty. There were a large number of *perfectae* living in their huts around the fortress; they were visited here by their sisters and daughters, who stayed with them for varying lengths of time, up to several months on occasion. Among the visitors who went up to the fortress during the years 1233–43, we hear chiefly of knights and men-at-arms, or of the wives, sisters and daughters of knights. *Credentes* of lesser rank may also have made the pilgrimage, but they did not attract any especial attention from the Tribunals. On the other hand the records do refer to those merchants or hawkers from neighbouring parts who went to Montségur to sell provisions, and by so doing fell foul of the law which forbade any person to give any sort of succour to a heretic.

In 1235 Raymond VII dispatched three knights to take formal possession of Montségur. These knights were admitted to the fortress, did obeisance [*adoratio*] before Guilhabert de Castres, and went back to Toulouse. Shortly afterwards the Count sent one of his bailiffs, Mancipe de Gaillac: he and his companions contented themselves with similarly 'adoring' the *bons hommes*, and coming back with nothing achieved. On the third occasion the Count sent back this same Mancipe de Gaillac, together with a body of men-at-arms. They seized a deacon named Jean Cambiaire (or Cambitor) together with three other *perfecti*, and haled them off to be burnt in Toulouse. This incident serves as an admirable pointer to the Count's policy where heretics were concerned: it was basically equivocal, and remained so till the end. All the evidence attests Raymond's sincere Catholicism. It is indeed quite possible (as several incidents in his life suggest) that he honestly detested heresy on account of all his country had suffered from it. He may on innumerable occasions have sided with the Cathars, but he sought primarily to use them as a weapon which might help him to regain his independence.

Raymond de Perella, *seigneur* of Montségur, also held lordship over the châteaux of Pereille [Perella], Laroque d'Olmes, and Alzen, or Nalzen as it is today. Montségur was not his sole place of residence, nor, it may be supposed, an especial favourite of the Perella family, since in 1204 it was falling down. The fortress must have antedated the Perella family's establishment in the area, but its foundations do not seem to go back before the ninth century. Its construction (or rather its ground-plan, since the walls were at least partially restored in 1204) reveals certain instances of technical and mathematical knowledge extremely rare at the time in Western Europe; indeed, the architecture of Montségur is unique of its kind, not only in the immediate area, but throughout the whole of Languedoc.

Since the rock was at least 3,500 ft. high [1,207 m.] and difficult of access, it offered a natural defensive position; but at first sight it looks as though whoever built the fortress made a mistake in setting it on so lofty and remote a pinnacle. There are ruined fortresses aplenty surviving today, perched on crests and hill-tops overlooking main roads, rivers, or mountain passes; Montségur is one of those unusual ruins which is so positioned as to dominate nothing, and lead nowhere. The building must have been influenced by the site's natural beauty rather than its practical advantages. We can find *churches* built in similarly improbable places—on rocky escarpments or isolated peaks, sites either designated by some miraculous vision or hallowed by a pagan tradition overlaid with Christianity. The choice of Montségur as a site may suitably be compared with that of Rocamadour or Saint-Michel de l'Aiguilhe; but the area shows hardly a trace of any cult that would have justified the erection of a temple in this precise spot. Furthermore, the architecture of this fortress does not resemble that of any religious edifice—though it is hardly that of a normal fortress, either. It is dictated in the first instance by the shape of the rock; but despite this it is constructed according to a plan which seems to have aimed, first and foremost, at catching the light, and orientating the walls in relation to the rising sun. The queerest detail about the structure, however, is to do with its two gates, and what is left of the windows in the main keep. No mediaeval fortress, if we except the outer walls of one or two major cities, can boast so monumental an entrance gate as the

Great Gate of Montségur. It is nearly two yards wide, and has no protecting tower or other defence-work. Once any attacker had stormed the rock itself he could walk into this impregnable fortress as though it were a windmill. Portals of this sort were a luxury reserved for churches, and whether the Great Gate was pierced in 1204, or left intact at the time of the reconstruction, a detail of this nature shows that the fortress was not regarded solely as a defensive military installation. There is something unusual about the mere idea of opening up such a gateway; it runs flat counter to all mediaeval rules of architecture.

All these considerations might well lead us to assume that, either originally or at some later point, Montségur was associated with the celebration of a cult—possibly a sun-cult. But it is hard to work out just what powerful person or persons could have reared this monumental edifice, at some time between the ninth and twelfth centuries, in order to practise there a religion which has left absolutely no trace of its existence in the area. The Cathars, so far as we can tell, did not pay any particular homage to the sun; the ancient Manichaeans did, but it is unlikely that a Manichaean sect could have survived for so long in this particular region. Still, if in such remote and unfrequented parts something of the Manichaean tradition *did* manage to survive, it would have aided the diffusion of Catharism; and thus Montségur would have gained favour among the heretics as having been a place of refuge for their religious predecessors. They cannot have attached overmuch importance to it before 1204, since the fortress became an abandoned ruin; but certain *perfectae* had already established themselves there, as they had in other isolated, mountainous spots. Perhaps they chose this site for its silence and its beauty. It seems highly probable that local tradition attached a certain importance to the fortress of Montségur, and regarded it as a relic left by the *boni Christiani* of olden times. As we have seen, the Cathars did not in any way consider themselves innovators, but claimed to be guardians of a tradition that was more ancient than Catholicism.

In 1233 the Catholics began to refer to Montségur as 'the Synagogue of Satan', a term borrowed from Catharist speech, where it was used, *per contra*, to describe the Church of Rome. Threatened with violent destruction, the Catharist Church in Languedoc created of its own accord an earthly capital, the bright rays of which were to counterbalance the steadily thickening darkness which Rome cast over the land. At a time when so many *credentes* were being forcibly sent off, all the way across Europe, to Catholic pilgrims' shrines, their spiritual leaders were making a Holy Place for them in the Pyrenees, the stern majesty of which could be set against the glories of Rome, or St James of Compostella, or Notre-Dame in Puy, or the great Cathedral of Chartres.

The reign of Montségur was a brief one: but nevertheless it constitutes the most enduring attempt by Catharism to establish itself as a national Church in Languedoc. The Inquisition on its own might well have failed to bring Montségur down; and this place, which had so rapidly come to symbolize all the hopes of a humiliated and hunted nation, might yet have had a lasting influence upon the history of Languedoc. But the Catharist citadel was only to pass into legend as a broken and desolate redoubt. So little trace is left of that impassioned way of life which was centred upon it; the men who lived there, admirable and heroic though they must surely have been, are less truly alive for us than the flames of their funeral pyre.

3. *Raymond VII's Rebellion and Defeat*

Despite the stubborn passive resistance put up by the population of Languedoc, the Inquisitors—Peter Seila and William Arnald in the Toulouse diocese, Arnald Cathala and Brother Ferrier within the jurisdiction of the French Crown—persisted in their task with exemplary doggedness. The revolt was brewing up; and its first open outbreak took place in 1240. In April of this year Raymond Trencavel, at the head of an army composed of *faidits*, exiles, and Aragonese and Catalan troops, crossed the mountains and advanced upon Carcassonne down the Aude Valley. Olivier de Termes raised the standard of rebellion in Les Corbières, and Jourdain de Saissac took up arms in the Fenouillèdes area.

The Occitan *seigneurs* were welcomed as liberators in Limoux, Alet, and Montréal: a few weeks, and they were masters of the entire region. Pépieux, Alzille, Laure, Rieux, Caunes and Minerve opened their gates to them; Montoulieu put up a resistance, was taken by storm, and its garrison massacred.

Carcassonne itself, where the Seneschal William of Ormes was trapped, together with Archbishop Peter Amiel and the Bishop of Toulouse, was invested on 7th September by the Trencavel army. They invaded the outlying quarters, and received a rapturous welcome there. The rebellion was, beyond a doubt, aimed as much at the Church as at the French—indeed, thirty-three priests captured in the outer borough were murdered by the populace, despite the safe-conduct granted them by the Viscount. The siege lasted for over a month. Despite Trencavel's energetic assault measures—he attempted to reduce the city by sapping and siege-engines—Carcassonne held out. On 11th October the advance guard of a French army commanded by Jean de Beaumont forced the assailants to raise the siege, however, and Trencavel's forces, together with some of the population of the outer borough, left Carcassonne. Before going they sacked the convent of the Friars Preachers and the Abbey of Notre-Dame, and set fire to several parts of the town.

Raymond Trencavel now withdrew into Montréal, where he was besieged in his turn, and forced to negotiate. The Count of Toulouse had not budged; he was waiting on the turn of events. When Peter Amiel and Raymond du Fauga bade him bring aid to the Seneschal, in accordance with the engagements he had given in the Treaty of Meaux, he had asked leave to consider the matter. He had not gone so far as to join the rebellion himself, and fly to his cousin's assistance: he was waiting for a more propitious opportunity. Together with the Count of Foix he undertook to negotiate peace with honour on Raymond Trencavel's behalf, and approached the King's representatives for this purpose. Raymond was authorized to go back into Spain, taking arms and baggage with him.

Those towns that had risen suffered stern reprisals. The outer borough of Carcassonne was burnt to the ground, while Limoux, Montréal and Montoulieu were all sacked, and the rest had to pay heavy indemnities. The King's army moved up in the direction of Les Corbières, and obtained the submissions of the *seigneurs* of Pierrepertuse and Cucugnan, and latterly that of the Lords of Niort as well.

Raymond VII, whose attitude during the rebellion had struck the French as something worse than equivocal, now found himself obliged to go to Paris and renew his oath of loyalty to the young King Louis IX, now aged twenty-five. He swore to wage war on all the King's enemies, to drive out heretics and *faidits*, and to capture and destroy Montségur. Furthermore, the Count gave the Legate a pledge of his loyalty by making peace with the Count of Provence, whom he had been attacking to further the policies of the Emperor Frederick II, the Pope's sworn enemy.

All the evidence suggests that Raymond VII had no intention of tangling with the King just now, at any price, and was anxious to wipe out the awkward impression which Trencavel's rising had produced. The revolt itself had been premature; and in any case it seems certain that neither time nor misfortune had succeeded in destroying the age-old rivalry between the Counts of Toulouse and the House of Trencavel. Young Raymond had not taken his cousin into his confidence, and the latter had not given Raymond any support. It is true, though, that he was planning an operation on a really large scale, and the hour to strike had not yet come.

Raymond VII had given up all hope of regaining his independence by means of a local uprising, which was doomed to failure in advance. He had already achieved the impossible: and his victory over De Montfort's troops had brought him to—the Treaty of Meaux. The only way in which he could restore peace and prosperity to his country was by weakening the power of the French Crown in some more or less permanent fashion; and there was no chance of his achieving this end with his own resources. So he began to mediate on rather grander political alliances. The right men to drive out the French were not Trencavel and Olivier de Termes, but the King of England, the German Emperor, and a league of the French King's major vassals, who could, in the event of victory, dictate terms to France. In order to lull the suspicions of the Pope and the King, the Count of Toulouse was ready to be as submissive and as orthodox as anyone could desire; besides, the monarchs whom he now wanted as allies were Catholic to a man, and it was more than ever essential that he should not be regarded as a supporter of heresy.

There were, moreover, two important favours he wanted to obtain from the Pope: authority to bury his father—and to repudiate his wife. It was, indeed, useless to try to shake off the yoke of France if, after the Count's death, Languedoc would still, whatever happened, automatically pass into the King's hands by right of inheritance. Now Raymond VII had not so far succeeded in getting a separation from his wife, who had been barren for the past twenty years: the Pope took great care not to authorize an annulment that might interfere with the French King's plans. In order to please the Pope, the Count sacrificed his alliance with the Emperor (though not for long, as we shall see) and thus found himself better placed to bring about the annulment of his marriage—all the more so since he had the support of the Countess's nephew, James I. Raymond claimed to have found out (after twenty-five years of wedded life) that his father, Raymond VI, had been one of Princess Sancha's godfathers, and thus he himself was married to his own father's godchild. He produced his witnesses, and the marriage was declared null—to the great indignation of the Bishop of Toulouse, and the still greater resentment of Alphonse of Poitiers and his wife Jeanne, Raymond VII's daughter.

Once rid of his wife, the Count of Toulouse became a highly eligible suitor for the daughters of the great feudal barons in the Midi. It happened that Raymond-Bérenger, Count of Provence (he was the son of Alfonso, Peter II of Aragon's younger brother), having first used the King of France's support to defend himself against the ambitions of the Emperor, was now thinking up a scheme to rid himself of the embarrassing protection of the French. After making war on the Count of Provence in 1239 to further the Emperor's interests, Raymond VII, by now proposing peace terms to him, brought off a double *coup*: on the one hand he gave satisfaction to the Pope, and on the other he acquired an ally for his coming struggle against the King.

Raymond-Bérenger's children were all daughters. The eldest girl was married to Louis IX, the next youngest to Henry III of England; two others remained to be disposed of. The Count of Provence had no more intention than did Raymond of letting the French King inherit his domains: ten years of French domination in the Carcassès and Albigeois regions must have given the Southern *seigneurs* a very clear idea of how their country would fare if the King finally got his hands on it. Raymond-Bérenger chose the Count of Toulouse as his third son-in-law in the hope that the two of them, together with his cousin James I of Aragon, might found a league of barons in the Midi powerful enough to hold the King's authority in check. This marriage was a matter of vital importance to Raymond VII, since only a male heir could—despite those clauses in the Treaty of Meaux—safeguard the independence of his domains.

In 1241 the Count was forty-four years old; there was no reason to suppose that he would lack for further offspring, and this fact might (as far as France was concerned) compromise the advantages gained by the Treaty of Meaux. Now unless he went and sought a bride in Denmark, no European prince could marry without a dispensation from the Holy Father; while the families of the great barons in the Midi were all interlinked by bonds of kinship. So Raymond VII found himself related by marriage to these daughters of Raymond-Bérenger's, his own repudiated wife being, by a stroke of irony, the young princesses' great-aunt. The dispensation seemed easy enough to obtain. King James I of Aragon represented the Count of Toulouse when he was married by proxy to Sancha, third daughter of the Count of Provence: the ceremony took place in Aix. The union was not destined to be consummated: Gregory IX died on 21st August, 1241, and his successor, Celestinus IV, had no time to deal with the question of dispensation, since his Pontificate only lasted a few weeks. After his death, in October 1241, the Holy See remained vacant for a year and eight months; and the Count of Provence, doubtless feeling that a dispensation which had suffered such delay might never materialize at all, married off his daughter to the King of England's brother, Richard.

The Count of Toulouse was now obliged to scout round for a new father-in-law. His choice fell on the daughter of Hugues de Lusignan, Count of the Marches [de la Marche]. Here too a dispensation was necessary: Marguerite de La Marche and Raymond VII had consanguinity in the fourth degree, being both descended from Louis VI ('The Fat'). For other reasons this dispensation was not obtained, either.

Hugues de Lusignan, Lord of Poitou, egged on by his wife Isabelle of Angoulême, John Lackland's widow, was also searching for allies against the King of France. In 1242 young Louis IX found a coalition forming against him. Those who, either more or less directly, had some part in it included Peter Mauclerc, Duke of Brittany; the Count of Toulouse; the Count of the Marches, and the Count of Provence. Supporting them on one side they had Henry III of England, and on the other James I of Aragon. But for all its apparent strength, this alliance lacked both unity and organization; it certainly could not control a young and aggressive French monarch. As we have already observed, on a purely military level the Northern Frenchmen were indubitably superior to the Southerners; and the swift defeat of Raymond Trencavel had demonstrated that even on enemy soil, and with relatively few troops, the French always got the upper hand in the end. Raymond VII's ambition was to encircle the King's domains and attack on several fronts simultaneously. This might have been a feasible plan if all his allies had been as anxious as he was to make war on the French Crown.

But the most deeply involved member of the coalition, the Count of Toulouse, was also the weakest. His strongholds had been dismantled; there were royal garrisons only a few score miles from his capital; and both Church and monarchy exerted an unrelenting control over him. Raymond spent the years 1240 to 1242 in intense diplomatic activity, travelling from Provence to Poitou, and from Poitou on to Spain, but at the same time taking every precaution to avoid rousing the suspicions of Blanche of Castille. Between 19th and 26th April, 1241, he signed a treaty of alliance with the King of Aragon, its joint objects being the defence of Catholic orthodoxy and the Holy See. Next he concluded a bilateral agreement, both for defence and attack, with Hugues de Lusignan. Finally he won over the Kings of Navarre, Castille and Aragon, together with Frederick II. No one could say that Raymond VII was lacking either in goodwill or diplomacy. But his future at the moment depended not so much on him as on his allies; and for them it was not a matter of vital importance that France should be defeated.

On 14th March, 1242, as he was returning from Aragon and on his way to Poitou, the Count fell ill at Penne d'Agenais—so seriously that he was thought to be at death's door. This illness came at a most inopportune time: the Count of the Marches did not wait for his ally to recover before denouncing the bond which held him in vassalage to the French Crown. Scarcely convalescent, Raymond hastily summoned his own vassals at the beginning of April, to assure himself of their loyalty, and all swore to stand by him to the end. Bernard, Count of Armagnac, Bernard, Count of Comminges, Hugues, Count of Rodez, Roger IV, Count of Foix, the Viscounts of Narbonne, Lautrec, Lomagne, and many others all undertook to aid the Count in his struggle against the King of France. It was a declaration of war.

Young Louis IX did not waste any time. He at once hastened with his army to Saintonge, where he wiped out the troops led by the Count of the Marches. The war had begun badly. Raymond, placing his reliance upon the strength of the English King and his other allies, never considered retreat: he knew there would be no second chance for him. But the swiftness of the King's decision had already compromised the success of the enterprise; and the Count's vassals, who were always ready to fight for their own domains, had no great urge to rush to the assistance of Hugues de Lusignan.

Among the common people rebellion had been smouldering like fire beneath the ashes, and the news of this imminent war made it flare up abruptly. But it was the massacre of Avignonet that gave the actual signal for revolt.

According to the testimony of witnesses who were closely concerned in the affair, this massacre was brought about by the direct instigation of the Count of Toulouse. Here is the account of the matter which was given to the Inquisitors by Fays de Plaigne, William de Plaigne's wife:[4]

William and Pierre-Raymond de Plaigne, two knights of the Mont-ségur garrison, were at the fortress of Bram when a certain Jordanet du Mas arrived, and told William that Raymond d'Alfaro was waiting for him in the Antioche Forest. D'Alfaro was a magistrate of Count Raymond's, and bailiff of the Château d'Avignonet. William de Plaigne met D'Alfaro at the place indicated, and the bailiff, after swearing him to secrecy, said: 'My master the Count of Toulouse cannot travel abroad as things are; nor can Pierre de Mazerolles or any of the other knights available to him. It is vital that Brother Arnaud and his companions should be done away with. I want Pierre-Roger de Mirepoix and every man-at-arms on Montségur to come to the castle of Avignonet, where the Inquisitors at present are. I also have letters for conveyance to Pierre-Roger. Act quickly, and after the Inquisitors are dead you shall have the finest mount to be found in Avignonet as a reward.'

This testimony involves the Count of Toulouse in the most explicit possible way. It seems at least conceivable that Fays de Plaigne only gave such evidence in order to relieve her own kin, at least partially, of responsibility in the affair. The person most directly responsible, in any case, was Raymond d'Alfaro, who sent for the men of Montségur: he alone made the murder a possibility. It is doubtful whether he can have been acting on his own initiative, or at least without the sure knowledge that he had Count Raymond's approval: moreover he had close ties with the Count, quite apart from his office as bailiff, being in fact Raymond's nephew—his mother Guillemette had been Raymond VI's illegitimate daughter. Despite his hatred for the Inquisitors, the Count could not order his own knights to carry out such a deed of violence. But the knights of Montségur were not his subjects; they were self-confessed rebels who, furthermore, lived in a reputedly impregnable fortress.

It was not, however, an unwelcome duty which the Count imposed upon these knights from Montségur: very far from it. It was a godsend, an unlooked-for favour, a holiday. These men hurried to their macabre rendezvous with the impatience of a lover anxious to be reunited with his sweetheart. William de Plaigne rode to Montségur at full gallop to break the good news to Pierre-Roger de Mirepoix, the garrison commander. Pierre-Roger at once assembled his knights and men-at-arms, and told them to prepare for action. 'An extremely important operation,' he said, 'and one from which we will reap great benefit!'[5]

The party numbered about sixty in all, roughly half the entire garrison of Montségur: fifteen knights and forty-two men-at-arms. All of them belonged to the lesser local nobility—Massabracs, Congosts, Plaignes, men from Montferrier and Arzeus and Laroque d'Olmes, Castelbon and Saint-Martin-la-Lande—and all of them Catharist *credentes*, probably for two or three generations back, since most of them were young men. Can we suppose that Pierre-

Roger de Mirepoix would have concealed the purpose of this expedition from the *perfecti*? Would he have risked taking such a responsibility upon himself without consulting the leader of the community, Bishop Bertrand Marty? The *bons hommes* may not have frequented the armouries and tiltyard, but they must have taken a passionate interest in everything that went on in the outside world, since they themselves travelled constantly, and maintained a close relationship with *credentes* throughout the area. The mission with which Raymond d'Alfaro had charged the men of Montségur was contrary to all notions of Christian charity; but that is no reason for our supposing that Bertrand Marty and his companions would have disapproved of it.

William Arnald had embarked on a new Inquisitorial tour, accompanied by the Franciscan Stephen de Saint-Thibéry, whom Pope Innocent IV had sent out to join him as a sop to the Count of Toulouse's protests. The two Inquisitors were assisted in their duties by a pair of Dominicans, Garsias d'Aure and Bernard de Roquefort. Their retinue also included a Franciscan companion of Saint-Thibéry's; Raymond Carbonier, Assessor to the Tribunal, who represented the Bishop; Raymond Costiran, known as Raymond the Scrivener, an ex-troubadour who was now Archdeacon of Lézat, and who, ten years before, had undertaken Bernard-Otho de Niort's defence at his trial; and four domestic servants.

Avignonet was situated in the heart of the Lauraguais district, on the borders of the Count of Toulouse's territory, and had a reputation for deep-rooted heresy. All the towns in the neighbourhood—Les Cassès, La Bessède, Laurac, Sorèze, Saissac, Saint-Félix—had a long-standing tradition of heretical allegiance; and it argues some courage in Arnald and his companions to have mounted this new Inquisition at a time when the Count of Toulouse had just declared war on the King of France. They travelled on horseback, unescorted, and spent the night in lodgings put at their disposal by the local authorities.

They reached Avignonet on the eve of Ascension Day, and were welcomed by Raymond d'Alfaro, who, in his capacity as the Count's bailiff, lodged them in his master's own house. He received them, as we may imagine, with great delight; and as we have already seen, he lost no time in passing on the news of their arrival to the proper quarters. The Montségur contingent, for their part, after a good hard ride (it is at least thirty-five miles as the crow flies between Avignonet and Montségur, and over sixty by road) halted at Gaja, where they were welcomed into Bernard de Saint-Martin's house. Here they were joined by another troop, composed of Pierre de Mazerolles, Jordan du Vilar, and several men-at-arms. Later, at Mas Saintes Puelles, the knight Jordan du Mas also joined them. There was no longer any need to keep the matter a close secret; the mere fact of knowing that the Inquisitors were within striking distance made every man of the population a fellow-conspirator.

The troop halted by the leper-house just outside Avignonet, where a messenger from Raymond d'Alfaro came to meet them, asking whether they were provided with axes. A dozen axes had in fact been got ready, and eight men from Gaja and four from Montségur chosen to lead the way. The conspirators were conducted into the town at nightfall; Raymond d'Alfaro himself, 'clad in a white surcoat', welcomed the men-at-arms and guided them by torchlight down the corridors of the house, to the door behind which the Inquisitors were sleeping. The bailiff was accompanied by a dozen or more inhabitants of Avignonet, who had expressed the wish to join the conspiracy.

The door was quickly battered in, and the seven monks, suddenly shot out of their sleep and seeing only too well what kind of trap they had fallen into, sank down on their knees and began to intone the *Salve Regina*. But they were not left the time to finish it. Raymond d'Alfaro strode forward with his armed posse at his heels, crying out '*Va be, esta be!*' ['This is it!']; the murderers all vied with each other for the honour of striking the first blows. We can imagine what sort of a shambles it all was simply from the number of conspirators who later boasted of having actually killed one of the victims. The monks' skulls were battered in with axes and maces, their bodies run through with innumerable spear-thrusts and dagger-strokes, many of which must doubtless have pierced mere dead flesh.

There then followed the sharing-out of booty: the Inquisitors' records, the few valuables they carried about with them on their travels, little enough indeed—some books, a candlestick, a box of ginger, a handful of coins, clothes and bedding, scapulars, knives. Though they were not wealthy, these men were not beggars either; but from the way they flung themselves on these trumpery objects, in a room still strewn with bleeding, mutilated corpses, they might have been sharing out trophies rather than indulging in mere pillage. Those conspirators who had not taken part in the massacre now joined them, each man being anxious to share the occasion personally.

Then Raymond d'Alfaro distributed candles and torches among the conspirators, and the procession passed out of the town to join the rest of the troop, who were still waiting for them by the leper-house. William de Plaigne mounted the fine horse that had been promised him: it was Raymond the Scrivener's palfrey. The Bailiff of Avignonet took leave of his accomplices, saying: 'All has gone well. Good luck!' Then he returned within the walls to proclaim the call to arms. The flaring torchlit procession which announced the Inquisitors' deaths also formed the signal for a general rising.

Pierre-Roger de Mirepoix was waiting for his men in the Forest of Antioche. Presently they arrived, horses laden with booty; and seven men (Pons de Capelle, P. Laurens, G. Laurens, Pierre de Mazerolles, P. Vidal, G. de la Ilhe, and G. Acermat) boasted of having struck the first, fatal blows upon the two Inquisitors. When he saw Acermat, Pierre-Roger cried out: 'Ah, traitor, where is Arnald's cup?'

'It is broken,' Acermat replied.

'Why did you not bring me the pieces? I would have bound them together with a circlet of gold, and drunk wine from this cup all the days of my life,'

The 'cup' in question was none other than Brother William Arnald's skull.[6]

On the morning of Ascension Day the troop reached Saint-Félix. The great news had already spread through the countryside: the parish priest came out at the head of his flock to congratulate the murderers, and they entered Saint-Félix with the crowd's acclamations ringing in their ears.

The Count's war of liberation had begun. The day after the massacre of Avignonet, Pierre-Roger de Mirepoix sent two men-at-arms to Isarn de Fanjeaux, bidding them ask him whether the Count of Toulouse's affairs were going well. In fact they were going very well indeed. In the space of three months, with Raymond Trencavel's help, Raymond VII made himself master of the Razès, Termenès, and Minervois districts, and rose triumphantly into Narbonne, which Viscount Aimery delivered up to him. To make it quite clear that the Treaty of Paris had been annulled, he solemnly resumed his old title of Duke of Narbonne [8th August, 1242]. The men of Languedoc could, briefly, believe that the hour of deliverance was at hand.

The murder of William Arnald and his companions was no military victory or act of heroism; indeed, when one examines the bare facts, it looks a decidedly sordid story. It is, all things considered, less sordid than the bonfires kindled in Christ's name: but acts of 'legal' justice very often tend to be favourably prejudged, even in the eyes of those who condemn them. The massacre at Avignonet was also, in its way, an act of justice—that rough justice which finally triumphs over laws, established authority, and the trend of the times. The Church never placed William Arnald amongst her Martyrs, and his murderers, despite the Inquisition's final victory, remained unpunished.

Raymond VII's rebellion was a failure. Doubtless the Count had under-estimated the vigour and military skill of the French leaders, just as he had over-estimated the strength of his own allies. This was a pardonable error, since his situation was so ghastly that he must have been tempted to treat his hopes as established reality. Time, too, was on the King's side. His ascendancy in eastern Languedoc progressively weakened the country's forces of resistance. He kept even stricter control over this area, increasing the number of French officials and knights, reducing the local burgher-class to penury, and gradually eliminating the native aristocracy altogether.

Since Raymond VII had no son and heir, his allies regarded him as a bruised reed on whom they should not risk too great a reliance. The County of Toulouse was no longer considered as a *country*, whether friendly or hostile, nor as a political key area; it was now scaled down to the somewhat frail person of the Count himself. And since Raymond's son was not yet born, it seemed unlikely that he would live long enough to see the boy come to manhood and hold his own against the King of France.

Following on the disaster suffered by Hugues de Lusignan, Henry III was beaten by the French army at Taillebourg, and retreated to Bordeaux. Neither the King of Aragon nor the Count of Provence were over-anxious to support such ill-fated allies; the vassals of the Count of Toulouse, realizing that the game was up, had no other thought than to avoid the reappearance of the King's forces in their territory. While Raymond VII (after signing a fresh treaty of alliance with the King of England) was away in the Agenais district, laying siege to the French-held fortress of Penne, Roger IV of Foix offered his submission to the King, and finally severed the bond of vassalship which tied him to the Count of Toulouse.

Finding himself thus deserted on all sides, Raymond had no option but to submit, and called in the Queen Mother, Blanche of Castille, to act as intermediary on his behalf. As a token of his surrender he returned to the King the two strongholds of Bram and Saverdun, and the whole Lauraguais region; and on 30th October, 1242, he signed a peace treaty at Lorris.

The revolt was over; so much so, in fact, that the King did not even see fit to mete out severe punishments to those vassals who, in despite of their oaths, had taken up arms against him. In January 1243 the Counts of Toulouse and of Foix betook themselves to Paris in order to renew their homage to the French Crown. It was to Blanche of Castille that, according to William de Puylaurens, the Count owed the comparatively mild conditions laid down in the new peace treaty: the Lady Regent had nothing to gain by impoverishing territory that would later revert to her son. The most effective way of rendering the Count of Toulouse harmless was still to prevent his remarriage—a task to which Blanche of Castille devoted herself, with some success, in the years that followed. Meanwhile Raymond promised, yet again, to purge his territories, once and for all, of heresy. Blanche of Castille took this matter of the Faith very much to heart; and the Count, for his part, asked nothing better than to persecute heretics, provided he was allowed to do it himself. Since he could not dislodge the King of France, at least he would try to rid himself of the Inquisition.

Scarcely was the Count back in Languedoc before he summoned a Council composed, for the most part, of the bishops and more important abbots resident in his domains. This he did without reference to the fact that he was still under ban of excommunication, imposed upon him by Brother Ferrier after the murder of the Inquisitors, and by Archbishop Peter Amiel after his entry into Narbonne. The purpose of this council was to organize the extermination of heresy; and the Archbishop of Narbonne himself presided over the meeting, which took place at Béziers, on 15th April 1243. As far as the Count was concerned, however, the real aim of the council was to eliminate the Inquisition, and restore its jurisdiction to episcopal authority.

This move was aimed rather at the Dominicans than at heresy *per se*; and the Order responded to it with a *démarche* that would have fulfilled all the Count's wishes if it had proved successful. They asked the Pope to relieve them of their Inquisitorial duties, which caused them nothing but trouble, and created great hostility against them. It is true that a number of Dominicans who were not Inquisitors at all had paid for their brethren's unpopularity: in many towns the convents of the Preaching Friars were attacked and plundered. On the other hand, William Arnald's fate was not liable to discourage the leaders of the Order; these men were as impervious to fear as they were to many other human sentiments.

On the contrary, it must rather have whetted their appetite for action. Such dour fighters could hardly have envisaged throwing in their hand when the enemy was half beaten and the French King triumphant. Their main purpose was to make the Pope realize what terror their activities produced, and, by implication, how efficient they were. Innocent IV ignored their request and confirmed them in all their existing powers, without putting them in any way under episcopal jurisdiction. The Preachers, for their part, were eager to placate the bishops, who might prove hostile otherwise, and therefore took care to give some prominence in their Tribunals' proceedings to the diocesan representative. This was a purely honorific concession, however, since the Dominican Inquisitors always remained the ultimate authority in matters of heresy, *de auctoritate apostolica*.

The Count's attempt, then, was a failure. Moreover, his excommunication had still not been lifted: it was deeds that were required of him, not words. At the Council of Béziers in 1243 the prelates of Languedoc decided to deal once and for all with Montségur (which the Count had already made a somewhat half-hearted attempt to capture) and which was the place where William Arnald's murderers had taken refuge. The Count's rebellion and defeat drove Church and King alike to increasingly harsh measures. Now he was beaten, Raymond VII's one aim was to cut his losses as far as possible, by sacrificing those of his subjects whom he could no longer defend, and taking care not to become embroiled with his conquerors and future allies.

Hugues des Arcis, the new Seneschal of Carcassonne, and Peter Amiel, Archbishop of Narbonne, accordingly resolved to assemble an army large enough to lay siege to this famous fortress, which, as public report had it, was the heretics' headquarters. In April 1243, when the last attempt at armed rebellion in Languedoc had failed, the general atmosphere was one of pessimism and defeat, and all that each person hoped for was to get out of the mess without individual loss. Montségur, stubborn and isolated, found itself—very much against the wishes of its defenders—fated to be the scapegoat of the Occitan resistance movement.

When Raymond de Perella agreed to let his fortress be used as the Catharist Church's official headquarters, he realized the danger to which he was exposing himself. Excommunicated and sentenced to death *in absentia*, he knew very well that only those thick walls stood between him and disaster. What he could not foresee was that one day King and Pope would use his tiny citadel as a symbol— a symbol of heresy poised to swallow up the Church.

CHAPTER XII

THE SIEGE OF MONTSEGUR

IN MAY 1243 HUGUES DES ARCIS, at the head of an army of French knights and men-at-arms, pitched camp below Montségur. He was expecting further reinforcements: to ring round a mountain of this size required considerable manpower. It seemed fairly clear that so lofty and remote a fortress could only be reduced by means of starving out the garrison. All the besieger needed to do was to sever all lines of communication and let the summer sun dry up the defenders' cisterns. There were several hundred persons collected in the fortress itself and the huts that clustered below its walls. These included the garrison (between a hundred and twenty and a hundred and fifty men), the families of knights and men-at-arms, and the 'heretics' proper, who must have numbered about two hundred, men and women together.

1. *The Siege*

The siege lasted far longer than any of those undertaken by Simon de Montfort—apart, that is, from the siege of Toulouse, where the situation was hardly comparable to that prevailing at Montségur. Carcassonne had held out for a fortnight only, Minerve and Termes for four months, Lavaur for two months and Penne d'Agenais slightly less than that, Montgaillard for six weeks, and so on. All these places were, militarily speaking, far stronger than Montségur. Fortresses such as Termes and Minerve also possessed natural defences which rendered them impregnable; thirst had defeated them. When we consider the tiny size of Montségur, it is clear that this fortress was overpopulated as no other château, Carcassonne excepted, had been during a siege.

Logically, Montségur should have surrendered at the end of the summer; but it held out long enough—that is, till the rainy season. Thereafter the besiegers could no longer rely on a water shortage. Nor, indeed, could they hope for famine: abundant gifts from *credentes*, rich and poor alike, had turned Montségur into one vast storehouse. There was always the possibility of a siege. If in 1235 the *credentes* were forced to organize collections because the *bons hommes* of Montségur had nothing to eat, the revictualling of the fortress in 1243 presented no greater a problem. Contributions poured in. The little village at the foot of the rock had become a market, and merchants from all the surrounding towns flocked thither; from all over the Toulousain and Carcassès regions convoys of wheat were put on the road for Montségur. The murder of the Inquisitors, moreover, had merely served to raise the Cathar citadel's prestige—it had become, as a result, a haven for heroes in freedom's cause. All through the siege the fortress continued to receive fresh supplies by means of partisans, who forced their way through the besieging army's blockade, and carried large quantities of corn to the top of the rock.

The garrison also received reinforcements of fresh troops. Men vowed to the Catharist cause got through the enemy's lines at night, clambered up to the fortress, and joined the defenders. Communication with the outside world continued throughout the siege. To cut off Montségur completely was a task of extreme difficulty. The mountain was a deep, sprawling, precipitous mass, a gigantic pyramid of limestone blocks topped off with a bare rocky summit, and dropping almost sheer into the valley below. Though the besiegers at times numbered some ten thousand men, they could not maintain a day-and-night watch on all the mountain paths and tracks: along them members of the garrison travelled to and fro regularly, bringing back friends, provisions, and news of the outside world. Indeed, the besiegers' difficulties were not solely due to their fortress's superb natural defences; at least half of them could be attributed to the local population's strong and unshakeable support for the besieged.

When Hugues des Arcis and his army arrived at the foot of this formidable rock (with the fortress seemingly mocking its assailants from the summit) they began by pitching camp on the Col du Tremblement—thus depriving the besieged of their easiest way down into the valley—and by occupying the village. There was not much else they could do except to sit and await reinforcements—such as the troops which the Archbishop of Narbonne conscripted from the burghers and common people of his city.

We have no precise evidence concerning the number of French knights that the Seneschal brought with him. It may have run into several hundreds, for Hugues des Arcis was preparing to face a hard

M

siege, and must have called upon the majority of fighting personnel at his disposal. Besides, the recent defeats of Trencavel and Raymond VII meant that the French now had a free hand. These knights might not have had the campaign experience of a Simon de Montfort, and were doubtless untrained for fighting in mountainous terrain; but they formed the core of a solid and well-disciplined army, quite capable of defeating the enemy by attrition if a frontal assault on the *pog* [fortress] proved impossible. But even counting all the squires and men-at-arms, it is clear that there were not enough French troops for the job. There were a good many more of the local auxiliaries, but these were primarily foot-soldiers, equipped and dispatched by various towns and boroughs at their own expense; some of them were not even professional soldiers at all. The majority can have had no great desire to fight against their fellow-countrymen, and were serving unwillingly. It was they who provided the detachments to encircle the mountain, and who patrolled the roads, tracks, and gorges. Throughout the siege, despite the Archbishop's efforts, this army suffered from desertions and—it goes without saying— from a passive complicity with the besieged. The latter penetrated the siege lines constantly, sometimes in numerous groups; and the blockade of Montségur, on which Hugues des Arcis was depending for the reduction of his adversaries, turned out to be a virtual impossibility. This eagles' eyrie could only be taken by assault—an enterprise which, at first sight, seemed quite hopeless.

Storming the fortress itself was out of the question; and the bare, exposed slope which led from the Col du Tremblement to the outer walls presented another insuperable hazard. Any attacking force which ventured on to this escarpment would be wiped out by the defenders' stone-guns before it was half-way to its gaol. This meant that the French were kept at a good distance from the fortress, and could use neither their siege-engines nor more normal weapons.

The only face that could be scaled in comparative safety was that on the eastern side; and this could only be reached by steep mountain tracks and forest paths which were familiar enough to local inhabitants, but very difficult of access. Furthermore, the crest itself was patrolled by sentries, and separated from the actual fortress by a drop of some thirty feet or more; thus it could not give attackers direct access to the citadel. But this narrow summit, no more than a hundred yards in length, formed the one possible approach. It was protected by a timber palisade, from which a defending force could easily push any assailants back into the depths below.

For five months besiegers and besieged alike remained in their respective positions—the one group perched on the summit of the mountain, the other spread out round the valleys and surrounding hillsides. There appear to have been some abortive attempts at an assault, since we know that three members of the Montségur garrison were mortally wounded before October 1243. That was just about all Hugues des Arcis had to show for a siege that had lasted five months, and which was proving a drain on finances and manpower alike.

Who *were* the defenders and inhabitants of the beleaguered fortress? The Inquisition's records tell us the names of three hundred persons who were in the fortress during the siege—not counting at least one hundred and fifty whose names are lost because it was not deemed profitable to interrogate them. The reason for this we shall see later.

The *seigneur* of the fortress, Raymond de Perella, had as it were put himself into the service of the *bons hommes*: he now found that he was not so much the proprietor of Montségur as its garrison commander and senior commissariat officer. He had his family living there with him: his wife, Corba de Lantar, his three daughters, and his son. The son, Jordan by name, must have been very young, since he seems not to have taken any active part in the defence. Two of the daughters were married, Philippa to Pierre-Roger de Mirepoix, Arpaïs to Guiraud de Ravat. The third, Esclarmonde, was an invalid, and had vowed herself to the service of God like her mother. The latter was not yet a *perfecta*, but later gave striking proof of the strength of her faith. Her mother was Marquésia de Lantar, who also lived at Montségur and had 'taken the robe' as a full heretic. Pierre-Roger de Mirepoix, the husband of the Castellan's eldest daughter, was (as we have seen) the garrison commander, and one of the finest knights in the country. He was a *faidit* (since the heirs of Guy de Lévis were at present settled in Mirepoix), and the scion of a family with strong heretical allegiances. Forneria, who was the mother of his kinsman Arnald-Roger de Mirepoix, had been one of the *perfectae* resident on Montségur in 1204. Forneria's daughter Adalays had likewise lived in the convent for *perfectae*, and her sons Otho and Alzeu de Massabrac were among the knights of the garrison. A daughter of this same Adalays had married William de Plaigne, already mentioned above. Bérenger de Lavelanet, a fellow-*seigneur* from the same district, was father-in-law to Imbert de Salas, the garrison's sergeant-at-arms, while one of his sisters was a *perfecta* at Montségur also. The knights and their squires all belonged to the local minor nobility, and formed what might be termed one large family. Each of them had at least one *perfecta* among his close relations.

In this context we may ask ourselves just what precise part women had to play in the Catharist faith. It is known that many high-born ladies (either widows or still married, but of an advanced age) withdrew from the world to lead a life of prayer together with other *perfectae*. These austere matrons brought up their children in an atmosphere of absolute devotion to their faith; the majority of the Catharist Church's leaders must have been vowed to the ministry since childhood by ardently religious mothers—a fact which doubtless explains the occasional glaring case of apostasy which we encounter among the *perfecti*. But none of these women would appear to have played an even remotely comparable role to that of the Catharist bishops and deacons. Though some of them certainly led an extremely active 'underground' existence, they nevertheless only filled junior positions in the Catharist hierarchy. Most of them lived segregated lives in hermitages and caves, praying and fasting and exhorting other women to follow their example. What does seem clear is that Catharism, which has been criticized for attempting to stamp out the natural affections, was in fact a highly patriarchal sort of religion. Its strength lay precisely in those family ties which ran from grandmother to grandchildren, from father-in-law to son-in-law, from uncle to nephew, and which finally won over to the Cathar Church a most powerfully united society, as solid in its faith as over the defence of its own interests. That is why women played so prominent a part in Catharism. In her capacity as guardian of the family, a woman also was responsible for that family's religious tradition. The knights and ladies who went up to Montségur to celebrate the feasts of Christmas or Pentecost also made their visit an occasion to call upon some venerable mother, aunt or grandmother, and receive her blessing.

Apart from the squires, who were all either related to the knights or at least their childhood friends, the garrison contained a round hundred soldiers or men-at-arms—local men for the most part, redoubtable warriors and fiercely loyal to their leaders. Some of them also had their wives with them in the fortress. Raymond de Perella's wife and daughters had their maidservants and companions. The two Lords of Montségur—authority in the fortress was split *de facto* between the Castellan and his son-in-law Pierre-Roger de Mirepoix, and the two men did not always agree—had their own bailiffs [*bailes*] whose business was to oversee their masters' estates. Apart from personnel connected with the knights' establishment,

Montségur also gave shelter to various guests who had fled thither through fear of the Inquisition—such as Raymond Marty, Bishop Bertrand's brother, or G. R. Golayran, who had played an active part in the Avignonet massacre.

At the time of the siege the number of persons shut up in the fortress rose, as has been stated above, to about three hundred, excluding the *perfecti*. The latter were very numerous, between a hundred and fifty and two hundred; but there is nothing surprising about this, since Montségur was the official asylum and Holy Place of their Church. The leaders of the Catharist Church in Languedoc had been established there ever since 1232, and did not deem it profitable to change their residence when a French army appeared at the foot of the mountain. In any case such a move would have increased the risk of their being captured; and it seems clear that Montségur had already acquired such importance in the eyes of local heretics that any flight elsewhere on the part of the *bons hommes* would have been construed as desertion. These men denied reality to all appearances and any material manifestation of divinity; yet they regarded their fate as being mysteriously bound up with this 'vessel of stone', this majestic cathedral sans cross, reaching up to heaven from its rocky eminence. Their supporters' moral fervour and conviction stemmed, perhaps, from the fact that they were defending something more than human lives—their very temple, the earthly image of their faith.

But was the fortress in fact a temple? Its structure would appear to hint as much; but the hint remains a hint only, since no one ever spoke of Montségur as a church. Whatever we may say about the Cathars, they made no mystery of their beliefs. They never claimed that Montségur housed some special secret which would have excepted the spot from their general doctrine concerning physical matter. This was no Golgotha or Holy Sepulchre, no Castle of the Grail.

Here was a well-fortified castle with not only one but *two* main gates; the great keep had windows let into it at first-floor level rather than arrow-slits. Clearly the Catharist cult must have been celebrated here with rather more solemnity than was the case elsewhere. Yet what we know of these Cathar ceremonies shows them to have been simple in the extreme. However, the upper chamber of the keep—the only possible room in which services and sermons could have been held—was small enough: about fifty square yards, a space which nowadays would be regarded as scarcely adequate to house a young married couple in any degree of comfort. A chamber of this size hardly suggests solemn ceremonial or vast congregations. Sermons might also have been delivered in the pentagonal courtyard which formed an extension of the keep, and was some six hundred yards square; but this space must have been largely given over to storage-sheds, stables, armouries and shot-piles, not to mention the defenders' quarters. In short, it must have been an extremely modest temple, as well as an uncomfortable one. We may deduce that the Cathars, with consistent logic, had chosen as their capital a place which had nothing to recommend it apart from its beauty and inaccessibility.

In this high place, which the Catholic Church had condemned to hellfire, an intense religious life flourished, remote for the most part, doubtless, from all earthly troubles. The *bons hommes* in their huts below the walls were probably far more concerned with the observances of their faith and the annotation of the Gospels than with following the progress of the siege. But the situation was nevertheless serious. In May, the deacon Clamens, together with three other *perfecti*, came down from Montségur and travelled as far afield as Causson, doubtless to establish contact with reliable friends who could, if things went badly, be entrusted with the guardianship of the Church's treasure. Both Clamens and his companions got back to Montségur without difficulty. About the same time two further *perfecti*, Raymond de Caussa and his companion, also came down and made their way to the fortress of Usson, where they celebrated the *apparelhamentum* and blessed bread. The men-at-arms who had escorted them returned to Montségur on their own.

The defenders of Montségur must have been primarily concerned with finding a safer retreat for the leaders of the Catharist Church, since if the fortress were taken, these latter would be condemned to death. The thing was perfectly feasible, since it had been possible to get in and out of the fortress for months on end, while the *perfecti* were hardened to every sort of endurance, and ought not to shrink from venturing out on the mountain tracks. But the majority of them stayed in Montségur to the end.

Among the great personalities of the Church of Languedoc who were at Montségur during the siege we find Bishop Bertrand Marty and Raymond Aiguilher, who had engaged in debate with St Dominic nearly forty years before, and in 1225 had been elected *filius maior* to the Bishop of Razès. Both these men must have been extremely old. Of the deacons Raymond de Saint-Martin (or Sancto Martino), William Johannis, Clamens and Peter Bonnet, only the first-named had any public reputation as a preacher. In addition, the testimony of witnesses questioned by the Inquisitors shows that at least eight Catharist deacons were officiating in the various districts of Languedoc *after* 1243; these deacons were not, apparently, in direct contact with Montségur. Of some thirty other deacons whose names and activities have been listed by Jean Guiraud in his work on the Inquisition, all trace is lost about 1240 or 1242. The best-known, such as Isarn de Castres, Vigoros de Baconia, or Jean Cambiaire, had been burnt at the stake, the first in 1226, the last two in 1233 and 1234 respectively; while William Ricard was taken and burnt in 1243, in the Lauraguais region. The deacons Raymond de Saint-Martin, Raymond Mercier (or de Mirepoix) and William Tournier belonged to the Montségur district, and had been working there for many years; but some doubt exists as to whether the two last-named were resident during the siege. Raymond Mercier had achieved great popularity in the area as early as 1210, and must have been dead some few years before 1243. William Tournier was still alive in 1240, and so was Bishop Guilhabert de Castres. But that same year we lose track of Guilhabert, too: he probably died in Montségur, though no document makes any mention of his fate. In any case, though he was surely eighty by now, he was still carrying on a life of nocturnal rides and secret meetings, from château to village, and from one forest to the next. Death must have overtaken him in the midst of such activities.

Therefore, with the exceptions of Raymond de Saint-Martin, Bishop Bertrand, and Raymond Aiguilher, none of the major figures in the Catharist Church were actually present at Montségur during the siege. Most of them were dead, or continuing their apostolic work clandestinely, in ever-increasingly dangerous conditions. Montségur was not the Catharist Church's last bastion, or indeed its last hope; but it did, as far as the great mass of *credentes* was concerned, symbolize that Church's continuing life.

It is possible that the many *perfecti* and *perfectae* in retreat at Montségur were, for the most part, either aged persons, or mystics given up wholly to contemplation and the study of Holy Writ, or neophytes accomplishing their period of probation. Montségur was one of the last Catharist convents and seminaries.

In the midst of the siege, during the summer of 1243, these cenobites and recluses were still living on the narrow strip that was all they had left to them. It lay along the stony face of the mountain, between the sheer fortress wall and the temporary defences thrown up around the small shelving slope that encompassed it. The broad stone-built edifice was ringed about with a collection of little wooden huts, to a depth in places of several dozen yards. These huts were exposed to all bad weather, and quite literally had no protection apart from their altitude and the sheerness of the rock-face. If this little colony had been within range of a stone-gun, it could have been smashed flat in a matter of hours.

The expression *infra castrum*[1] which appears in testimony given by Bérenger de Lavelanet and Raymond de Perella has led people to suspect the existence of underground dwellings to which access might have been gained from the interior of the fortress. It has very reasonably been asked why Guilhabert de Castres sought permission from De Perella to live *beneath* the fortress rather than in it, and how the knight Del Congost managed to spend three months beneath the fortress while the siege was going on. The present state of the ruins is such that we can find no trace of any opening leading to an underground passage; but the comparatively large number of caverns and excavations that turn up in other parts of the mountain allow us to speculate on the possible existence of a fair-sized underground cave, which might even have been situated beneath the fortress itself, and which the defenders walled up at the end of the siege. On the other hand it would be rash to excogitate the existence —as Peyrat does in his *Histoire des Albigeois*—of a veritable underground fortress, with corridors, staircases, armouries, dormitories, cells, and burial vaults. If such an establishment had existed, a great many people would have known about it; but no contemporary witness makes any reference to it.

The expression 'to live beneath [or below] the fortress' is probably to be explained by the existence of the wooden huts put up around the walls. When we consider their size, and the fact that they were built on a steep slope, under walls anything from forty-five to sixty feet high, we see that it was quite reasonable for people to say that they stood *beneath* the fortress rather than *beside* it. These Cathar hermits lived, not in some remote and labyrinthine underground fortress, but beneath the open sky, in temporary quarters the cramped discomfort of which would have scarified the most hardened modern slum-dweller. Before the siege some of them had probably lived up on the mountain itself, in the forest that covered the eastern flank. When the enemy armies approached they would have been driven to retreat in the direction of the fortress. We read that such-and-such a *perfecta* or male 'heretic' had their 'house'. To these 'houses' there came *credentes*, members of the garrison, or the castellans' wives, to share in the blessing of bread and to do obeisance [*adoratio*] before the *bons hommes*; the dying were carried thither to receive the *consolamentum*. The bishops' and deacons' houses (as opposed to those of the other *perfecti*) were doubtless inside the fortress's perimeter. Till the very last months of the siege these wretched hovels could be inhabited. The vast emptiness which stretched away beyond those wooden palisades protected them better than any rampart could have done.

Generally speaking, these men and women lived in pairs, although —no doubt on account of shortage of space—cases are cited of *perfectae* who had several companions. We may assume that the men's 'village', if we may so describe it, was separate from that of the women. Most of the *perfecti* had kinsmen or intimate friends among members of the garrison: during the siege, especially, life upon Mont-ségur must have been that of a community, united for better or worse.

It has hard to picture the existence of a group of several hundred persons, nearly half of whom were candidates for the stake. Even in the Early Christian Church martyrs remained noble exceptions, universally venerated heroes. For the *perfecti* martyrdom was, in certain circumstances, an absolute and previously recognized obliga-tion. Even though they had doubts concerning the outcome of the siege—and they must have gone on hoping till the very end—as they watched, from their mountain-top, the ant-like swarms of troops spread out across the pass and down the valley, they surely prepared themselves for death as the months went by. There is nothing to show us that they were pure spirits whom fear and sorrow could not touch; but the majority did remain. That is a fact. Doubtless they preferred to face this danger together, prayerfully and in the free profession of their faith, rather than endure the risks of a lonely, hunted, and humiliating existence—with the same flaming faggots at the end of their journey.

For long the defenders of Montségur still hoped to exhaust their adversaries' patience. Winter was approaching; in the mountains bad weather comes as early as October. It was in October that the assailants at last contrived to obtain a success which looked like seriously compromising the chances of the besieged. Hugues des Arcis signed on a detachment of Basque mercenaries, hardy moun-taineers who were not in the least disconcerted by the terrain round Montségur. These Basques climbed along the ridge of the mountain, and got a foothold on the narrow ledge at the eastern face—only some eighty yards downhill from the fortress.

The position of the besieged was not yet desperate. Though their adversaries could now get both men and equipment up to the ridge, and establish a firm bridgehead there, the strip which they occupied was perilously narrow, and offered no scope for manoeuvre on a large scale. The defenders still controlled the summit of the mountain, and maintained their lines of communication with the outside world. When they learnt that the Bishop of Albi had built a siege-engine to bombard Montségur, the Cathars' supporters (their identity has been the subject of much discussion) rushed an engineer of their own into the beleaguered fortress. His name was Bertrand de La Baccalaria, from Capdenac; he broke through the blockade, got up into the fortress, and at once had another machine mounted in the eastern barbican which could return the episcopal stone-gun's fire, shot for shot. There they lay, attackers and besieged, on a narrow mountain-top with the void on both sides of them: their relative strength was about equal. The besieged had an advantage in the protection of the fortress: the French, on the other hand, had to camp out on the ridge, around their siege-engine, and suffered from wind, snow, and bitter cold. Bishop Durand must have needed all his courage to supervise the firing, and keep his men up to scratch amid the storms and sleet. December was nearly over, and the positions of the opposing forces were still the same as they had been in October, with the two siege-guns exchanging a more or less continuous fire.

But the Crusaders had one considerable advantage over those inside the fortress: they could bring up relief forces as and when they liked. The garrison of Montségur had already lost quite a few men, while the reinforcements they received were a mere trickle—two or three soldiers at a time, and that infrequently. The men-at-arms were under a severe strain: holding out month after month had told on them, and however advantageous their position, they were a hundred against six to ten thousand. There were no reliefs or replacements for them: they were trapped in a ridiculously tight perimeter, with large numbers of women, old men, and other non-combatants on their hands. In such conditions, even in the company of the most saintly men on earth, life must have been quite unbearable.

There was no question of their courage failing, and indeed they were to hold out for a long time yet. But there can be no doubt that weariness was beginning to tell on them. During these winter months Pierre-Roger de Mirepoix several times sent messengers to find out 'whether the Count of Toulouse's affairs were prospering'.[2]

The reply—not from the Count himself, of course, but from people who were doubtless in touch with him—was always in the affirmative. The garrison continued to hold out. What were these 'affairs' of the Count's? Did they mean some future attempt at revolt, which would allow Raymond to send an army and raise the siege of Montségur? Were negotiations in hand more specifically concerned with the men of Montségur themselves? What is clear is that the Count insisted on the garrison's continued resistance, even though, *qua* official persecutor of heretics, he could not have any direct communication with the besieged.

There was little help the *perfecti* were able to give the troops in their task of defence, though their own fate hung upon it. They appear to have done what they could, however, to soften the hard lives of the soldiers a little. At least, we find some of the knights, and indeed certain men-at-arms, being invited in to the quarters of the *bons hommes*, taking meals with them, and receiving gifts at their hands. For instance, the *perfecta* Raymonde de Cuq invited Pierre-Roger de Mirepoix to visit her, while Raymond de Saint-Martin the deacon received Guillaume Adhémar, Raymond de Belvis, Imbert de Salas and the engineer Bertrand de La Baccalaria; later, Bishop Bertrand Marty was to distribute salt and pepper among the men-at-arms.[3] We may guess that even those soldiers who had no ties of kin or friendship with the *perfecti* came in the end to feel drawn to them by the common ordeal they were undergoing, and to regard them in some sort as members of their own family, rather than superior beings whom one could 'adore', but no more. When you rub shoulders with a man twenty times daily, *adoratio* becomes an impossibility. Some sergeants of the garrison were later to give no uncertain proof of their adherence to the faith which these *bons hommes* professed.

Some of the defenders, exhausted by the hardships of the siege, must have hoped to end it at any price. We know that Imbert de Salas had a personal interview with Hugues des Arcis himself. But why, and in what circumstances? At all events Pierre-Roger de Mirepoix criticized him for having done so, and as a punishment took from him the armour of Jordan du Mas, who had been killed in a skirmish near the barbican.[4] The garrison commander had issued an order that the only greetings his men were to send the Crusaders in future were crossbow quarrels—which not only shows that the attackers made occasional efforts to establish contact with their opponents, but suggests that such overtures were not always ill-received.

The garrison's morale was at a very low ebb; yet in spite of this, surrender remained out of the question, and to take the fortress by storm still seemed an impossibility. However, either shortly before or shortly after Christmas, the attackers gained a decisive step: they succeeded in rushing the barbican, and thus found themselves only a few score yards from the fortress. Despite this, the fortress itself remained almost as inaccessible to them as before: to reach it they would have to make their way along a ridge less than six feet wide, with a sheer drop on either side. But at least they had driven the defenders back from the barbican, and installed their own siege-gun there instead. The southern and eastern walls of the fortress were now within range of their projectiles, and the hutments below them had to be evacuated. The inhabitants of these huts must doubtless have sought refuge within the walls, where there was scarcely any room to accommodate them. By now the attacking force controlled the entire mountain, and were almost into the last stronghold; and the Bishop of Albi's stone-gun battered away ceaselessly, without respite, at the eastern wall.

The eastern barbican (or tower) was divided from the Crusaders' bridgehead by a difficult and well-defended path. How, despite this, did the attacking force manage to storm it? According to William de Puylaurens, they followed a trail cut out of the very rock-face; the troops were guided by 'a group of keen local mountaineers, light-armed, and with an extensive knowledge of the terrain'.[5] This must have been a secret route, for the Basques, themselves no mean mountaineers, had not succeeded in discovering it. It was not a proper path, but a series of craggy footholds in the rock, linked in all likelihood by a few steps chipped out here and there, and unknown to all but a handful of people—either villagers from Montségur itself, or the guides who habitually escorted *perfecti* in their comings and goings. Even so, this route could not have been employed very often. According to William de Puylaurens, it went up 'horrible precipices', and the soldiers who scaled it at night later confessed that they would never have dared to do so in broad daylight. Having thus clambered up a practically sheer rock-face, they reached the barbican. This was manned by members of the garrison, who, however, let the party approach without suspecting that anything was amiss: perhaps they were deceived by the guides' voices into supposing that they had to do with friends.

So the eastern defences were taken by surprise: though the sentries had time enough to give the alarm, the men who had just toiled up that secret approach must have been a sizable body, and brave enough to surmount any ordeal. We do not know the number of troops guarding the barbican, but they were probably all slaughtered before their comrades from the fortress had time to come to their aid. Now the Crusaders dominated the entire peak, and could bring troops up to the summit with no fear of any counter-attack. The narrow space between fortress and barbican protected the defenders, but did not allow them any room to manoeuvre for offensive action. On this occasion, it seems clear, the defenders of Montségur were the victims of treachery, or quasi-treachery at the very least. The guides, who must have been heavily bribed by the Crusaders, were beyond any doubt in the confidence of the garrison: otherwise it is impossible to see why the besiegers did not find out about the secret approach months earlier.

It was only from this day forward that the defenders of Montségur appeared to realize that, short of a miracle, they were doomed. It was after the capture of the eastern barbican that the two heretics Matheus and Peter Bonnet left the fortress, taking with them gold and silver bullion, and a great quantity of money, *pecuniam infinitam*[6] —the treasure, in fact, which must now be safely bestowed elsewhere. Imbert de Salas afterwards revealed, during his interrogation that these two men had a secret understanding with the enemy sentries posted by the last road out still accessible to the besieged garrison. The sentries turned out to be from Camon-sur-l'Hers, in the fief of Mirepoix. Despite this the evacuation of the treasure was an appallingly risky operation, since the route that had to be followed was far harder and more dangerous than the one by which the Crusaders had come up on the night they stormed the barbican. If the garrison of Montségur waited till this was the only escape-line available to them before thinking of removing their treasure to safety, the reason must have been that till then they believed the fortress to be impregnable. The gold and silver—doubtless a very considerable sum—was cached by the two *perfecti* in the woods on the Sabarthès mountains, till the day arrived when a safer hiding-place could be found for it.

The siege dragged on. A French attempt to surprise the garrison was beaten off without difficulty. The eastern wall was both short and unusually thick; the battering it was getting from the stone-gun could not make any serious impression on it, let alone knock it down. Bertrand de La Baccalaria hurriedly set up another machine of his own. The *perfectus* Matheus returned to the fortress towards the end of January, bringing with him two crossbowmen—a meagre reinforcement, but better than nothing. Only very dexterous and intrepid men could have risked the climb up the Porteil chimney; and to return to the fortress at such a moment must have required a boundless devotion to the heretics' cause. This same Matheus then went down a second time to seek reinforcements: he came back with one man only, and some promises which were never fulfilled, doubtless because of the increased vigilance shown by the troops blockading the mountain.

Yet the garrison still had hope. The men-at-arms smuggled in by Matheus were, according to Imbert de Salas' testimony, sent by Isarn de Fanjeaux, and brought a message from him to Pierre-Roger de Mirepoix: the Count of Toulouse wanted to know if Montségur could hold out on its own till Easter. The two men asserted that the Count (with the Emperor's help) was levying an army to march on Montségur and raise the siege. Could Pierre-Roger de Mirepoix have placed any trust in so vague and impracticable a promise? It seems more likely that the statements made by Matheus and the two men-at-arms were intended to raise the garrison's morale. Yet the Count had good reasons for asking the men on Montségur to hold out as long as possible. Matheus' second venture might well have achieved very tangible results. He had persuaded two local *seigneurs*, Bernard d'Alion and Arnald d'Usson, to get in touch with a man well capable of saving the situation. This was an Aragonese mercenary captain called Corbario: the two knights promised him fifty *livres melgoriennes* if he would bring twenty-five of his men-at-arms to Montségur. It is clear that these troops belonged to an Aragonese *corps d'élite*, where each man was versed in all the arts of war, and a match for any knight. With the aid of the garrison these mercenaries would have been quite capable of driving the French back from their advanced position and setting fire to their siege-engine. But Corbario could not break through the lines of the besieging army, which were closer-drawn than ever before. This time Montségur really was cut off from the outside world with a vengeance, and could no longer rely on any external assistance.

The fortress held out all through February. William de Puylaurens says that 'no rest was given to the besieged, either by day or night'.[7] The stone-gun kept up a constant barrage, making it impossible to erect any defensive fortifications on the wall under fire. Inside the fortress shortage of space was making life quite unbearable: hundreds of people were literally jostling against one another. One odd thing is that right to the very end the majority of the garrison—its senior officers, at any rate—had their own 'houses'. A great number of these so-called houses must still have been outside the walls, on the sides facing north and west, where the enemy's missiles could not penetrate. But the space between the fortress wall and the cliff-edge was, if we may judge by present-day appearances, extremely narrow, and shelved down steeply. It is true that even now we find mountain villages perched above similar sheer drops. But at Montségur there are no signs either of house-foundations in the rock or of stone buildings—apart from the remains of a somewhat clumsy perimeter wall which doubtless served as the base for a wooden stake-palisade. It was here that the defenders of Montségur spent that winter. Many of them lived out on the bare, icy slope, in tiny wooden huts which —we may be certain—it was impossible to keep warm. Inside the fortress itself the scanty living-quarters by stores or cistern were reserved for the elderly, the sick, and the wounded. And daily those stone missiles came crashing into the walls.

Pierre-Roger de Mirepoix took counsel with Bishop Bertrand and Raymond de Perella, and decided to attempt a night sortie, with the object of retaking the barbican, throwing the Crusaders off it, and setting their siege-engine on fire. A detachment from the garrison crawled along the ridge below the peak and managed to approach the enemy's encampment. They were driven off, and the sortie proved a failure. The fight took place on a steep slope, with a sheer drop below, and many of the garrison must have fallen to their deaths during the struggle. The survivors were forced to retreat over the narrow ridge between the barbican and the fortress, dragging their wounded with them, and fighting a rearguard action against the enemy, who tried to utilize this situation to force the garrison's final defences.

The wounded and the dying were hastily set down on the first available beds, in the nearest huts. Meanwhile the remainder of the garrison hastened to the ramparts and the barricades to repel the Crusaders, who had already gained a footing in the forecourt. The knights' wives and daughters—Raymond de Perella's wife Corba, Cecilia, the wife of Arnald-Roger de Mirepoix, Pierre-Roger's wife Philippa, Arpaïs de Ravat, Fays de Plaigne, Braïda de Mirepoix, Adalays de Massabrac and others—hurriedly asked for the *convenensa* [the initiation ceremony for a *credens*] and then rushed off to help their menfolk defend the fortress.[8]

In all the tumult of clashing arms and the screams of the wounded, the Bishop and his deacons only had time to go from one dying man to the next, administering the last sacraments. Bernard Roainh, Peter Ferrier the Catalan, Bernard of Carcassonne, man-at-arms, and Arnald de Vensa all died that night after receiving the *consolamentum*.[9] With a final spurt of energy the garrison managed to throw back its assailants, who retreated towards the barbican. When we remember that the battlefield had a sheer drop on either side of it, we may deduce that those killed must have outnumbered the wounded who got back to the fortress.

On the morning after this night of tragedy, a horn sounded on the ramparts. Raymond de Perella and Pierre-Roger de Mirepoix had decided to negotiate for surrender.

2. *The Massacre*
Negotiations began on 1st March, 1244. After a siege that had lasted over nine months, Montségur had capitulated. The Crusaders too had been exhausted by this over-protracted siege, and kept the discussions very short. Conditions for the surrender were as follows:

(1) The garrison were to remain in the fortress for another fifteen days, and give up hostages meanwhile.

(2) They would receive pardons for all their past crimes, including the Avignonet affair.

(3) The men-at-arms would be allowed to retire with their arms and baggage, but would thereafter be required to appear before the Inquisition and make confession of their errors. They would be liable to receive light penances only.

(4) All other persons in the fortress would remain at liberty, and would similarly be subject to light penances only, provided that they abjured their heretical beliefs and made confession before the Inquisitors. Those who did not recant would be burnt at the stake.

(5) The fortress of Montségur would pass into the hands of the Church and the French Crown.

By and large these conditions were fair enough: it would certainly have been hard to obtain better ones. Thanks to their heroic resistance, the men of Montségur were to be spared a death sentence, and their relatives to escape life imprisonment. Those responsible for the Avignonet massacre found themselves guaranteed not only their lives, but their freedom as well.

How could the Church—as represented by those of her servants who took part in the siege—have ever agreed to grant absolution for so heinous a crime? The punishment of William Arnald's murderers must have seemed no less vital to them than that of the heretics themselves. Yet it looks as though the speedy agreement reached by both sides on this point was due to previous preparation of the ground. The protracted exchange of messages between the Count of Toulouse and the beleaguered garrison in Montségur must have dealt, *inter alia*, with the Avignonet affair.

In point of fact, at the time of the siege the Count was in diplomatic communication with the Pope, his aim being to procure a reversal of the excommunication he had incurred after this crime—of which he declared himself innocent. It was towards the close of 1243 that Pope Innocent IV revoked Brother Ferrier's sentence of excommunication, and declared the Count of Toulouse his 'faithful and Catholic son'. The second ban of excommunication, that imposed by the Archbishop of Narbonne, was rescinded on 14th March, 1244, two days before French troops occupied Montségur. This coincidence of dates may be fortuitous. But there is a possibility that the Count's diplomatic manoeuvres and the fate of the garrison at Montségur—in particular Pierre-Roger de Mirepoix, who took so close an interest in the progress of the Count's affairs—were very closely connected. The Count may have counselled the besieged to hold out, not with the intention of bringing them a relief force (a prospect which he seems scarcely to have envisaged) so much as to obtain a complete pardon over the Avignonet affair. The testimony of the men of Montségur was to implicate many people outside the fortress, over and above the Count himself; yet these named persons were never troubled by the authorities.

On the other hand the personal courage shown by the garrison, and the necessity of concluding the siege (if the reprieve had been refused, it might still have been going on) had led Hugues des Arcis and his knights to put pressure on the Archbishop and Brother Ferrier. The murder of the Inquisitors had been a political crime; and the French, who perhaps were beginning to understand by now both what was going on in Languedoc and how the native population felt about it, probably did not feel the need for excessive reprisals. The Montségur troops were simply men who had fought bravely, and earned the right to their adversaries' respect.

So Montségur was granted a fifteen days' truce, during which period the fortress could deny entry to enemy forces, even though it had already surrendered. During those fifteen days the two sides, abiding by their sworn word, remained where they were, making no attempt either to attack or to flee. Bishop Durand's siege-engine stood idle, and there was no longer any need for sentries to patrol the ramparts; nor did the troops have to live in constant expectation of the alarm sounding. Montségur passed its last days of freedom peacefully—if one could call it peace, with the enemy keeping a vigilant eye on the fortress from their position less than a hundred yards away, and nothing to look forward to save parting and death.

Still, in comparison with the tragic hours they had lately lived through, for the inhabitants of Montségur this *was* peace—and for many of them, their last respite. It has been asked why the besieged demanded this stay of surrender, which only prolonged, to no purpose, an already impossible existence. Could the answer possibly be that Brother Ferrier and the Archbishop of Narbonne could not on their own responsibility absolve the Inquisitors' murderers, and deemed it necessary to refer the matter to the Pope? A more likely solution is that it was the besieged themselves who asked for this respite, and that what they wanted was a little more time with friends and loved ones whom they might never see again once the fortress had finally capitulated. As F. Niel suggests, it is very likely that Bishop Bertrand Marty and his companions wanted, before they died, to celebrate for the last time the feast which, in their ritual, corresponded to Easter. We know that the Cathars did observe such a festival, since one of their major fasting-periods came immediately before Easter.

Can we deduce that this was their version of the Manichaean festival known as the *Bema*, which took place more or less at the same time of year? There is no documentary evidence which would allow the point to be established with any certainty; and, as we have seen, though the Catharist Ritual quotes the Gospels and Epistles with insistent frequency, it never once mentions the name of Mani. Could it be possible that there were two distinct levels of teaching in Catharism, and that the *consolamentum*, generally regarded as the highest sacrament, was in fact no more than a pious gesture reserved for the benefit of the uninitiated? Such a supposition seems highly unlikely. Though the doctrines of Catharism were Manichaean, this religion was profoundly Christian both in the form and the expression of its thought. The Cathars offered their devotion too single-mindedly to Christ for there to be an important place in their cult for Mani. All the same, evidence is lacking to tell us just what the feast of Easter —or the *Bema*—meant to them.

It is not only intrinsically likely, but a very human desire, that these people should have wanted one last respite before they were parted for ever. It was little enough to ask; and no doubt they would have had difficulty in obtaining more.

Hostages were surrendered during the first week in March. As we learn from the records of interrogation, they consisted of the old

knight Arnald-Roger de Mirepoix, a relative of the garrison commander; Raymond de Perella's son Jordan; Raymond Marty,
Bishop Bertrand's brother; and others whose names remain unknown, the full list of hostages not having survived.

Certain writers have supposed that Pierre-Roger de Mirepoix
himself withdrew from the fortress before the truce period was up,
that is, before the signing of the Act of Surrender. This thesis is
scarcely tenable, since, according to Alzeu de Massabrac's testimony,
Pierre-Roger was still in the fortress on 16th March. We know that
afterwards he retired to Montgaillard, after which all trace of him
vanishes for ten years. It may well be the silence surrounding his
name which has led to his being accused of desertion, if not of actual
treason. It would be reasonable enough to assume, however, that the
conquerors found the presence of the prime mover in the Avignonet
coup somewhat embarrassing, and that they requested him to vanish
as discreetly as might be. The man who had expressed so lively a desire to drink his wine from William Arnald's skull could only obtain
his reprieve under the counter, so to speak. Eleven years later he is
mentioned by the King's commissioners as 'a *faidit*, dispossessed of
his estates for defending and abetting heretics in the fortress of Montségur'. He was not to have his civil rights restored until 1257. This
makes it hard to believe that Pierre-Roger ever trafficked with the
enemy, in any kind of way.

We may assume, then, that both Pierre-Roger de Mirepoix and his
father-in-law Raymond de Perella stayed in the stronghold till the
conclusion of the truce period, together with the majority of the
garrison, their families, and the *haeretici*—those, that is, who would
not abjure their faith, and thus became liable, under Clause Four of
the Act of Surrender, to be burnt at the stake. The fifteen days must
have been spent in religious ceremonies, prayer, and private farewells.

All we know of what went on in the fortress of Montségur during
this last tragic fortnight is derived from such questions as the
Inquisitors chanced to ask the witnesses they afterwards interrogated. The deliberate bareness of these precise, clipped details cannot
wholly obliterate the stirring nobility of mood that underlies them.
First there is the final sharing out of all property belonging to those
who were about to die. In gratitude for his devoted support, the
haeretici Raymond de Saint-Martin, Amiel Aicart, Clamens,
Taparell, and William Peter presented Pierre-Roger de Mirepoix
with a coverlet full of deniers. Bishop Bertrand Marty, too, gave a
present to Pierre-Roger: oil, salt, pepper, wax, and a piece of green
cloth. No doubt the austere old man had no more valuable posses-

sions. It was Pierre-Roger de Mirepoix, again, whom the *haeretici* presented with large quantities of corn, and fifty jerkins for his men. The *perfecta* Raymonde de Cuq presented William Adhémar, sergeant-at-arms, with a wagon-load of wheat—which shows that the provisions in the fortress were regarded as belonging to the Catharist Church rather than to the owners of the fortress.[10]

Old Marquésia de Lantar gave all her belongings to her granddaughter Philippa, Pierre-Roger's wife. Other heretics gave the soldiers a handful of *sous melgoriens*, wax, pepper, salt, a pair of shoes, a purse, breeches, a felt hat—everything, in fact, that the *bons hommes* still possessed. The chief value of some of these objects must have been as relics.

The evidence goes on to describe the ceremonies at which witnesses were present during this period—the only ones concerning which they were asked detailed questions. These were the *consolamenta*. At a time when to enter the Catharist Church meant certain and imminent death, there were at least seventeen persons whose faith was strong enough to make them aspire to this favour. Six of them were women, and eleven men—the latter all knights or men-at-arms.

One of the women was the wife of the *seigneur* of Montségur, Corba de Perella. Corba was the daughter of the *perfecta* Marquésia; her invalid daughter had in all probability already received the *consolamentum*, and Corba herself must have been preparing to take this decisive step for some time. She actually did so on the last possible day, the evening before the truce period ran out, abandoning her husband, her two married daughters, her grandchildren, and her son, whose presence had doubtless held her back till this moment. But now they all took second place to her self-martyrdom for the faith she held. Ermengarde d'Ussat was a noble lady living in the Montségur district. Guillelme, Bruna, and Arssendis were the wives of men-at-arms; the two last-named went to the stake with their husbands, who also became voluntary converts at the eleventh hour. They were not old women, since men-at-arms were normally in the prime of life. Guillelme de Lavelanet may have been older, however, since she was married to the knight Bérenger de Lavelanet.

Amongst the men who received the *consolamentum* during the truce there were two knights: William de l'Isle, who had been seriously wounded some days earlier, and Raymond de Marciliano. The list of men-at-arms included Raymond-William de Tornaboïs, Brasillac de Calavello (both these two had taken part in the Avignonet massacre), Arnald Domerc, Bruna's husband, Arnald Dominique, William of Narbonne, Pons Narbona (Arssendis's husband), Johan Reg,

William of Puy, William John de Lordat, and, lastly, Raymond de Belvis and Arnald Teouli, who both came to Montségur when the situation was already desperate, and who seem to have braved so many dangers in their journey thither simply with the intention of becoming martyrs. All these soldiers could have marched out of the fortress with full military honours, their heads held high; yet they chose to be hunted like beasts, dumped on piles of dry faggots, and burnt alive beside their masters in the faith.

Concerning these latter we have very little knowledge, except for the fact that Bishop Bertrand, Raymond de Saint-Martin, and Raymond Aiguilher granted the *consolamentum* to those who desired it, and distributed their possessions. The *perfecti* and *perfectae* must have numbered about a hundred and ninety, since we know that the total number of *haeretici* burnt at Montségur was between two hundred and ten and two hundred and fifteen. The persons' names that we have certain knowledge of are almost all those of ordinary *credentes*, who were converted at the very last moment.

It is an impressive fact that a good quarter of what remained of the garrison consisted of men prepared to die for their faith—not in a sudden burst of enthusiasm, either, but after day upon day of conscious preparation. The martyrs of a defeated creed never achieve canonization, but these men and women, whose names were only recorded so that those who witnessed their initiation could be blacklisted, richly deserve to be remembered as true martyrs.

Of the *perfecti* shut in the fortress at the time of the surrender, at least three escaped the stake. This fact constituted a violation of the terms agreed upon, but it was not discovered until after the occupation of the fortress by the French. During the night of 16th March Pierre-Roger had ropes let down the west face of the rock, and got four men away—the *haeretici* Amiel Aicart, his companion Hugo, another named Poitevin, and one more whose name is unrecorded, perhaps a mountain guide. When the Crusaders entered Montségur these men were hidden in a cave, and thus escaped the fate of their brethren. Their task was to conceal all of the heretics' treasure that still remained in the fortress, and to mark down the cache where they had buried the money evacuated two months previously. In fact, Pierre-Roger and his knights were the last to leave the fortress, after the *perfecti* and the women and children; up to a point they remained masters of their own castle. The escape plan seems to have been completely successful, since neither the four *haeretici* nor the treasure ever fell into the hands of the authorities.

According to Alzeu de Massabrac's evidence, Arnald-Roger de Mirepoix testified as follows:[11]

When the *haeretici* came forth from the fortress of Montségur, which was perforce rendered up to the Church and the French Crown, Pierre-Roger de Mirepoix held back within the said fortress Amiel Aicart and his friend Hugo, they being *haeretici*; and the night on which the other *haeretici* were burnt, he concealed the said heretics, and did cause them to escape; and this was done that the Church of the heretics might not lose its treasure, which was hidden in the forest; and the fugitives knew the place where it lay . . .

Bérenger de Lavelanet tells us that Amiel Aicart, Poitevin, and two other men were let down on ropes, and remained hidden underground when the Crusaders entered the fortress. Montségur might have fallen, but the Catharist Church fought on.

Apart from these three (or four) men, who were charged with an important and dangerous mission, none of the *perfecti* escaped the stake, or perhaps even wished to. When the truce period expired, the Seneschal and his knights presented themselves at the main gate of the fortress, accompanied by representatives of the ecclesiastical authority. The Archbishop of Narbonne had returned home before the end of the truce. The Church was represented on the spot by the Bishop of Albi and two Inquisitors, Brothers Ferrier and Duranti. The task of the French forces was now over: they had promised the combatants that their lives would be spared. The fate of Montségur's defenders now rested solely with the ecclesiastical Tribunal.

By surrendering the fortress Raymond de Perella was condemning his own wife and his youngest daughter to the hands of the executioner. The centuries-old law condemning impenitent heretics to the flames was so universally accepted that those fathers, husbands, brothers or sons who must needs be so brutally parted from their loved ones could only see in their loss the working of blind Fate, the logical consequence of defeat. How were those who had no chance of pardon distinguished from the rest? Probably they isolated themselves of their own volition, pointed themselves out. In their present circumstances it was useless putting them through repeated interrogations simply to make them confess what they never had any intention of denying.

William de Puylaurens states that 'they were vainly begged to recant and be converted'.[12] By whom were they begged to do so, and how? It seems likely that the two hundred and more heretics formed a group apart, whom the Inquisitors and their assistants brought out

of the fortress for token admonition. That evening Philippa de Mirepoix and Arpaïs de Ravat, Corba de Perella's daughters, took fare-
well of their mother, who had just attained—though for too short a
time—the dignified status of a *perfecta*. One of these young women,
Arpaïs, without daring to go into details, hints at the horror of this
moment, when her mother, and all the rest of the *haeretici*, went to
meet their deaths: 'they were *brutally* dragged forth from the fortress
of Montségur . . . ', she testified.[13]

Bishop Bertrand Marty clearly was at the head of these condemned persons. The *haeretici* were fettered and dragged roughly
down the slope between the fortress itself and the place where the
pyre had been prepared. On the south-west face of the mountain,
opposite Montségur—the only side comparatively easy of access—
there is an open space known today as the Field of the Burnt Ones
[*cramatchs=crémats*]. This spot is less than two hundred yards from
the fortress, and the ground slopes steeply enough towards it. William de Puylaurens tells us that the heretics were burnt 'close to the
foot of the rock', and this probably refers to the *Champs de
Cramatchs*.

While up on the summit of the rock the *perfecti* were preparing to
meet their fate, and saying goodbye to their friends, a party of men-
at-arms from the French camp must have been working on the final
labour of the siege: the erection of a pyre large enough to consume
the bodies of two hundred persons. (The rough number of those
condemned was doubtless known in advance.) 'They built a palisade
of stakes and pales', William de Puylaurens tells us,[14] as a means of
marking out the area of the pyre. Inside they heaped up 'countless
faggots', and possibly straw and pitch too, since in March the firewood would be damp and difficult to ignite. With so great a number
of victims there was probably no time to erect individual stakes for
each one of them; at all events William de Puylaurens merely says
that they were shut inside the palisade.

The sick and wounded must have simply been thrown on to the
faggots. Perhaps the remainder were able to seek contact with their
socii or kinsmen; perhaps the Lady of Montségur contrived to die
beside her aged mother and her invalid daughter, and the two men-
at-arms' wives beside their husbands. Perhaps the Bishop managed a
few last words of exhortation to his faithful followers, though what
he said would be half-drowned by groans of misery and the chink of
weapons, by the shouts of the executioners as they set fire to the
palisade at each of its four corners, by the clergy chanting their
psalms. Once the flames had caught well, both executioners and sol-

diers perforce retired to some distance off, in order to avoid suffering from the smoke and heat that the vast pyre discharged. In a few hours' time the two hundred living torches heaped together inside the palisade were no more than a mass of raw, blackened, bleeding flesh, slowly burning to a cindered crisp, spreading a ghastly stench of burnt meat right down the valley, and up to the very walls of the fortress.

Those of the garrison still behind the ramparts could look down and watch the flames of the pyre rising and spreading far below them, then gradually dying away for lack of fuel, while a pall of thick, blackish smoke spread out over the mountainside. As the flames diminished, this acrid, sickening smoke must have increased. Throughout the night the furnace slowly burnt itself out. Soldiers sitting outside their tents round camp-fires, scattered across the slopes, could still see those red embers glowing through the smoke. During that night the four guardians of the treasure let themselves down the rock-face by ropes, almost opposite the place where this gigantic bonfire, fuelled on human flesh and blood, was gradually dying.

The Cathar Church did not surrender. But she was never really to recover from the blow dealt her at Montségur.

EPILOGUE

FIVE YEARS AFTER the fall of Montségur Raymond VII died at the age of fifty-two, still without a legitimate heir. The County of Toulouse passed into the hands of Alphonse of Poitiers, who was married to the Count's only daughter, the Countess Jeanne. Both of them died in the same year, 1271, without leaving any issue. These two deaths finally brought under the French Crown a country which for the past twenty years had been, *de facto*, a French province, in the ancient, traditional sense of that term: i.e., an area of secondary importance which is colonized, exploited, and dominated both intellectually and with regard to its administration by a powerful metropolis well aware of its own best interests.

In twenty-two years Alphonse of Poitiers only went to Toulouse twice: in 1251, on the day that he appeared there to receive homage from his new vassals, and in 1270, a year before his death. He was a good administrator, and chiefly concerned with the organization of a harshly efficient fiscal system, which would permit him to levy from his domains such monies as he needed for the achievement of his political ambitions—or rather, those of his brother: for St Louis the reconquest of the Holy Land remained the prime objective of French policy. It seems clear that Alphonse never took his position as Count of Toulouse at all seriously, and was only a faithful executor of his brother's wishes. The people who, in 1249, followed Raymond VII's coffin from Millau to Fontevrault, weeping as they went, knew that what they wept for was the end of their existence as a nation.

A few months before his death the Count had burnt at Agen some eighty heretics, or persons suspected of heresy, after a summary judgment that even the Inquisition might have disallowed. No doubt he thought to win back the Church's favour by this act of violence; but it is possible that he also wanted to make the heretics expiate the evils they had brought upon his country. It was, indeed, more than enough. Exhausted by persecution, humiliated, demoralized by the progressive stifling of all their living traditions, the people of Languedoc—or at least its privileged classes, those who had most to lose—

abandoned the Catharist faith and ranged themselves, in bitter resignation, on the side of the conquerors.

Languedoc was incorporated into France; it is pointless to ask whether this unification, which after all was demanded by the country's geographical and political position, could not have been accomplished in a less brutal fashion. Did there really exist such incompatibilities of interests and beliefs between North and South that it took a most savage war of conquest to bring about a union in which both partners were Frenchmen? Before 1209 there may have been mutual lack of understanding, but no hatred. After Raymond VII's death his people grew weary of hatred and suffering; they gradually resigned themselves—though it came hard to them, and there were further rebellions still—to seeing their language degenerate into a mere *patois*.

Who has ever calculated what a people must lose with their independence? How can one draw a line between regional idiosyncrasies and legitimate national aspirations? We may say, as a rule, that might always appears to be right in the end, and that what *is* always has more immediate reality than what might have been.

The French monarchy emerged from this ordeal with added strength, more conscious than ever of its Divine Rights; very soon it was to defy the Papacy, which had both served and made use of it. In her desire to extirpate heresy, the Church had exposed herself to the danger of seeing her too-powerful ally trampling on her temporal authority.

The Catholic Church had certainly not been unaware of this danger. Her struggles against the Empire, and her recent experiences with Frederick II in particular, had enabled her to take its measure very clearly; but in her eyes the peril that heresy represented was something far more terrible still. Yet though, thanks to the Inquisition, the Papacy finally triumphed, first over Catharism, and then over numerous other heretical movements which arose during the thirteenth and fourteenth centuries, her victory was to cost her dear. The humiliation inflicted at Anagni did not compromise the Church in its basic dignity; it was simply one episode in that unending battle which the Church was forced to wage in order to safeguard her moral and material independence. But the repressive terrorism which the Inquisition for several centuries imposed, as a policy, on the nations of the West—this was to undermine the Church's edifice from the inside, and to bring about a terrible lowering of Christian morality and Catholic civilization.

Before the Albigensian Crusade and the Inquisition, bishops and abbots still raised their voices in protest against the burning of heretics, and preached compassion towards such strayed brethren. In the thirteen century, however, St Thomas Aquinas justified such *autos-da-fé* in terms that are ill-suited to any Christian.[15] Excesses that could previously be attributed to ignorance or the brutal *mores* of the period were now given the stamp of approval, consecrated *ex cathedra theologica* by one of the greatest philosophers of Christianity. This fact is too serious to be minimized. From the thirteenth century onwards we no longer find saint or doctor in the Catholic Church bold enough to assert (as for instance St Hildegarde had done in the twelfth century[16]) that a man who errs in religious matters is still one of God's creatures, and that to deprive him of his life is a crime. The Church which so resolutely forgot this very simple truth no longer deserved the title of 'Catholic'; in this sense we may claim that heresy had dealt the Church a blow from which it never recovered.

The victory was bought at too great a price. Even if the Roman Church, by taking the strong line against heresy that she did, spared Western Christendom grave troubles which might have brought the whole social and cultural structure crashing down in ruins—and this is by no means certain—she only did so at the cost of a moral capitulation the consequences of which she is still suffering today.

APPENDIX A

A CATHARIST RITUAL

This abridged version has been translated from L. Clédat's French rendering of the Ritual. The complete text can be consulted in Clédat's Le Nouveau Testament traduit au XIIIe Siècle en Langue Provençale *(Paris 1887). The original manuscript is preserved in the Municipal Library of the Palais Saint-Pierre at Lyons, and a photostatic reproduction of it has been published in Vol. 4 of the* Bibliothèque de la Faculté des Lettres de Lyon.

If a Believer [that is, a *credens*, one initiated into Catharist beliefs, but not yet fully received] has performed his Abstinence [*abstinentia*, a preparatory period of trial]; and if the Christians [as the Cathar *perfecti* described themselves] are agreed that his prayerful request should be granted, let them first wash their hands; and let the Believers (if there be any present) do likewise. Then let one of the *bons hommes*, he who is next in precedence after the Elder, do obeisance to the Elder thrice; and let him make ready a table, and [do obeisance] thrice more, and set a cloth upon the table, and then again [do obeisance] three times. Then let him say: *Benedicite parcite nobis.* Then let the postulant perform his *melioramentum* [a ritual gesture of veneration, consisting of three genuflections and a request for a blessing] and take the Book from the Elder's hand. Then the Elder is to address fitting words of Scripture to him for his admonishment [such passages being drawn from the New Testament] . . .

Then the Elder is to say the Lord's Prayer, with the Believer following him; and then let the Elder say [to the Believer]: 'We entrust this holy Prayer into your keeping; receive it then, from God and us and the whole Church; may you have strength to say it all the days of your life, night and day, alone or in company; may you never eat or drink without first uttering it. And if you fail of this, you needs must do penance therefore.' Then he [*i.e.* the Believer] is to say: 'I do accept it from God, and you, and the Church.' Then let him perform his *melioramentum* and give thanks; and then let those Christians present say a *double* [prayer twice repeated] with *veniae* [prostration and genuflection], and the Believer after them.

Bestowal of the Consolamentum

And if he [*i.e.* the Believer who has just been received as a Christian] is to be granted the *consolamentum* forthwith, let him perform his *melioramentum* and take the Book from the hand of the Elder; and the Elder is to address fitting words of Scripture to him for his admonishment, with such exhortations as may be appropriate to a *consolamentum* [see below, Appendix B] . . .

Then let him say: 'I have the will; pray God give me the strength.' Then one of the *bons hommes* is to make his *melioramentum* with the Believer before the Elder, and say: '*Parcite nobis*. Good Christians, we pray you for the love of God to bestow the gift which God has granted you upon our friend here present.' Then let the Believer perform his *melioramentum*, and say: '*Parcite nobis*. For every sin that I may have committed, by deed, word, thought or action, I beg forgiveness of God, the Church, and all those here present.' Then let the Christians say: 'May God and the Church and all those here present forgive you these sins, and we pray God absolve you of them.' Then are they to give him the *consolamentum*. Let the Elder take the Book and place it upon his head, and the other *bons hommes* each take him by the right hand, and say the *parcias*, and the *Adoremus* thrice [names of Catharist prayers], and afterwards these words: *Pater sancte suscipe servum tuum in tua justitia et mitte gratiam tuam et spiritum sanctum tuum super eum*. Then let them pray to God with the Lord's Prayer, and let the minister conducting Divine Service repeat the *sixaine* [? the Lord's Prayer repeated six times]; and when the *sixaine* is said, he must then say the *Adoremus* thrice and the Lord's Prayer once, aloud, and after that the Gospel. And when the Gospel is said, the congregation must say the *Adoremus* thrice, and the *gratia*, and the *parcias*. This done, they are to give one another the kiss [of peace], and to kiss the Book likewise. If there are any Believers present, let the men among them also exchange the kiss [of peace]; and let the women too, if any there be, exchange the kiss [of peace] amongst themselves, and kiss the Book. Then let them pray to God with *double* and *venia* [see above]; and [this done], they will have bestowed the gift of prayer [upon the postulant].

Rules of Conduct

The right of *double* and the utterance of the Lord's Prayer shall not be granted to a layman.

If Christians go into a perilous place, let them pray God with the *gratia*.

And if any Christian goes a journey on horseback, let him pray with *double*. Also he is to say the Lord's Prayer when boarding a ship or entering a town, or when about to cross a rickety bridge or gangplank.

And if they find themselves obliged to hold converse with some person while they are praying to God, an eightfold repetition of the Lord's Prayer duly accomplished may be reckoned as a single orison; and a sixteenfold repetition as a *double*.

And if they find some article of property by the wayside, they are not to touch it unless they are certain they can return it to its owner. And if they see at the time that other persons have passed that way ahead of them, to whom the article might be surrendered, then let them take it, and surrender it if they can; but if they cannot, they must put it back where it was. And if they find bird or beast caught in a trap, let them not meddle with such things.

And if the Christian wishes to drink during the hours of daylight, he must pray to God twice or more after eating. And if he drinks after the evening *double*, he must offer a second *double*. And if there are Believers present, let them stand up when the Christians make their orisons before drinking. And if male and female Christians are praying together, let the prayer always be led by a man. And if a Believer on whom the gift of prayer has been bestowed finds himself with female Christians, let him go apart and pray by himself.

Conversion of the Sick

If those Christians to whom the service of the Church is entrusted receive a message from a sick Believer, they must go to him, and ask of him in confidence what his conduct towards the Church has been since he received the Faith, and whether he owes the said Church any reparation, or has caused her harm. And if he owes her aught and has the wherewithal to discharge his debt, let him do so; but if he refuses, he is not to be received. For a prayer to God on behalf of some guilty or disloyal person shall profit him nothing. If, however, he cannot pay, he is not on that account to be rejected.

And the Christians shall expound to him concerning *abstinentia* [see above] and the customs of the Church. Then they must ask him whether, if he is received, he intends to observe these customs. And unless his intention to do so is true and steadfast, he should not give them his word. For as St John says, liars shall have their part in a lake which burneth with fire and brimstone. But if he declares himself steadfast enough to endure all *abstinentia*, and if the Christians agree to receive him, then let them impose *abstinentia* upon him. . . .

Then they are to ask him whether he is willing to receive the gift of the Lord's Prayer, And if he says he is, then let them clothe him in shirt and breeches (if this be possible), and make him sit erect in his bed, if he can lift his hands. Then let them spread a napkin or some other cloth before him upon the bed. And upon this cloth let them place the Book, and say the *Benedicite* once, and thrice repeat the *Adoremus patrem et filium et spiritum sanctum*. Then is he to take the Book from the hand of the Elder; and thereupon, if he can endure for so long, the minister conducting the ceremony is to address fitting words of Scripture to him for his admonishment. Then he must ask of the sick person concerning the promise he has given: whether he truly intends to observe and keep it as sworn. And if he says Yes, let them then confirm him. Then they are to communicate the words of the Lord's Prayer to him, and he must repeat it. Then shall the Elder say to him: 'This is the prayer that Christ Jesus brought into the world, and taught to the *bons hommes*. Never eat or drink again without repeating this prayer first; and if you fail of this duty, you must needs do penance therefore.' To this the sick person must reply: 'I receive this Prayer from God, and the Church, and you.' Then let them salute him as it were a woman [salutations differed according to whether the recipient was male or female; a sick woman receiving the *consolamentum* was greeted like a man]. Then they are to pray to God with *double* and *veniae*; and this done, the Book shall be replaced before the sick person, after which all repeat the *Adoremus* thrice. Then shall he take the Book from the hand of the Elder, and the Elder shall address fitting words of Scripture to him for his admonishment, with such exhortations as may be appropriate to a *consolamentum*. . . .

Then the Elder is to take the Book, and the sick person must bow his head and say: '*Parcite nobis*. For every sin I have committed by word or deed, I ask pardon of God, and the Church, and all here present.' Then shall the Christians say: 'May God and the Church and all those here present pardon you; and we pray God grant you His forgiveness.' Then they are to grant him the *consolamentum* by placing their hands, and the Book, upon his head. . . . Then they are to exchange the kiss of peace amongst each other, and to kiss the Book. And if any Believers be present, whether men or women, let them too exchange the kiss of peace. Then shall the Christians ask salutation of them, and return it.

And if the sick person dies, and gives or bequeaths them any article, they are not to make use of it or keep it for themselves, but must place it at the disposition of the Order. If the sick person recovers, then the Christians must present him before the Order, and beg that he will receive the *consolamentum* a second time, as soon as may be, and with ready willingness.

APPENDIX B

PRELIMINARY DISCOURSE

Addressed to the Postulant by the Elder

———————————◆———————————

Peter [fictitious postulant's name], you wish to receive that spiritual Baptism from which comes the Holy Spirit into the Church of God, together with the holy Lord's Prayer, and the laying on of hands by the *bons hommes*. Of this Baptism our Lord Jesus Christ says, in the Gospel according to St Matthew [28.19–20]: 'Go ye therefore, and teach all nations, baptizing them in the name of the Father, and of the Son, and of the Holy Ghost: teaching them to observe all things whatsoever I have commanded you: and lo, I am with you always, even unto the end of the world.' And in the Gospel according to St Mark [16.15] He says: 'Go ye into all the world, and preach the Gospel to every creature. He that believeth and is baptized shall be saved; but he that believeth not shall be damned.' And in the Gospel according to St John [3.5] He says to Nicodemus: 'Verily, verily I say unto thee, Except a man be born again, he cannot see the kingdom of God.' And St John the Baptist spoke of this Baptism when he said [St John I.26–7; St Matthew 3.11]: 'I indeed baptize you with water unto repentance: but he that cometh after me is mightier than I, whose shoes I am not worthy to bear: he shall baptize you with the Holy Ghost, and with fire.' And Christ Jesus says, in the Acts of the Apostles [1.5]: 'For John truly baptized with water; but ye shall be baptized with the Holy Ghost.' Holy Baptism by the laying on of hands was instituted by Christ Jesus, according to St Luke's testimony; and as St Mark testifies [16.18] He said that his disciples would do so: 'They shall lay hands on the sick, and they shall recover'. Further, Ananias [Acts 9.17–18] bestowed this Baptism upon St Paul at his conversion. And afterwards Paul and Barnabas did the like in many places. And St Peter and St John did the same for the Samaritans. For St Luke writes as much in the Acts of the Apostles [8.14–17]: 'Now when the apostles which were at Jerusalem heard that Samaria had received the word of God, they sent unto them

N

Peter and John: who, when they were come down, prayed for them, that they might receive the Holy Ghost: (for as yet he was fallen upon none of them . . .). Then laid they their hands on them, and they received the Holy Ghost.'

From the time of the Apostles to this present the Church of God has preserved this holy Baptism by means of which the Holy Spirit is bestowed; it has been passed on from one generation of *bons hommes* to the next, and so it will continue until the end of time. You must understand, too, that power has been given to God's Church to loose and to bind, to pardon sins or to retain them, as Christ says in the Gospel according to St John [20.21–3]: 'As my Father hath sent me, even so send I you.' And when he had said this, he breathed on them, and saith unto them: 'Receive ye the Holy Ghost: whose soever sins ye remit, they are remitted unto them; and whose soever sins ye retain, they are retained.' And in the Gospel according to St Matthew [16.18–19] He said to Simon Peter: 'And I say also unto thee, that thou art Peter, and upon this rock I will build my church; and the gates of hell shall not prevail against it. And I will give unto thee the keys of the kingdom of heaven: and whatsoever thou shalt bind on earth shall be bound in heaven: and whatsoever thou shalt loose on earth shall be loosed in heaven.' And in another passage [Matthew 18.18–20] He said to His disciples: 'Verily I say unto you, Whatsoever ye shall bind on earth shall be bound in heaven: and whatsoever ye shall loose on earth shall be loosed in heaven. Again I say unto you, that if two of you shall agree on earth as touching any thing that they shall ask, it shall be done for them of my Father which is in heaven. For where two or three are gathered together in my name, there am I in the midst of them.' And in yet another passage [Matthew 10.8] He said: 'Heal the sick, cleanse the lepers, raise the dead, cast out devils.' And in the Gospel according to St John [14.12] He said: 'He that believeth on me, the works that I do shall he do also.' And in the Gospel according to St Mark [16.17–18] He said: 'And these signs shall follow them that believe; In my name shall they cast out devils; they shall speak with new tongues; they shall take up serpents; and if they drink any deadly thing, it shall not hurt them; they shall lay hands on the sick, and they shall recover.' And in the Gospel according to St Luke [10.19] He said: 'Behold, I give unto you power to tread on serpents and scorpions, and over all the power of the enemy: and nothing shall by any means hurt you.'

And if you wish to receive this power and strength, you must keep the commandments of Christ and the New Testament so far as in you lies. And know that His commandments forbid a man to lie, or to kill, or to commit adultery; or to swear any oath; or to take or steal; or to do unto others what he would not wish done unto himself. He must pardon those who harm him, love his enemies, pray for those who slander or accuse him, and give them his blessing. If he is struck on the one cheek, let him turn the other; and if a man takes his coat, let him give up his cloak also; and let him neither judge nor condemn. All these commandments, and many others ordained by our Lord and his Church, you must needs observe. You must, besides, hate this world and all its works and everything in it. For St John writes in his First Epistle General [2.15–17]: 'My little children . . . love not the world, neither the things that are in the world. If any man love the world, the love of the Father is not in him. For all that is in the world, the lust of the flesh, and the lust of the eyes, and the pride of life, is not of the Father, but is of the world. And the world passeth away, and the lust thereof: but he that doeth the will of God abideth for ever.' And Christ said to the nations [St John 7.7]: 'The world cannot hate you; but me it hateth, because I testify of it, that the works thereof are evil.' And in the Book of Solomon [Ecclesiastes 1.14] it is written: 'I have seen all the works that are done under the sun; and, behold, all is vanity and vexation of spirit.' Jude the brother of James also spoke for our enlightenment in his Epistle General [v. 23] of 'hating even the garment spotted by the flesh'. From this and much other testimony you must learn to abide by God's commandments and hate this world. And if you do so steadfastly to the end, we have hope that your soul will attain everlasting life.

APPENDIX C

A CATHARIST PRAYER

Translated from the French version published by René Nelli in his anthology Spiritualité de l'hérésie: le Catharisme *(Toulouse 1953), which also contains the Provençal text of this prayer.*

Holy Father, Thou just God of all good souls, Thou who art never deceived, who dost never lie or doubt, grant us to know what Thou knowest, to love what Thou dost love; for we are not of this world, and this world is not of us, and we fear lest we meet death in this realm of an alien god.

Pharisees, seducers, you who sit at the gates of the Kingdom: you hold back others who would enter, yet will not go in yourselves; and because of this I pray to the Holy Father of all good souls, who has the power of salvation, and through the merit of the saved causes our souls to germinate and flourish, and for the sake of the virtuous grants life to sinners—and will continue to do so as long as there are good men in the world, till none of my little children are left. These are they who come from the Seven Kingdoms, and fell from Paradise when Lucifer lured them thence, with the lying assurance that whereas God allowed them the good only, the Devil (being false to the core) would let them enjoy both good and evil; and he promised to give them wives whom they would love dearly; and that they should have authority one over another, and that some amongst them should be kings, or emperors, or counts; and that they would learn to hunt birds with birds, and beasts with beasts.

All those who acknowledged his mastery would descend below and have the power to work both good and evil, as God did in heaven above; but it would (said the Devil) profit them much more to be below where they could work both good and evil, seeing that in heaven God granted them the good alone. Then they rose up on a sky of glass, and for every one that rose aloft, another fell and was lost; and God came down from heaven with the twelve Apostles, and took ghostly shape in Holy Mary.

APPENDIX D

REPRESSIVE MEASURES AND DECREES

Promulgated against the Cathars by Councils between 1179 and 1246

---

1. *The Eleventh Ecumenical, or Third Lateran, Council of* 1179
Can. 27:
. . . For that in Gascony, and in the regions about Toulouse, Albi,
and other places, the madness of those heretics known variously as
Cathars, Patari, or Publicani, has risen to such heights that they no
longer practise their malignities in secret only, but proclaim them
openly, to the corruption of simple or weak-willed folk, We do pronounce an Anathema against them, and against all who shall henceforward adhere to or defend their doctrines; and We forbid any person, under pain of Anathema, to give such heretics shelter, or to
have any commerce with them. . . . Whosoever shall associate himself with these heretics shall be debarred from Holy Communion,
and all persons shall be released from any duties or obedience they
may owe him . . . The whole body of the Faithful must fight this
pestilence vigorously, and even at need take up arms to combat it.
The goods of such persons shall be forfeit, and all princes shall have
the right to enslave them. Whosoever shall, according to the counsel
of the Bishops, take up arms against these heretics shall earn two
years' remission of penance, and shall be placed under the Church's
protection, exactly like a Crusader.

2. *The forty-five 'Capitula' promulgated by the Council of Toulouse
in* 1229.
1. In every parish, whether within or beyond the city limits, the
Bishops shall nominate a priest and two or three lay persons (or yet
more if there be need) of unblemished reputation, who shall take an
oath to search out, loyally and assiduously, such heretics as may be

resident in the said parish. They shall make a close inspection of all suspect houses, their chambers and cellarage, and likewise all concealed hiding-places, the which should be demolished. If they discover any heretics, or persons giving favour or credit, protection or asylum to heretics, they shall take such measures as will prevent their escape, and lodge a denunciation against them with all possible speed, to the Bishop and the local *seigneur* or his bailiff.

2. Abbots of autonomous foundations shall do likewise in respect of such lands as are not under episcopal jurisdiction.

3. The lords temporal shall diligently hunt out heretics in such towns, houses, and forests as they use for their meetings, and shall cause these haunts of theirs to be destroyed.

4. If any person whatsoever permits a heretic to sojourn on his land, whether for money or any other consideration, let him confess to it; else on conviction he will forfeit his lands in perpetuity, and be liable to personal punishment at the hands of his *seigneur*, according to the degree of his guilt.

5. A person on whose lands heretics are frequently to be found—without his connivance, but due to negligence on his part—shall be equally liable to punishment.

6. The house in which a heretic is discovered shall be razed to the ground, and the land on which it stands confiscated.

7. If the resident bailiff [*bailli*] of a locality suspected to be a haunt of heretics does not hunt the said heretics down zealously, he shall lose his position without compensation.

.   .   .   .

9. All persons may search out heretics on their neighbours' land. . . . In this way the King may search out heretics in the Count of Toulouse's domains, and *vice versa*.

10. A *haereticus vestitus* who of his own free will abjures heresy is not to remain living in the same place if the area is believed to harbour other heretics. He must be moved to a staunch Catholic district, of good repute. Such converts are to wear two crosses on their outer garment, one on the right and the other on the left side, and of a different colour from the garment itself. This does not release them from the obligation of obtaining testimonial letters of reconciliation from the bishop. They shall be ineligible for public office or any legal function till their rehabilitation (after suitable penance) by the Pope or his Legate.

11. Those who return to unity with the Catholic Church through fear of death or for some other motive rather than of their own free will, shall be cast into prison by the bishop; here they shall do pen-

ance, under proper supervision, that they may not corrupt their
fellow-prisoners. . . .

12. All faithful Catholics of adult years shall swear an oath before
their Bishop to preserve the Catholic Faith and to persecute heretics
according to their means. This oath must be renewed every two
years.

·   ·   ·   ·

14. Lay persons are forbidden to possess the Books of the Old
and the New Testament, with the exception of the Psalter, the
Breviary, and the Book of Hours of the Blessed Virgin; and it is
rigorously forbidden to possess even these in the vernacular tongue.

15. Any person accused or suspected of heresy cannot practise as a
doctor. When any sick person has received Holy Communion from
his parish priest, great care must be taken to prevent any heretic or
suspected heretic from coming near him; for such visits can have
very ill consequences.

·   ·   ·   ·

18. The label of 'heretic' shall be properly applied to any so regarded by common public consent, or whose ill repute amongst
honourable folk shall have been legally proved before the bishop.

·   ·   ·

42. Women such as widows or heiresses who own strongholds or
fortresses shall not marry enemies of the Faith or of the peace.

3. *Ordinances of the Council of Béziers*, 1233

1. *Perfecti* and *credentes*, together with their protectors, defenders
and other adherents are to be excommunicated each Sunday. Any
guilty party who, after a warning and a pronouncement of excommunication, still fails to mend his ways within a forty-day
period, shall himself be treated as a heretic.

2. Any private person has the right to arrest a heretic, provided he
then hands him over to the bishop.

·   ·   ·   ·

4. Any reconciled heretic who fails to display the two crosses upon
his garments shall be treated as a case of relapse, and his goods shall
be confiscated.

4. *Canon of the Synod of Arles*, 1234

6. Many heretics merely feign conversion, and thereafter are
doubly dangerous. Henceforth all those convicted of heresy who do

not suffer the [death] penalty shall—even if their conversion is sincere—be subject to life imprisonment, and maintained with the revenues from their property.

. . . .

11. The bodies of heretics and their *credentes* shall be exhumed and delivered to the secular arm for judgment.

. . . .

13. Whosoever shall remain for more than a month under ban of excommunication must, when he solicits absolution, pay fifty *solidi* for each additional month of delay. Half of this fine is to go to the penitant's temporal lord, and half to his Bishop, for pious causes.

. . . .

21. Wills are to be made in the presence of the priest or his chaplain; failing which the notary shall be excommunicated, and the testator deprived of burial in consecrated ground.

5. *Council of Narbonne*, 1243

1. Such heretics, together with their adherents or protectors, as furnish proof of their repentance by telling the whole truth concerning both themselves and their fellows, and who thereby obtain remission of imprisonment, shall notwithstanding be subject to the following penances: they are to wear the cross, and every Sunday between the reading of the Epistle and the Gospel they shall present themselves before the priest with a rod, to receive chastisement. The like punishment is to be inflicted upon them during all solemn processions. . . .

. . . .

4. Prisons are to be erected for the housing of poor persons converted from heretical beliefs. Their upkeep is to be the concern of the Inquisitors, to ensure that the diocesan bishops are not excessively burdened with such expenses.

. . . .

9. Since the number of heretics and *credentes* liable to life imprisonment is very large—so large, indeed, that there is a shortage of stones for the construction of the necessary prisons—not to speak of the other various costs incurred through having such a multitude of prisoners, their incarceration shall be deferred until the Pope's intentions in this matter have been ascertained. Howbeit the most notorious suspects will be committed without delay.

. . . .

11. Whosoever shall relapse into heresy after abjuring the same

shall, without further trial, be handed over for punishment to the secular arm.

. . . .

17. The Dominican Inquisitors are not to impose fines by way of penance, since such a course is not fitting for their Order. On this matter they should refer to the bishops, and to the Papal Legate responsible for penances.

. . . .

19. No person can have a prison sentence remitted on the grounds of age or ill-health, or out of consideration for his marriage, his parents, or his children.

. . . .

22. The names of witnesses are to be kept secret. However, an accused person may list the names of his enemies. . . .

23. No person shall be condemned without sufficient proof or a personal confession. . . .

24. In a case of heresy any person whatsoever may be admitted as accuser or witness, not excluding criminals, evil-livers, or the accomplices of such.

25. Only those depositions inspired by malice or personal enmity are to be set aside as valueless.

6. *Instructions drawn up by the Council of Béziers* (1246) *for the use of Inquisitors.*

1. Inquisitors who find it difficult to visit every separate locality shall, in accordance with the Pope's orders, select a special place of residence and exercise their Inquisitorial functions from here over the entire region. They are to summon clergy and people, read out their mandate of authority, and direct all persons fallen into heresy or having knowledge of heretics to appear before them and reveal the truth concerning such matters.

. . . .

20. Condemned or relapsed heretics, together with those who have fled or absconded from justice, those who have failed to present them-selves within the prescribed time-limit, or have done so only after a personal summons, and those who, in disregard of their oath, persist in concealing the truth, shall, in accordance with Apostolic instruc-tions, be condemned to life imprisonment; howbeit if these guilty persons, on the advice of those prelates to whom they are answerable, show themselves repentant, the Inquisitors may thereafter mitigate or commute their sentences.

21. But first they must guarantee to accomplish their penance fully and exactly, and take an oath to fight against heresy; and if they then relapse, they shall be punished without mercy.

22. Furthermore the Inquisitors have the right, if it seem good to them, to commit again to prison those who have been reprieved.

23. Imprisoned persons shall, in accordance with the requirements of the Holy Apostolic See, be placed in separate isolated cells, that they may not be able to corrupt others, or suffer further corruption themselves. . . .

24. The penalty of life imprisonment shall not be wholly remitted except for very serious reasons, e.g. if the prisoner's absence might expose his children to the risk of death.

25. A wife may visit her husband in prison, and a husband his wife. Cohabitation is not to be refused, whether both are imprisoned or one only.

[Text from Hefele-Leclercq, *Histoire des Conciles*, Vol. 5², Part ii.]

APPENDIX E

SENTENCES OF THE INQUISITION

---

1. *Condemnation of a relapsed person*

In the name of the Father, and of the Son, and of the Holy Ghost. Amen.

We, Brother Jacques, by Divine authority Bishop of Pamiers, having special licence from the Reverend Father in God, Peter, by the Grace of God Bishop of Carcassonne, and being in this place, day, and hour his diocesan deputy; and We, Brother Jean de Prat, of the Order of Friars Preachers, Inquisitor appointed to investigate heresy in the Kingdom of France, being the representative of Apostolic Authority resident in Carcassonne for the purpose of hunting out all those tainted with the poison of heresy or suspect thereof; have found and had it proved before us that you, Guilhelmette Tornier, wife of Bernard Tornier, formerly of Tarascon, in the diocese of Pamiers, . . . having been sentenced and condemned to life imprisonment, did make solemn abjuration before the judgment-seat of all heretical beliefs and acts, and of the harbouring of heretics, under pain of suffering such penalties as are reserved for relapsed persons.

Howsobeit, despite your solemn oath sworn upon the Holy Gospels, to which you set your hand, that you would persecute all heretics, together with their supporters and harbourers and defenders, revealing their evil deeds, arresting them (or causing them to be arrested) by all the means at your disposal, and, above all, maintaining and preserving the Catholic Faith . . . you have nevertheless fallen again into a depraved state of heresy, as a dog being gorged with rotten meat will return to its vomit, in that you did both follow and hearken to Peter and William Antérieu, they being persons condemned for depraved and heretical beliefs, and did on divers occasions praise their bounty, their saintliness, their exemplary lives, together with their faith and beliefs, declaring that the sect of the above-mentioned heretics led to salvation, and that every human being could through them be saved; and did assert that our Holy Father the Pope and the prelates of Holy Church were miscreants;

and did speak out against our Catholic Faith and all those who kept it, and did give aid and comfort by divers means to this heretical sect.

All this being attested by the two witnesses required in law; and you yourself having been warned, begged, supplicated and exhorted at several days' interval (with a view to preventing the state of affairs described above) that you would speak truthfully upon oath concerning the beliefs and deeds of the said heretical sect; and inasmuch as you did then, and do now, refuse to take such an oath, being stiffnecked and impenitent, a heretic and supporter of heretics. . . . We, therefore, the Bishop and Inquisitor abovementioned, after duly consulting the opinions of many worthy men, lay and religious alike, and well-versed in Civil and Canon Law; and having as our sole purpose the fulfilment of God's Will . . . do declare and pronounce Guilhelmette Tornier a relapsed person, fallen into crime and the support of heresy, and herself an impenitent heretic; and since the Church can do nothing with a heretic of your stamp, we do hereby abandon you to the secular courts; recommending them nevertheless, as strongly as we may, according to the prescription of Canon Law, to preserve your life and limbs from peril of death [*as we know, the secular arm could not, and was not expected to take any notice of this charitable recommendation*], if you, the aforesaid Guilhelmette Tornier, do fully admit the charges of heresy laid against you, and do show that your heart is touched with repentance, and do no longer persist in denying the Sacraments of Penance and the Holy Eucharist . . . [Doat, Vol. 28, p. 158].

2. *Destruction of houses 'defiled' by the Cathars*
In the name of our Lord, Amen. Inasmuch as after due investigation, and the depositions of witnesses summoned to testify on oath, We have found it proved that in the houses of William Adémar, lawyer, Raymond Fauret, and Raymond Aron, and upon the estate of Peter de Medens, situate near Réalmont, the above-named persons did (during the several illnesses they suffered, and which led to their decease) receive in the said houses various heretics, according to the execrable practices of their damned sect; We therefore, the Inquisitors and Vicars-delegate of the Bishopric of Albi . . . having consulted with wise and learned men, and availing ourselves of the Apostolic Authority vested in us, do declare and pronounce, by irrevocable sentence, that the aforesaid houses and the aforesaid estate, together with all their appurtenances and dependencies, shall be razed to the ground utterly, and we hereby order their destruction; further-

more we decree that the material stuff of the said houses shall be delivered to the flames, unless it seem profitable to us, according to our will, to employ the said material for pious ends.

Furthermore we decree that it shall be forbidden to attempt any rebuilding in the aforesaid places, or to enclose the plots; and that the aforesaid places shall remain unfenced, uninhabited, and uncultivated for ever, in that they have harboured heretics, and for this alone should become forbidden territory. . . .

This sentence given in the year of our Lord 1329, the Sunday after the Octave of the Blessed Virgin Mary's Nativity, in the market-place of the Borough of Carcassonne. [Doat, *op. cit.*].

APPENDIX F

THE DEBATE BETWEEN IZARN AND SICART

A thirteenth-century Provençal poem, composed shortly after the capture of Montségur, at the instigation of those responsible for Catholic propaganda: its object was to cast maximum discredit upon the militant Cathars. The text has been published, with notes and a French translation, by Paul Meyer, in the Annuaire-Bulletin de la Société de l'histoire de France (1879). *This is an abridged version of Meyer's French rendering.*

IZARN: Before the fire consumes you, heretic, and ere you feel the flames, I would know—if you fail to recant tonight—why it is you refuse to believe in our true and holy Baptism. Tell me your reasons. . . . You reject your godfather and the chrism wherewith you were anointed; for you have denied Christian baptism, and have received baptism in another sort according to your own beliefs, which is accomplished by the laying on of hands. . . . You tell countless lies of which I do not believe one word. . . . You have separated man from God, and given him over to the Devil; you have deluded him into believing that he passes from one body to another while he progresses towards salvation, and that he will [in the end] recover all he has lost. . . . Every place, every land that has suffered your presence should perish and sink into the abyss, so vast is the evil web you have woven, the seed of persuasion you have scattered. . . . If you do not confess at once, why, the fire is kindled, the crier goes about the streets, and the crowds are gathered to see justice done; for you are for the stake.

SICART: Izarn [the heretic said], if you promise—and make others promise—that I shall not be burnt, or otherwise destroyed, or cast into prison, then, provided you save me from these torments, I will endure all others with resignation. And if I receive an assurance that you will not cut me off from your presence, but grant me honourable treatment, without violence, then shall you learn so much concerning our missions (I say this for the kindness you yet offer me) that all the knowledge gained by Berit and Razolz [two well known Inquisitors] will be worthless in comparison with the answers I shall give to your questions touching both Heretics and Believers. But I wish to remain anonymous; for if I tell you my secrets, and afterwards you betray me and publish my confession; and if, lastly, you do not take me under your protection, you and the Friars Preachers, then I should be lost indeed. And I shall tell you why; I want you to know. With these hands of mine I have saved a good five hundred people since I was consecrated Bishop, and dispatched them to Paradise. If now I cut myself off from these five hundred souls and abandon them, I rob them of all chance of salvation. By my act I plunge them into the torments of hell and damnation, and consign them to the brutal mercies of a host of devils: there is no hope of any of them ever being saved. And what would become of me if thereafter I met with friends of these people? Supposing you did not admit me [among your adherents]? Supposing I were mocked and made an object of scorn in your Courts, and lost the see of Son where I was installed, and could no longer return thither? This would be great folly; which is why (whether I refuse or accept) I would like a personal guarantee, effective from the moment I arrived here under safe-conduct. And in the first place, I want you to know that it was neither hunger nor thirst nor any other such deprivation which impelled me to present myself before you: be quite sure of that. It is true that we have been warned to be on our guard against pursuit by those summoned before the Inquisition, since the only way such persons can win some sort of a fair and honourable agreement in their own behalf is by undertaking (if they wish to be spared) to deliver up to the Court every heretic they discover, wheresoever they find them. This policy has amazing results, greater than you could possibly imagine. Our dearest friends, those most closely bound to us, throw us over and become our adversaries and foes. Having greeted us they take us and throw us into bonds, hoping thus to procure their own acquittal and the price of our condemnation. By selling us they hope to redeem their sins. But I decided to act before they could lay hands on me; I came before this Court not under constraint, but of my own free will, and have done you a favour which (as those familiar with the comfortable conditions of my life will be aware) is much greater than you might suppose. On this point I would like to tell you somewhat more, if this would not weary you. I have numerous friends, wealthy and opulent friends, and not one of them is happy till he has entrusted me with his cash or bullion, if he has any. I am well furnished with movable chattels and goods on deposit—so much so, indeed, that I can keep all our followers provided from this source, which is why you will find very few of them clad in rags or otherwise poverty-stricken. I have an abundance of clothes, shirts, breeches, sheets, coverlets, counterpanes and the like available from those in use among my private friends; I only have to ask to get the loan of them. Though I fast frequently, you have no reason to pity me, since I often also feed extremely well, with clove-flavoured sauces and good fish-pies. Fish is just as good as bad meat, and fine clove-wine as any barrel-vintage; whole-meal bread is no worse than monastery crumbs. On occasion, too, to be dry and warm is better than getting a soaking. You pass your nights in the wind and rain, and arrive wet through, while I lie snug under cover, very much at peace, with colleagues and assistants to hunt for my fleas and scratch me when the itch takes me. And if at times I conceive a desire for one of my little cousins, whether male or female, the sin costs me nothing; when I have finished I can give myself absolution. There is no sin or impiety so mortal that its author (whoever he be) cannot gain salvation by coming to us, believe you me, either from myself or the deacon who serves at my side. Such is the happy situation in which I find myself. If I admit that it is sinful, and consent to abandon it and embrace the Roman Faith, I would like you to show me proper gratitude by receiving me as an honoured friend.

IZARN: May God bless you, Sicart, the upright God who alone and unaided created heaven and earth, waters and tempests, sun and moon; may He grant you a place amongst those loyal workers whom He has set in His vineyard, giving latecomers no less payment for their labour than the first arrivals! If you are willing to show yourself sincere, and as true and open towards the Faith as erstwhile you were perversely deceitful, then you shall be numbered among them indeed. Yet it is hardly to be expected that those who repent and are converted out of fear will ever be good labourers, or fight manfully to overcome their guilt. When a man has been a heretic, a leader in sin, a steward with charge over the bad grain which fills the store-rooms, so stubborn is the disease that it will take a skilled physician to prescribe for it, and a well-stocked pharmacy to make up the medicine required—one capable of drawing out the rottenness and the root of the complaint. If you are not of this sort, Sicart, you must prove it by your deeds; you must show yourself strong and zealous, not sluggish and faint-hearted; all your efforts must be directed towards the eradication of heresy. And if you are willing to show yourself open, loyal and persevering in the work of Christ which Brother Ferrier is pursuing, great will be your recompense, and generous your hire. . . .

CHRONOLOGICAL TABLE

1002 First executions of Cathars in France, at Orléans and Toulouse. Ten Canons of the Collegiate Church of the Holy Cross sent to the stake.

1049 First discussion (at the Council of Rheims) concerning the appearance of a new heresy in France.

1077 A Cathar condemned as a heretic in Cambrai, and burnt at the stake.

1114 Several heretics snatched from prison by the mob in Soissons, and burnt.

1126 Peter de Bruys sent to the stake at Saint-Gilles in Languedoc.

1160 [+ or −] BIRTH OF THE WALDENSIAN MOVEMENT IN LYONS.

1163 The Council of Tours denounces the threatening advance of the 'new heresy', i.e. Catharism.

1165 The Council of Lombez pronounces against the *boni homines* (*bons hommes*).

1167 COUNCIL OF ALBIGENSIANS HELD AT SAINT-FELIX-DE-CARAMAN, UNDER THE PRESIDENCY OF A BULGARIAN BISHOP, TO DEFINE THE SECT'S ORGANIZATION AND CULT.

— An ecclesiastical conference held at Vézelayx condemns seven Cathars to the stake.

1172 A cleric accused of heresy is burnt at Arras.

1177 Raymond V, Count of Toulouse, reports to the Chapter-General of Cîteaux on the 'alarming development' of the Catharist heresy.

1179 The eleventh Ecumenical (Third Lateran) Council at the instigation of Pope Alexander III pronounces an Anathema against the Albigensian heretics.

1180 The Pope causes his Legate Henry, Cardinal-Bishop of Albano, to preach a Crusade against the heretics in the French Midi.

1181 Capture of Lavaur.

1184 Pope Lucius III excommunicates the Waldensians.

1194 Raymond VI succeeds his father Raymond V as Count of Toulouse.

1198 ENTHRONEMENT OF POPE INNOCENT III. Papal commission for action against heretics delivered to the

Cistercians Reynier and Gui: first establishment of the so-called episcopal or Legates' Inquisition.

1200 Five men and three women burnt at Troyes on a charge of heresy.

1201 A knight owing allegiance to the Count of Nevers burnt at the stake in Nevers.

— Persecution of the Catharist colony at Charité-sur-Loire.

1203 Peter of Castelnau as Legate.

1204 Raymond de Perella rebuilds Montségur, at the request of Cathars in the area.

— February: Theological debate between Catholics and Cathars held at Carcassonne, at the instigation of King Peter II of Aragon.

1206 Esclarmonde, sister of the Count of Foix, receives the *consolamentum*.

— St Dominic establishes a foundation at Prouille to serve as an asylum for converted Catharist women.

1207 The Pope confirms the sentence of excommunication pronounced against the Count of Toulouse by Peter of Castelnau [29th May].

1208 PETER OF CASTELNAU MURDERED [15th January].

— Peter of Castelnau canonized [10th March].

— St Francis of Assisi decides to devote his life to apostolic work.

1209 RAYMOND VI MAKES HIS SUBMISSION TO THE CHURCH AND IS SCOURGED IN PUBLIC AT SAINT-GILLES [18th June].

— The Crusaders' army marches on Languedoc [early July].

— BÉZIERS SACKED AND BURNT [22nd July].

— CAPTURE OF CARCASSONNE [15th August].

— Simon de Montfort is granted by the Legates the title of Viscount of Carcassonne and Béziers [late August].

— A Council held at Avignon utters twenty-one canonical decrees against heretics and Jews [September].

— Death of Raymond-Roger Trencavel, Viscount of Carcassonne and Béziers [10th November].

— The following towns fall into the Crusaders' hands: Albi [surrendered], Castres, Caussade, Fanjeaux, Gontaud, Mirepoix, Puy-la-Roque, Saverdun, Tonneins, and others.

1210 Capture of Minerve: one hundred and forty Cathars burnt [22nd July].

— The Papal Legates summon the Count of Toulouse before a Council held at Saint-Gilles, and excommunicate him a second time [September].

— Termes falls after a nine months' siege [23rd November].

— The Franciscan Order founded.

— Philip II has Amaury de Bène's disciples burnt at the stake in Paris [20th December].

— The Crusaders gain control of the strongholds of Alayrac (garrison massacred), Bram (garrison mutilated), Pennautier, and others.

1211 Fall of Lavaur: four hundred Cathars burnt [3rd May].

— Fall of Cassès: ninety-four Cathars burnt.

— First Siege of Toulouse [end of May].

— Siege of Castelnaudary [September].

— The following places fall into the Crusaders' hands: Cahuzac, Coustaussa, Gaillac, La Garde, La Grave (garrison massacred), La Guépie, Montaigu, Moncuq, Montferrand, Montgey (complete destruction), Puy-Celsi, Rabastens, and others.

1212 [+ or —] Nearly eighty heretics put on trial at Strasburg, and the majority sent to the stake.

1212 Pierre des Vaux de Cernay goes to the Albigeois district.

— Simon de Montfort captures Agen.

— Simon de Montfort summons an Assembly at Pamiers, charged with settling the political and legal status of the conquered [1st December].

— The following fall into the hands of the Crusaders: Ananclet (massacre), Auterive (burnt), Biron, Castelsarrasin, Cauzac, Hautpoul (siege and massacre), L'Isle, Moissac (siege and massacre of mercenaries), Montaut, Muret, Penne d'Agenais (siege), Penne d'Albigeois (siege), Saint-Antonin (sack of the outer borough), Saint-Gaudens, Saint-Marcel, Saint-Michel, Samatan, Verdun-sur-Garonne.

1213 Philip II's son Prince Louis joins the Crusade [end of the year].

— THE BATTLE OF MURET [12th September].

— Siege of Casseneuil: capture, massacre, and demolition of walls.

1214 Battle of Bouvines [27th July].

— Capture of the fortresses of Dome, in Périgord (keep demolished) and of Montfort.

1215 First Crusade of Prince Louis, and Simon de Montfort's entry into Toulouse [April–October].

— The wealthy Toulouse burgher Peter Seila (or Cella) presents St Dominic with several houses which afterwards become the home of the Inquisition.

1215 OPENING OF THE LATERAN COUNCIL [11th November].

— Persecution of heretics at Colmar.

1216 Simon de Montfort receives investiture at the King's hands as Lord of Languedoc [10th April].

— SIEGE OF BEAUCAIRE AND THE CRUSADERS' FIRST DEFEAT [May–August].

— Death of Innocent III [16th July].

— Simon de Montfort's entry into Toulouse; the crushing of the revolt and the dismantling of the city's defences.

— A Bull of Honorius III solemnly confirms the Order founded by St Dominic.

1217 Persecution of heretics at Cambrai.

— Simon de Montfort captures the fortresses of Crest in the Dauphiné, La Bastide, Monteil, Montgrenier, and Pierre-pertuse.

— Opening of the Siege of Toulouse [October].

1218 DEATH OF SIMON DE MONTFORT [25th June].

— Death of Pierre des Vaux de Cernay [late December].

1219 Prince Louis's second Crusade. Capture of Marmande and unsuccessful siege of Toulouse [May–June].

1220 Heretics persecuted at Troyes.

1221 Death of St Dominic [6th August].

1222 Death of Raymond VI [August].

1223 Death of Raymond-Roger, Count of Foix [April].

— Death of Philip II [14th July].

— Louis VIII crowned at Rheims [6th August].

1224 AMAURY DE MONTFORT LEAVES LANGUEDOC [15th January].

1225 Assembly of Catharist Churches at Pieusse.

— Death of Arnald-Amalric, Archbishop of Narbonne [29th September].

1226 Raymond VII excommunicated by the Council of Bourges [28th January].

— LOUIS VIII'S CRUSADE [June–November].

— Death of St Francis of Assisi [3rd October].

— Louis VIII dies at Montpensier [8th November].

1227 Gregory IX becomes Pope.

1229 THE TREATY OF MEAUX SIGNED. RAYMOND VII SCOURGED BEFORE THE ALTAR OF NOTRE-DAME IN PARIS [12th April].

— COUNCIL OF TOULOUSE [November].

1231 MONTSÉGUR BECOMES THE CENTRAL STRONGHOLD OF CATHARISM

— Death of Foulques of Marseilles, Bishop of Toulouse.

1232 Guilhabert de Castres convenes the Synod of Montségur.

1233 GREGORY IX GIVES DEFINITIVE POWERS TO THE MONASTIC

INQUISITION AND GRANTS THE DOMINICANS A GENERAL AUTHOR-
ITY FOR THE EXERCISE OF THIS OFFICE [13th April].

— The Pope ratifies the foundation of the University of Toulouse
'to cause the Catholic Faith to flourish in these parts' [29th
April].

1233 Three Dominicans thrown into a well at Cordes.

1234 Raymond VII publishes his 'statutes against heretics'.

— The Inquisitor Arnald Cathala has sundry dead heretics exhumed at Albi, and is roughly handled by the mob.

— The Inquisitors William Arnald and Peter Seila condemn two
hundred and ten persons to the stake at Moissac.

— The Dominican convent in Narbonne sacked by the mob.

1235 The Dominicans are expelled from Toulouse on the orders of
the Count and the consuls [November].

1239 At Montwimer (Marne) one hundred and eighty-three Cathars
are burnt in the presence of the Count of Champagne.

1240 Carcassonne besieged by Raymond Trencavel [September].

1241 Raymond VII promises Louis IX to destroy the fortress of
Montségur.

1242 Raymond VII's rebellion [April–October].

— THE MASSACRE OF AVIGNONET [28th May].

1243 THE TREATY OF LORRIS [January].

— The Council of Béziers decides to destroy Montségur.

— OPENING OF THE SIEGE OF MONTSÉGUR [13th May].

— Ramon Damors brings letters from the Catharist Bishop of
Cremona to Bertrand Marty at Montségur [before November].

— Durand, Bishop of Albi, brings reinforcements for the army
besieging Montségur [November].

1243 Pope Innocent IV grants Raymond VII absolution [2nd Decem-
ber].

— Council held at Narbonne, attended by the army commanders
besieging Montségur.

1244 Night attack attempted by the besiegers of Montségur [?
5th January].

— Night sortie by the garrison: a failure [1st March].

— Truce concluded between besiegers and besieged [2nd March].

— Capitulation of Montségur [14th March].

— THE MASSACRE OF MONTSÉGUR [16th March].

1246 St Louis ordains the erection of special prisons to house heretics in Carcassonne and Béziers.

1249 The Count of Toulouse has eighty *credentes* burnt at Barleiges
(Agen).

— DEATH OF RAYMOND VII [27th September].

1255 Capture of Quéribus, one of the Cathars' last places of refuge in Languedoc.

1271 Death of Alphonse of Poitiers and his wife Jeanne of Toulouse. Languedoc passes under the French Crown [21st–24th August].

NOTES AND REFERENCES

Chapter I: The Background of the Crusade
1 *Historia Albigensis*, ch. 3
2 *Chronique sur la guerre des Albigeois*, ch. 10
3 Ch. 6, vv. 131–4
4 Letter dated 9th February, 1209
5 Op. cit., ch. 64
6 Ibid., ch. 4
7 Letter to Raymond VI, 20th May, 1207
8 Op. cit., ch. 13
9 William de Puylaurens, op. cit., ch. 9
10 Cf. the *Lettres d'Etienne de Tournai*, ed. Desilve (Paris 1893)

Chapter II: Heresy and Heretics
1 See *Interrogatio Johannis*, or *The Secret Supper*, ap. Doat, Vol. 36, fols. 27 *et seq.*, and *Liber de duobus principiis*, ed. Dondaine [*Un traité manichéen du XIIIe siècle*, '*Liber de duobus principiis*', Istituto storico Dominicano, S. Sabina, Roma, 1939]
2 De Cernay, op. cit., ch. 4
3 Douais, *Les Albigeois*, p. 10
4 Bibliothèque de Toulouse, MS. 609, fol. 239
5 Innocent III, *Epistles*, vol. 7, p. 79
6 Op. cit., Prologue
7 William de Puylaurens, op. cit., ch. 8
8 *Chanson de la Croisade*, 145.3292–3
9 Doat, Vol. 24, pp. 59–60
10 *Practica Inquisitionis*, p. 130
11 Bibl. de Toulouse, MS. 609; Doat, Vol. 22, p. 15
12 Dom Bouquet, *Chronicon de Rodolphe, abbé de Coggeshall*, Vol. 18, p. 59
13 See Dom Vaissette, *Histoire du Languedoc* (ed. Molinier), Vol. 6, p. 227
14 De Cernay, op. cit., ch. 4
15 Bibl. de Toulouse, MS 609, fol. 130
16 De Cernay, op. cit., ch. 46

17 De Cernay, op. cit., ch. 2
18 *Mansi Concil.*, Vol. 22, col. 477
19 Douais, Vol. 2, p. 109
20 Bernard Gui, *Practica Inquisitionis*, Vol. 1, p. 63

Chapter III: The Pre-heretical Church
1 *Epistles*, 365
2 *Epistles* 241=Migne, *Patrol. Lat.*, Vol. 182, col. 434
3 Jordanis de Saxonia, *Opera* (Freiburg 1891)
4 Op. cit., ch. 10
5 Jordanis, ibid., p. 549
6 William de Puylaurens, ch. 10
7 Balme and Lelaidier, *Cartulaire de saint Dominique*, Vol. 1, pp. 186–8
8 Humbert de Romans, *L'Enquête de Toulouse pour la canonization de saint Dominique*, ch. 13
9 Dante, *Paradiso*, Canto 9

Chapter IV: The Campaign of 1209
1 *Chanson de la Croisade*, 9.193–202
2 Ibid., 17.395–400
3 Ibid., 18.430–40
4 Ibid., 19.450–5
5 Ibid., 20.467–71
6 Ibid., 20.471–6
7 Ibid., 21.481–9
8 Ibid., 21.500–5
9 Ibid., 22.523–6
10 Ibid., 23.532–6
11 Ibid., 30.685–702
12 Ibid., 32.742–3
13 Ibid., 33.774–6
14 Ibid., 33.769–70
15 Ibid., 15.343–52
16 Ibid., 34.796
17 De Cernay, ch. 17
18 Ibid., ch. 21
19 *Chanson de la Croisade*, 36.826–8

Chapter V: Simon de Montfort
1 *Chanson de la Croisade*, 35.800–2
2 De Cernay, op. cit., ch. 19

3 De Cernay, op. cit., ch. 56

4 Ibid., ch. 86

5 Ibid., ch. 86

6 Ibid., ch. 34

7 Ibid., ch. 37

8 Ibid., ch. 37

9 Ibid., ch. 40

10 Ibid., ch. 33

11 Letter of Pope Innocent III to the Abbot of Cîteaux

12 De Cernay, op. cit., ch. 39

13 *Chanson de la Croisade*, 59.1360–6

14 De Cernay, ch. 47

15 *Chanson de la Croisade*, 68.1552–3

16 Ibid., 1560–1

17 Op. cit., ch. 11

18 Ibid.

19 De Cernay, ch. 51

20 Letter of Pope Innocent III to Arnald-Amaury, 15th January, 1213

21 Letter of Pope Innocent III to the King of Aragon, 21st May, 1215

22 *Cronica o commentari del rey en Jac me* (new ed., Barcelona)

23 De Cernay, op. cit., Appendix IV

24 Letter of Pope Innocent III to Simon de Montfort, 15th January, 1213

25 *Chanson de la Croisade*, 131.2756–65

26 De Cernay, ch. 71

27 *Chanson de la Croisade*, 139.3046–7

28 William de Puylaurens, ch. 22

29 Cf. the original edition of Dom Vaissette's *Histoire du Languedoc*, Vol. 3, p. 252, and A. Molinier's note *ad loc.* in his 1879 edition (Vol. 6, p. 427)

30 De Cernay, ch. 78

31 Ibid., ch. 81

32 Ibid., ch. 82

Chapter VI: The Consecration and Failure of the Crusade

1 De Cernay, ch. 83

2 *Chanson de la Croisade*, 144

3 Ibid., 145.3265–74

4 Ibid., 150.3547–53

5 De Cernay, ch. 83

6 *Chanson de la Croisade*, 153
7 De Cernay, ch. 83
8 Ibid.
9 William de Puylaurens, ch. 29
10 *Chanson de la Croisade*, 172.5112–3
11 Ibid., 5542–8
12 Ibid., 179.5640–7
13 De Cernay, ch. 84
14 *Chanson de la Croisade*, 182.5861–8
15 Ibid., 5852–8
16 Ibid., 183.5952–63
17 Ibid., 189.6486–8
18 Ibid., 200.7913–7
19 William de Puylaurens, ch. 30
20 *Chanson de la Croisade*, 205.8452–6
21 Ibid., 8479–84
22 Ibid., 208.8681–93

Chapter VII: The King of France
1 *Chanson de la Croisade*, 212.9306–21
2 William the Breton, *Bouquet*, 17, 11d.
3 William de Puylaurens, ch. 33
4 Ibid., ch. 34
5 Cf. Dom Vaissette, op. cit., Vol. 23, ch. 65; *Poètes provençaux* (1879), Vol. 6, pp. 556–9
6 William de Puylaurens, ch. 38
7 Ibid., ch. 39

Chapter VIII: The Final Years of Occitan Independence
1 *Chanson de la Croisade*, 165
2 Ibid., 154.3812
3 William de Puylaurens, ch. 40
4 See Dondaine, *Un traité manichéen du XIIIe siècle: le 'Liber de duobus principiis' suivi d'un fragment du 'Rituel cathare'*. Istituto storico domenicano, S. Sabina (Rome 1939)
5 Taken from the list of *seigneurs faidits*: see Dom Bouquet, *Recueil des historiens des Gaules et de France*, Vol. 24
6 Balme and Delaidier, *Cartulaire de saint Dominic*
7 Thibaut of Champagne, *Oeuvres poètiques*
8 Bernard de La Barthe: '. . . *patz forsada* . . .' Cf. Dom Vaissette (1885 ed.), Vol. 10, p. 337
9 William de Puylaurens, ch. 39

Chapter IX: The Church's Peace

1 See Marcel Fournier, *Les Statuts et Privilèges des Universités françaises avant* 1879, Vol. 1, p. 439
2 *Recueil des historiens des Gaules*, Vol. 21, p. 599
3 William de Puylaurens, ch. 40
4 G. Pelhisson, *Chronicon* (ed. Douais), p. 84
5 William de Puylaurens, ch. 40
6 Pelhisson, op. cit., p. 92
7 William de Puylaurens, ch. 42
8 Letter to the Legate Gautier de Tournay, 18th February, 1232

Chapter X: The Inquisition

1 Pelhisson, op. cit., p. 95
2 Ibid., p. 98
3 Ibid.
4 Bernard Gui, *Libelli de Ordine Praedicatorum* [*Recueil des historiens des Gaules*, Vol. 21, pp. 736–7]
5 Ibid.
6 *Registres de Grégoire IX*, no. 3187
7 Innocent IV's Bull *Ad Extirpanda* of 15th May, 1252
8 Bernard Gui, *Practica Inquisitionis*, ch. 1, §5
9 Doat, Vol. 22, p. 142; 23, p. 165

Chapter XI: The Cathar Resistance

1 Doat, Vol. 23, pp. 2–39
2 *Chanson de la Croisade*, 145.3265
3 Op. cit. (1879 ed.), Vol. 6, p. 768
4 Testimony given before Brother Ferrier, 18th March, 1244; Doat, Vol. 22, pp. 293 v°–294 v°
5 Doat, ibid., 295 v°
6 Ibid., p. 287

Chapter XII: The Siege of Montségur

1 Doat, Vol. 24, fol. 44, testimony by Raymond de Perella; cf. ibid., fol. 58, testimony by Bérenger de Lavelanet
2 Ibid., pp. 170–1, 181
3 Ibid., p. 180
4 Ibid., p. 174
5 William de Puylaurens, ch. 46
6 Doat, Vol. 24, p. 172; testimony by Imbert de Salas
7 Op. cit., ch. 46

8 Doat, Vol. 22, p. 263; Vol. 24, pp. 202–3, 207

9 Ibid., Vol. 24, pp. 80, 207; Vol. 22, pp. 247, 255

10 Concerning these gifts see Doat, Vol. 24, p. 173

11 Doat, Vol. 22, p. 129

12 Op. cit., ch. 46

13 Doat, Vol. 22, p. 259

14 Op. cit., ch. 46

15 *Summa, Secunda Secundae*, 2.46; 2.50; ibid., *questio* 12, art 2

16 Hildegarde, *Epist.* 139

BIBLIOGRAPHY

—————————•—————————

PRIMARY SOURCES

BERNARD GUI, *Practica inquisitionis hereticae pravitatis*, ed., C. Douais, Paris (1886).

BERNARD GUI, *Manuel de l'Inquisiteur*, ed., G. Mollat, 2 Vols., Paris (1926–27).

Bullaire de l'Inquisition française, ed., J. M. Vidal, Paris (1913).

Bullarium ordinis fratrum praedicatorum, ed., T. Ripoll, 8 Vols., Rome (1779–90).

Bullarium Franciscanum, ed., J. H. Sbaralea *et al.*, 8 Vols., Rome (1759–1908).

Cartulaire de Notre-Dame de Prouille, ed., J. Guiraud, 2 Vols., Paris (1907).

Cartulaire et archives des communes de l'ancien diocèse et de l'arrondissement administratif de Carsassonne, ed., A. Mahul, 7 Vols., Paris (1857–82).

Catalogue des actes de Philippe Auguste, ed., L. Delisle, Paris (1856).

Chanson de la croisade contre les Albigeois, ed., P. Meyer, *Société de l'histoire de France*, 2 Vols., Paris (1875 and 1879); and ed. with trans., M. Chabot, Tome I, Paris (1931).

Chartes inédites des comtes Raymond VI et Raymond VII, ed., J.-B.-G. Belhomme. *Mémoires de l'Académie de Toulouse* (1854).

Collection Doat, Les Registres de l'Inquisition, Bibliothèque Nationale, Paris.

Concilia Galliae Narbonensis, ed., J. C. de Baluze, Paris (1668).

Corpus Iuris Canonici, ed., E. Friedberg, 2 Vols., Leipzig (1879 and 1881).

Débat d'Izarn et de Sicart de Figueiras, trans. with notes, P. Meyer, *Société de l'histoire de France* (1879).

Documents inédits sur l'histoire des Albigeois, ed., J.-B.-G. Belhomme, *Mémoires de la Société archéologique du Midi de la France*, VI, Toulouse (1852).

Documents pour servir à l'histoire de l'Inquisition dans le Languedoc, ed., C. Douais, *Société de l'histoire de France*, 2 Vols., Paris (1900).

Epistolae Innocentii papae III, ed., J. P. Migne, *Patrologiae Cursus Completus, Series Latina*, Paris, CCXIV–CCXVII (1855).

GUILLAUME DE PUYLAURENS, *Historia Albigensium*, in M. Bouquet *et al.*, edd., *Recueil des historiens des Gaules et de la France*, XIX (1833).

GUILLAUME DE PUYLAURENS, *Chronique sur la guerre des Albigeois*, trans., C. Lagarde (1864).

GUILLAUME DE PUYLAURENS, *Historia Albigensium et sa chronique*, ed., J. Beyssier, *Bibliothèque de la Faculté des Lettres de Paris*, XVIII (1904).

GUILLAUME DE TUDÈLE [William of Tudela], *Histoire de la croisade contre les hérétiques albigeois*, ed. and trans., M. C. Fauriel, Paris (1847); re-publ., Mary-Lafon (1868), P. Meyer (1875–79) and M. Chabot (1931–54).

Histoire des croisades contre les Albigeois, edd., J. J. Barrau and B. Darragon, *Nouveaux documents sur l'histoire de France au XIe, XIIe and XIIIe siècles*, 2 Vols., Paris (1840).

JEAN DE GARLANDE, *De triumphis Ecclesiae*, ed., T. Wright, Roxburghe Club, London (1856).

Nouveau Testament traduit au XIIIe siècle en langue provençale, ed., L. Clédat, *Bibliothèque de la Faculté des Lettres de Lyon*, IV, Paris (1888).

PELHISSON, GUILLAUME, *Chronicon fratris Guillelmi Pelisso*, ed., C. Douais, *Sources de l'Inquisition dans le Midi de la France*, Paris (1881).

PIERRE DE CASTELNAU [Peter of Castelnau], *Bullaire du bienheureux Pierre de Castelnau martyr de la foi*, ed., A. Villemagne, Montpellier (1917).

PIERRE DES VAUX DE CERNAY, *Petri Vallium Sarnaii monachi Hystoria Albigensis*, edd., P. Guébin and E. Lyon, 3 Vols., Paris (1926–1939).

PIERRE DES VAUX DE CERNAY, *Histoire albigeoise*, trans., P. Guébin and H. Maisonneuve, Paris (1951).

Regesta Honorii papae III, ed., P. Pressutti, 2 Vols., Rome (1888 and 1895).

Registres de Grégoire IX, ed., L. Auvray, *Bibliothèque des Écoles françaises d'Athènes et de Rome*, 3 Vols., Paris (1896–1910).

Registres d'Innocent IV, ed., E. Berger, 3 Vols., Paris (1884–97); index (1911).

Rerum Gallicarum et Francicarum Scriptores: Recueil des historiens des Gaules et de la France, edd., M. Bouquet et al., Paris (1738–1876, 1894, 1899–).

Traité cathare inédit du début du XIIIe siècle, d'après le 'Liber contra Manicheos' de Durand de Huesca, ed., C. Thouzellier, *Bibliothèque de la Revue d'histoire ecclésiastique*, XXXVII, Louvain (1961).

Traité inédit du XIIIe siècle contres les Albigeois, ed., C. Molinier, *Annales de la Faculté des Lettres de Bordeaux* (1883).

Traité neo-manichéen du XIIIe siècle, le 'Liber de duobus principiis', ed., A. Dondaine, *Instituto storico Dominicano*, Rome (1939).

SECONDARY WORKS

ALBE, E., 'L'Hérésie albigeoise et l'Inquisition en Quercy', *Revue d'histoire de l'église de France* (1910).

ALPHANDÉRY, P., 'Les idées morales chez les hétérodoxes latins au début du XIIIe siècle, *Bibliothèque de l'École des hautes études sciences religieuses*, XVI, Paris (1903).

ASTRUC, J., *L'Albigéisme et la prise de Carcassonne par les croisés en 1209*, Carcassonne (1908).

ASTRUC, J., *La Conquête de la vicomté de Carcassonne par Simon de Montfort*, Carcassonne (1912).

BARRAU, J. J., and DARRAGON, B., *Histoire de la croisade contre les Albigeois*, 2 Vols., Paris (1843).

BEAUSOBRE, I. DE, *Histoire critique de Manichée et du Manichéisme*, 2 Vols., Amsterdam (1734–39).

BELPERRON, P., *La Croisade contre les Albigeois et l'union du Languedoc à la France*, Paris (1945).

BENNETT, R. F., *The Early Dominicans*, Cambridge (1937).

BENOIST, J., *Histoire des Albigeois et des Vaudois ou Barbets*, 2 Vols., Paris (1691).

BENOIST, J., *Suite de l'histoire des Albigeois contenant la vie de saint Dominique*, 2 Vols., Toulouse (1693).

BERGER, G., *Histoire de Blanche de Castille*, Paris (1895).

BERNE-LAGARDE, P. DE, *Bibliographie du catharisme languedocien*, Toulouse (1957).

BESSÉ, G., *Histoire des comtes de Carcassonne*, Béziers (1645).

BEYSSIER, J., 'Guillaume de Puylaurens et sa *Chronique*', *Bibliothèque de la Faculté des Lettres de Paris*, XVIII (1904).

BLOCH, M. L. B., 'La France sous les derniers Capétiens, 1223–1328', *Cahiers des Annales*, XIII, Paris (1958).

BORST, A., *Die Katharer*, Stuttgart (1953).

BOUCHE, H., *Histoire de Provence*, Aix (1664).

BOUTARIC, M. E., 'La Guerre des Albigeois et Alphonse de Poitiers', *Revue des questions historiques*, II (1867).

BOUTARIC, M. E., *Saint Louis et Alphonse de Poitiers: Réunion des provinces du midi et de l'ouest à la couronne*, Paris (1870).

BREILLAT, P., *Recherches albigeoises*, Albi (1948).

BROECKX, E., *Le Catharisme*, Hoogstraten (1916).

CALMETTE, J., 'Le Monde féodal', *Clio: Introduction aux études historiques*, IV, Presses Universitaires de France (1935).

CASTILLON, H., *Histoire du comté de Foix*, 2 Vols., Toulouse (1852).

CATEL, G., *Histoire des comtes de Toulouse avec quelques traités et chroniques anciennes concernant la même histoire*, Toulouse (1623).

CATEL, G., *Mémoires de l'histoire du Languedoc, tirés des archives de la même province et autres circonvoisines*, Toulouse (1633).

CAUZONS, T. DE, *Histoire de l'Inquisition en France*, 2 Vols., Paris (1909 and 1912).

CHASSANION, J., *Histoire des Albigeois touchant leur doctrine et religion*, Geneva (1595).

COMPAYRÉ, C., *Études historiques et documents inèdits sur l'Albigeois*, Albi (1841).

COMTE, P., 'Le Catharisme dans les contes populaires de la Gascogne', *Bulletin de la Société archéologique et historique du Gers* (1953).

COURREHT, P., *Montségur, son rôle pendant la croisade des Albigeois*, Carcassonne (1932).

DELPECH, H., *La Bataille de Muret et la tactique de la cavalerie au XIIIe siècle*, Paris (1878).

DELPOUX, C., 'Le Siège de Carcassonne et l'Inquisition', *Cahiers d'études cathares*, XI (1951).

DEVIC, C., and VAISSÈTE, J., *Histoire générale de Languedoc*, ed., A. Molinier, 16 Vols., Toulouse (1872–1915).

DOGNON, P., *Les Institutions politiques et administratives du pays de Languedoc du XIIIe siècle aux guerres de religion*, Toulouse (1895).

DONDAINE, A., 'Nouvelles sources de l'histoire doctrinale du neomanichéisme au moyen âge', *Revue des sciences philosophiques et théologiques*, XXVIII (1939).

DOSSAT, J., 'La Société méridionale à la veille de la croisade des Albigeois', *Revue du Languedoc* (1944).

DOSSAT, J., 'Le Clergé méridional à la veille de la croisade des Albigeois', *Revue du Languedoc* (1944).

DOUAIS, C., *Les Albigeois: leurs origines*, Paris (1879).

DOUAIS, C., 'Les Sources de l'histoire de l'Inquisition dans le midi de la France', *Revue des questions historiques*, XXX (1881).

DOUAIS, C., *Les Frères Prêcheurs en Gascogne au XIIIe et au XIVe siècle*, Paris (1888).

DOUAIS, C., *Les Hérétiques du midi au XIIIe siècle*, Paris (1891).

DOUAIS, C., *Les Hérétiques du comté de Toulouse d'après l'enquête de 1245*, Paris (1891).

DOUAIS, C., *L'Albigéisme et les Frères Prêcheurs à Narbonne au XIIIe siècle*, Paris (1894).

DOUAIS, C., *L'Inquisition: ses origines, sa procédure*, Paris (1906).

DUCOS, F., 'Note sur Guillaume de Puylaurens', *Mémoires de l'Académie de Toulouse* (1857).

DUCOS, F., 'Notice sur un historien de la croisade contre les hérétiques albigeois: Pierre des Vaux de Cernay', *Mémoires de l'Académie de Toulouse* (1856).

EMERY, R. W., *Heresy and Inquisition in Narbonne*, New York (1941).

FAWTIER, R., *The Capetian Kings of France: Monarchy and Nation, 987–1328*, trans., L. Butler and R. J. Adam, London (1960), from *Les Capétiens et la France: leur rôle dans sa construction*, Presses Universitaires de France (1942).

FLICHE, A., FOREVILLE, R., and ROUSSET, J., 'Du Premier Concile du Latran à l'avènement d'Innocent III, 1123–98', *Histoire de l'Église depuis les origines jusqu'à nos jours*, edd., A. Fliche and V. Martin, IX, in 2 Vols., Paris (1946 and 1953).

FLICHE, A., THOUZELLIER, C., and AZAIS, Y., 'La Chrétienté romaine', *Histoire de l'Église depuis les origines jusqu'à nos jours*, edd., A. Fliche and V. Martin, X, Paris (1950).

GAY, J., *L'Histoire des schismes et hérésies des Albigeois*, Paris (1561).

GRÉGOIRE, H., 'Cathares d'Asie Mineure, d'Italie et de France', *Mémorial Louis Petit: Mélanges d'histoire et d'archéologie, Archives de l'Orient Chrétien*, I, Bucharest (1948).

GUIRAUD, J., *St Dominique*, Paris (1899); English trans., K. de Mattos, London (1901).

GUIRAUD, J., 'Le *Consolamentum* ou l'initiation cathare; le répression de l'hérésie au moyen âge', *Questions d'histoire et d'archéologie chrétiennes*, Paris (1906).

GUIRAUD, J., L'Albigéisme languedocien aux XIIe XIIIe siècles', introduction to *Cartulaire de Notre-Dame de Prouille*, 2 Vols., Paris (1907).

GUIRAUD, J., 1. 'Albigeois'; 2. 'Croisade contre les Albigeois', *Dictionnaire d'histoire et de géographie ecclésiastiques*, edd., A. Baudrillart, A. Vogt and U. Rouziès, I, Paris (1912), cols. 1619–94.

GUIRAUD, J., *Histoire de l'Inquisition au moyen âge*, 2 Vols., Paris (1935 and 1938).

HAVET, J., 'L'Hérésie et le bras séculier au moyen âge jusqu'au

XIIIe siècle', *Bibliothèque de l'École des chartes*, XLI (1880).

HEFELE, C. J., *Histoire des Conciles*, trans. and ed., H. Leclercq, Tome V, 2nd Part, Paris (1913).

JACOB, E. F., 'Innocent III', *Cambridge Medieval History*, edd., J. R. Tanner, C. W. Previté-Orton and Z. N. Brooke, VI, Cambridge (1929), pp. 1–43.

JEANJEAN, J.-F., *La Croisade contre les Albigeois à Carcassonne*, Carcassonne (1941).

JORDAN, E., 'La Responsabilité de l'Église dans la répression de l'hérésie au moyen âge', *Annales de philosophie chrétienne*, CLIV, CLVI, CLVIII and CLIX (1907–9).

LACGER, L. DE, 'L'Albigeois pendant la crise de l'Albigéisme', *Revue d'histoire ecclésiastique*, XXIX (1933).

LANGLOIS, J.-B., *Histoire des croisades contre les Albigeois, depuis la naissance de cette hérésie en 1106 jusqu'au 1270*, Rouen (1703).

LAVISSE, E., *Histoire de France*, Vols. II and III, Paris (1901–3).

LEA, H. C., *History of the Inquisition of the Middle Ages*, 3 Vols., New York reprint (1908–11).

LONGNON, A., and DELABORDE, H. F., *La Formation de l'unité française*, Paris (1922).

LOT, F., and FAWTIER, R., *Histoire des institutions françaises au moyen âge*. Tome I: *Institutions seigneuriales*; Tome II: *Institutions royales*, Presses Universitaires de France (1957–58).

LUCHAIRE, A., *Innocent III*, Vol. II: *La Croisade des Albigeois*, Paris (1905).

LUCHAIRE, A., *Social France at the Time of Philip Augustus*, trans., E. B. Krehbiel, London (1912), from 2nd French ed., Paris (1909).

MAILLET, H., 'L'Église et la répression sanglante de l'hérésie', *Bibliothèque de la Faculté de Philosophie et Lettres de l'Université de Liége*, XVI, Liége (1909).

MAISONNEUVE, H., *Études sur les origines de l'Inquisition*, Paris (1942).

MANDONNET, P., *St Dominic and his Work*, trans., M. B. Larkin, London (1945), from *Saint Dominique: L'Idée, l'homme et l'oeuvre*, Paris (1937).

MEYER, P., 'Recherches sur les auteurs de la *Chanson de la Croisade albigeoise*', *Bibliothèque de l'École des chartes*, XXVI (1865).

MIROT, A., *Manuel de géographie historique de la France*. Tome I: *L'Unité française*, 2nd ed., Paris (1947).

MOLINIER, A., 'Catalogue des actes de Simon et d'Amauri de Montfort', *Bibliothèque de l'École des chartes*, XXXIV (1873).

MOLINIER, C., *L'Inquisition dans le midi de la France au XIIIe et au XIVe siècle*, Paris (1880).

MOLINIER, C., 'L'*Endura*, coutume religieuse des derniers sectaires albigeois', *Annales de la Faculté de Bordeaux*, III (1881).

MOLINIER, C., 'L'Église et la société cathare', *Revue historique*, XCIV (1907).

NAZ, R., 1. 'Innocent III: La croisade contre les hérétiques'; 2. 'Inquisition', *Dictionnaire de droit canonique*, ed., R. Naz, VI, Paris (1953), cols. 1416–26.

NELLI, R., 'Les deux tentations chez les Cathares du XIIIe siècle', *Cahiers d'études cathares*, Arques (1949).

NELLI, R., *Écritures cathares: Textes précathares et cathares*, Paris (1959).

NIEL, F., 'La Capitulation de Montségur', *Cahiers d'études cathares*, Arques (1951).

NIEL, F., 'Béziers pendant la croisade contre les Albigeois', *Cahiers d'études cathares* (1953).

NIEL, F., *Albigeois et Cathares*, Collection *Que sais-je?*, Presses Universitaires de France (1955).

PETIT-DUTAILLIS, C., *Étude sur la vie et le règne de Louis VIII, 1187-1226*, Paris (1894).

PETIT-DUTAILLIS, C., 'Saint Louis', *Cambridge Medieval History*, VI (1929), pp. 331-61.

PEYRAT, *Histoire des Albigeois*, 2 Vols., Paris (1880 and 1882).

POWICKE, F. M. 'The Reigns of Philip Augustus and Louis VIII of France', *Cambridge Medieval History*, VI (1929), pp. 285-330.

RAMET, H., *Histoire de Toulouse*, Toulouse (1935).

ROCHÉ, D., 'Le Catharisme', *Institute d'études occitanes*, Toulouse (1938).

ROCHÉ, D., 'La Capitulation et le bûcher de Montségur', *Mémoires de la Société archéologique de l'Aude* (1944-46).

ROCHÉ, D., 'Études manichéennes et cathares', *Institute d'études occitanes*, Toulouse (1952).

RUNCIMAN, S., *The Medieval Manichee*, Cambridge (1955 imp.).

SCHMIDT, C., *Histoire et doctrine de la secte des Cathares ou Albigeois*, 2 Vols., Paris (1848 and 1849).

SHANNON, A. C., *The Popes and Heresy in the Thirteenth Century*, Pennsylvania (1949).

SMEDT, C. DE, 'Les Sources de l'histoire de la croisade contre les Albigeois', *Revue des questions historiques*, XVI, Paris (1874).

SÖDERBERG, H., *La Religion des Cathares: Étude sur le Gnosticisme de la basse antiquité et du moyen âge*, Uppsala (1949).

SOMMARIVA, L., 'Studi recenti sulle eresie medievali, 1939-52', *Rivista storico italiana*, LXIV (1952).

TANON, L., *Histoire des tribunaux de l'Inquisition en France*, Paris (1893).

THOMAS, L. J., 'Quelques aspects peu connus de la croisade contre les Albigeois', *Cahiers d'histoire et d'archéologie*, I, Nimes (1931).

TURBERVILLE, A. S., 'Heresies and the Inquisition in the Middle Ages, c. 1000-1305', *Cambridge Medieval History*, VI (1929), pp. 699-726.

VACANDARD, E., 'Les Origines de l'hérésie albigeoise', *Revue des questions historiques*, LV (1894).

VACANDARD, E., *The Inquisition*, trans., B. Conway, New York (1908).

VARAGNAC, A., 'Croisade et marchandise: Pourquoi Simon de Montfort s'en alla défaire les Albigeois', *Annales: économies, sociétés, civilisations*, I (1946).

VICAIRE, M.-H., *Histoire de saint Dominique*, 2 Vols., Paris (1957).

VIDAL, J. M., 'Les Derniers ministres d'Albigéisme en Languedoc', *Revue des questions historiques*, XXXV, Paris (1906).

WARNER, H. J., *The Albigensian Heresy*, London (1922).

INDEX